Worshipping Walt

✣ Worshipping Walt ✣

THE WHITMAN DISCIPLES

Michael Robertson

Princeton University Press
Princeton and Oxford

Published by Princeton University Press, 41 William Street, Princeton,
New Jersey 08540
In the United Kingdom: Princeton University Press, 6 Oxford Street,
Woodstock, Oxfordshire OX20 1TW

Library of Congress Cataloging-in-Publication Data

Robertson, Michael.
Worshipping Walt : the Whitman disciples / Michael Robertson.
p.   cm.
Includes bibliographical references.
ISBN 978-0-691-12808-5 (acid-free paper)
1. Whitman, Walt, 1819–1892—Appreciation. I. Title.
PS3231.R58 2008
811′.3—dc22   2007019088

British Library Cataloging-in-Publication Data is available

This book has been composed in Fournier

Printed on acid-free paper. ∞

press.princeton.edu

Printed in the United States of America

1 3 5 7 9 10 8 6 4 2

FOR MARY PAT AND MIRANDA

I know . . . that a kelson of the creation is love

CONTENTS

ACKNOWLEDGMENTS

IN THE LAST DECADES of his life Walt Whitman was surrounded and supported by a large group of exceptionally generous people. While working on this book, I've had the same experience.

At the beginning of this project a number of friends and colleagues—Tim Clydesdale, Jonathan Greenberg, Dan Rodgers, Paul Sorrentino, and Eric Ziolkowski—helped in important ways. Ed Folsom offered crucial support from beginning to end. Beth Harrison, former manager of the English Department at Princeton University, helped to make my year there as a visiting fellow exceptionally pleasant and productive. My time at Princeton was supported by a fellowship from the National Endowment for the Humanities. I also received sustained support from the College of New Jersey SOSA committee.

Can a book have godparents? If so, David Blake and Lynn Powell fill the bill. These two gifted writers took time from their own book projects to read drafts of every chapter. They understood what I was trying to do more clearly than I did, and I'm immensely grateful for their guidance.

Ellen Friedman, Bryan Garman, Janet Gray, Alex Liddie, Eric Lubell, Steve Marsden, Michelle Preston, Gary Schmidgall, Leigh Schmidt, and Mildred Thompson also read drafts of chapters. Early versions of two chapters were published in *History Today* and the *Mickle Street Review*; my thanks to editors Peter Furtado and Tyler Hoffman.

My research in Bolton and Manchester, England, was pure pleasure, thanks to the generosity of Jacqueline Dagnall, Carolyn Masel, and Paul Salverson, as well as Penny and Paul Element and Janet and Gerry Thorpe. I'm grateful to the staff of the John Rylands Library of the University of Manchester, and I owe a special debt to members of the staff of Bolton Central Library, who with modest resources have done a superb job of maintaining their important Whitman collection. I also relied on the resources of the Library of Congress and the libraries of Princeton University, Rutgers University, the College of New Jersey, and the Walt Whitman House in Camden, New Jersey.

Thanks to Marion Alcaro, Bill Behre, Marjorie Ormrod Lee, Bob Mehlman, and Jesse Zuba for their help with research and to Melinda Roberts and Suzanne and Peter Robertson for their support. Anne Matthews, Richard Preston, Ken Price, Christine Stansell, and Geri Thoma contributed crucially to this book's publication. It has been a privilege to work with Peter Dougherty, director of Princeton University Press, editor Hanne Winarsky, production editor Ellen Foos, and copy editor Polly Kummel. Thanks to all the people mentioned in my afterword who spoke to me so frankly and movingly about what Walt Whitman means to them. I also interviewed a number of people not mentioned in the afterword who were equally helpful: Tony Adler, Judith Crompton, Susan Veronica Rak, Gale Smith, and Robert Strassburg.

My greatest thanks go, as always, to the two Whitmanesque women to whom this book is dedicated: Mary Pat and Miranda Robertson.

R. M. BUCKE (1837–1901): Canadian psychiatrist. His 1883 biography of Whitman boosted the poet's reputation, and Bucke's *Cosmic Consciousness* (1901), which features Whitman prominently among its case studies, continues to be an important, if eccentric, study of mysticism.

JOHN BURROUGHS (1837–1921): American nature writer. An enormously popular writer in his time, he published two books and numerous essays on Whitman.

EDWARD CARPENTER (1844–1929): English writer and social activist. The several editions of his volume of poems *Towards Democracy* (1883–1905) led to his reputation as the English Walt Whitman. He made pilgrimages to Camden in 1877 and 1884.

ANNE GILCHRIST (1828–1885): English writer. Widowed at thirty-three, in 1876 she moved to Philadelphia in order to be near the poet she was convinced was her soul mate. Unsuccessful in her intention to become Whitman's wife, she became, along with Carpenter and Rossetti, one of his most important British champions.

THOMAS HARNED (1851–1921): American attorney. Married to Horace Traubel's sister Augusta and a resident of Camden, Harned was one of Whitman's closest friends and supporters. The poet named Harned, along with Traubel and Bucke, as coexecutor of his literary estate.

JOHN JOHNSTON (1853–1927): Scottish physician. After establishing a practice in Bolton, England, he became a central figure in the Eagle Street College, a Whitmanite group. His 1890 pilgrimage to Camden resulted in the book *Visits to Walt Whitman in 1890–1891, by Two Lancashire Friends*, coauthored with J. W. Wallace.

WILLIAM O'CONNOR (1832–1889): American civil servant and writer. His polemical 1866 pamphlet "The Good Gray Poet" was a major turning point in Whitman's reputation.

WILLIAM MICHAEL ROSSETTI (1829–1915): English civil servant, poet, and critic. He rejected the bohemian lifestyle of his brother Dante Gabriel and served for fifty years in the British Office of the Treasury while maintaining a vigorous second career as a writer and editor. He edited the first British edition of Whitman's poems (1868).

JOHN ADDINGTON SYMONDS (1840–1893): English man of letters. Late in his life Symonds became an historian and theorist of what he called "sexual inversion" and in 1890, while planning a book about Whitman, wrote him a notorious, unsuccessful letter attempting to pin down the sexual meanings of his poetry.

HORACE TRAUBEL (1858–1919): American writer. As a Camden teenager, he befriended Whitman and in 1888 began recording their daily conversations, an effort that resulted in the nine-volume *With Walt Whitman in Camden*. Traubel's monthly journal, the *Conservator* (1890–1919), was the major Whitmanite organ for three decades, featuring work by all the disciples and reviewing or excerpting virtually everything published about Whitman worldwide.

J. W. WALLACE (1853–1926): English architect's assistant. Leader of the Whitmanite Eagle Street College group in Bolton, he was also a prominent socialist activist.

WALT WHITMAN (1819–1892): American poet. He published his first book, *Leaves of Grass*, in 1855 and issued ever-expanding editions until his death. He gained his first disciples, John Burroughs and William O'Connor, after publishing the third edition of *Leaves* (1860) and moving to Washington, D.C., during the Civil War. He remained in Washington for ten years (1863–73) before moving to Camden, New Jersey, where he lived with his brother George for eleven years before buying his own house on Mickle Street.

OSCAR WILDE (1854–1900): Irish poet, novelist, and dramatist. He made two pilgrimages to Camden during his 1882 American lecture tour.

Worshipping Walt

INTRODUCTION

*Have you reckon'd a thousand acres much? have you reckon'd the
earth much?*
Have you practis'd so long to learn to read?
Have you felt so proud to get at the meaning of poems?

*Stop this day and night with me and you shall possess the origin
of all poems.*

WHEN I WAS IN MY TWENTIES and living in New York City, I quit
my job teaching English at a private school and was, for a period,
seriously underemployed. I taught part–time and worked as a freelance journalist, both of which paid miserably, and a lot of my interior life consisted of trying to decide what I wanted to be when I
grew up. I probably spent as much time, though, trying to decide
what I believed.

I grew up Presbyterian in Oklahoma, a religion and a place that
took belief seriously. In my junior high school confirmation class a
bunch of bright kids, loosely guided by a young minister, wrestled
with Calvinist theology. *Predestination, foreordination, infant damnation*—we gnawed on the dense polysyllabics like puppies, though
splinters kept catching in our throats: *How can we be free to choose if
God has foreknowledge of our choices? Doesn't salvation have anything
to do with good works?* By the time I left Oklahoma for college,
I'd concluded that Calvinism was logically elegant but emotionally
repellent, and I put religion behind me.

Until a few years later in New York when, professionally un-
moored, I found myself with time on my hands and a desire for
some sort of spiritual life. This was the late 1970s and I was living

on the Upper West Side, fertile ground for a spiritual seeker. Within a few blocks of my apartment were a Zen temple, a Vedanta group, and a Society for Ethical Culture. I sampled them all. The theologies of Vedanta and Ethical Culture were appealing—both replaced the angry God and selective salvation of Calvinism with a democratic sense of equality and a conviction of the holiness of everyday life— but their services, with hymns and sermons and readings, seemed aimed at reproducing the forms of the conventional Protestantism I'd fled in Oklahoma. The meetings at the Zen temple were nothing like Oklahoma Presbyterianism, but I never felt completely comfortable in the temple's Japanese austerity.

I turned to books. Bookstores with extensive religion sections were strung along Broadway and Columbus Avenue, and I climbed the stairs to my fifth-floor walk-up with shopping bags full of titles by Alan Watts and Ram Dass, with translations of the Dhammapada and the Tao-te ching. Yet the book to which I kept returning was one I'd had since college, a paperback reprint of the first edition of *Leaves of Grass*. I'd bought the book for my freshman English course. At the time Walt Whitman's poetry was so far over my head that it might as well have been some sort of nineteenth-century dirigible. Still, it had made an impression, and, years later, searching for spiritual guidance, I turned to the dimly remembered volume.

The timing was perfect. A few years before, the poems in *Leaves of Grass* had meant nothing to me. Now they seemed as profound as the Eastern-tinged mysticism of Alan Watts, though much more powerful and vivid. I was helped along in my spiritually charged interpretation of *Leaves of Grass* by Malcolm Cowley's elegant introduction to my edition. Cowley wanted to replace the commonly accepted views of Whitman as American nationalist or political democrat with an image of him as a religious visionary and *Leaves of Grass* as a nineteenth-century Yankee equivalent of Indian spiritual classics like the Bhagavad Gita and the Upanishads. Cowley pointed to passages in *Leaves of Grass* that were virtually identical to reports of ecstatic mystical experiences in both Eastern and Western religious traditions:

Swiftly arose and spread around me the peace and joy
and knowledge that pass all the art and argument of
the earth;
And I know that the hand of God is the elderhand of
my own,
And I know that the spirit of God is the eldest brother of
my own,
And that all the men ever born are also my brothers . . . .
and the women my sisters and lovers.

He juxtaposed an excerpt from *The Gospel of Sri Ramakrishna* with
a spiritually playful passage from "Song of Myself":

Why should I wish to see God better than this day?
I see something of God each hour of the twenty-four,
and each moment then,
In the faces of men and women I see God, and in my
own face in the glass;
I find letters from God dropped in the street, and every
one is signed by God's name,
And I leave them where they are, for I know that others
will punctually come forever and ever.

In college I'd studied Whitman in the context of American literary
traditions, but now those traditions seemed less important than the
book's urgent religious messages. "Folks expect of the poet [. . .] to
indicate the path between reality and their souls," Whitman wrote
in his preface to the first edition, and with Cowley's guidance I saw
Leaves of Grass as a guide to a spiritualized apprehension of reality.
"I swear I see now that every thing has an eternal soul!" Whitman
wrote in one of the poems of the first edition. "The trees have,
rooted in the ground . . . . the weeds of the sea have . . . . the
animals. / I swear I think there is nothing but immortality!" *Leaves
of Grass* proved more helpful than anything I'd yet come across as
I attempted to construct a belief system that was more flexible and
joyous than my childhood Presbyterianism, oriented not toward fu-

ture salvation through supernatural agency but toward the beauty and immortality of the here and now.

At the time I wasn't conscious of how representative my spiritual quest was. As a baby boomer, born in the 1950s, I was one among hundreds of thousands of my contemporaries who spent the 1970s searching for enlightenment among a variety of religious traditions and writings. By the 1980s pop sociologists were already deriding the trend as *spiritual shopping* or *cafeteria spirituality*. However, recent work in religious studies has demonstrated that spiritual seeking didn't originate about the same time as the musical *Hair*, as the pop sociologists would have it, but instead has a long history in the United States.

The concept of *spirituality* (individualistic, mystical, pluralist) as distinct from *religion* (institutional, creedal, orthodox) arose in the 1830s with the flowering of Emersonian romanticism. Emerson resigned as pastor of Boston's Second Church before he was thirty; he spent the rest of his career preaching a highly individual spirituality that mixed German idealism, Asian religion, and nature mysticism. The transcendentalists surrounding Emerson were the nation's first spiritual seekers; their numbers swelled as the century progressed. The major churches were ill prepared to respond to the rapid advances in nineteenth-century science that undermined the biblical account of creation and to address the new scholarship that regarded the Bible not as a divinely inspired work but as a disparate collection of historical texts. Before the Civil War most spiritual seekers abandoned the church and turned for inspiration to some combination of Emersonian transcendentalism and non-Western religious writings and traditions. From the 1860s on, many turned as well to Walt Whitman's *Leaves of Grass*.

I first came across Whitman's nineteenth-century disciples through biographies of the poet that mentioned, briefly, some of the women and men who regarded him as a religious teacher, a prophet—even a messiah—rather than as a poet equivalent to Longfellow or Tennyson. John Burroughs, for instance, who met Whitman during the Civil War and began writing about him soon after, said that "*Leaves of Grass* is primarily a gospel and is only secondarily a poem." Burroughs scoffed at the notion of classing Whitman with "minstrels and edifiers"; he belonged among the "prophets and saviours." The disciples R. M. Bucke and Edward Carpenter published books that placed quotations from *Leaves of Grass* alongside passages from the New Testament, Buddhist scriptures, the Upanishads, the Bhagavad Gita, and the Tao-te ching.

In the twenty-first century, with aesthetic and political interpretations of literature dominant, moral interpretation—that is, reading literature as a guide to life—seems faintly embarrassing, and it is left to conservatives like William Bennett. Yet the disciples, all of whom came from the political and cultural left, insisted that *Leaves of Grass* should be interpreted in primarily moral and spiritual terms. "Whitman means a life as much as Christianity means a life," Burroughs said. Most people today encounter Whitman through individual poems printed in anthologies, a situation that would have appalled the disciples. They insisted on the "essential unity" of *Leaves of Grass*; the book had to be taken whole, not read as "merely a collection of pretty poems." *Leaves of Grass* offered "a religion to live by and to die by," in the words of Thomas Harned, a Camden attorney. "I can never think of Whitman as a mere literary man," he said. "He is a mighty spiritual force."

The disciples' reactions to Whitman and *Leaves of Grass* can seem extreme, a charge that bothered Whitman himself not at all. "Someone was here the other day and complained that the Doctor [Bucke] was extreme. I suppose he is extreme—the sun's extreme, too: and as for me, ain't I extreme?" Whitman said in conversation. Whitman himself insisted on the spiritual dimensions of *Leaves of Grass*: "When I commenced, years ago, elaborating the plan of my poems," he wrote in 1872, "one deep purpose underlay the others, and has underlain it and its execution ever since—and that has been the religious purpose." Critics have explained away Whitman's statement—at other times he emphasized other purposes; he became more religious as he got older—but it struck me that the disciples, who took Whitman at his word, might have been on to something. "No one will get at my verses who insists upon viewing them as a literary performance, or attempt at such performance, or as aiming mainly toward art or aestheticism," Whitman wrote, and the disciples concurred. Paul Zweig speaks of the puzzle that Whitman's work creates for his readers: "Do we respond to his poem as we might to a poem by a more conventional poet—Wordsworth, say, or Shelley—or as followers of an impassioned saint speaking radical new words?" The disciples chose the latter response.

Whitman's disciples were a large, diverse, loosely affiliated international group. "Dear Walt, my beloved master, my friend, my bard, my prophet and apostle," wrote one in an homage from Melbourne, Australia. Another, the French critic Léon Bazalgette, applauded the German writer Johannes Schlaf for translating a Whitman biography; the book, Bazalgette said, "will further the knowledge of the poet-prophet in Germany whom in a few centuries, humankind will place among their Gods." A comprehensive history of the Whitman disciples would include hundreds of figures across several continents. I've limited this study to nine of the principal disciples, all of whom were from North America and Great Britain and knew Whitman personally. Focusing on those who not only worshipped but actually encountered Walt offers the opportunity to study the interactions between Whitman and his disciples.

Most disciples, primed by their reading of *Leaves of Grass*, came to their first meeting with Whitman prepared to be overwhelmed. They were not disappointed. "Whitman's magnetic quality was peculiar," wrote one. "I never knew a person to meet him for the first time who did not come under its spell; most people going away in such a curious state of exaltation and excitement as to produce a partial wakefulness, the general feeling not wearing off for a fortnight." The magnetism likely was a result of the disciples' own receptiveness combined with the mature Whitman's personal qualities. Whitman was a late bloomer who did not publish his first book of poetry until he was thirty-six; he gained his first disciples when he was past forty. The late start gave him plenty of time to cultivate his image. Daguerreotypes of the young Walter Whitman reveal an urban dandy in a stylish black suit with a cravat and cane. By the 1860s, when the first disciples came onto the scene, he had perfected his mature style: long hair and full beard, wide-brimmed hat, open-collared shirt—working class with a bohemian flair. He worked on perfecting his manner also. In a notebook he outlined a sketch of a "superb calm character": "He grows, blooms, like some perfect tree or flower, in Nature, whether viewed by admiring eyes, or in some wild or wood, entirely unknown." That this superb, calm character was a goal rather than an achieved reality is demonstrated by the entry's placement in his notebook; it occurs just after a passage recording his extreme emotional turbulence surrounding his friendship with Peter Doyle, a young working-class man. Still, there is much evidence that, from his forties on, Whitman largely succeeded in projecting the image of benign wisdom that the disciples sought in a spiritual master. Bucke, the most fervent of the disciples, invited Whitman on a three-month visit to his home in Canada expressly to observe the poet for a biography he was writing. In the published book Bucke paid lavish tribute to Whitman's "personal magnetism" and concluded that he never experienced common human feelings of fretfulness, antipathy, anger, or fear. Whitman was a bit taken aback by the resulting portrait—"I am by no means that benevolent, equable, happy creature you portray," he wrote Bucke—but he let the encomium stand.

Whitman basked in his disciples' attention. *Leaves of Grass* never won a wide audience during his lifetime, and it produced only a modest income. In compensation, however, it brought him ardent followers. He welcomed the adoring young men who gathered round him, from William O'Connor and John Burroughs during the Civil War years to Oscar Wilde, who made two pilgrimages to Camden in the early 1880s, and Horace Traubel, a Camden bank clerk who served as a volunteer literary assistant during the last years of Whitman's life while, on the side, keeping a voluminous record of their daily conversations. Whitman was made uneasy at times by the more effusive demonstrations of devotion—"You all overrate me too much, immensely too much," he wrote to a group of disciples in Lancashire, England, who raised the money to send one member, J. W. Wallace, on a trans-Atlantic pilgrimage—yet at the same time Whitman was flattered by the attention.

One English disciple, John Addington Symonds, figures prominently in this book even though he never met Whitman in person. Stretching my criteria to include this purely epistolary relationship allows me to examine the reception of *Leaves of Grass* among a set of British male intellectuals who revered Whitman both for his religious message and for his poems about love between men. Symonds began corresponding with Whitman in the early 1870s, decades before the word *homosexual* entered the English language. Immersed in a moralistic culture that condemned his desires as sodomitical and perverse, Symonds seized on Whitman's "Calamus" poems, which portray intimate male friendships as pure and ennobling. During a twenty-year period Symonds wrote Whitman a series of devotional, cagey, inquisitive letters attempting to pin down the meaning of "Calamus."

Through his reading of *Leaves of Grass* and his correspondence with its author, Symonds constructed a unique "Walt Whitman," a figure in accord with Symonds's religious yearnings, psychological needs, and erotic desires. All the disciples did the same. Anne Gilchrist, for example, a distinguished British woman of letters, was certain that Walt Whitman was the soul mate she was seeking. She first read *Leaves of Grass* in 1869, eight years after her husband died, leaving her with four young children. The book transformed her life: the astonishing intimacy of the verse; the frank recognition of female sexuality; the calls to reject conventionality and embrace freedom. ("Hark close, and still, what I now whisper to you, / I love you—O you entirely possess me, / O I wish that you and I escape from the rest, and go utterly off—O free and lawless, / Two hawks in the air—two fishes swimming in the sea not more lawless than we.") She wrote Whitman a series of letters professing her love for him, proposing marriage, offering to come to him. When he tried to put her off, flustered that a woman was actually taking him up on the erotic invitations offered in his verse, she ignored him and in 1876 sailed for America, taking with her three of her children and a houseful of furniture. She returned to England three years later, frustrated in her attempt to become Whitman's wife but comfortable in the role of friend and disciple. Her final essay on Whitman, published shortly before her premature death, is titled "A Confession of Faith"—it could be the ur-title for all the disciples' writings.

All the disciples in this book are writers, people who left behind copious letters and diaries and memoirs that allow us to trace their relationships with Whitman, and who, even more significantly, composed essays and books intended to spread the Whitmanite gospel. "A Confession of Faith," "The Gospel according to Walt Whitman," "The Poet of the Cosmos," *Cosmic Consciousness*—the disciples' writings argue that Whitman is a successor to Jesus and Whitman's book *Leaves of Grass* a new scripture. "Do you suppose a thousand years from now people will be celebrating the birth of Walt Whitman as they are now the birth of Christ?" asked William Sloane Kennedy, a Harvard Divinity School dropout-turned-Whitman disciple, in December 1890. "If they don't—the more fools they."

As I describe in my afterword, many readers still regard Whitman as a religious poet, but few imagine that Whitman's May 31 birthday will supplant Christmas. Why did the disciples think that Whitmanism might become an organized religion, possibly rivaling Christianity? The answer has to do with the late nineteenth-century "crisis of faith," the intellectual upheaval that resulted from new discoveries in biology and geology that shattered the biblical account of Creation and turned the book of Genesis into one myth among many. At the same time textual studies of the Bible revealed it to be not a unified, univocal revelation but a patchwork of historically diverse texts by a variety of authors. In the standard account the crisis of faith spurred by modern science and historical scholarship led to a secularized modern culture. More recently, historians have questioned the secularization thesis, arguing that, rather than diminishing religion, modernity led to different forms of religious expression. Many Whitman disciples, for example, had loose ties to two successful new religious movements of the late nineteenth century, Spiritualism and Theosophy. Both movements arose in response to the era's crisis of faith, offering belief systems that seemed to many to fit more comfortably with a modern, scientific, pluralist worldview. Spiritualism claimed to replace dogma and superstition with empirical investigation into the spirit world; many eminent scientists were attracted to the movement, despite regular revelations of fraud on the part of mediums. Theosophy rejected Christianity's claims to unique truth and incorporated elements of Hinduism and Buddhism into its doctrines, attracting intellectuals and bohemians interested in non-Western culture.

More broadly, the religious liberalism associated with Emersonian transcendentalism can be seen as one of the nineteenth century's earliest and most enduring responses to the shocks delivered to conventional Judeo-Christian belief. Emerson promoted an individualistic spirituality that, to many people later in the century, seemed to find its highest expression in *Leaves of Grass*. Unlike Spiritualism or Theosophy, Whitman's verse rejected all forms of supernaturalism, offering instead a pantheistic affirmation of the sacredness of the everyday. Unlike the Bible and Judeo-Christian theological tradition, *Leaves of Grass* celebrated modern science, incorporating catchphrases from recent discoveries in biology, geology, and astronomy. In contrast to Judeo-Christian prohibitions surrounding sexuality, *Leaves of Grass* celebrated sex and the body. It challenged religious and social hierarchies, insisting on the absolute equality of all women and men. And in place of Christianity's claim to offer the sole means of salvation, *Leaves of Grass* suggested that every religion had contributed its mite to the truth that Whitman now announced:

> Magnifying and applying come I,
> Outbidding at the start the old cautious hucksters,
> Taking myself the exact dimensions of Jehovah,
> Lithographing Kronos, Zeus his son, and Hercules his
>   grandson,
> Buying drafts of Osiris, Isis, Belus, Brahma, Buddha,
> In my portfolio placing Manito loose, Allah on a leaf, the
>   crucifix engraved,

> With Odin and the hideous-faced Mexitli and every idol
>   and image,
> Taking them all for what they are worth and not a
>   cent more,
> Admitting they were alive and did the work of their days,
> . . .
> Accepting the rough deific sketches to fill out better
>   in myself, bestowing them freely on each man
>   and woman I see

Leaves of Grass fit perfectly with the progressive optimism common among nineteenth-century spiritual seekers, the notion that earlier religions had been rough sketches for a fully realized democratic spirituality that was manifested equally in every man and woman and expressed in the inspired verse of a modern poet-prophet.

The disciples were ready to regard Whitman as a successor to Jesus, Kronos, Buddha, and every other religious figure of the past because of the widespread openness at the time to the concept of the poet-prophet. Few readers in North America and Great Britain today turn to poetry for religious inspiration, but the idea of the poet-prophet remains alive in non-Western cultures such as India, where "poet-saints" like Kabir are revered, and Vietnam, where the Cao Dai sect regards Victor Hugo as a prophet. One hundred fifty years ago many Americans and Britons were similarly prepared to accept the creative writer as a divinely inspired figure. William Blake was the first modern artist to be widely regarded as a poet-prophet; the disciples saw Whitman as his heir. More than a century after the disciples were at their peak, many of their ideas have entered the mainstream of academic Whitman studies: William O'Connor's insistence that Whitman was not a minor figure of controversy but a major artist who belonged with Dante and Shakespeare; John Burroughs's interest in Whitman as a nature writer; Anne Gilchrist's emphasis on Whitman's celebration of women and sexuality; John Addington Symonds's and Edward Carpenter's stress on same-sex passion. However, the notion of Whitman as a religious prophet is seldom discussed by scholars.

Yet Whitman insisted on his religious purpose from the beginning of his career to its end. "Laws for Creations," an early poem, poses a series of powerful rhetorical questions:

> What do you suppose I would intimate to you in a
>   hundred ways, but that man or woman is as good
>   as God?
> And that there is no God any more divine than Yourself?
> And that this is what the oldest and newest myths finally
>   mean?

Talking with Horace Traubel in his old age, Whitman commented, "I claim everything for religion: after the claims of my religion are satisfied nothing is left for anything else: yet I have been called irreligious—an infidel (God help me!): as if I could have written a word of the Leaves without its religious root-ground." Like every religious prophet, Whitman was interested in transforming the lives of those who attended to him, and he virtually grabs his readers by the lapels as if to shake them—*you*—into the realization that divinity inheres within yourself.

The disciples offer an alternative way of understanding Whitman, one largely excluded from modern criticism. Thirty years ago, fresh out of college, I read *Leaves of Grass* the same way I read the Bhaga-vad Gita or the Tao-te ching—as inspired wisdom that could help me make sense of fundamental spiritual questions: *Who am I? Where am I going? What's the nature of my relationship to other people and to the world at large?* While researching this book, I kept encountering people who read Whitman the same way. In my afterword I write about some of them. I describe attending services at a Unitarian chapel in Bolton, England, where the minister salted his sermon with quotations from *Leaves of Grass*; participating in a guided meditation session at a Quaker meetinghouse in Washington, D.C., that used Whitman's words as a guide to higher states of consciousness; meet-ing with the New Jersey secretary of commerce in his office to talk about how, as a teenager living in Camden, he felt a mystical connec-tion to Whitman as he jogged past the poet's tomb in Harleigh Cem-etery. These twenty-first-century readers of Whitman don't deify the poet as did disciples like Bucke, who fell under the spell of Whitman's personal magnetism, and modern readers are not inclined to make *Leaves of Grass* the basis of a movement to transform society in the way that Wallace and Traubel imagined was possible. But *Leaves of Grass* is important to many readers today not just as a book of poetry but as a foundation of their spiritual lives.

These contemporary readers are often well aware of recent Whitman criticism, and they don't imagine that a religious approach to Whitman is the only valid one. In that they are unlike the disciples, who were actively hostile to academic approaches. The disciples tended to think in stark binaries: either you regarded Whitman as an inspired religious figure and accepted *Leaves of Grass* as a scriptural whole, or you missed the point. Most academic critics have returned the favor. As Michael Warner has pointed out, literary critics define themselves as professionals in opposition to what they see as amateurish enthusiasm, and Whitman critics have a long tradition of scoffing at the disciples as "hot little prophets," "subliterary minds," "the lunatic fringe." I think it's possible to be a *both/and* rather than an *either/or* reader, to value the rich aesthetic and historical and political interpretations of Whitman that have flourished since the 1950s while still learning from the disciples' religious appreciation. "Stop this day and night with me and you shall possess the origin of all poems," Walt Whitman promised; he believed that reading *Leaves of Grass* could change your life. Here are the stories of some people who prove that.

CHAPTER ONE

William O'Connor and John Burroughs:
Reading Whitman's New Bible

*No one will get at my verses who insists upon viewing them
as a literary performance, or attempt at such performance,
or as aiming mainly toward art or aestheticism.*

IN THE SUMMER OF 1857 Walt Whitman, who had just turned thirty-eight, was living with his mother in a working-class Brooklyn neighborhood. Three of his five brothers also were living at home. Space was tight for the Whitman family, and Walt shared a bed in the attic with Eddie, his youngest brother. No member of his family had read either of the two books of poetry Walt had written in the previous two years, and sales of the books, both self-published, had been virtually nonexistent.

Despite what many might have considered his unpromising prospects, he was in an optimistic mood. It's likely that his sanguine view of his poetic career was based almost entirely on a single letter that he had received after the publication of his first book. On a venture Whitman had sent a copy to America's greatest man of letters, Ralph Waldo Emerson. Within days of receiving it, Emerson responded:

> Concord, Massachusetts, *21 July, 1855.*
> Dear Sir—I am not blind to the worth of the wonderful gift
> of "Leaves of Grass." I find it the most extraordinary piece of

wit and wisdom that America has yet contributed. I am very happy in reading it, as great power makes us happy. . . . I give you joy of your free and brave thought. I have great joy in it. I find incomparable things said incomparably well, as they must be. I find the courage of treatment which so delights us, and which large perception only can inspire. I greet you at the beginning of a great career.

Whitman carried the letter around with him for weeks afterward, showing it to friends and acquaintances. After two months he slipped a copy to friends on the *New-York Tribune*, and they published it in full. It was an indiscreet move—he never asked Emerson's permission, and the sage of Concord was said to be displeased—but it was critical for Whitman's career. Emerson's approval could not guarantee that Whitman's poems would become popular, but it meant that at least they would not be ignored. Still floating on the great man's praise, Whitman rushed out a second edition of *Leaves of Grass* in 1856, with twenty new poems inside and "I Greet You at the Beginning of a Great Career" stamped in gold on the spine. In an appendix Whitman printed Emerson's letter—again without permission—along with a lengthy reply that began, "Here are thirty-two Poems, which I send you, dear Friend and Master, not having found how I could satisfy myself with sending any usual acknowledgment of your letter." With the blithe disregard for facts that distinguished his efforts as self-publicist, Whitman claimed that he had printed a thousand copies of the first edition, "and they readily sold," and that he intended to print "several thousand copies" of the second edition. He hinted that he was about to embark on a national lecture tour, "but the work of my life is making poems." He would keep on till he had made a hundred, then more—"perhaps a thousand." The way was clear, he claimed: "A few years, and the average annual call for my Poems is ten or twenty thousand—more, quite likely." The audacity and boasting of this open letter must have made Emerson wince, but he no doubt understood Whitman's motivation. Whitman was a late bloomer, already pushing forty, who had not yet been able to find a commercial publisher for his unconventional, challenging verse. He was a middle-aged man in a hurry, determined to clear a path for his poems, and still half-drunk on Emerson's 1855 praise. His Master had said that he had written the greatest work yet published in America—why not envision a limitless future?

In this buoyant mood Whitman began planning during 1857 for a third edition of *Leaves of Grass*. He wrote to a friend in June claiming that he had a hundred poems ready for publication. The same month he confided an alternative, grander plan to his notebook: "*The Great Construction* of the *New Bible*. Not to be diverted from the principal object—the main life work—the Three Hundred & Sixty five—(it ought to be read[y] in 1859." In another notebook entry he wrote: " 'Leaves of Grass'—Bible of the New Religion."

Whitman's ambition seems stunning, but in midnineteenth-century America such pronouncements were not uncommon. It was an era of tremendous religious tumult, and *Leaves of Grass* was only one among numerous new bibles jockeying for position in the antebellum United States. The Book of Mormon (1830) is the best known of the era's new scriptures, but Joseph Smith and the Mormons were not unique. The 1830s and the decades following witnessed an unprecedented number of new sects and a flood of new bibles. From its publication in 1611 until the early nineteenth century, the King James Version had been accepted by virtually every Protestant in Great Britain and North America as the definitive and only Bible, but beginning in the 1830s and continuing through the Civil War, a new English-language version or translation of the Bible appeared on average every two years. The impulse for the creation of new Bibles came in part from scholars who recognized the errors and shortcomings of the King James Version, in part from sectarian differences, and in part from a confluence of democratic and romantic ideologies that made it seem reasonable for every church—or why not every person?—to have its own Bible.

Among Protestant sects seemingly minor differences—should the Greek *baptizein* be interpreted as *baptism* or *immersion?*—resulted in competing Bible translations. In the larger culture romantic writers, beginning with William Blake, believed that the poet was called to provide an alternative to orthodox Christian belief, a unique mythology that could revivify spirituality and serve as a secular scripture. "The priest departs, the divine literatus comes," Whitman wrote in 1871; by that time he was announcing a commonplace. "Make your own Bible," Emerson had commanded in an 1836 journal entry. When he spoke to the graduates of Harvard Divinity School two years later, he described the "Hebrew and Greek scriptures" as fragmentary and urged each graduate to become "a newborn bard of the Holy Ghost." When Whitman proposed *Leaves of Grass* as a new bible in 1857, he was not making an unprecedented claim but responding to a widespread demand among progressive intellectuals and artists.

He imagined that the new bible would be ready in 1859, but by the summer of that year he had fallen into a self-described "Slough" and had to write self-admonitory messages in his notebook: "It is now time to *Stir* first for *Money* enough *to live and* provide for *M*"— "M" most likely was his mother. His plan was to set aside poetry for fiction. Early in his career, during the 1840s, Whitman had published several short stories as well as a temperance novel. His fiction was undistinguished—conventional and sentimental—but unlike his verse, it brought in money. He sketched out ideas for a few short stories in his notebooks, but early in 1860 he received a letter out of the blue that made him abandon for good his plan to become a commercial fiction writer. The letter was from Thayer and Eldridge, a recently founded Boston publishing firm:

> Dear Sir. We want to be the publishers of Walt. Whitman's Poems—Leaves of Grass.—When the book was first issued we were clerks in the establishment we now own. We read the book with profit and pleasure. It is a true poem and writ by a *true* man.
>
> When a man dares to speak his thought in this day of refinement—so called—it is difficult to find his mates to act amen to it. Now *we* want to be known as the publishers of Walt. Whitman's books, and put our name as such under his, on title

pages.—If you will allow it we can and will put your books into good form, and style attractive to the eye; we can and will sell a large number of copies; we have great facilities by and through numberless Agents in selling. We can dispose of more books than most publishing houses (we do not "puff" here but speak *truth*).

We are young men. We "celebrate" ourselves by acts. Try us. You can do us good. We can do you good—pecuniarily.

This letter was almost as electrifying as Emerson's had been. Within a few weeks Whitman took up residence in Boston, where he spent two months supervising the printing of the third edition of *Leaves of Grass*.

The speed with which Whitman put together the 1860 *Leaves of Grass* meant that it lacked the numerical perfection he had imagined for the New Bible—it contains only about half the 365 poems he projected—but in other ways it evidences Whitman's scriptural ambitions. The stanzas of every poem are numbered, as if they were verses in a bible, and the volume opens with a new poem, "Proto-Leaf"—later titled "Starting from Paumanok"—that boldly announces, "I too, following many, and follow'd by many, inaugurate a Religion." Directly addressing the reader, Whitman continues:

> O I see the following poems are indeed to drop in the
>   earth the germs of a greater Religion.
> My comrade!
> For you, to share with me, two greatnesses—And a third
>   one, rising inclusive and more resplendent,
> The greatness of Love and Democracy—and the
>   greatness of Religion.

The 1860 *Leaves of Grass* is particularly insistent upon Whitman's religious intentions, but his interest in writing a new American bible is evident in every version of *Leaves of Grass*, from the 1855 first edition on.

"I celebrate myself, / And what I assume you shall assume, / For every atom belonging to me as good belongs to you." So begins the first poem of the first edition. The statement is political—it asserts a democratic equality between poet and reader—but it is also religious. *I* and *you* are not simply equal but identical in a way that makes sense only in metaphysical terms. Whitman's poetic self constantly assumes other identities—not only the reader but anyone who comes within sight of the wide-ranging hero of "Song of Myself." Near the end of one of the longest catalogues in the poem—after Whitman has written of himself as a farmer, prospector, explorer, balloonist, and hunter, among other identities—he describes a shipwreck, then a hunted slave, and says, "I am the man, I suffer'd, I was there." He continues: "Agonies are one of my changes of garments, / I do not ask the wounded person how he feels, I myself become the wounded person." Whitman displays an empathy so strong that it becomes identity. "In all people I see myself," he writes, "none more and not one a barley-corn less." John Updike has written that the common charge against Whitman of egotism won't stick; rather, the self of *Leaves of Grass* is an example of "egotheism." "Divine am I inside and out," Whitman writes, but since *I* and *you* are interchangeable, you are as divine as I. Whitman offers a radically democratic theology: "Did you suppose there could be only one Supreme?" he asks in the 1855 preface. "We affirm there can be unnumbered Supremes[. . . . There is nothing] in the known universe more divine than men and women."

If egotheism is one key element of Whitman's religious message, immanence is another. The divine is immanent throughout the universe of *Leaves of Grass*: every mouse "is miracle enough to stagger sextillions of infidels." Looked at another way, Whitman's notorious catalogues, often seen as tedious assemblages of objects, can be understood as inventories of the sacred. "The pismire is equally perfect, and a grain of sand, and the egg of the wren," he writes. These three objects could be multiplied indefinitely. Whitman offers lists of objects as incantations designed to help us see the world afresh and recognize the spirituality of the material. In place of Christianity's condemnation of the flesh and elevation of the soul, Whitman offers a sensual spirituality, or a spiritual sensuality, that refuses to recognize any distinction between body and soul. "If the body were not the soul, what is the soul?" he asks at the beginning of his great 1855 poem "I Sing the Body Electric." "If any thing is sacred the human body is sacred," he insists. He overthrows hierarchies and obliterates distinctions between the sacred and profane. "If I worship one thing more than another it shall be the spread of my own body, or any part of it," he writes in "Song of Myself."

Whitman's celebration of the body was a direct challenge to conventional Christian concepts of shame and sin. *Leaves of Grass* has a strong anti-institutional, anticlerical dimension. Whitman saw a link between "ecclesiasticism" and "feudalism"—that is, the institutional church, with the minister in his pulpit preaching to the congregation below him, seemed as antidemocratic as the notion of a divinely appointed king or inherited nobility. "Really what has America to do with all this mummery of prayer and rituals and the rant of exhorters and priests?" he wrote in an early notebook. Whitman wanted to sweep away "sects, churches, creeds, pews, sermons, observances, Sundays, etc." in favor of "real religion." In "Democratic Vistas," his great post–Civil War jeremiad, he called for a new religion that would have as its foundation "the divine ride of man in himself." Like Emerson and the other transcendentalists, Whitman extended self-reliance to the sphere of religion. "Nothing, not God, is greater to one than one's self is," he wrote in "Song of Myself."

He was never a systematic theological thinker, but in "Democratic Vistas" he sketched out a religion appropriate for American democracy, one freed from all links to Old World feudalism. Individuality was at the core of the new American religion. "Bibles may convey, and priests expound," he wrote, "but it is exclusively for the noiseless operation of one's isolated Self, to enter the pure ether of veneration, reach the divine levels, and commune with the unutterable." Like other religious liberals of his era, Whitman mistrusted all religious authority. Once direct, authentic experience of the divine is formulated into a creed to which others are expected to assent, individuality has been violated. The only church to which Whitman could assent was a Church of One.

Yet Whitman recognized that, crucial as it was, individuality was not sufficient. His religious vision also included empathy, compassion, and love. "Not that half only, individualism, which isolates," he writes in "Democratic Vistas." "There is another half, which is adhesiveness or love, that fuses, ties and aggregates, making the races comrades, and fraternizing all. Both are to be vitalized by religion, (sole worthiest elevator of man or State,) breathing into the proud, material tissues, the breath of life. For I say at the core of democracy, finally, is the religious element." Whitman's thought cannot be split into political and religious dimensions; the two realms are completely intertwined.

Whitman well recognized the paradox at the heart of his religious message. Priests and sermons were to be shunned because they substituted formulaic creeds for direct individual experience of the divine. Yet the new American religion demanded advocates, since the people could not be expected to leave the churches without being exhorted by someone who would point the way. He solved the problem by replacing priests with poets. Whitman believed that poets could be—should be—prophets, a belief shared by many of his contemporaries. Emerson, Carlyle, and Ruskin were all regarded as prophets—not diviners of the future but, like the prophets of the Hebrew Bible, inspired figures whose aim was to transform the lives of individuals and move their societies toward righteousness. Whitman cast himself as a poet-prophet from the start of his career.

Each of the first three editions of the *Leaves* foregrounded Whitman's prophetic purpose in a different way. The 1860 edition, his "New Bible," commences with "Proto-Leaf" ("Starting from Paumanok"), intended as a preview of his "programme of chants," *Leaves of Grass* as a whole. "Proto-Leaf" trumpets Whitman's ambition to be the poet of the New World, glides over images that will appear later in the book, and with a crescendo of capital letters announces his two great themes of Love and Democracy and a third, inclusive of the other two and even "more resplendent": Religion. "I . . . announce that the real and permanent grandeur of These States must be their Religion," he proclaims. Whitman does not systematically describe the new American religion that he envisions—like all his best long poems, "Paumanok" proceeds not through logically reasoned steps but through dreamlike, associative leaps—but he repeatedly emphasizes the sacredness of the individual ("I say no man . . . has begun to think how divine he himself is") and the divinity immanent within the material world ("Was somebody asking to see the Soul? / See! your own shape and countenance—persons, substances, beasts, the trees, the running rivers, the rocks and sands"). The 1860 *Leaves of Grass* may have been hurriedly produced, but it was perfectly positioned to become the bible of a liberal, post-Christian American spirituality.

✝ ✝ ✝

Thayer and Eldridge followed through on their promise to produce the 1860 *Leaves of Grass* in an attractive form and to promote it heavily. The book was widely reviewed, and controversy over the poems' frank sexuality spread Whitman's name widely across North America and Great Britain. The initial printing of one thousand copies quickly sold out, and Thayer and Eldridge printed more and began negotiating with Whitman for a second volume of poems. Unfortunately for their plans, the election of Abraham Lincoln in November 1860 precipitated a national political and financial crisis. Thayer and Eldridge, financially overextended, went into bankruptcy early in 1861, and Whitman's new American bible sank out of sight. He retreated to his mother's home in Brooklyn as the nation plunged into war, and he entered a period that he later referred to as his "New York stagnation."

His stagnation ended abruptly in December 1862 when he read in a newspaper report that his brother George, a Union army officer, had been wounded at the Battle of Fredericksburg. Whitman rushed to northern Virginia, to find that his brother had suffered only a superficial wound to his face and had already returned to active duty. However, the few days that he spent with his brother in camp changed the direction of his life. Whitman was powerfully affected by the suffering he saw in a field hospital at Fredericksburg, full of wounded and sick young men desperate not only for treatment but for human affection. He determined to settle in Washington, D.C., find a government clerkship, and devote his free time to visiting the soldiers pouring by the thousands into the city's army hospitals. Within days of arriving in Washington he found work as a part-time copyist in the army paymaster's office and began daily visits to the military hospitals. Furnished with fruit, tobacco, writing paper, and small change, he walked through the wards, talking to the soldiers, writing letters for them, distributing gifts, sitting by the bedside of the sickest men for hours at a time. "I never before had my feelings so thoroughly and (so far) permanently absorbed, to the very roots, as by these huge swarms of dear, wounded, sick, dying boys," he wrote to his brother Jeff two months after arriving in Washington. Walt's heart went out to the boys, and they clung to him. "Mother, I have real pride in telling you," he wrote during his first summer in Washington, "that I have the consciousness of saving quite a little number of lives by saving them from giving up & being a good deal with them—the men say it is so, & the doctors say it is so—& I will candidly confess I can see it is true, though I say it of myself—I know you will like to hear it, mother, so I tell you." It was as if, amid the fever and suffering and amputated limbs of the army hospitals, he had transformed himself into the outsized, compassionate, lifesaving hero he had imagined in "Song of Myself." In Washington he found a new vocation that would sustain him through the rest of the war years. He also found his first disciples: William O'Connor and John Burroughs.

✟ ✟ ✟

Neither man was comfortable with the label of disciple. Burroughs was too prickly and independent to want to be associated with Whitman's principal North American disciples of later years, R. M. Bucke and Horace Traubel. O'Connor said he preferred to be thought of as Whitman's "champion," in the way that Ruskin had championed the painter J. M. Turner or Boccaccio defended Dante. Yet both

FIGURE 1.1. Walt Whitman in Washington, D.C., 1863. Library of Congress, Prints and Photographs Division.

Burroughs and O'Connor responded, as no one before them had, to the religious dimensions of *Leaves of Grass*. Burroughs combined Whitman's poetry with his own love of nature to produce a pantheistic religious vision that suffused his many books and essays. O'Connor, a lifelong hero worshiper, was the first person to compare Whitman to Jesus.

O'Connor and Whitman met in Boston in the spring of 1860. Whitman was there to supervise the third edition of *Leaves of Grass*; O'Connor had been commissioned by Thayer and Eldridge to write an abolition novel. O'Connor was only twenty-eight, twelve years younger than Whitman, but he already had a substantial reputation as a fiction writer, journalist, and fiery antislavery polemicist. He had been one of the few Americans to read the first edition of *Leaves of Grass*, and he had enthusiastically reprinted a great swath from the 1855 preface in a magazine he was editing at the time. Meeting

Whitman at the Thayer and Eldridge office, O'Connor was instantly smitten. "The great Walt is very grand & it is health & happiness to be near him," O'Connor wrote to a friend. "He is so large & strong—so pure, proud & tender with such an ineffable *bon-hommie* & wholesome sweetness of presence; all the young men & women are in love with him." The attraction, according to Whitman, was mutual, "instant on both sides." O'Connor was "so bright, magnetic, vital, elemental"; Whitman called O'Connor "the most attractive man I had ever met." Whitman and O'Connor's relationship was chaste but erotically charged, a textbook case of what has been called the "erotics of discipleship." All the male disciples include a lovingly detailed physical description of Walt Whitman in their works about him, writing breathlessly of his "striking masculine beauty." The phrase is from O'Connor, but it could have come from any of them: a paean to Whitman's physical beauty was as obligatory as explications of his religious themes. Whitman, for his part, clearly thrived on the younger men's adoration. Talking years later about O'Connor's writings in his defense, the old poet said, "I must say I like them. They are comforting. Just as any woman likes a man to fall in love with her—whether she returns it or not—so to have once aroused so eloquent and passionate a declaration is reassuring and a help to me."

Having established a warm relationship with O'Connor in Boston, Whitman immediately looked up his friend when he found himself in Washington two and a half years later. O'Connor had moved to Washington with his wife and daughter in order to take a clerkship in the Treasury Department, and they found Whitman a room in the same building in which they lived. Whitman took all his meals with O'Connor; his wife, Ellen (Nelly); and their daughter, Jean. Whitman was delighted with this surrogate family, and he wrote his mother after a few months in Washington, "I can never forget their kindness & real friendship & it appears as though they would continue just the same, if it were for all our lives." The O'Connors were at the center of a circle of friends who gathered at their flat on Sunday evenings to discuss literature and politics. William, brilliant and voluble, was a passionate conversationalist; Nelly, who had

FIGURE 1.2. William O'Connor, c. 1855. Library of Congress, Prints and Photographs Division.

written for William Lloyd Garrison's abolitionist journal and been active in the women's rights movement, was as interested in politics and current affairs as he. Whitman, absorbed in his hospital work, delighted with his new friends, was as happy as he had ever been. Years later, remembering his time in Washington, he said, "The O'Connor home was my home: they were beyond all others—William, Nelly—my understanders, my lovers: they more than any others. I was nearer to them than to any others—oh! much nearer."

Still, for all the pleasure he took in his friends' company, Whitman observed the tensions in their marriage. William O'Connor was prone to depression, and for long stretches he would scarcely speak to Nelly and would come home late at night, claiming that he had been working at the office, though he hinted to male friends that he was having affairs. Nelly O'Connor had talked her husband into giving up literature for the safety of a government salary, and he said that he felt like "a caged tiger walking around and around

FIGURE 1.3. Ellen O'Connor, c. 1870. Library of Congress, Prints and Photographs Division.

endlessly—mad as I can be that I am wasting my life in this infamous office." Nelly O'Connor took care of their daughter, entertained their many friends, and found an outlet for her frustrated romantic longings in an unfortunate but not unprecedented manner: she fell in love with her husband's best friend.

Her infatuation with Walt Whitman is obvious in a letter she wrote him less than a year after they first met, when he left Washington to visit his family in Brooklyn: "Dear Walt, we long for you, William sighs for you, & I feel as if a large part of myself were out of the city—I shall give you a good big kiss when you come, so depend upon it." As time passed, her hints became broader. When Whitman became ill the next summer and went to Brooklyn to recuperate, Nelly wrote, "I have missed you terribly every minute of the time. . . . Ah! Walt, I don't believe other people need you as much as we do. I am *sure* they don't need you as much as *I* do." Whitman never responded in a like key, but his lack of ardor did not discourage her. Eight years after first meeting Whitman, she wrote him a remarkably frank love letter:

> My very dear friend—It is good to feel so assured of one's love as not to need to express it, & it is very good to know that one's love is never doubted or questioned. . . . I always know that you know that I love you all the time, even though we should never meet again, my feeling could never change, and I am *sure* that you know it as well as I do. I do flatter myself too, that *you* care for *me*,—not as I love you, because you are great and strong, and more sufficient unto yourself than any woman can be,—besides you have the great outflow of your pen which saves you from the need of personal love as one feels it who has no such resource. You could not afford to love other than as the Gods love; that is to love *every body*, but no one enough to be made unhappy, or to lose your balance.

Even at the height of her infatuation with Whitman, Nelly O'Connor was able to coolly appraise their relationship: he cared for her, certainly, but not the way she loved him. But she was wrong about his never loving one person enough to be made unhappy; it was just that no woman could ever throw him off balance. Men were another matter.

During his years in Washington with the O'Connors, Whitman had a series of intense, often unhappy, romantic entanglements with working-class men. While visiting in the hospitals in 1863–64, he fell in love with a succession of wounded soldiers. These simple young men, physically weakened and far from home, responded gratefully to Whitman's gestures of affection, as he held their hands, wiped their brows, kissed them at parting. "Many a soldier's kiss dwells on these bearded lips," Whitman wrote in his great Civil War poem "The Wound-Dresser," and there is no reason to doubt him. Relations between men were often more physically demonstrative in the nineteenth century than now, and many a soldier doubtless kissed the gray-haired visitor, returned home after Appomattox, got married, and forgot about him. Whitman's relationships with a handful of soldiers were more intense, but even they eventually abandoned their older friend. For example, soon after his arrival in Washington, Whitman was taken with Thomas Sawyer, a former soap maker from Massachusetts. After Sawyer recovered and left the hospital, Whitman wrote him a series of ardent letters, first proposing that they live together after the war, then, when the young soldier did not reply, beseeching him for some response. After Sawyer finally sent a stilted reply—obviously composed for him by someone else—Whitman was reduced to writing plaintively, "My dearest comrade, . . . I do not expect you to return for me the same degree of love I have for you." By the end of his first year in Washington, Whitman could not help falling in love with other soldiers, but he had given up the notion of a lasting relationship. Private Elijah Fox wrote Whitman from his home in Illinois at the end of 1863, "Since coming here I have often thought of what you told me when I said to you I am certain I will come back to Washington. You said to me then that a gret [sic] many of the boys had said the same but none had returned."

As the war wound down, Whitman found a comrade who would not, like the soldiers, leave Washington, never to return. Early in 1865 Whitman encountered Peter Doyle, a twenty-one-year-old Irish immigrant who had served briefly in the Confederate army before taking a job as a Washington streetcar conductor. They met on a winter's night, when Whitman was the only passenger on Doyle's Pennsylvania Avenue car. "It was a lonely night," Doyle recalled years later, "so I thought I would go in and talk with him. Something in me made me do it and something in him drew me that way. He used to say there was something in me had the same effect on him. Anyway, I went into the car. We were familiar at once—I put my hand on his knee—we understood. He did not get out at the end of the trip—in fact went all the way back with me. . . . From that time on we were the biggest sort of friends." Doyle and Whitman never lived together, but they saw one another frequently. Whitman would ride along on Doyle's streetcar during the day;

after dark they took long moonlit walks along the Potomac. It is not clear that the relationship ever became sexual, and his deep feelings for Doyle at times sent Whitman into an emotional tempest. In 1870, the same year that Nelly O'Connor told Whitman that he could never love anyone enough to be made unhappy or to lose his balance, he wrote an anguished journal entry, full of capital letters, underlining, and childish attempts at disguise. He referred to Peter Doyle as "16.4"—"P" and "D" are the sixteenth and fourth letters of the alphabet—and he changed the pronoun "him" to "her":

> Always preserve a kind spirit & demeanor to 16. BUT PURSUE HER NO MORE. . . . TO GIVE UP ABSOLUTELY & *for good from the present hour this* FEVERISH, FLUCTUATING, *useless* UNDIGNIFIED PURSUIT OF 16.4—*too long, (much too long)* persevered in,—so humiliating,— —*It must come at last* & had better come now —*(It cannot possibly be a success)* . . . —*avoid seeing her, or meeting her, or any talk or explanations*—or ANY MEETING WHATEVER, FROM THIS HOUR FORTH, FOR LIFE

Anyone who has ever written a similarly intense resolution can predict what happened next: Whitman ignored his self-administered advice. He saw Doyle again less than two weeks later, late at night, before leaving for a lengthy visit to his mother. The letter he wrote Doyle from Brooklyn reveals that the turbulence had given way to a satisfying calm: "Pete, there was something in that hour from 10 to 11 oclock (parting though it was) that has left me pleasure & comfort for good—I never dreamed that you made so much of having me with you, nor that you could feel so downcast at losing me. I foolishly thought it was all on the other side."

In his relations with wounded soldiers and with Peter Doyle, Whitman underwent emotional storms that Nelly O'Connor never suspected. His relationship with William was different. Although their friendship contained an erotic undercurrent, Whitman never had a romantic relationship with a man as close to his own age and intellectual level as William O'Connor. The tumult in their relationship was political, not romantic: the radical O'Connor liked to argue vociferously, even violently, with his more conservative

FIGURE 1.4. Walt Whitman and Peter Doyle, Washington, D.C., c. 1869. Bayley/ Whitman Collection of Ohio Wesleyan University.

friend. Nelly worried constantly that the two men's vehement arguments would break apart their friendship, but throughout the 1860s O'Connor overlooked their political differences, convinced that his friend was the greatest poet the nation had yet seen. When, shortly after the war's end, Whitman suffered a minor setback, O'Connor sprang to his side with an élan that justified the nickname he had been given as young fencing student: D'Artagnan, the hotheaded fourth Musketeer.

O'Connor hurtled into action in the summer of 1865 when Whitman was fired from a position as clerk in the Department of the Interior. Whitman's dismissal from his government post was inevitable from the moment in May 1865 when James Harlan, U.S. senator from Iowa and an ordained Methodist minister, was appointed secretary of the interior. Harlan determined on a moral cleansing of his department, and shortly after taking office he asked his bureau chiefs for the names of any employees who disregarded "the rules of decorum & propriety prescribed by a Christian Civilization." The next month he fired every woman in the department—on the ground that their presence might be injurious to the morals of the men—and several men, including first-class clerk Walter Whitman. Whitman's immediate superior had refused to supply the names of anyone whom the secretary might consider morally degenerate, but Harlan himself, snooping about the office after hours, found Whitman's personal copy of *Leaves of Grass*. The former clergyman would have encountered much to offend his sensibility. The provocatively titled "To a Common Prostitute" begins, "Be composed—be at ease with me—I am Walt Whitman, liberal and lusty as Nature," and continues, "My girl, I appoint with you an appointment—and I charge you that you make preparation to be worthy to meet me." Virtually anywhere Harlan dipped into the volume he could have found Whitman making good on his promise to express "forbidden voices, / Voices of sexes and lusts—voices veiled, and I remove the veil." Harlan believed in keeping veils firmly in place.

The moment O'Connor heard that Whitman had been fired, he rushed in a fury to call on his friend J. Hubley Ashton, an assistant attorney general. Almost forty years after the event Ashton could recall vividly O'Connor's "terrific outburst": "I fancy that there never was before such an outpouring of impassioned eloquence in the presence of an audience of *one*. The wrong committed, as O'Connor said, was the ignominious dismissal from the public service of the greatest poet America had produced, an offence against the honor and dignity of American letters, and against humanity itself as consecrated in 'Leaves of Grass.' " Ashton tried to calm the volatile O'Connor by promising to intervene with Harlan. When that effort failed, Ashton quickly got Whitman an even better position in the Attorney General's Office. Whitman was satisfied with this outcome; O'Connor was not. Still gripped by righteous indignation, he began to compose a long essay on the affair. "The Good Gray Poet: A Vindication," a forty-six-page pamphlet, appeared a few months later. It is likely that few people read the entire pamphlet. O'Connor, in his wrath, believed in adding every possible scrap of fuel to his fire, and many of his paragraphs, dense with allusions to world literature, run six to ten pages long. But his title entered the popular consciousness, and Whitman, previously considered by many to be a licentious, disreputable author, became widely regarded as a virtuous, benign figure. H. L. Mencken paid indirect tribute to the transformative effect of O'Connor's essay on Whitman's reputation in his comment on the Harlan-Whitman clash: "Let us repair, once a year, to our accustomed houses of worship," Mencken wrote a half century after the event, "and there give thanks to God that one day in 1865 brought together the greatest poet that America has ever produced and the damndest ass."

"The Good Gray Poet" defends Whitman's morality, calling him "the grandest gentleman that treads this continent," and argues that *Leaves of Grass* ranks among the greatest works of world literature, earning its author a place beside Shakespeare, Aeschylus, Cervantes, Dante, and Homer—"the bards of the last ascent, the brothers of the radiant summit." Most famously, O'Connor relies on a lengthy account of Whitman's Civil War service as a volunteer nurse. In a passage heavy with Victorian sentiment O'Connor depicts his friend at work:

There, in those long wards, in rows of cots on either side, were stretched, in all attitudes and aspects of mutilation, of pale repose, of contorted anguish, of death, the martyrs of the war; and among them, with a soul that tenderly remembered the little children in many a dwelling mournful for those fathers, the worn and anxious wives, haggard with thinking of those husbands, the girls weeping their spirits from their eyes for those lovers, the mothers who from afar yearned to the bedsides of those sons, walked Walt Whitman in the spirit of Christ, soothing, healing, consoling, restoring, night and day, for years.

Despite his comparison of Whitman to Christ and a description of *Leaves of Grass* as an American Bible, O'Connor's argument in "The Good Gray Poet" is not primarily religious. O'Connor preferred to compare his defense of Whitman to great literary battles of the past—Scott's praise of Byron or Aristophanes defending Aeschylus—and O'Connor saw himself as part of a tradition of "that old chivalry of letters, which in all ages has sprung to the succor and defence of genius."

"William's onslaught is terrifying," Whitman said. He compared O'Connor's polemical style to "a battle-ship firing both sides and fore and aft: no man in America carries as big an armament for controversy as William—can do as heavy immediate execution. I would hate to be in his way myself." O'Connor's friends convinced him to tone down some of the most outrageous invective in "The Good Gray Poet," though he could not forgo calling Whitman's opponents "the devotees of a castrated literature, the earthworms that call themselves authors, the confectioners that pass for poets, the flies that are recognized as critics, the bigots, the dilettanti, the prudes and the fools." However, for the most part O'Connor held his talent for insult in check and instead relied on sentiment, decrying the injustice of the saintly Whitman's being removed from office for the offense of writing one of the great works of world literature. Two years after publishing "The Good Gray Poet," O'Connor decided to burnish the halo that his essay had successfully planted on

Whitman's head and wrote a novella that depicted Whitman not just as a saint but a messiah, uniquely able to unite and heal a divided nation still suffering from the wounds of war.

"The Carpenter: A Christmas Story" was published in the popular *Putnam's Magazine*, appearing on newsstands in December 1867. O'Connor apparently composed it with "A Christmas Carol" propped in front of him, but he translated Dickens's very English story into a uniquely American narrative. "The Carpenter" takes place on Christmas Eve 1864, just before the fall of the Confederate capital of Richmond. The Scrooge figure is Elkanah Dyzer, owner of an estate in the border state of Maryland; his lame granddaughter, Lilian, stands in for Tiny Tim; and the three spirits are rolled into the figure of Walt Whitman. Whitman's name is never mentioned— the character is known only as "the carpenter"—but readers familiar with the poet, who had supposedly worked as a house builder in Brooklyn, recognized him immediately. The story begins with the Dyzer family legend that the carpenter Jesus did not die on the cross but continued to live on Earth, growing old and gray as he wandered about the world doing good. Just as Elkanah Dyzer finishes telling the legend, there is a knock at the door, and the carpenter enters. In the few hours that this good gray messiah spends at the Dyzers' home, he cures Elkanah of his greed, reconciles the patriarch and his wife, gives the youngest son courage to win the hand of his sweetheart, heals Lilian's lameness, and finds a fortune in gold hidden in the woodwork. So far, so Dickens. However, O'Connor introduces plot elements that make the story quintessentially Whitmanesque. Like Whitman's Civil War "Drum-Taps" poems, "The Carpenter" emphasizes reconciliation between North and South, here embodied in the figures of two sons the family thought lost— one a Union soldier, one Confederate—whom the carpenter has nursed back to health in a Washington hospital and delivers into the bosom of their family. Like the "Calamus" poems, "The Carpenter" also stresses comradeship—"the love passing the love of women," as the carpenter calls it. As the story opens, the dashing Michael Faulkner is about to seduce his friend John Dyzer's wife; after his tête-à-tête with the carpenter, Faulkner renounces "amativeness"—

Whitman's preferred term for male-female passion—in favor of comradeship. "My son," the carpenter says to him following his conversion, "with this kiss I dedicate you to a manly life."

The story was widely read and favorably received. A reviewer for *The Nation* recognized the title character as Walt Whitman, approved of the portrayal, and called the carpenter "the grand incarnation of friendliness and brotherhood." The story fit in squarely with mainstream American values of the time: reconciliation between North and South, childhood innocence, and the sanctity of marriage, motherhood, and home. Later disciples would portray Whitman as a cultural radical who figuratively blessed their socialist politics and bohemian lifestyles. O'Connor's Whitman, however, was a thoroughly Victorian hero capable of restoring the (national) family.

Years later O'Connor protested when another disciple wrote that in "The Carpenter" he had identified Whitman with Christ. O'Connor said he was after something "different and more subtle"—not Christ but the spirit of Christ. Still, his mythmaking in "The Carpenter" and "The Good Gray Poet" served to license the extravagance of later disciples who abandoned fine distinctions and declared Walt Whitman to be a modern Christ. O'Connor knew Whitman too well to think him a divinely perfect figure. Five years after "The Carpenter" was published, he and Whitman quarreled so violently that they ceased speaking to one another for a decade.

The immediate cause was an argument about civil rights. O'Connor, the ardent former abolitionist, was appalled by southern resistance to black suffrage; Whitman, always more egalitarian in his poetry than in his personal life, cared little what happened to southern blacks. He and O'Connor "were in the habit of goring each other in argument like two bulls," John Burroughs recalled, "and that time Walt was, I guess, rather brutal and insulting. . . . O'Connor fired up and turned on him. Walt took his hat and went home in a pet." The next day when they met on the street, Walt put out his hand in a gesture of reconciliation, but O'Connor walked right past him: "The iron had entered his soul." O'Connor detested Walt's social conservatism, but the two men had been arguing about slavery and civil rights for years. The break must also have been precipitated by Nelly O'Connor's deepening infatuation with Whitman. That fall of 1872, after ten years of living in an emotionally intense ménage à trois, William O'Connor called it quits: he broke off with Whitman and separated from Nelly.

For all the iron in his soul O'Connor could not abandon Whitman permanently. When the poet was attacked in the press in 1876, then again six years later, O'Connor came to his defense. He had never wavered in his belief in *Leaves of Grass*; besides, he loved a good fight. Whitman compared him to "a knight of chivalric ages, flying to the defense of the injured and maimed. It was always his *forte*— that seemed what he was made for." O'Connor came fully alive only in opposition. When *Leaves of Grass* was banned in Boston in 1882, he wrote Burroughs a nearly illegible letter, explaining that he was "trembling with fury." He continued, "I don't let the grass grow under my feet when an outrage of this kind is committed—one which makes Harlan's insignificant—and I am going to make the [Boston] District Attorney regret that he was ever born. . . . It is the greatest outrage of the century." Reading over this letter years later, Whitman mused, "William had unlimited capacity for raising hell . . . he was a human avalanche: nothing could defy him: stand up before him: nothing." The Boston affair fully reconciled O'Connor and Whitman; they began corresponding, and three years later O'Connor visited his old friend in Camden. When O'Connor was dying in Washington in 1889 and Whitman was too ill to travel to his old friend, he sent Horace Traubel instead. He told Traubel nothing about their lengthy estrangement, choosing instead to talk about his friend's "vehement magnificence." When O'Connor died soon after, Whitman was distraught: "The grand O'Connor! Who can take his place today? Who can take his place for *me*?"

✛ ✛ ✛

During O'Connor's final illness and for months after his death, Whitman talked about him almost daily in his chats with Horace Traubel. Occasionally, Whitman would compare O'Connor to the

other disciples: with his Celtic heritage O'Connor was more imaginative than Bucke, more emotionally volatile than Burroughs. Whitman dwelled most often on the contrast between O'Connor and
Burroughs, his first two disciples. "John and William are very different men," he emphasized to Traubel. "John is a placid landscape—
William is a landscape in a storm." The two men came from radically different backgrounds: O'Connor was a self-taught Boston
street urchin who fled his abusive Irish immigrant father when he
was only eight years old, Burroughs the son of a farmer in New
York's Catskills region, the only one among his nine brothers and
sisters to settle more than a few miles from the family farm. He
had a farmer's emotional equanimity, the ability to accept whatever
squalls or droughts came his way.

He brought his gift for calm observation and his countryman's
familiarity with the natural world to his enormously popular nature
essays. Today Burroughs is little known outside academic circles,
but for fifty years, from the 1870s to the 1920s, he was America's
most popular nature writer, more famous than either his predecessor
Henry David Thoreau or his contemporary John Muir. Burroughs
was extremely prolific, publishing three hundred essays and twenty-
seven books. At the turn of the century his publishers had the idea
of packaging his essays into special editions for schools; by 1912
virtually every school district in the country had at least one book
by Burroughs in the curriculum. Burroughs did not write for children, but his essays offered a vision of America that appealed to
school superintendents in a nation that was being transformed by
industrialization and immigration. Burroughs's most typical subject
was birds—not the exotic raptors of the wilderness but species familiar to farmers and city dwellers alike: warblers, thrushes, sparrows.
His anecdotal essays have a cozily familiar tone: "Have you ever
heard the song of the field sparrow? If you have lived in a pastoral
country with broad upland pastures, you could hardly have missed
him." Relatively few of Burroughs's readers lived near broad upland
pastures, but his assumption that they once had attracted both city
dwellers only a generation removed from the farm and school offi-
cials eager to Americanize the immigrant children pouring into the

nation's schools. There is nothing nostalgic about Burroughs's essays; he wrote what he knew. Except for the nine years he spent in Washington with Whitman and O'Connor, he lived all his life—more than seventy years of it—in rural New York State. Yet his essays satisfied a national nostalgia for a life lived close to the land. Burroughs's ambition as a young man was to be an "Audubon of prose"; in his contemporaries' eyes he succeeded.

It took Burroughs several years of false starts to find his vocation as a nature writer. In 1854, at the age of seventeen, he left the family farm to become a schoolteacher. Soon after, he discovered Emerson. "I read him in a sort of ecstasy," he recalled later. "I got him in my blood, and he colored my whole intellectual outlook." The teenaged schoolteacher determined to become a writer, and in the cramped spare bedrooms where he boarded with his students' families and in intervals snatched from summertime work on his father's dairy farm, he began composing Emersonian essays—imitations good enough that eventually one was published in the prestigious *Atlantic Monthly*, though the editor, James Russell Lowell, held it back for several months until he could verify that it was not plagiarized from Emerson.

By the time Burroughs broke into the *Atlantic*, he was married, but his bride took no pleasure in her husband's literary success. Ursula North Burroughs was the daughter of a successful farmer, a conventional young woman who saw her husband's "scribbling" as a waste of energy that should have been expended in making a comfortable home for them. She and John were mismatched from the moment they met as teenagers. He was powerfully attracted to the dark-eyed beauty, writing during their courtship that she "wets my taste and makes the saliva run." Ursula, however, coolly kept John at a distance before their marriage; afterward she complained about his "unending" sexual demands. Five years into their marriage she left her husband for an extended visit to relatives, writing him that he should use the period to learn chastity and self-control: "Just as there is more than a bedroom to a house, there is more than the activity of a bedroom to a marriage. I would like to think that I share more than just that part of your life." Instead of learning chas-

FIGURE 1.5. John Burroughs, 1862, the year before he met Walt Whitman. American Museum of Natural History Library.

tity, John learned how easy it was for a tall, good-looking, articulate young man to find more ardent female companions. And Ursula had no real interest in sharing John's intellectual life. She called him a fool for "masquerading" as an author and forbade him from using the parlor of their rented house to write his essays.

When in 1861 Burroughs discovered the work of a poet who quickly displaced Emerson as his literary hero, he said little of it to Ursula. On his own he used a school holiday to travel to New York City, where, he had heard, he was likely to find Walt Whitman at Pfaff's, a bohemian saloon. Whitman was often at Pfaff's in those days but not during the brief period that a schoolteacher could afford to stay in Manhattan. Burroughs returned to rural New York State and corresponded with his friends Myron Benton and Elijah Allen, who were as enthusiastic about Whitman as he. Allen even succeeded in meeting the poet. Early in the Civil War Allen had moved

FIGURE 1.6. Ursula North, 1857, the year she married John Burroughs. American Museum of Natural History Library.

to Washington and opened an army supply store. When Whitman came to Washington at the beginning of 1863, Allen befriended him and began writing Burroughs tantalizing letters, telling how on hot afternoons Whitman would come in from the street, sink into a camp chair in Allen's store, and fan himself while chatting. Allen told Whitman about his friend John Burroughs, and the poet said that he would like to meet the young writer-schoolteacher. Finally, Burroughs could stand it no longer. He quit his teaching job and headed for Washington in the fall of 1863. He took the first job he could find, burying the bodies of Union soldiers in mass graves, even though he found the work so gruesome that he frequently had to retreat to the nearby woods to vomit. In his free time he lingered about Allen's supply store, hoping that Whitman would drop in. Finally, he did. "Walt, here's the young man from the country I told you about," Allen said. Walt enclosed Burroughs's fine-boned hand in his great fist. "I have seen Walt and think him glorious," Burroughs wrote to Ursula, whom he had left behind to live with her relatives.

Within a few weeks Burroughs quit the burial detail, sent for Ursula, and found an undemanding position as a clerk in the Treasury Department, which gave him time to write and to see Walt Whitman. They quickly became close friends. As with O'Connor, there was a powerful homoerotic undercurrent to their relationship. Burroughs's published writings about Whitman contain lovingly detailed physical descriptions, and in a letter to a friend he talked about observing Walt bathing: "Such a handsome body, and such delicate rosy flesh I never saw before. I told him he looked good enough to eat." Whitman, for his part, kissed Burroughs "as if I were a girl." "I have been much with Walt," he wrote proudly soon after arriving in Washington. "Have even slept with him. I love him very much." In the face of such comments, Burroughs's most recent biographer hastens to assure readers that in the nineteenth century to sleep with someone signified sharing only a bedroom, not necessarily a bed, and that Burroughs was noted for his "voracious" heterosexuality. True enough. Yet while it would be wrong to overstate the erotic dimension of Burroughs's attraction to Whitman, it would be just as misleading to ignore it. Burroughs, like all the disciples, was drawn to both poet and poems, believing the man to be indistinguishable from his work. Whitman "is by far the wisest man I have ever met," he wrote early in their relationship. "There is nothing more to be said after he gives his views. It is as if Nature herself had spoken."

The link, seemingly unmediated, between Walt Whitman and nature inspired all of Burroughs's writing about Whitman: two books and fifty essays, stretching from 1866, when Burroughs was twenty-nine, to 1920, a year before his death at eighty-three. Burroughs understood that *Leaves of Grass* could not be defended by the conventional standards of nineteenth-century poetry. Instead, he argued that the *Leaves* was not a work of art but a direct manifestation of nature, as elemental as waves or weather. "Whatever else 'Leaves of Grass' may be, it is not poetry as the world uses that term," he wrote. "It is an inspired utterance. . . . Lovers of Whitman no more go to him for poetry than they go to the ocean for the pretty shells and pebbles on the beach." Burroughs did not consider Whitman to be a nature writer in the way he himself was in his detailed, genial essays about birds and landscape. After all, Whitman spent most of his childhood and all his adult life in cities, and he depended on others for the details of flora and fauna—it was Burroughs who told him about the hermit thrush, the bird that became one of the principal images in the great Lincoln elegy "When Lilacs Last in the Dooryard Bloom'd." Rather, Burroughs thought of Whitman as the poet of "a larger more fundamental nature, indeed of the Cosmos itself."

Whitman's reliance upon "absolute nature" meant that he was inevitably, in Burroughs's mind, a fundamentally religious poet. By the time he met Whitman, Burroughs had begun to craft the "gospel of nature" that would be central to his life and work. Burroughs's farmer father was an Old School Baptist, a fundamentalist who discouraged his son's literary inclinations because he feared they might lead to Methodism. Burroughs, in fact, flirted with Methodism as a teenager and had an ecstatic religious experience at a camp meeting. However, he soon recanted and rejected all Christian theology as "irrational and puerile." Then at nineteen he got Emerson the way his father got religion. When he met Whitman a few years later, Burroughs thought that here was "the man Emerson invoked and prayed for." During the Civil War, embarking on his career as a nature writer, Burroughs combined Emersonian transcendentalism, Walt Whitman, and nature into a post-Christian creed that had wide appeal to Gilded Age spiritual seekers, as Americans increasingly left the countryside for rapidly growing cities. Urbanization was a "spiritual catastrophe," he believed, but nature offered salvation. "Amid the decay of creeds," Burroughs wrote, "love of nature has high religious value. This has saved many persons in this world. . . . [Nature] is their church, and the rocks and the hills are the altars, and the creed is written in the flowers of the field and in the sands of the shore. . . . Every walk to the woods is a religious rite, every bath in the stream is a saving ordinance."

"Under the influence of Christianity," Burroughs wrote, "man has taken himself out of the category of natural things." Walt Whitman put humans back into nature. The outsized persona of "Song of Myself" recalls the mythological Green Man, repeatedly describing himself in ways that blur distinctions between the human and the natural: "I find I incorporate gneiss, coal, long-threaded moss, fruits, grains, esculent roots, / And am stucco'd with quadrupeds and birds all over." O'Connor was the first of the disciples to compare Whitman to Christ, but it was Burroughs who first explicated the Whitmanian creed. He called *Leaves of Grass* "the most religious book I ever met" and described it as "the broad hymn of the praise of things; all the works of the Creative Father are sung in joyous strains." Burroughs later abandoned the concept of a personalized God (even as a metaphorical Creative Father), but he never wavered in his belief that *Leaves of Grass* was "primarily a gospel and . . . only secondarily a poem." He saw the *Leaves* as the foundation of a religion uniquely suited to a democratic and scientific age. Recalling his own Baptist father but speaking for many in his generation, Burroughs wrote that "the old religion, the religion of our fathers, was founded upon a curse. Sin, repentance, fear, Satan, hell, play important parts." However, Whitman "sings a new song. . . . The earth is as divine as heaven, and there is no god more sacred than yourself." Just as *Leaves of Grass* was more gospel than poem, Whitman was less a poet than "a great and astounding religious teacher."

Burroughs's friendship with Whitman continued unabated throughout their nine years together in Washington. The two men would take long hikes together along Rock Creek, Burroughs teaching Whitman about birds, Whitman encouraging his young disciple's newfound passion for nature writing. Every Sunday Whitman took his breakfast at the Burroughs house on Capitol Hill, somewhat to the dismay of Ursula, who could never count on him to arrive anywhere near the appointed hour. "The coffee would boil, the griddle would smoke, and car after car would go jingling by, but no Walt," Burroughs recalled years later. "But at last a car would stop, and Walt would roll off it and saunter up to the door—so cheery, and so unaware of the annoyance he had caused." Afterward the two friends would stroll outdoors and have long talks while sitting on the Capitol building's "cataract of marble steps."

Inevitably, despite their wildly different temperaments, Burroughs and O'Connor became friends through their mutual admiration of Whitman. When O'Connor had to find new quarters after the Civil War, he and his family boarded with Burroughs for a brief, disastrous period. The fastidious Ursula could not bear the O'Connors' bohemian circle, the empty liquor bottles tossed in a pile outside their room, William's predilection for sneaking women into the house when Nelly and their daughter were away. Burroughs was more tolerant; what concerned him was O'Connor's "suicidal" work schedule. O'Connor wrote his Christmas story "The Carpenter" while living with Burroughs, feverishly composing the piece in every hour he could snatch from his government job, fueled by tea and tobacco. Burroughs, working in his garden, would throw plums through O'Connor's open window, hoping to distract his friend. The O'Connors moved out after a few months, and Whitman and Burroughs established a regular Sunday routine: breakfast with Ursula, supper with William and Nelly. Unlike Nelly, Ursula took no interest in Whitman's poetry, but she eventually warmed up to the man; Whitman, for his part, was quite fond of Sula, as he called her. The problems in the couple's marriage were John's fault, not hers, Whitman said, and he chastised John for his "wantonness," which hurt Ursula "more than she or anyone deserves to be hurt. The urges of your biology spark the one great and only flaw in your otherwise generous and noble character."

Burroughs meekly accepted the admonitions. He was in awe of Whitman throughout the Washington years. He confided to his journal, "It is a feast to me to look at Walt's face; it is incomparably the grandest face I ever saw—such sweetness and harmony, and such strength. . . . If that is not the face of a poet, then it is the face of a god. None of his pictures do it half justice." Earlier Burroughs wrote of Whitman's "incredible and exhaustless" magnetism. The phrase occurs in *Notes on Walt Whitman as Poet and Person*, which Burroughs wrote and published at his own expense in 1867, four years after first meeting Whitman. Burroughs permitted Whitman to become a silent collaborator in the book's composition; the poet supplied biographical material, polished Burroughs's prose, and wrote all of one chapter. However, the intense, hagiographic praise of Whitman is Burroughs's own. He writes at the book's beginning, "In History, at wide intervals, . . . there come . . . individuals whom their own days little suspect, and never realize, but who, it turns out, mark and make new eras, plant the standard again ahead, and in one man personify vast races and sweeping revolutions. I consider Walt Whitman such a man." Burroughs never retreated from the fervid estimation of Whitman's stature that he offered at age thirty. In his final essay on Whitman, written at eighty-three, Burroughs said the same thing more forcefully: "I look upon him as the greatest personality . . . that has appeared in the world during the Christian era."

Whitman did what he could to help along his young disciple's budding career as a nature writer, including suggesting the title for Burroughs's first, highly popular collection of nature essays, *Wake-Robin* (1871). Burroughs later recalled how he wrote the essays in *Wake-Robin*, dense with details of the outdoors, while sitting at a desk facing an iron wall as keeper of a Treasury Department vault. Less than two years after the book was published, buoyed by its success, he quit his job and bought a large abandoned orchard in New York's Hudson Valley. He found a position as a part-time bank examiner, tended the orchard, and devoted more of his time to writing. Three weeks after Burroughs left Washington at the beginning of January 1873, Walt Whitman had a massive stroke that left him paralyzed on the left side. Ursula, who had temporarily stayed behind in Washington, urged him to come live with her, but Whitman preferred to remain in his rented room until a few months later when, realizing that he would not fully recover, he moved into the home of his brother George in Camden, New Jersey.

Separated by almost two hundred miles, Burroughs and Whitman nevertheless maintained their close friendship in the years after Burroughs built Riverby, his stone house overlooking the Hudson River. Burroughs sprinkled references to Whitman through his essays, and in 1877 he concluded his book *Birds and Poets* with a lengthy essay on Whitman, "The Flight of the Eagle." By this time Burroughs had a considerable reputation as a nature writer, and in the preface to the volume he fretted about his readers' reactions to Walt Whitman: "I hope [the reader] will not be scared away when I boldly confront him . . . with this name of strange portent, Walt Whitman, for I assure him that in this misjudged man he may press the strongest poetic pulse that has yet beaten in America, or perhaps in modern times." He ends "The Flight of the Eagle" by warning any reader who might be moved to take up *Leaves of Grass* that it is not poetry "in the Virgilian, Tennysonian, or Lowellian sense." Mindful of his reputation, Burroughs was not about to rush into print with an over-the-top panegyric like O'Connor's "The Good Gray Poet" or "The Carpenter." Yet for all Burroughs's caution, he never concealed his admiration of Whitman and his religious awe for *Leave of Grass*. He writes in ecstatic tones of Whitman's "warm, breathing, towering, magnetic Presence" and classes *Leaves of Grass* with human history's "great inspired utterances, like the Bible."

The same year that Burroughs published "The Flight of the Eagle," Whitman made the first of his visits to Riverby. That first year he was accompanied by his young working-class companion Harry Stafford, a successor to Peter Doyle. ("They cut up like two boys and annoyed me sometimes," Burroughs wrote in his journal. "Great tribulation in the kitchen in the morning. Can't get them up to breakfast in time.") Whitman adored the steamer trip up the Hudson to Burroughs's West Park home and fell in love with Burroughs's "honeysuckle-and-rose-embower'd cottage." Whitman devotes several chapters in *Specimen Days*, his casual collection of memoirs, to Riverby; the first is titled "Happiness and Raspberries," referring to Ursula's breakfasts of coffee, cream, and home-grown fruit. The summer of the raspberries was also marked by the birth of Burroughs's son, Julian. It is likely that even Whitman did not know for sure, though he may have suspected, that forty-two-year-old Ursula was not the infant's mother; the child was born to a young Irish servant on a neighboring estate who, at Ursula's insistence, returned to Ireland immediately after giving birth. At the same time Ursula also insisted that John stop his affairs with other women; in this demand she was less successful.

The pattern of Whitman's annual visits to Riverby was broken in 1880, when he spent the entire summer in Canada with R. M. Bucke, a fervent new disciple intent on writing a book about Whitman that would supersede Burroughs's *Notes on Walt Whitman*. However, Burroughs visited Whitman regularly and encouraged him to leave Camden—"that half-dead place," Burroughs called it—and settle near Riverby. He was unsuccessful in his appeals, but in 1883 he lured Whitman to join him for several days at Ocean Grove, New Jersey. Burroughs was exhilarated to be reunited with his old friend, writing that Whitman's "presence and companionship act like a cordial upon me that nearly turns my head." As convinced as ever that the poet had a special affinity with nature, Burroughs rhapsodized about the sight of Whitman upon the New Jersey strand: "The great bard on my right hand, and the sea upon my left—the thoughts of the one equally grand with the suggestions and elemental heave of the other. From any point of view W.W. is impressive."

The next year Whitman moved into his own house on Mickle Street, and the two men began to drift apart. By 1888 Whitman lamented to Horace Traubel, "For years and years John has seemed to avoid me. I never try to guess why. Sometimes I think he is a little afraid of my friends." The old poet was exactly right. Talking about the Mickle Street years, Burroughs explained that he "had not grown cold toward [Whitman], but I saw less of him, and was not so active a disciple as I had been. I had absorptions of my own. Then the crowd that surrounded him was not altogether to my liking." Burroughs was referring primarily to Bucke, who frequently traveled to Camden from his home in Canada, and the ubiquitous Horace Traubel, who made a point of visiting Whitman daily. Burroughs thinks that you and Bucke "are too boisterously radical,"

Whitman told Traubel. Burroughs disliked the reverential tone of the birthday dinners Traubel organized for Whitman and made a point of avoiding the events, sending a cranky, terse greeting in May 1891 on the occasion of Whitman's seventy-second birthday: "Walt, I keep your birthday pruning my vineyard and in reading an hour from your poems under my fig tree. I will let you eat your dinner in peace, as I shall want to do if I ever reach my 72d." When the letter was read aloud to the assembled guests, Whitman leaned over to Traubel, who was seated next to him: "The only trouble with John is, he has a bit of a suspicion of us all—thinks I must have fallen in bad company." Then the old man laughed heartily.

Despite his distaste for the Camden disciples, Burroughs rushed to Mickle Street in late December of that year when Traubel telegraphed him that Whitman was dying. Burroughs spent Christmas Eve by the bedside of the man whom he regarded as the greatest religious teacher since Jesus. "Walt on the bed with eyes closed," Burroughs recorded in his journal, "but he knows me and speaks my name as of old, and kisses me. He asks me to sit beside him awhile. I do so, holding his hand. . . . After a while I go out for fear of fatiguing him. He says, 'It is all right, John,' evidently referring to his approaching end."

Whitman held on for three more months, dying on March 26, 1892. Three weeks later, still devastated, Burroughs wrote in his journal, "I am fairly well these days but sad, sad. Walt constantly in mind. I think I see more plainly how Jesus came to be deified—his followers loved him; love transforms everything." Burroughs assuaged his grief through his pen. In the first month after Whitman's death he published four articles on the poet; during the next four years he published a total of nineteen works on Whitman, culminating with the book *Whitman: A Study* (1896). This critical analysis, which remains one of the most perceptive books published about Whitman, repeatedly emphasizes the same point Burroughs had made thirty years earlier: Whitman's work cannot be judged against other poetry; it is inspired utterance intended to transform its readers' lives. Whitman "is not a poet in the usual . . . sense," Burroughs writes, "but poet-prophet or poet-seer. . . . We have all been slow to see that his cherished ends were religious rather than literary."

Burroughs took essentially the same awestruck, spiritualized view of Whitman as did the later disciples, such as Bucke and Traubel. Yet Burroughs's prose was ever artful, his view always nuanced, his tone that of the genial, popular nature writer. Burroughs detested Traubel's break into imitative Whitmanesque verse and Bucke's strident philosophizing. In 1895, when the other disciples elected Burroughs president of the recently formed Walt Whitman Fellowship in absentia, he wrote curt letters to both Traubel and Bucke refusing the position. To Bucke he explained, "I am too jealous of my literary reputation to have it associated with such things as Horace is doing. I refer to [his] ridiculous imitations of Walt. . . . To me they are positively inane, & his prose is not much better." As for Bucke, Burroughs complained to Traubel that the doctor's writing on Whitman and cosmic consciousness would provoke ridicule: "I do not like it."

Burroughs surely would not like it any better to find himself linked to Bucke and Traubel in these pages. Yet he pioneered the spiritualized interpretation of *Leaves of Grass* that was furthered by subsequent disciples. Burroughs was the first reader of the *Leaves* to regard it as Whitman intended: a New Bible. From the 1860s through the 1920s Burroughs reached thousands of readers with his interpretation of *Leaves of Grass* as post-Christian scripture, a gospel of nature and individuality. The ends of Whitman's poetry were religious, not literary, Burroughs emphasized over and over; Whitman was not a mere poet but "a great religious teacher and prophet." To read Whitman aright was to have your life transformed: "Whitman means a life as much as Christianity means a life," Burroughs wrote. He knew what he was talking about. Thanks to *Leaves of Grass*, a twenty-six-year-old schoolteacher had been inspired to quit his job, move to a new city, and seek out the master. Burroughs's journey to Washington in 1863 was the first Whitman pilgrimage. It would not be the last.

CHAPTER TWO

Anne Gilchrist:

Infatuation and Discipleship

Are you the new person drawn toward me?
To begin with take warning—I am surely far different from what
*   you suppose;*
Do you suppose you will find in me your ideal?
Do you think it so easy to have me become your lover?

THE LOBBY OF THE MONTGOMERY HOUSE HOTEL in Philadelphia was bustling with activity on September 13, 1876. In addition to the usual contingent of businessmen and commercial travelers, Philadelphia's hotels were filled with tourists who had come to see the celebrated Centennial Exposition in Fairmount Park, the grandiose one-hundredth birthday party that the United States was throwing for itself. Few of those hurrying through the Montgomery House parlor would have noticed the plump middle-aged Englishwoman seated in a corner, obviously waiting for someone. She seemed a completely conventional, soberly dressed matron. No one could have guessed that Anne Gilchrist, forty-eight years old, was expecting the love of her life. That the two had not yet met seemed to her a minor detail.

Her soul mate was Walt Whitman. She had encountered him through his poetry, which she first read in 1869, eight years after she had been widowed in London at the age of thirty-three with four young children to raise. A woman of letters from a genteel family, she supported herself on a small inheritance and the royalties from a biography of William Blake that she had completed for her husband after his death. Her response to *Leaves of Grass* had been immediate and overwhelming: "I had not dreamed that words could cease to be words, and become electric streams like these," she wrote her friend William Michael Rossetti, who had edited an English edition of Whitman's poetry. "I do assure you that, strong as I am, I feel sometimes as if I had not bodily strength to read many of these poems." Her reaction to the poems was physical and deeply sexual, though the language of her letters to Rossetti was veiled. She was more direct when, two years after first reading Whitman, she obtained his address from Rossetti and wrote him a letter. "Dear Friend," she began, decorously enough, but within a few pages her tone was panting, ecstatic: "O come. Come, my darling: look into these eyes and see the loving ardent inspiring soul in them. Easily, easily will you learn to love all the rest of me for the sake of that and take me to your breasts for ever and ever." When Whitman failed to respond within a month, she wrote him a second letter, this one more ardent and, certainly, more explicit about her desires: "I am yet young enough to bear thee children, my darling." Whitman was finally jolted into action, and he wrote what he hoped would be a placating reply: brief, tactful, vague, an attempt to move from his correspondent's intensely personal plane to the safely general: "I am not insensible to your love. I too send you my love. And do you feel no disappointment because I now write so briefly. My book is my best letter, my response, my truest explanation of all." But Anne Gilchrist would not be put off so easily. She continued her ardent letters for the next five years, at which point she set sail for America, bringing with her three of her four children, her pianoforte, and a houseful of good furniture. She intended to set up housekeeping as Walt Whitman's wife.

‡ ‡ ‡

The background of Anne Burrows Gilchrist was conventionally Victorian. Her father, a solicitor, and mother, a clergyman's daughter, were respectable middle-class Church of England Londoners. Yet

FIGURE 2.1. Anne Gilchrist, 1874. Collection of Marion Alcaro.

by her teenage years she had a reputation as an intellectual rebel and religious freethinker. "Rhoda and I have already commenced correspondence, and she tells me she is going to be confirmed," seventeen-year-old Anne Burrows wrote to her school friend Julia Newton. "Poor girl, she is very pleased. I never will be confirmed with my own consent. If I am forced, I must submit; but I trust I shall escape." Under the influence of Emerson's essays the teenaged Anne Burrows cobbled together a liberal theology similar to that developed by John Burroughs and other spiritual seekers of the era. "I feel deeply grateful for the warm, true affection that prompts your anxiety about my views of religion," she later wrote Julia Newton in a letter. However, Burrows continued, "I cannot help thinking you attach too much importance to creeds and doctrines. . . . I think, dear Julia, we start with a different aim; those who take your view of religion . . . think that our sole object is to get to Heaven and escape damnation; and this necessarily results from their view of human nature and of God. But to me it seems, that our great aim should be to fulfil the ends for which we were created; that is to say, develop to the utmost the nature which God has given us; and I cannot think of Heaven as a place, but as a state of Being."

At eighteen Anne Burrows met Alexander Gilchrist. Alexander, two months younger than Anne, was immediately smitten and for two years waged a relentless campaign for her love. He never won it. But he wore her down, and in 1848 they were engaged to be married. She told him she could not love him "as a wife should love"; he said he was glad to have her on any terms. When Alexander, a freelance art critic, received a commission to write a biography of the recently deceased painter William Etty, Alexander and Anne married on the strength of his prospects.

In an essay written after her husband's death, Anne Gilchrist gives a decorously veiled account of her wedding night. She argues that the high-flown sexual ignorance promoted by middle-class Victorian culture made the reality of intercourse a "hateful, bitter humiliation" for women. "Do you think," she asks rhetorically, "there is ever a bride who does not taste more or less this bitterness in her cup?" The Victorian system of sexual/gender apartheid—to use one historian's term—ensured that the odds were virtually nil that a well-brought-up middle-class bride would find sexual satisfaction early in her marriage. Kept in ignorance of their own physiology and human sexuality, women were deprived even of the language for discussing sexual matters; sexual vocabulary for women was limited to the veiled language of pregnancy and childbirth, the circumlocutions of *confinement* and *blessed event* or, for the daring, the French *enceinte*. Sexual experience before marriage was out of the question for middle-class women, who were, in any case, widely presumed to be virtually without sexual desire. "As a general rule, a modest woman seldom desires any sexual gratification for herself," Dr. William Acton wrote in a well-known Victorian health manual. "She submits to her husband's embraces, but principally to gratify him; and, were it not for the desire of maternity, would far rather be relieved from his attentions." It is questionable how accurately Acton described the reality of nineteenth-century marriages, but his views reflect a cultural discourse that minimized women's sexuality.

If middle-class Victorian culture dismissed women's sexual needs, it recognized the power of male sexuality and condoned sexual experimentation with prostitutes and lower-class women. However, at the same time an ethic of male "restraint" circulated in the culture, and it is likely that Alexander Gilchrist—sensitive and artistic, eager to wed the woman he met at eighteen—came to their wedding night as inexperienced as Anne Burrows. But at least he was passionately in love with his bride. She, who had reasoned herself into marriage with a man she could not love deeply, found the first months of marriage "dark and gloomy."

The gloom lifted when she found herself *enceinte*. Percy Carlyle Gilchrist was born eleven months after the wedding. Three more children followed in the next seven years. During the same period her husband completed *The Life of William Etty, R.A.* The book's greatest significance was that it won Alexander Gilchrist the friendship of Thomas Carlyle. If his oldest son's middle name is any indication, Alexander had long been enamored of the Sage of Chelsea, and when 6 Cheyne Row, the house next door to Carlyle's, became vacant in 1856, Alexander inquired, tentatively, about taking it for his family. "I dare not advise anybody into a house," the great man wrote his young friend, "(almost as dangerous as advising him to a wife, except that divorce is easier); but if Heaven should please to rain you, accidentally, into that house, I should esteem it a kindness." The Gilchrists rained into Chelsea soon after, and Alexander began writing a biography of William Blake. The project brought him into contact with the luminaries of the London art and literary worlds, and the Gilchrists soon became friends of the brilliant Rossetti family, including siblings Dante Gabriel, William Michael, and Christina. Anne entertained frequently—the Gilchrist home became an artistic social center—even though her third child was born just a few months after their move to Chelsea. Moreover, she quickly gained the demanding friendship of Jane Carlyle, who peppered her with gossip and notes and requests for aid in the household arts that the unconventional older woman had never mastered: "Can you conveniently come in and *stand over me* while I make the bread myself to-day? . . . A precious Bother I am to be sure to you! But if I can never reward you on earth you are pretty certain to have two little additional wings for it in heaven!" Between children and friends and her work with Alexander—his prose style was, Anne noted, atrocious, and he depended on her to untangle his syntax—Anne Gilchrist must have been frantically busy. Yet during the years in Chelsea she somehow managed to forge her own literary career as a freelance popular science writer.

It was not unusual for a midnineteenth-century literary person to be interested in science. New discoveries in geology, biology, chemistry, and physics were shaking the Victorian worldview, and the editors of popular magazines were eager to enlist writers who could lucidly explain new scientific developments to a general audience. However, it was virtually unprecedented for a woman to write about science. In the 1850s postsecondary training in science was unavailable to Englishwomen; careers in university teaching, engineering, and medicine were all restricted to men. Anne Gilchrist, whose education ended at sixteen, not only had no one to aid her in her scientific education but also had to confront cultural taboos that deemed science as "unwomanly." Her science writing was a continuation, by other means, of the war against Victorian orthodoxy that she had declared as a teenager. One of her first articles, published in Charles Dickens's new magazine, *All the Year Round*, took direct aim at conservative religion. Writing about gorillas in 1859, the year of Darwin's *On the Origin of Species*, Anne Gilchrist titled her article "Our Nearest Relation." Her other articles take up botany, astronomy, electricity, and physics. Her most ambitious article, "The Indestructibility of Force," which appeared in the prestigious *Macmillan's Magazine*, ranges widely over new developments in physics, concluding with an eloquent peroration that attacks the hostility to science displayed by both clerics and poets. Even Wordsworth, the revered giant of English poetry, cannot escape Anne Gilchrist's censure; she scoffs at his romantic notion that scientific inquiry destroys the beauty and mystery of nature.

During her residence on Cheyne Row, Gilchrist showed herself to be a devoted mother, accomplished housekeeper, expert editor, fine writer, and bold progressive thinker. All those strengths would be needed at the conclusion of her fifth year in Chelsea when two of her children came down with scarlet fever. Heedless of her own safety, she sent her two uninfected children to the countryside and nursed the two sufferers by herself around the clock; she would not allow Alexander to do more than peek his head into the sickroom. The two children recovered, but Alexander, worn out with long hours of work on his Blake biography, caught the infection and died within a week. It was near the close of 1861; he and his wife were only thirty-three years old, and she was left with four children younger than ten. Jane Carlyle pleaded with her to stay in Chelsea, but the young widow was desperate to establish a new, independent life. Early in 1862 Anne Gilchrist and her four children moved to a cottage in Surrey, not far from London.

The proximity to London was critical; Gilchrist was determined to finish her husband's biography of Blake. Within weeks after his death she began firing off letters to Alexander Macmillan, her husband's publisher, and to the Rossettis. With their assistance she completed the massive two-volume biography within a year; *The Life of William Blake* was published in 1863. The income from the book, combined with money from her family, meant that Gilchrist could live comfortably, if frugally, without working for pay, and in the years following the publication of the *Life of Blake* she devoted herself to educating her four children. (She would "skin, and bury herself alive for the benefit of her children," Jane Carlyle had observed.) Sociable Anne Gilchrist kept up old friendships—London was only a train ride away—and made new ones, becoming close to Alfred Tennyson when the poet laureate and his wife took a house nearby in Surrey. Her life was rich in family and friends but completely devoid of romance. Her forty-first birthday passed before she fell in love. Fittingly for a woman of letters, it was with a character in a book.

✢ ✢ ✢

Strictly speaking, Walt Whitman did not write *Leaves of Grass*. The copyright notice in the first (1855) edition is in the name of "Walter Whitman," and no name at all appears on the title page. Instead, facing the title page is an engraving of what appears to be an idealized workingman, hat on his head, arm cocked negligently, collar open to reveal his undershirt. The name *Walt Whitman* is not mentioned until page twenty-nine, when it appears as abruptly as if conjured from thin air: "Walt Whitman, an American, one of the roughs, a kosmos, / Disorderly fleshy and sensual." The context makes clear that "Walt Whitman" is a persona, an invented mythic character along the lines of Paul Bunyan. Paradoxically, at the same time as the writer stands apart from his tall-tale creation, he encourages his readers to conflate poet and persona, reaching out to them with an intimacy never before seen in literature.

Whitman was not the first poet to test the limits of his printers' stock of *I*'s, but he was the first to deplete their stock of *y*'s, *o*'s, and *u*'s. "I celebrate myself, / And what I assume you shall assume, / For every atom belonging to me as good belongs to you," he wrote in the opening lines of his first book, and throughout *Leaves of Grass* the poet reaches out to the reader, conjuring a relationship as deftly

FIGURE 2.2. Engraving of Walt Whitman by Samuel Hollyer; frontispiece to the 1855 *Leaves of Grass*.

as he conjures the outsized figure of Walt Whitman. The long initial
poem of the 1855 first edition (later titled "Song of Myself") ends
on a lyrical, intimate note—as if, over forty-four pages, poet and
reader have become the closest of friends:

> Failing to fetch me at first keep encouraged,
> Missing me one place search another,
> I stop some where waiting for you

From 1860 on he concluded every edition of *Leaves of Grass* with
"So Long," a poem that attempts to break the boundaries of the
page and make direct physical contact with readers:

> Camerado, this is no book,
> Who touches this touches a man,
> (Is it night? are we here together alone?)
> It is I you hold and who holds you,
> I spring from the pages into your arms

The book is filled with similar erotic appeals, and the edition Gilchrist read had even more intimate passages that Whitman later
thought better of and deleted, such as the original opening to "A
Song for Occupations":

> Come closer to me;
> Push close, my lovers, and take the best I possess;
> Yield closer and closer, and give me the best you possess.
>
> This is unfinished business with me—How is it with you?
> (I was chill'd with the cold types, cylinder, wet paper
>   between us.)
>
> Male and Female!
> I pass so poorly with paper and types, I must pass with
>   the contact of bodies and souls.

"Male and Female!" Whitman cries, appealing to both sexes to push
closer and yield to him. In the twenty-first century we have become
so used to thinking of Whitman as the Good Gay Poet that it's easy
to overlook his crossover appeal, his textual bisexuality. During his

lifetime he received countless romance-tinged letters from women who responded to the erotically charged invitations scattered throughout *Leaves of Grass*; Anne Gilchrist happened to be one of the first, and certainly the most serious among them.

She discovered *Leaves of Grass* in June 1869, fourteen years after Whitman published his first edition. Early in his career Whitman was fiercely nationalistic, and he made no effort to have his work published in Great Britain. However, a few remaindered copies of the 1855 first edition made their way to England via an itinerant book peddler. One of these fell into the hands of the poet and critic William Michael Rossetti, who loved the book and circulated copies to family and friends. Not always with success—his brother Dante Gabriel said that he had "not been so happy in loathing anything for a long while." But William's enthusiasm was undiminished, and in 1868 he arranged to publish an edition of Whitman in England. Rossetti's *Poems by Walt Whitman* was the first introduction to Whitman for a generation of English artists and intellectuals. It was something of a peculiar introduction. Rossetti, certain that no English publisher would tolerate Whitman's frank sexuality, initially toyed with the idea of bringing out an expurgated edition. Whitman protested, and Rossetti dropped the idea. He would change nothing, he proudly declared; rather than alter a word, he would simply exclude the poem. There was a lot to exclude: one half of *Leaves of Grass*, including "Song of Myself," Whitman's longest and greatest poem; "The Sleepers" and "I Sing the Body Electric," poems now central to Whitman's reputation; and virtually all of the sequence known as "Children of Adam," poems celebrating heterosexual love. Rossetti claimed that he had refused to play the role of Bowdler, but his edition is a bowdlerized *Leaves of Grass*. Whitman's eroticized celebration of the human body—one of his most important themes—is absent from the collection, and in reprinting Whitman's 1855 preface Rossetti omitted words that were even marginally questionable, such as *womb* and *prostitute*. Rossetti fussed over *Leaves of Grass* like an English nanny pulling up stockings and buttoning collars. Even then, he apologized in his introduction for the poems' frequently "gross" and "crude" qualities, and he assumed the book would be distasteful to women; he did not bother to send a copy to Anne Gilchrist, with whom he had worked so closely on the Blake biography.

Gilchrist came across the Rossetti edition more than a year after it was published. When a friend loaned her a copy, she wrote to Rossetti in a state of intense excitement, saying that she was "spell-bound"; for the two weeks since she had received the book, she could read nothing else. Pleased, Rossetti wrote back immediately and—after a great deal of hedging about Whitman's "bluntness" and "directness"—concluded that anybody who valued Whitman as much as Gilchrist should read the whole of him and offered to lend her the complete *Leaves of Grass*. She immediately took him up on the offer; the next few days, as she made her way through the poems, were to alter radically the course of her life.

In the complete *Leaves of Grass* that Rossetti loaned her, Gilchrist found poems even more intensely intimate than anything in the Rossetti edition, as in this parenthetical aside:

(Hark close, and still, what I now whisper to you,
I love you—O you entirely possess me,
O I wish that you and I escape from the rest, and go
    utterly off—O free and lawless,
Two hawks in the air—two fishes swimming in the sea
    not more lawless than we;)

Moreover, this intimate address to the reader was contained within poems marked by a sexual frankness unlike anything to be found in nineteenth-century literature—aside, of course, from the vast body of pornography to which a middle-class woman like Anne Gilchrist was unlikely to have access. The last passage is from a poem that begins, "From pent-up, aching rivers; / . . . From my own voice resonant—singing the phallus, / Singing the song of procreation." Other poems in the "Children of Adam" sequence are even franker. One can only try to imagine the effect of a passage like the following on a vibrant woman who had never before encountered an artistic representation of sexual intercourse:

[L]ove-flesh swelling and deliciously aching;
Limitless limpid jets of love hot and enormous, quivering
    jelly of love, white-blow and delirious juice;
Bridegroom night of love working surely and softly into
    the prostrate dawn;
Undulating into the willing and yielding day,
Lost in the cleave of the clasping and sweet-flesh'd day.

However, Whitman's metaphor of intercourse as daybreak in this passage distinguishes it from pornography; on the other, the metaphor sexualizes nature, eroticizing the entire visible world. In addition, the passage differs from most pornography in its attention to women's active sexuality; the feminized day may yield to bridegroom night, but she also clasps him.

Leaves of Grass was unprecedented in its recognition of women's sexuality. At a time when medical experts like Acton proclaimed that respectable women "seldom desire any sexual gratification," Walt Whitman wrote, "Without shame the man I like knows and avows the deliciousness of his sex, / Without shame the woman I like knows and avows hers." Whitman's emphasis on women's sexual equality was part of a larger emphasis on gender equality unmatched by any male writer of the nineteenth century aside from John Stuart Mill. Whitman's great poems of the 1850s were written in dialogue with the vigorous woman's rights movements of that decade, as Sherry Ceniza has pointed out; among his close friends at the time were some of the era's leading feminists. "I am the poet of the woman the same as the man, / And I say it is as great to be a woman as to be a man," Whitman declared in 1855; he immediately followed his declaration with, "And I say there is nothing greater than the mother of men." The last line indicates the limits of Whitman's feminism. His proclamations of women's equality are set within poems that not only accept but promote the Victorian idealization of motherhood. Whitman was capable of writing about women:

They are not one jot less than I am,
They are tann'd in the face by shining suns and blowing
    winds,

Their flesh has the old divine suppleness and strength,
They know how to swim, row, ride, wrestle, shoot, run,
   strike, retreat, advance, resist, defend themselves,
They are ultimate in their own right—they are calm,
   clear, well-possess'd of themselves.

However, this passage occurs in a poem in which women's ultimate role is bearer of future generations.

Anne Gilchrist, mother of four, embraced both Whitman's celebration of motherhood and his emphasis on women's sexual and spiritual equality. Within days after she received the complete *Leaves of Grass*, she wrote Rossetti an extraordinary lengthy letter about the book. "I had not dreamed that words could cease to be words, and become electric streams like these," the letter begins. If Gilchrist's response to Whitman was electric, Rossetti proved the perfect conductor. In the course of his work on *Leaves of Grass*, Rossetti had shifted his role from editor to advocate, and he immediately began to consider how he could use Gilchrist's letters for "the cause." Without telling her, he copied passages from her letters and sent them to William O'Connor in the United States, knowing that the fiercely partisan O'Connor would show them to Whitman and be ready, at a moment's notice, to publish them. At the same time Rossetti wrote to Gilchrist, encouraging her to work up the letters for publication. Gilchrist was agreeable, and so Rossetti confessed. He might as well "make a clean breast of it," he wrote. He had sent her letters to the United States because "it wd. be a sin not to give Whitman a chance of knowing what cd. not fail to be a real pleasure & internal triumph to him—the immense enthusiasm his book had succeeded in inspiring in a thoroughly cultivated Englishwoman."

Gilchrist's status as an educated middle-class woman was what made her letters golden to Whitman advocates like Rossetti and O'Connor. If the initial hostility to *Leaves of Grass* focused on the poems' supposed formlessness, the increasing sexual frankness of the first three editions drew critics' fire to their sensuality. The charge that *Leaves of Grass* was "an outrage upon decency, and not fit to be seen in any respectable house" was representative of the criticism Whitman received in the 1860s, following the publication of the

"Children of Adam" sequence of poems. The critics' emphasis upon the respectable home served as a coded warning in the Victorian gender system: these poems were not fit for women. Even Whitman's defenders conceded that *Leaves of Grass* was unsuitable for the parlor; they simply argued that Whitman was no worse than Shakespeare or Rabelais.

Anne Gilchrist took a different approach. In her letters to Rossetti she suggested that only a woman could fully appreciate Whitman's message, only a wife and mother could recognize the essential purity of his treatment of sex and the body. All *Leaves of Grass* needs to become a success, she told Rossetti, is "acceptance from a woman. . . . I think they will take from a woman's lips, what they seem as though they could not from a man's." Her letters to Rossetti reveal that she was as entranced by Whitman's profeminist stance as by his erotic appeal. She contrasted Whitman's gospel of the sanctity of sex with what she saw as the culturally pernicious effects of the Hebrew Bible and its "astounding invention" that Adam and Eve were innocent of sex until they were expelled from Eden. The "Fall of Man," Gilchrist wrote, was "such a sneaking invention too, 'She did it'!"

When Gilchrist's letters to Rossetti, shaped into essay form, appeared in print, they were shrewdly titled "A Woman's Estimate of Walt Whitman." Rossetti's brief introduction claimed that the essay to follow was the "fullest, farthest-reaching, and most eloquent appreciation of Whitman yet put into writing" and also the most valuable—because, he emphasized, it was by "*a woman.*" He went on to vouch for her middle-class bona fides: this was no bohemian but a woman of the highest character, intellect, and culture. The assurances were necessary because Rossetti had convinced Gilchrist that she ought to publish the essay anonymously. Displaying the same timidity that marked his edition of Whitman, Rossetti worried that Gilchrist's defense of the poetry's sexual content might expose her to censure. Gilchrist agreed, but as soon as the essay was published, she regretted giving in.

Reading "A Woman's Estimate," one tends to agree with Gilchrist: there is nothing in the essay to offend. An experienced professional writer, Gilchrist couched her defense of the poems' sexual frankness in the most discreet of terms, and she shrewdly used her era's ubiquitous religiosity to support her case. She does not touch on the poetry's sexual content for the first few pages of the essay. When she finally introduces the topic, she does so with a rhetorically brilliant maneuver: "If the thing a word stands for exists by divine appointment (and what does not so exist?), the word need never be ashamed of itself." Gilchrist wins readers to her side with her blandly devout question, and she repeats the tactic later in the essay when she speaks of the shame that a prudish culture forces on the young bride in her first encounter with the realities of sex: "It must surely be man's fault, not God's, that she has to say to herself, 'Soul, look another way—you have no part in this. Motherhood is beautiful, fatherhood is beautiful; but the dawn of fatherhood and motherhood is not beautiful.' Do they really think that God is ashamed of what he has made and appointed? And, if not, surely it is somewhat superfluous that they should undertake to be so for Him." Gilchrist executes a Victorian double play in this passage, bringing both religion and the family to Whitman's defense. The essay includes a number of other key nineteenth-century touchstones: nature, democracy, progress, science. But religion is paramount, and she begins the essay with the claim that reading *Leaves of Grass* has brought her "a new birth of the soul."

O'Connor, who had difficulty finding a publisher for Gilchrist's essay, wound up placing it in a religious magazine. It was an appropriate venue. Gilchrist's use of religious language was not merely strategic. A true disciple, she regarded Whitman as, first, a great spiritual liberator and only secondarily a poet. She wrote to Rossetti, "Whitman is, I believe, far more closely akin to Christ than to either Homer or Shakespeare or any other poet." On seeing the famous engraving of Whitman in workingman's clothing, she had exclaimed, "Here at last is the face of Christ, which the painters have so long sought for," and in a letter to Rossetti she systematically laid out the parallels to Jesus: Whitman has "the same radiant glowing consciousness (it *is* a consciousness, not a belief) of the divine and immortal nature of the human soul—the same fearless, trusting, loving attitude towards God, as of a son, the same actual close embracing brothers' love of every human creature." Gilchrist, like many Victorian religious progressives, believed that "Christ's beautiful life and teaching" had been distorted by Christianity. Whitman, the new Christ, rejected what she saw as the primitive religious conceptions that the church had imposed on Jesus's teaching: supernaturalism, belief in the devil, the notion of a vindictive, angry God. And in place of the church's tradition of misogyny and asceticism, Whitman declared the equality of women and men, the glories of the body, and the sanctity of sex.

As intoxicated with Whitman as Rossetti was, he was pulled up short by Gilchrist's declaration of faith. In an answering letter he conceded that Whitman was no mere littérateur, but still, "there is a range of considerations pertinent to the case, in which you and I must differ." Rossetti took issue with Gilchrist's conception of Whitman as a modern Christ and declared that, great as the American poet might be, he was no different in kind from Homer or Shakespeare. Rossetti's resistance to what Gilchrist saw as Whitman's true stature only confirmed her belief that she was uniquely able to apprehend his message of spiritual ecstasy. And did it not make sense that, once Whitman read her words, he would understand that she was uniquely suited to share other forms of ecstasy with him as well? "A Woman's Estimate" was published anonymously, but Walt would know how to find her through Rossetti. The essay appeared in May 1870. All she had to do now was wait.

And wait. For months no word came. When O'Connor first showed Whitman the extracts from letters by an anonymous woman that Rossetti had sent him, the poet was deeply touched; he wrote Rossetti late in 1869 that he "had hitherto received no eulogium so magnificent." Authorizing Rossetti to give his letter of thanks to "the lady," Whitman considered the episode closed. He was deeply grateful when "A Woman's Estimate" appeared in print and proudly sent a copy to his lightly educated but shrewd mother, who wrote her son, "That Lady seems to understand your writing better than ever any one did before as if she could see right through you." Walt no doubt agreed. But he saw no reason to attempt to contact the unknown Englishwoman.

For her part Anne Gilchrist believed that her essay showed her to be the loving, responsive reader that Whitman seemed to long for in *Leaves of Grass*. The poetic persona of *Leaves* is both a self-sufficient "kosmos" and a perpetually yearning lover who casts the reader as the object of his affections: "I whisper with my lips close to your ear, / I have loved many women and men, but I love none better than you." Whitman's poetic program is deliberately paradoxical: he wants to reach the entire American nation, yet he longs to establish an intimate relationship with the individual reader. As an Englishwoman, Gilchrist was oblivious to the first part of Whitman's program; as a lonely widow desperate for the passionate love she never had with her husband, she was hypersensitive to his intimate appeals. Reading a poem like "Among the Multitude," Gilchrist imagined herself to be the first one ever to understand it fully and respond as Whitman intended:

> Among the men and women, the multitude,
> I perceive one picking me out by secret and divine signs,
> Acknowledging none else—not parent, wife, husband,
>   brother, child, any nearer than I am;
> Some are baffled—But that one is not—that one
>   knows me.
>
> Ah, lover and perfect equal!
> I meant that you should discover me so, by my faint
>   indirections;
> And I, when I meet you, mean to discover you by the
>   like in you.

As far as Gilchrist knew, she was the only living person able to respond to the desire evident in this and so many other poems in *Leaves of Grass*. Whitman's situation in the United States, as conveyed by the excitable William O'Connor, was deplorable. Hounded out of his job by fanatical puritans, Whitman was a prophet without honor or ready cash. In England only Rossetti and a few others shared Gilchrist's enthusiasm for the poet, but Rossetti's devotion was imperfect, as demonstrated by his carping about Whitman's "gross" and "crude" language and his rejection of her comparison of the poet to Christ. Gilchrist assumed that she was the sole woman in either England or the United States ready to respond fully, mind and body, to the poet's passion. Surely, her essay proved that to Whitman. Why did he not contact her?

Four months after "A Woman's Estimate" was published, Gilchrist collapsed, wrought to a high pitch of anticipation and concern. The physicians could find nothing wrong with her and diagnosed "exhaustion of the nervous energy"; Gilchrist thought she was going to die. She was prostrated for months, gradually recovered during 1871, but faced another crisis in August of that year when Whitman sent Rossetti two copies of his new edition of *Leaves of Grass*, one for him and one for "the lady." Rossetti dutifully passed on the books, but Gilchrist was aghast. Was there no note for her? Surely, he had overlooked it. He had not? In that case would it be appropriate for her to write to Mr. Whitman? Rossetti replied affirmatively, and on the same late-summer day that she received his letter, Gilchrist went into the fields outside her home to compose a message to Walt Whitman.

"Dear Friend," she began and, after thanking him for the books, set out to tell the story of her life. She began with her meeting of Alexander Gilchrist and painted the portrait of a marriage, initially "dark and gloomy," that was entered into without love on her part. Scholars have pointed to ebullient letters that she wrote during her engagement and suggested that she is fictionalizing her relationship with her husband. Of course she is. She begins her account by writing, "When I was eighteen I met a lad of nineteen"—though she was actually two months older than Alexander. Gilchrist's letter to Whitman paints her as a young woman swept into marriage by the devotion of a more mature man. However, there is no reason to doubt her assertion that she never overcame a certain reserve toward her husband—or, in the fervent language of her letter, that her "soul dwelt apart & unmated."

Then in 1869, after nearly eight years of widowhood, "came the voice over the Atlantic to me—O, the voice of my Mate: it must be so—my love rises up out of the very depths of the grief & tramples upon despair." "It must be so"—you can see Gilchrist trying to assuage her own doubts, creating a story of true love across the ocean as compelling as the narrative of a young woman's marrying an older man out of a sense of duty. And in the rest of this long, passionate letter she creates another fiction—that "A Woman's Estimate," her critical essay on *Leaves of Grass*, served as an encoded love letter. What seemed to the rest of the world to be an appreciative analysis was surely read by its subject as an impassioned personal call: "O dear Walt, did you not feel in every word the breath of a woman's love? did you not see as through a transparent veil a soul all radiant and trembling with love stretching out its arms towards you?" Since Walt evidently did not, she makes clear her desire: "O come. Come, my darling." Then, in a sudden drop from the sublime to the prosaic, she notes that her home in Surrey is on the main railroad line between London and Portsmouth. Did she half hope that Walt might impulsively take the next steamer to England and suddenly appear at the village train station?

If so, Whitman resisted the impulse. Seven weeks passed with no word from him. At the end of October she wrote a second letter, much shorter, poignant in its desperation:

> Dear Friend,
> I wrote you a letter the 6th September & would fain know whether it has reached your hand. If it have not, I will write its contents again quickly to you—if it have, I will wait your time with courage with patience for an answer; but spare me the needless suffering of uncertainty on this point & let me have one line, one word, of assurance that I am no longer hidden from you by a thick cloud.

The letter is beseeching, but it is also a masterpiece of dignity and courage. She justifies conduct that she knows virtually everyone in her world would condemn:

> Do not say I am forward, or that I lack pride because I tell this love to thee who have never sought or made sign of desiring to seek me. Oh, for all that, this love is my pride my glory. . . . Besides, it is not true thou has not sought or loved me. For

when I read the divine poems I feel all folded round in thy love: I feel often as if thou wast pleading so passionately for the love of the woman that can understand thee. . . . I know that a woman may without hurt to her pride—without stain or blame—tell her love to thee. I feel for a certainty that she may.

Anne Gilchrist was not the first woman who felt compelled to tell her love to Walt Whitman. Sara Payson Parton, known to readers as "Fanny Fern," gave the virtually unknown poet a flirtatious puff in her New York City newspaper column, "Peeps from under a Parasol," in April 1856, writing not of his book but of his "muscular throat," broad shoulders, and "fine, ample chest." A month later she reviewed *Leaves of Grass*, calling the book "unspeakably delicious"; she applied the same savory adjective to Whitman himself in a private note. Parton was married, however, and their relationship did not go beyond her flirtatious admiration. Four years later, the 1860 edition of *Leaves of Grass*, the first to contain the erotic "Children of Adam" sequence, occasioned a letter to Whitman from yet another woman that seems to bear some resemblance to Anne Gilchrist's 1871 letters:

Know Walt Whitman that I am a woman! I am not beautiful, but I love you! . . . Know Walt Whitman that thou has a child for me! A noble beautiful perfect manchild. I charge you my love not to give it to another woman. The world demands it! It is not for you and me, *is our child*, but for the world. My womb is clean and pure. It is ready for thy child my love. Angels guard the vestibule until thou comest to deposit our and the world's precious treasure. . . . I am willing. My motives are pure and holy. Our boy my love! do you not already love him? He must be begotten on a mountain top, in the open air. Not in *lust*, not in mere gratification of sensual passion, but in holy ennobling pure strong deep glorious passionate broad universal love. I charge you to prepare my love.

I love you, I love you, come, come. Write.

> Susan Garnet Smith
> Hartford, Connecticut

Whitman's response to this extraordinary missive was unsurprising: he wrote on the envelope "? insane asylum" and tossed it into a pile. Ten years later he did not do the same with Anne Gilchrist's letters. Like Susan Smith, Gilchrist offered in her second letter to bear Walt's children, but she was clearly not insane. Whitman knew through Rossetti that she was a respectable widowed mother, and her essay on *Leaves of Grass* showed a sensitive, highly intelligent woman familiar with literature and science. When he received her second letter, pleading for a response from him, he at last sat down to write:

> I have been waiting quite a while for time & the right mood to answer your letter in a spirit as serious as its own, & in the same unmitigated trust and affection. . . . I wished to give to it a day, a sort of Sabbath or holy day apart to itself, under serene & propitious influences—confident that I could then write you a letter which would do you good, & me too. But I must at least show without further delay that I am not insensible to your love. I too send you my love. And do you feel no disappointment because I now write so briefly. My book is my best letter, my response, my truest explanation of all. In it I have put my body & spirit. You understand this better & fuller & clearer than any one else. And I too fully & clearly understand the loving letter it has evoked. Enough that there surely exists so beautiful & delicate a relation, accepted by both of us with joy.

"Ah, that word 'enough' was like a blow on the breast to me," Gilchrist wrote in reply. Yet, though wounded, she showed in this letter, as she would throughout her correspondence with Whitman, a remarkable self-awareness of her infatuation: "Ah, foolish me! I thought you would catch a glimpse of it in those words I wrote—I thought you would say to yourself, 'Perhaps this is the voice of my mate,' and would seek me a little to make sure if it were so or not. O the sweet dreams I have fed on these three years nearly." She waited two months—an interval she adhered to throughout most of the five years of their trans-Atlantic correspondence—then sent Whitman a letter that, to some extent, attempted to normalize their relationship. She enclosed pictures of her family, talked about her children and her elderly mother. In grateful response Whitman, who was genuinely fond of children, wrote back promptly, attempting to establish an avuncular relationship to Gilchrist's children and, more important, to her. He was not successful. She wrote him an impassioned letter, which drew a rebuke from Whitman: "Dear friend, let me warn you somewhat about myself—& yourself also. You must not construct such an unauthorized & imaginary ideal Figure, & call it W.W. and so devotedly invest your loving nature in it. The actual W.W. is a very plain personage, & entirely unworthy such devotion."

Gilchrist tried to tone down her expressions of passion after receiving Whitman's warning—"I will not write any more such letters"—but she was only intermittently successful. Two years after Whitman's rebuke she was asking him to "please . . . be indulgent . . . of these poor letters of mine with their details of my children & their iterated and reiterated expressions of the love and hope and aspiration you have called into life within me." Gilchrist's spot-on summary of her correspondence demonstrates exceptional self-awareness, and at times during her lengthy epistolary courtship of Whitman she showed her understanding that she was not the only reader to feel personally drawn to him: "I am sure it is not possible for any one,— man or woman, it does not matter which, to receive these books, not merely with the intellect . . . but with an understanding responsive heart, without feeling it drawn out of their breasts so that they must leave all & come to be with you." On one level Gilchrist knew that her love for Whitman was not unique. On another she was convinced that he needed her, a conviction that increased once she realized the severity of the stroke that he had suffered in January 1873, leaving him partially paralyzed on his left side. In August of that year she wrote that he needed her more than ever, now that she could serve him not only as wife but as nurse. Ironically, her letter crossed the Atlantic at the same time that a packet from him was heading toward England. Whitman had mailed her a ring, "taken from my finger, & [sent to] you, with my love."

It was an act of spectacularly bad judgment. Yet Whitman's action is completely understandable; 1873 was a year of horrors for him. One month after his paralytic stroke his beloved sister-in-law Mattie Whitman died in St. Louis, leaving two young daughters. In the spring came "the great dark cloud" of his life when his mother— "inexpressibly beloved" by her bachelor son—died. In late summer Whitman was suffering from the after-effects of the stroke. Too ill to live on his own in Washington, he was staying with his brother and sister-in-law in Camden, New Jersey, virtually housebound, mourning the loss of his mother and Mattie. For two years Anne Gilchrist had been begging him for signs of affection, or at least recognition; she was immoderately grateful when Whitman began mailing her a newspaper as a signal that he had received a letter from her. To send her the ring along with a letter explaining the year's disasters, knowing that it would bring showers of affectionate concern from a safely distant woman, was an irresistible temptation.

Whitman got the sympathy he bargained for—and much more. Two months after she received the ring, Gilchrist began making plans to emigrate to America. Her oldest child, Percy, was starting his career as a metallurgical engineer and could make his way without her; her younger son and daughter, Herbert and Grace, still teenagers, could easily relocate; and her older daughter, Beatrice, would find America an advantage over England, since Beatrice was determined to become a physician at a time when no British medical school would admit women. Only the need to care for her elderly mother kept Gilchrist in England. And on August 15, 1875, Henrietta Burrows, eighty-nine years old, died peacefully in her sleep. Five months later, in January 1876, Whitman received a letter from England that began, "Do not think me too wilful or headstrong, but I have taken our tickets & we shall sail Aug. 30 for Philadelphia." She clearly intended a permanent relocation: "This is the last spring we shall be asunder."

Whitman must have been emotionally paralyzed by this stunning announcement. It was not until two months later that he wrote in return. "My dearest friend, I do not approve your American trans-settlement. . . . Don't do any thing towards such a move, nor resolve

on it, nor indeed make any move at all in it, without further advice
from me. If I should get well enough to voyage, we will talk about
it yet in London." Gilchrist was not deceived by the transparent
ploy of the voyage to London, and her reply to Whitman revealed
an iron fist within the velvet glove of her affection: "Yesterday *was*
a day for me, dearest Friend. In the morning your letter, strong,
cheerful, reassuring—dear letter. In the afternoon the books . . .
with inscription making me so proud, so joyous. But there are a few
things I want to say to you at once in regard to our coming to
America. I will not act without 'further advice from you'; but as to
not resolving on it, dear friend, I can't exactly obey that, for it has
been my settled, steady purpose (resting on a deep, strong faith)
ever since 1869." Whitman did not reply to this letter and remained
silent for the rest of the year. Gilchrist wrote only twice more; she
was busy packing a lifetime's accumulation of goods for her move
to America.

✠ ✠ ✠

Anne Gilchrist and her three younger children sailed from Liverpool
on the steamship *Ohio* on August 30, 1876, landing in Philadelphia
eleven days later. During their voyage fifty-seven-year-old Walt
Whitman betrayed an adolescent's agitation. Although Gilchrist had
twice told him the date of her departure, he wrote to Rossetti on
September 1, only two days after she sailed, that he could not understand why he had not yet heard of her arrival. On September 10,
the day the Gilchrists' ship landed, he wrote again, petulantly concluding his letter, "*I want to hear about Mrs. Gilchrist,*" as if Rossetti
might be concealing her in his London home. Yet once she arrived,
he was paralyzed; he waited three days before taking the brief ferry
ride across the Delaware River from Camden to Philadelphia. Once
across the river he would have taken a streetcar, mounting and de-
scending the steps with some difficulty; his left leg still dragged from
his stroke three years earlier. Leaning on his cane, he entered the

Montgomery House hotel to meet the woman who had come across the Atlantic to become his wife.

That was not to be. Neither he nor Gilchrist ever described their first meeting, yet it is clear what must have happened. At this supreme test of her life Anne Gilchrist somehow summoned the courage to behave with extraordinary wisdom and strength. She managed to overcome all her expectations and nervousness, was able to set aside the speeches she must have rehearsed, the gestures she had practiced. "O, I could not live if I did not believe that sooner or later you will not be able to help stretching out your arms towards me & saying, 'Come, my Darling,' " she had written him. But the large, gentle white-haired man who stood before her did not take her into his arms, did not address her as "Darling." He was kindness itself, but there was not a hint of romantic attraction, not a glimmer of erotic fire in his greeting. She somehow managed to set aside seven years' worth of hopes and dreams. She and Whitman would be friends, just friends.

Her success in overturning, in an instant, the plans she had been elaborating for years is proved by Whitman's immediate sense of comfort. Their meeting could have been—*should* have been—horrendously difficult. It took Whitman three days to work up the nerve to go to Philadelphia after the Gilchrists arrived; he had tried to prevent the meeting from ever occurring. On her part Gilchrist came to the encounter with years' worth of illusory expectations. Yet by the time he left the Montgomery House parlor, Whitman was already planning his next visit. While the Gilchrists stayed at the hotel, Whitman visited them every day. They had dinner together, spent the evenings chatting. John Burroughs, who happened to be in Philadelphia at the time, saw not a hint of discomfort between them. He was delighted that Whitman had so quickly been accepted into the heart of this charming English family. "Walt came over every evening from Camden and took supper with us, and we had much talk," Burroughs wrote to his wife. "He likes Mrs. Gilchrist and her family, and they like him. They are going to housekeeping and expect to spend several years in this country. It will be a god-send to Walt, and he anticipates much pleasure in visiting them."

Walt commenced his visiting with extraordinary rapidity. Within days after the Gilchrists settled into a rented house, he came to stay for two weeks. That visit concluded, he adopted the habit of dining with them six evenings a week. They set aside a room for him so that he could stay overnight whenever he wished, and he was soon issuing orders to Anne's teenage son: "Herbert, see about the stove [for Whitman's bedroom] & have put up as soon as convenient—& have some *dry oak wood* sawed the right length, split, & carried up there, & piled in the room. Send me word before the end of the week."

Obviously, within a short time after their arrival Whitman felt himself one of the Gilchrist family. Burroughs knew that the poet needed a surrogate family, which was why he immediately sized up the Gilchrists as "a god-send to Walt." Shortly after his 1873 stroke, Whitman had left Washington, D.C., to move into the Camden, New Jersey, home of his younger brother George, the Civil War veteran, and sister-in-law Louisa. They all got along well enough, but George, an inspector at a foundry, did not share his brother's interests. "George believes in pipes, not in poems," Walt quipped. Three months after moving to Camden, Whitman wrote Peter Doyle, "I don't know a soul here—am utterly alone—sometimes sit alone & think, for two hours on a stretch—have not formed a single acquaintance here, any ways intimate." Later the same year he wrote, "I am very comfortable here indeed, but my *heart* is blank & lonesome utterly." The Gilchrist home—once the stove was installed—proved a haven for Whitman. "I have been over here with the Gilchrists for a week," he wrote Burroughs in January 1877. "I have a nice room here with a stove and oak wood—everything very comfortable and sunny—most of all *the spirit* (which is so *entirely lacking* over there in Camden, and has been for more than three years)."

The spirit could only have come from Anne, who was able to make the about-face from infatuated would-be lover to friend, hostess, and disciple with extraordinary facility and grace. Her first letter to Rossetti was full of praise for Philadelphia and for her frequent houseguest: "Our greatest pleasure is the society of Mr. Whitman, who fully realizes the ideal I had formed from his poems, and brings such an atmosphere of cordiality and geniality with him as is indescribable." She was dissembling to some extent; the ideal of Mr. Whitman that she had formed from his poems went far beyond that of cordial and genial friend. Yet her success in establishing a new basis for their relationship is proved not only by Whitman's ease with her and her family but by his testimony about their relationship. In later years he frequently discussed her with Horace Traubel, trying to convey to the young man the depth of his admiration for the woman he called "Mrs. G." "I have that sort of feeling about her," Whitman told Traubel, "which cannot easily be spoken of—put into words—indeed, the sort of feeling that words will not fit: love (strong personal love, too), reverence, respect—you see, it won't go into words: all the words are weak and formal." Whitman, who was known for his many friendships with women, called Mrs. G "my noblest woman-friend." Yet even that description seemed inadequate to him: "She was more than my friend. I feel like Hamlet when he said forty thousand brothers could not feel what he felt for Ophelia." On another occasion he said, "I am not sure but she had the finest and perfectest nature I ever met." He also said of her, "She was *all* courage, bravery, power, yet all *womanly*, too—not a jot of the womanly abated for all the force. She was never conventional, unless she chose to be—unless she thought it as well to be conventional as not." Whitman had read and admired her scientific essays, but "the best of her was her talk," he told Traubel. "I shall never forget—never forget: she is over there now . . . eyeing me, overflowing with utterance. She was marvellous above other women in traits in which women are marvellous as a rule—immediate perception, emotion, deep inevitable insight. She had such superb judgment—it welled up and out and I only sat off and wondered: welled up from a reservoir of riches, spontaneously, unpremeditatedly." He summed up to Traubel his happiness in Gilchrist's presence: "After all, Horace, we were a family—a happy family."

"Never saw Walt look so handsome—so new and fresh," John Burroughs wrote in his journal after spending a night at the Gilchrists'. Burroughs was only one of Walt's many friends whom the poet invited to stay with Mrs. G, whose Philadelphia home became a sort of Whitmanite boardinghouse. Delighted to have an alternative to his brother's rigid establishment in unlovely Camden, Whitman preferred to do his socializing at the Gilchrists'. When Edward Carpenter came to the United States on a pilgrimage, Whitman had him stay with the Gilchrists. Carpenter left a record of the summer's week he spent there in 1877, describing how the entire family would spend the evenings chatting on the front stoop, Whitman in an armchair, the moonlight shining on his long white hair and beard. That same summer Whitman wrote to a young friend about his daily routine during one of his many extended stays with the Gilchrists: "It is all very pleasant here, every thing is so gentle & smooth, & yet they are all so jolly & much laughing & talking & fun—we have first rate times, over our meals, we take our time over them, & always something new to talk about. . . . I dont suppose it would be so much fun for you here—but it suits an old man like me, (& then it pleases one's vanity to be made so much of)." None of the gaiety Whitman described is evident in our only visual record of Whitman at the Gilchrists', Herbert Gilchrist's painting *The Tea Party*, which he completed from memory after the family left Philadelphia. In this rather odd group portrait a sketchily rendered Whitman smells a flower; Anne Gilchrist gazes into the distance—just as Burroughs described her, "a rosy woman without a gray hair in her head"; and her younger daughter, Grace—"fresh and comely, like [a] soft, light-skinned peach," according to Burroughs—looks obliquely at the viewer, as a servant pours tea.

Anne's older daughter, Beatrice, is missing from the painting, though Whitman delighted in her. "There are two grown daughters," he wrote to a friend; "the eldest one is a *first class trump*, she is my favorite every way." The trump was able to establish a warm relationship with Whitman despite working ferociously hard on her medical studies. By the time she was eighteen, Beatrice Gilchrist had determined to become a doctor. The few British women physicians had all studied abroad, and Anne Gilchrist, who warmly supported her daughter, more than once cited Beatrice's ambition as support for her decision to relocate to the United States. Beatrice's career

FIGURE 2.3. Herbert Gilchrist, *The Tea Party*. Annenberg Rare Book & Manuscript Library, University of Pennsylvania.

may have served to some extent as a cover for her mother's secret passion, but the move to Philadelphia unquestionably benefited Beatrice, who enrolled at the Woman's Medical College of Pennsylvania within weeks of their arrival.

American women medical students may have had more opportunities than their British counterparts, but they were the subject of extraordinarily vehement opposition from the male medical establishment. The Philadelphia college, founded in 1850, was the oldest women's medical school in the world, but its students were barely tolerated by brother institutions. Only seven years before Beatrice arrived, the school's directors had gingerly attempted to give their students the same advantages that Philadelphia's male medical students enjoyed. The directors took a class to a clinical lecture at Pennsylvania Hospital. According to a contemporary account, when the women entered the amphitheater, they were "greeted by yells, hisses, 'caterwaulings,' mock applause, [and] offensive remarks upon personal appearance. . . . During the last hour missiles of paper, tinfoil, tobacco-quids, etc. were thrown upon the ladies, while some of the men defiled the dresses of the ladies near them with tobacco-juice." When the women left, men followed them into the street shouting insults. Despite their treatment, the women students tried to attend subsequent lectures. But the entire Philadelphia medical establishment—medical school professors, hospital staffs, and other physicians—voted, "out of respect for their profession and for the interests of the public," to prohibit joint attendance by male and female students at clinical demonstrations. Beatrice must have been frustrated by the restrictions imposed on her and her classmates, but she did not complain.

Grace, the comely younger daughter, was seventeen when the family moved to Philadelphia. Lacking her sister's ambition—she took singing lessons in Philadelphia but seems never to have seriously attempted a professional career—she also lacked Beatrice's fondness for Walt Whitman. Anne's children knew something of their mother's feelings for Whitman; during Anne's nervous breakdown in 1870, when Grace was eleven, Anne told her children "all they could rightly understand" about her love for the American poet. Once they were in Philadelphia, Grace observed how the rest of the family pampered Whitman, jumping to his commands about a stove and firewood, fixing him his favorite meals. It was not as if Whitman were trying to replace the father who died when she was only two; rather, it must have seemed to Grace, he had assumed her role as youngest child. She acknowledged her resentment of Whitman in an unpublished memoir. Describing the last evening they spent with Whitman before their return to England, she wrote,

We were all gathered in the parlour of our boarding house,
. . . [and] Walt kissed each in turn, my mother, brother and
sister. When it came to my turn, I drew back, I hardly know
what youthful caprice actuated me, or whether it was caprice.
In some part it was constitutional dislike to being kissed by
"bearded lips" but the larger part lay in a jealous concern for
my family. Subconsciously I felt they had invested so large a
capital of love and devotion in the wayward poet, that by a
certain rough, youthful justice, I was constrained to give no
more. "Not a kiss for Walt?" argued the "good grey poet." I
shook my head, and remained silent.

Years later Grace fully unleashed her antagonism in a letter: "There
have always appeared to me two distinct beings—the super man
who wrote Leaves of Grass, and the Walt Whitman of Camden,
somewhat wayward and capricious with a child-like vanity and love
of applause and notoriety."

Whitman's love of applause was fed by Grace's brother Herbert.
Encouraged by his mother, Herbert read *Leaves of Grass* when he
was sixteen and was filled with "loving admiration" for Whitman.
When the family moved to Philadelphia two and a half years later,
Herbert was as emotionally ready as his mother to be overwhelmed
by Whitman. But while she faced disappointment, Herbert seems
to have fallen into the infatuation that his mother was forced to
abandon.

Herbert, set on becoming an artist, was somewhat adrift in Philadelphia. The Pennsylvania Academy of Fine Arts—until then a sec-
ond-rate provincial art school—had moved into a handsome new
building just before the Gilchrists arrived in the United States and
at the same time hired an iconoclastic young artist named Thomas
Eakins to teach painting. However, Herbert seems never to have
taken classes there. He had been warned that opportunities for artists
were meager in Philadelphia, and he had evidently determined to
practice his craft on his own. For much of his time in America that
meant drawing pictures of Walt Whitman at Timber Creek outside
Camden.

During the year and a half that the Gilchrists remained in Philadelphia, Whitman divided his time among their house on North 22nd Street, his brother's house in Camden, and the farm of George and Susan Stafford, located on Timber Creek. Eighteen-year-old Harry Stafford, one of George and Susan's six children, was working in a Camden printing office when Whitman met him early in 1876. By April Whitman was writing letters to friends, asking them to help Harry find a job; the same month Harry took Whitman home to meet his parents. The meeting went well, and in June Whitman made the first of many extended visits to the family farm. During the next two years Whitman was as likely to be at Timber Creek or North 22nd Street as at his brother George's, his nominal residence. At the Gilchrists' he stayed in the "prophet's chamber" they had prepared for him; at the Staffords' he slept in Harry's room.

George and Susan Stafford were extremely fond of Whitman, and he returned their affection; however, his friendship for the parents did not hinder Whitman's love affair with their son. A series of tortured letters and anguished diary entries records the progress of their tempestuous affair. Harry—handsome, uneducated, and most likely manic depressive—would frequently explode in anger, then contritely supplicate Walt's forgiveness: "I will have to *controol* [*sic*] [my temper] or it will send me to states prison or some other bad place. Can't you take me back and [love] me the same," he wrote after one spat. In the fall of 1876 Whitman made to Harry the same gesture that he had extended to Anne Gilchrist three years earlier: he gave the young man a ring. Gilchrist had gladly and serenely slipped onto her finger the ring from a man she had never met; Harry, who knew Walt well by this point, was less acquiescent. For several months the ring flew back and forth between them like a shuttlecock slammed in anger.

One cause of Harry's anger was his resentment of Herbert Gilchrist. Whitman treated the Stafford farm with the same freedom as the Gilchrist house, inviting his friends to join him there. One of the most frequent visitors was Herbert, who quickly charmed George and Susan Stafford. Harry was less impressed. Herbert began to spend extended periods at Timber Creek, sketching Walt and the surrounding scenery, even remaining at the farmhouse when Walt was not present. On one of these occasions he and Harry got into a tiff. Harry angrily recalled the scene to Walt: "Herbret [*sic*] cut me pretty hard last night at the supper table, you must not let on if I tell you; he called me a 'dam fool,' I wasn't talking to him any way! we was all talking of telegraphing, and father said he was reading of a man who was trying to overdo it and I said that I did not think he could do it and the[n] Herbret stuck in that, it did not sit very well, and if I had been near enough to smacked him in the 'Jaw' I would of done it." Walt, in the avuncular tone he often used with Harry, counseled patience. The peaceable Whitman no doubt genuinely wanted the two young men to get along; at the same time it would have greatly inconvenienced him if two of his admirers were fighting.

Herbert, who never married, maintained his close friendship with Whitman for years. After his mother's death in England he returned to the United States, painted Whitman's portrait, visited the old poet regularly, and delivered a fulsome tribute at his seventieth birthday celebration. Whitman did not think much of Herbert's abilities as an artist, but he basked in the lionizing that he received from Herbert, Beatrice, and Anne during their time in Philadelphia. Whitman's frequent notes to his friend and hostess Anne suggest a relation that on his part was serene and untroubled. Was the relationship equally untroubled for Anne Gilchrist? It is impossible to know. While living in Philadelphia, she kept no diary and did not reveal her deepest feelings about Whitman in her letters to English friends. However, when Beatrice received her medical degree after two years of study and left Philadelphia for an internship in Boston, Anne departed also. She put her household goods into storage and headed to New England, where she and the two younger children could be close to Beatrice.

During the summer of 1878, which she spent at a resort hotel in Northampton, Massachusetts, Anne Gilchrist decisively demonstrated that she had freed herself of the erotic fantasies that had dominated her emotionally and intellectually for years before she came to the United States. The letters that she addressed from New

FIGURE 2.4. Walt Whitman at Timber Creek. Sketch by Herbert Gilchrist. Annenberg Rare Book & Manuscript Library, University of Pennsylvania.

England to her "dearest friend" are radically different from her earlier ones. Now she sent chatty, relatively brief notes that suggest an easy familiarity with Whitman; the desperate passion of her English letters is entirely absent.

In the winter of 1878–79 the Gilchrists moved to New York City, where Herbert studied with William Merritt Chase at the Art Students League. The following spring Beatrice finished her Boston internship and decided to go to Europe for further study. Anne Gilchrist was at a turning point. With what seems to have been relative ease, she decided to return to England, informing Whitman of her decision in a chatty letter.

Now it was the poet's turn to be emotionally overwhelmed. The Gilchrist household in Philadelphia had been the happy family he had not known as a child, and he could not bear to see his adoptive family disperse. He appealed plaintively to Herbert, suggesting that the Gilchrists get a "big cheap house in Brooklyn" large enough that he could move in with them. However, Anne was determined to go back to England. In April Whitman came to New York, where he stayed for two months until the Gilchrists' departure. On the family's last day in the city J. H. Johnston, Whitman's host in New York, decorously left Walt and Anne alone in the parlor for a long, private conference; they emerged deeply moved, although neither ever revealed what was said between them. Walt kissed the family—all but Grace—good-bye, and the Gilchrists sailed for England on June 7, 1879, after almost three years in the United States.

✣ ✣ ✣

The Gilchrists' return to England was triumphal. Friends told Anne she looked ten years younger, and she reveled in her new role as grandmother to Archie Gilchrist, born the previous fall to her oldest child, Percy, who had stayed behind in England. Anne saw Beatrice off to Bern, Switzerland, for further medical studies, then with Herbert and Grace went house hunting in Hampstead, at that time a charming village on the heaths outside London. Grace continued voice lessons and began performing occasionally, and Herbert landed his first commissions as an artist. For her part Anne was soon caught up in a social and professional whirl, dining with Henry James and corresponding with the publisher Alexander Macmillan about a second edition of the *Life of William Blake*.

Then Beatrice suddenly appeared in Hampstead. She would not be returning to Bern—had decided, in fact, that she was giving up medicine. Anne struggled to make sense of her daughter's decision and in a letter to Whitman—still her "dearest friend"—she tried to present Beatrice's change of heart as a rational decision. In this prepsychiatry era Anne lacked the knowledge—even the vocabulary—to understand that her daughter was suffering from severe depression. In any case, after a few months Beatrice changed her mind and arranged to assist Dr. Sophia Jex-Blake, a highly regarded Edinburgh physician. All seemed well again. Beatrice wrote a long, happy letter to her friend Walt Whitman in December 1880, after she had been in Edinburgh a few months, and the next June her mother came for an extended visit. Beatrice seemed content, her patients adored her, and she was studying for advanced examinations. Anne was relieved, and after several weeks in Edinburgh she returned to Hampstead in July 1881, assured that Beatrice had found her way.

Soon after her return Anne received an urgent summons to Edinburgh. Beatrice had vanished. The police were called in, but they could find no trace of her. Finally, on August 15, nearly four weeks after Beatrice had last been seen, a farmer near Edinburgh discovered in his fields the badly decomposed body of a young woman. The coroner ruled suicide by overdose of hydrocyanic acid.

Anne was devastated—for years she and Beatrice had been more like sisters than mother and daughter—and took the blame on herself. If only she had stayed in Edinburgh! She could not let go of the thought, and the normally composed Anne wrote Herbert and Grace a hysterical letter from Edinburgh after the discovery of the body: "You would not want me to live if you knew how I suffered."

However, Anne had enormous reserves of emotional strength—her quick and successful transformation of her relationship with Whitman after she arrived in Philadelphia had proved that. She invented a plausible story to explain Beatrice's death: a laboratory accident involving ether. In tribute to her daughter and in an act of healing for herself, she wrote a long, emotional obituary for the Alumnae Association of the Woman's Medical College of Pennsylvania that stressed Beatrice's professional success and the admiration and affection she had won from her patients. And she composed the epitaph for Beatrice's tombstone in Edinburgh: "Many hearts mourn her. In her short career did she by skill tenderness and unwearied devotion to duty bring healing and comfort to many both here and in America."

Fortunately, Anne was able to immerse herself in what Freud called the only two stays against despair: love and work. Herbert and Grace were still living with her in Hampstead; she frequently saw her older son, Percy, and her grandson; and early in 1882 she was asked to write a biography of Mary Lamb. Anne poured herself into the task, completing the book by the end of the year. In Mary Lamb, best known as coauthor of *Tales from Shakespeare*, Gilchrist found a subject as familiar with tragedy and suffering as she was. At the age of thirty-two, in a fit of insanity, Lamb had killed her mother with a kitchen knife; for the rest of her life she alternated between periods of productive literary work and confinement in asylums. Gilchrist did not conceal the tragedies of Lamb's life, but the core of her narrative is not Lamb's psychosis but rather her relationship with her brother and literary collaborator, Charles. Gilchrist opens her biography by stating, "The story of Mary Lamb's life is mainly the story of a brother and sister's love." Gilchrist's "mainly" may seem stupefying to modern readers, but the pure, nonsexual love of brother and sister seemed to many Victorians the highest possible relation between man and woman. In her emphasis on the Lambs' deep mutual affection in the face of tragedy, Gilchrist was reinforcing a Victorian ideal; at the same time she was validating her own sisterly relationship with Walt Whitman.

Throughout the turbulent years following her return to England, Gilchrist maintained her correspondence with Whitman. He sent characteristically brief notes; she wrote letters that were intimate, loving, and entirely free of the sexual obsession that had gripped her for years before her trip to America. She could calmly appraise both Walt Whitman and her own earlier feelings for him now. With the Mary Lamb biography published in 1883, she could take up the task that Whitman's admirers had been pressing on her. "I . . . hope . . . that before long you will give yourself up and write the article on

Walt Whitman, that we are all looking for," John Burroughs wrote her. "I feel sure that you will cut your way to the heart of this matter as no one has yet done." Gilchrist replied that she would accept the challenge and "put my heart into an article on Walt." As a professional writer she knew that, realistically, it would not be easy to place a long essay about Whitman, "but anyhow I must try once more and give a reason for the faith that is in me."

The faith that is in me. The words reveal Gilchrist's religious devotion to Whitman, a feeling deeper and more enduring than her seven years' infatuation. Initially, she had imagined that this great American poet-prophet was her personal savior, poised to rescue her from lonely, celibate widowhood. When that fantasy was shattered at their meeting in Philadelphia, she did not abandon her sense of *Leaves of Grass* as a modern scripture. It seemed only natural to title her essay, this letter to the Gentiles who had not yet glimpsed the revelation of *Leaves of Grass*, "A Confession of Faith."

The only problem was that the Gentiles were not interested. She had a devil of a time placing the article. "A Confession of Faith" is longer, denser, and more complex than her first essay on Whitman, "A Woman's Estimate." In 1884, fifteen years after the earlier article, Whitman was no longer a fresh voice from America, and a woman's defense of him was not a novelty. In addition, this time she did not have the imprimatur of William Michael Rossetti. Gilchrist never asked Rossetti for a preface to "A Confession of Faith"; she likely knew he would balk at her messianic interpretation of Whitman. In her earlier essay Gilchrist had used religious rhetoric to offer a defense of the poems' sexual decency. This time she used scientific rhetoric to defend her religious view of the poetry.

Gilchrist, the former freelance science writer, sprinkles quotations from eminent scientists throughout her essay. She acknowledges that the discoveries of the great nineteenth-century physicists and biologists shattered the religious faith of many, but that was only because their beliefs were shallow and dogma bound. Interpreted rightly, modern science is not atheistic and materialist; rather, it reveals that "what we thought poor, dead, inert matter is (in Clerk Maxwell's words) 'a very sanctuary of minuteness and power.'" Gilchrist seizes on Maxwell's religious metaphor to defend Whitman, the poet who shouted, "Hurrah for positive Science!" In Gilchrist's view atomic theory had animated the material world, and evolutionary biology affirmed an optimistic, teleological view of human progress toward a spiritualized goal. Humanity was not just existing on the earth; it was—she repeats the phrase—"going somewhere!" Science, she writes, has "annihilated our gross and brutish conceptions of matter, and . . . revealed it to us as subtle, spiritual, energetic beyond our powers of realization." This opens the way for the Poet, who can "increase these powers of realization. He it is who must awaken us to the perception of a new heaven and a new earth here where we stand on this old earth." And who better to fulfill this role of poet as spiritual guide than Walt Whitman?

In Gilchrist's view Whitman's entire poetic project is to bring to humanity a new faith to replace the imperfect religious doctrines shattered by the discoveries of modern science. In an essay that is largely sober and impersonal, she includes an autobiographical conversion story of her first encounter with *Leaves of Grass*: "Fifteen years ago, with feelings partly of indifference, partly of antagonism—for I had heard none but ill words of them—I first opened Walt Whitman's poems. But as I read I became conscious of receiving the most powerful influence that had ever come to me from any source. What was the spell? It was that in them humanity has, in a new sense, found itself; for the first time has dared to accept itself without disparagement, without reservation. For the first time an unrestricted faith in all that is and in the issues of all that happens has burst forth triumphantly into song." Gilchrist devotes much of the essay to long quotations from *Leaves of Grass*; in this spiritualized context Whitman's sometimes tedious catalogues are not assemblages of objects but signifiers of divine perfection. She combines passages from two poems to form a Whitmanian creed:

> Why! Who makes much of a miracle?
> As to me, I know of nothing else but miracles,
> To me, every hour of the light and dark is a miracle,
> Every cubic inch of space is a miracle,

> Every square yard of the surface of the earth is spread
> with the same, . . .
> Every spear of grass—the frames, limbs, organs, of men
> and women, and all that concerns them,
> All these to me are unspeakably perfect miracles.

"A Confession of Faith" was designed to bolster the beliefs of the faithful and convert skeptics. To read *Leaves of Grass* with understanding, Gilchrist suggests, is to embrace a faith in a divinely infused universe that is inevitably progressing toward the good. A sympathetic reading leads, in addition, to an intimate connection with Walt Whitman. In a moving passage Gilchrist writes that Whitman "has infused himself into words in a way that had not before seemed possible; and he causes each reader to feel that he himself or herself has an actual relationship to him, is a reality full of inexhaustible significance and interest to the poet." These words reveal that, fifteen years after first reading Whitman and eight years after meeting him, Gilchrist had achieved a wise and distanced perspective on her infatuation. The intimate connection with Walt Whitman that she had felt on first reading him was not an illusion; the relationship was embedded in the very substance of his verse. Her error had been to imagine that her connection was unique. In "A Confession of Faith" Gilchrist generously gives up any special claim to her "dearest friend" in order to convince her readers that each can achieve a personal relationship with this spiritual savior.

The next task was to find readers. Gilchrist shopped the article around London without success. In the end she relied on her children. Herbert and Grace had recently joined the Fabian Society, where Grace attracted the attention of a young red-haired Irish playwright. Her romance with George Bernard Shaw soon dissolved, but she and Herbert maintained their socialist connections, and they helped to place their mother's essay in the leftist journal *To-Day*. Anne was less than ecstatic. "I could not get my Whitman article into the 'Nineteenth Century' or 'Fortnightly,'" she wrote John Burroughs. "It is, I believe, coming out in a Socialist magazine,

'Today,' which is a somewhat feeble affair, or, at any rate, with which I am but partially in sympathy, but it seemed my only chance." Gilchrist adored her children and wanted to like their new friends, but she found herself both amused and dismayed by the Fabians. "I am seeing a good deal of your socialists just now," she wrote Whitman, "& I confess that though they mean well, I think they have less sense in their heads than any people I ever saw." Gilchrist was a crusader but not for a political cause; her campaign was for Walt Whitman and his *Leaves*.

Shortly after the publication of "A Confession of Faith," Rossetti received a letter from an acquaintance who had visited Whitman in Camden and found him living in what seemed appalling poverty. Rossetti immediately enlisted Gilchrist in an effort to raise money for their friend. They wrote countless letters seeking contributions; Rossetti even wrote a naive but touching appeal to President Grover Cleveland requesting federal aid for the poet. By the time the campaign was concluded in 1886, they had raised nearly $1,000 from more than eighty contributors, including Henry James and Robert Louis Stevenson.

However, Anne's name was absent from the letters accompanying the checks to Camden. Shortly after commencing the fund-raising effort, she took to her bed. For years she had kept a secret from her closest friends and even from her children: she was dying of breast cancer. Herbert wrote a terse note to Whitman in September 1885, saying only that "Mother is very sickly." He revealed the full truth to the poet in late November: "Her condition is critical. Four years ago our dear mother was attacked by cancer with left breast [*sic*]. . . . Her strength seems daily ebbing and her heart is very weak." In response on December 8 Whitman sent a cheery letter designed to buck Anne up: "I . . . cannot but trust your illness is less gloomy than Herbert states it." The letter never reached her. Anne Gilchrist had died a week earlier. When the poet received the news in a letter from Herbert on December 15, he sent a response that reflects his devastation:

Dear Herbert

I have rec'd your letter. Nothing now remains but a sweet &
rich memory—none more beautiful, all time, all life, all the
earth—

I cannot write any thing of a letter to-day. I must sit alone
& think.

Walt Whitman

Whitman's thoughts resulted in a poem, "Going Somewhere," that
echoes Gilchrist's repeated phrase in "A Confession of Faith."

> My science-friend, my noblest woman-friend,
> (Now buried in an English grave—and this a memory-
>   leaf for her dear sake,)
> Ended our talk—"The sum, concluding all we know of
>   old or modern learning, intuitions deep,
> "Of all Geologies—Histories—of all Astronomy—of
>   Evolution, Metaphysics all,
> "Is, that we all are onward, onward, speeding slowly,
>   surely bettering,
> "Life, life an endless march, an endless army, (no halt,
>   but it is duly over,)
> "The world, the race, the soul—in space and time the
>   universes,
> "All bound as is befitting each—all surely going some-
>   where."

Whitman's memorial poem pays tribute to Gilchrist's status as a
scientific essayist and her role as devoted friend. However, at the
same time it serves as a back-patting tribute to Whitman himself. In
its stress on the optimistic sense of inevitable progress that both
Gilchrist and Whitman derived from nineteenth-century science, the
poem subtly casts the former as a supporting player in the uplifting
drama of *Leaves of Grass*.

Colossal, as always, in his egotism, Whitman was not entirely
wrong. If Anne Gilchrist had not fallen in love with Walt Whitman

and his *Leaves*, she would not be remembered now. Her modern biographer claims that she was "one of the great pioneers in the crusade for the equality of women," but this overstates the case. Her sole crusade was on behalf of Walt Whitman. In her essays on science and literature she showed herself the equal of any man, but she never linked the personal and the political, never connected her own quest for equality with the larger movement for women's rights or made common cause with women engaged in the political sphere. Of course, that does not mean there was no political dimension to her life and work. It is possible to see Anne Gilchrist as a progressive political thinker who went against the grain of mainstream Victorian feminism in powerful and provocative ways.

Although some British feminists of the late nineteenth century stressed women's right to sexual pleasure, most were more concerned with protecting women from male lust—"banishing the beast," to borrow the title of a recent study of sexuality and the early feminists. Feminists of the era believed that unrestrained male carnality threatened women and families, not only through the extensive, informally sanctioned networks of prostitution and its attendant diseases but through the institution of marriage. With little access to birth control in an era of high rates of infant mortality and death in childbirth, even married women were endangered by male lust. Victorian feminists emphasized an ideal of sexual restraint that applied equally to women and men. They did not fight for "free unions"—that call would not come until the rise of the "New Woman" in the 1890s—but for the right to choose celibacy as a socially acceptable alternative to marriage. In this atmosphere a middle-class woman "conscious of her own unsatisfied sexual needs faced a problem of self-definition," in the words of Janet Murray.

Anne Gilchrist, middle aged and widowed, refused to define herself according to the model provided by the most famous middle-aged widow of the era, Queen Victoria. Not for Gilchrist the role of asexual mother and grieving wife. The thrill she experienced on reading *Leaves of Grass* at age forty-one was not just that she imagined she had found in the author the love of her life; it was that she had found a writer who acknowledged female sexual desire as the powerful, positive force she herself felt it to be. "Without shame the man I like knows and avows the deliciousness of his sex, / Without shame the woman I like knows and avows hers," Whitman writes in one of his "Children of Adam" poems, and he continues:

> Now I will dismiss myself from impassive women,
> I will go stay with her who waits for me, and with those
>   women that are warm-blooded and sufficient for me,
> I see that they understand me and do not deny me,
> I see that they are worthy of me, I will be the robust
>   husband of those women.

Whitman offered a portrait of active, sexually vibrant women unlike anything to be found elsewhere in nineteenth-century literature. "These beautiful, despised poems," Gilchrist called this and the other "Children of Adam" poems. "A Woman's Estimate of Walt Whitman" is filled with cautiously phrased but stalwart defenses of Whitman's value to middle-class Victorian women who were steeped in a culture that deemed sex too shameful to discuss in mixed company. Whitman, she wrote, had broken the evil spell of silence and let in daylight to the dark regions of female sexual ignorance. Her language throbs ecstatically as she praises Whitman's frank treatment of intercourse and conception and his liberating effect on women: "Wives and mothers will learn through the poet that there is rejoicing grandeur and beauty there wherein their hearts have so longed to find it." Whitman's own romantic longings were for men, but Gilchrist's ecstatic response to his poetry highlights the hetero-sexual, profeminist dimensions of *Leaves of Grass*.

Anne Gilchrist was among the first women to respond passion-ately and publicly to *Leaves of Grass*, but she was not the last. In the final decade of Whitman's life, as his work became increasingly available in the United States and abroad, he frequently received admiring letters from women readers. These letters show that many women responded to the same elements of his poetry that attracted Gilchrist: his intimate appeals to the reader, his equal treatment of women and men, and his celebration of women's physicality. An 1882 letter from the Chicago journalist Helen Wilmans is typical:

"No man ever lived whom I have so desired to take by the hand as you. I read Leaves of Grass, and got new conceptions of the dignity and beauty of my own body and of the bodies of other people; and life became more valuable as a consequence." Like Wilmans, an extraordinary number of the women who wrote to Whitman responded to his often-repeated invitations to establish physical contact with him. ("Touch me, touch the palm of your hand to my body as I pass, / Be not afraid of my body," Whitman had written.) "Sometimes I think I must put out my hand to you," one woman wrote in the 1880s. "I cannot forbear in this way to take you by the hand," wrote another. "If I could I would clasp your hand," said a third. A fourth wrote from England, "I have already reached across the water and clasped your hand."

In the face of these intimate messages from nineteenth-century women readers, Anne Gilchrist's letters to Walt Whitman appear less singular and strange. Male critics' dismissals of her as a "pathetic Victorian lady" seem misogynistic in the face of her essays about the poet, which remain among the most perceptive analyses of Whitman written in the nineteenth century. Moreover, Anne Gilchrist stands with John Burroughs as the first of the disciples to argue that Walt Whitman merited not just aesthetic appreciation but religious devotion. "Whoever takes up Walt Whitman's book as a student of Poetry alone, will not rightly understand it," she wrote to Rossetti. "What I, in my heart, believe of Whitman is, that he takes up the thread where Christ left it; that he inaugurates, in his own person, a new phase of religion." Anne Gilchrist's belief and devotion would be elaborated upon by a host of disciples in the years to come.

CHAPTER THREE

R. M. Bucke:

Whitman and Cosmic Consciousness

I too, following many and follow'd by many, inaugurate a religion.

THE PAPERS DELIVERED AT THE 1894 MEETING of the American Medico-Psychological Association in Philadelphia were, for the most part, what one might expect from a convention of specialists at a moment of transition. Only months before, the group had marked its fiftieth anniversary by changing its name from the Association of Medical Superintendents of American Institutions for the Insane; it would be another twenty-seven years before it became the American Psychiatric Association. In 1894 the group's members still referred to themselves as "alienists," and the speeches they gathered to hear alternated between the mundane realities of their role as institutional administrators ("Asylum Dietaries") and scientific reports that reflected their common training as physicians ("Frequent Disorder of Pneumogastric Functions in Insanity"). However, one speech delivered in Philadelphia veered wildly from the usual format. Dr. Richard Maurice Bucke, medical superintendent of the London, Ontario, Asylum for the Insane, had titled his talk "Cosmic Consciousness." Bucke, fifty-seven years old, was a highly regarded member of the association and four years later would serve a term as its president. As he walked to the podium he cut an impressive figure, with long white hair swept back from his high forehead and a massive beard covering his chest, his quick gait only slightly impeded by his limp and reliance on a cane. He began his speech conventionally enough with references to biological evolution and an argument for analogous evolution in the human mind. However, within a few minutes he had left biology far behind, as his references shifted from Darwin to an eclectic group of religious and artistic figures who, he contended, exemplified an evolving mental faculty that he dubbed cosmic consciousness: the Buddha, St. Paul, Muhammad, Dante, Shakespeare, and, greatest of all, Walt Whitman. In his peroration Bucke predicted that in the future cosmic consciousness would become common to every human, in much the same way as bodily consciousness and consciousness of self had evolved. "The simple truth," he confidently announced, "is, that a new race is being born from us, and this new race will in the near future possess the earth." Bucke went on to deliver the address to a different audience later the same day, thus becoming, it seems safe to say, the only member in the history of the American Psychiatric Association to give the same speech to both the association's national gathering and the local chapter of the Theosophical Society.

Bucke's paradoxical status as eminent alienist and religious enthusiast was a source of some amusement to his acquaintances in the medical community. In a reminiscence of Bucke, a colleague noted that the doctor in his appearance and dress seemed to be imitating Walt Whitman—indeed, people on the streets of Camden frequently took Bucke for the poet, though the doctor was almost twenty years younger. Bucke's colleague, well aware of the doctor's Whitman obsession, described how one evening after dinner with a group of physicians, he drew Bucke on to talk about the poet: "It was an experience to hear an elderly man, looking a venerable seer, with absolute abandonment tell how *Leaves of Grass* had meant for him spiritual enlightenment, a new power in life, new joy, in a new existence on a plane higher than he had ever hoped to reach. All this with accompanying physical exaltation expressed by dilated pupils and an intensity of utterance that were embarrassing to uninitiated friends."

Bucke was well aware that his championing of Walt Whitman made him a laughingstock in some circles, but he plowed ahead,

unfazed. The way he put it to himself was that the greatness of
Socrates or Jesus or Muhammad had not been recognized by most
of their contemporaries; Bucke happened to possess the prescience
to recognize Whitman's superior status. More strongly than any of
Whitman's other disciples, he argued for a religious interpretation
of *Leaves of Grass* and a messianic view of the poet. John Burroughs
and Anne Gilchrist regarded *Leaves of Grass* as a spiritual text, but
they were well aware of its author's human failings. William O'Connor portrayed Whitman as a Christ figure in "The Carpenter," but
during his long estrangement from Whitman he had ample time
to reflect on his former friend's shortcomings. In Bucke's view of
Whitman, however, no failings or shortcomings existed. Immediately after meeting the poet Bucke wrote to a friend that he had
encountered "a god," a position from which he never retreated.
"Whitman lived in an upper spiritual stratum above all mean
thoughts, sordid feelings, earthly harassments," Bucke wrote years
later. Like O'Connor, he compared Whitman to Christ, but it was
to the latter's disadvantage. Bucke took the typically Victorian belief
in progress and applied it to the religious realm: human consciousness was evolving, and Walt Whitman was the latest, best, and most
perfect example of a fully evolved spiritual being. Let the members
of the American Medico-Psychological Association laugh; Bucke devoted more than twenty years of his life to the service of what he
often referred to simply as "the Cause"—that is, promoting Walt
Whitman as the greatest religious figure in history.

✠ ✠ ✠

Bucke's father, Horatio Walpole Bucke, was an unlikely candidate
for the role of pioneer farmer. Great-grandson of the British prime
minister Sir Robert Walpole and grand-nephew of the writer Horace
Walpole, Horatio Bucke took holy orders after his graduation from
Cambridge and was appointed curate in the Cambridgeshire village
of Methwold. All signs pointed to a career as the sort of complacent
clergyman who served as satirical fodder for Anthony Trollope. Yet

FIGURE 3.1. R. M. Bucke in the 1890s. John Rylands University Library, University of Manchester.

FIGURE 3.2. Walt Whitman, 1872. Bayley/Whitman Collection of Ohio Wesleyan University.

in 1838 the Reverend Mr. Bucke herded his wife and seven children—including his infant son, Richard Maurice—aboard an emigrant ship bound for Canada. The family settled on an Ontario farm near what became the city of London and began squeezing a livelihood out of the Canadian wilderness. Richard Maurice—he was called Maurice, pronounced "Morris"—remembered an idyllic early childhood of farm chores interrupted by rural pleasures: swimming in the farm's creek, searching for flowers and birds' eggs, skating and sledding in the long winters. None of the Bucke children attended school, but their father taught them to read at least two languages and set them loose in his library of several thousand volumes brought over from England. This haphazard educational system was remarkably successful: of the five male children, three became physicians, one a lawyer, and one a civil servant.

Maurice's childhood idyll ended abruptly with his mother's death when he was seven years old. In an autobiographical sketch Bucke revealed little about his reaction to her death, saying only that his life "in some respects became more unhappy than can readily be told"—the terseness of the statement underscoring the pain of a sensitive boy in a family of ten children where a mother's attention must have been a scarce and precious commodity. Bucke's father soon remarried, but his stepmother died a few months after the marriage. When his father sold the farm in 1853 to move to another part of Ontario, sixteen-year-old Maurice headed for the States; he would not return to Canada for five years.

He began by wandering through the Midwest and South, working odd jobs. In 1856 he hired on as a driver in a wagon train from Leavenworth, Missouri, to Salt Lake City, then kept heading west, teaming up with other wagon drivers looking for adventure in the mining territory. Following the Humboldt River through the mountains, they found more adventure than they had bargained for: an attack by a band of one hundred Shoshone warriors. The sixteen drivers had only five rifles, a shotgun, and two revolvers among them. Still, they were better armed than the Shoshone, most of whom had only bows and arrows. The Shoshone carried on the battle for several hours, then abruptly gave up and fled—luckily for

Bucke and his companions, since at that point most of them had run out of ammunition.

Bucke pushed on, finally stopping in Gold Canyon on the eastern slopes of the Sierra Nevada. There he joined a few dozen miners looking, with little success, for gold. Bucke gravitated toward two brothers from Pennsylvania, Hosea and Allen Grosh. When Hosea died a horrible death in September 1857 after accidentally wounding himself in the foot with a pickaxe, Allen formed a close bond with Bucke, who had helped to nurse and bury his brother. Allen even let Bucke in on the brothers' secret: while the other miners had been searching for gold in the canyon, he and Hosea had discovered what appeared to be an extraordinarily rich vein of silver. When Hosea's accident occurred, they had been about to leave for California, where they planned to file their claims and get backing from investors. Allen stood to become extraordinarily wealthy: Would Bucke like to join him as a partner?

Bucke would, and the two young men prepared to go to California. However, various setbacks delayed their departure, and it was late November before they began ascending the Sierras, knowing that winter came early to the high peaks. More experienced men might have hesitated before making a winter crossing; Bucke and Grosh, with the conviction of immortality common to young men, pushed on. Within days they were lost in waist-deep snow. They killed their pack donkey for food, threw away everything they were carrying—including Grosh's claim papers—and pushed on with nothing but blankets and knives. On December 6, twelve days after they had killed the donkey, Bucke pleaded with Grosh to let him lie down and die, but Grosh insisted they push on. The next day the two young men heard a dog bark, saw smoke, and, unable to walk any longer, literally crawled three-quarters of a mile into a California mining camp called Last Chance. But it was too late for Allen Grosh, who died twelve days later. At first it did not seem that Bucke, severely frostbitten, would survive either, but the miners were able to send for a surgeon. When Bucke recovered in the spring, he was missing all of one foot and half the other. With no record of the Groshes' silver find surviving, Bucke had no reason to stay in the West, and he headed home.

Back in Canada in the fall of 1858, his father dead and his family dispersed, twenty-one-year-old Maurice Bucke followed two of his older brothers to McGill University's medical school, which was considered the best medical school in North America at the time. Yet even at McGill medicine had not entirely broken free of its eighteenth-century connections to metaphysics. While his classmates conducted experimental research, Bucke tried to combine physiology and philosophy. He was obsessed with the theory of vitalism, which held that animate life forms must have originated through a divine force. His thesis, "The Correlation of the Vital and Physical Forces," represented a last-gasp effort to hold back the scientific materialism that was coming to dominate medical studies.

Bucke's prize-winning thesis reveals much about its author. The twenty-five-year-old medical student was wildly ambitious: he announced in his introduction that his subject was nothing less than "the nature of life." This largely self-educated provincial young man was bold enough to swim against the tide of modern scientific research, naive enough to imagine that, working largely on his own, he could discover the key to life's secrets. He later described this period of his life as "one passionate note of interrogation," a time of "unappeasable hunger for enlightenment on the basic problems." He channeled much of his enormous energy into spiritual seeking, reading voluminously and trying out various religious and philosophical paths.

His search for enlightenment initially led in the direction of liberal Protestantism. Matriculating at McGill's medical school, Bucke's two older brothers had dutifully identified their religion as Church of England, their father's denomination. Bucke defiantly wrote "Universalist." Universalism, the country cousin of Unitarianism, thrived among freethinking farmers and tradespeople who, like the Unitarians, rejected Calvinist doctrines of predestination and divine election in favor of an optimistic theology that held the possibility of redemption for all and a very American confidence that this belief could constitute a new world religion.

Spiritually and professionally restless, Bucke headed to Europe after graduation for further study. His first destination was London, where he befriended two young literary men, the brothers Harry and Alfred Forman. Harry later edited a massive twelve-volume edition of Percy Shelley's works; Alfred was the English translator of Wagner's operas. The young Canadian's friendship with these soon-to-be-eminent writers reflects his intellectual ability and his attractive personality. All Bucke's friends admired his high energy, but all acknowledged that he was extreme in his intellectual enthusiasms. "I love the Doctor, like him near me mostly," Walt Whitman was to say in later years, but "there are times when his boisterous vehemence gets on my nerves."

After more than a year in England Bucke continued his study of medicine in Paris, where he quickly learned enough French to read the Forman brothers' favorite philosopher, Auguste Comte. Virtually overnight Bucke became a boisterously vehement Comtean. Comte was a grand synthesizer who founded the Universal Church of the Religion of Humanity and claimed that his philosophy of positivism "comprehend[s] human life under every aspect"—an appealing prospect to a young physician whose medical school thesis had purported to explain the foundations of life. Bucke, who had left behind his clergyman father's Anglican religion but not his religious disposition, was a perfect candidate for conversion to Comtean religion.

Bucke returned to Canada in 1864, established a medical practice in Sarnia, Ontario, and the next year married Jessie Gurd, a young woman much more conventional than her husband. Given his intelligence and training, he seemed poised to become a highly successful physician. Yet for several years after his wedding he flailed about in both his professional and personal life. He took long breaks from his practice—and his marriage—by making three trips to England for vaguely defined health problems that seem to have been largely psychosomatic in origin. He abandoned medical practice for two years after his final trip to England and tried to make a living speculating in oil and land. His dissatisfaction with the practice of medicine and his restlessness with family life—he and Jessie would have seven children—are reflected in his ceasing, in 1866, his long-time practice of keeping a diary, writing, "My life [now] that I am fairly married and settled down to work is so monotonous that what is said of it one day answers for every other day." Most disturbingly, he suffered from a mental affliction that he described, using the diagnostic terms of the period, as "violent attack[s] of nervous depression from Dyspepsia"—that is, acute anxiety disorder with recurrent panic attacks. During the eight years after his return from Europe, the normally high-spirited Bucke was suffering psychologically and physically. "My health has completely broken down again," he wrote Harry Forman in the spring of 1872. Fortunately, during the 1870s Bucke's life changed for the better. Walt Whitman, he firmly believed, was responsible for the transformation.

✢ ✢ ✢

Bucke first heard of Walt Whitman from a friend in 1868 and soon afterward obtained William Michael Rossetti's edition. Within months Bucke was transformed from Comtean to Whitmanite. He wrote Harry Forman early in 1869, "Here is a man who receives images of spiritual and material things from without and transmits them again without the least thought of what will the world say of this idea and how will the world like this form of expression. . . . He speaks from his own soul with the most perfect candor, sincerity and truth. There is nothing in modern literature like it." Bucke began pressing Forman to set aside work on Shelley in order to publish a complete *Leaves of Grass* in England, and Bucke determined to collect everything published so far by and about Whitman. In pursuit of that goal in 1870 he wrote Whitman a respectful "Dear Sir" letter, ordering copies of *Leaves of Grass*, *Passage to India*, and "Democratic Vistas" and inquiring how to obtain a copy of the 1855 *Leaves*. Unlike Anne Gilchrist's first letter to Whitman, Bucke's prosaic letter does not reveal the depth of his reaction to the poet. Whitman presumably sent Bucke his books, but he did not bother to respond with a letter to the bibliophile Canadian physician. Bucke was undeterred. He continued his study of *Leaves of Grass* and in 1872, primed by Whitman's verse, he had the first of his transformative spiritual experiences.

Bucke was on a recuperative visit to the Forman brothers in England. The three friends spent an evening together reading and talking about poetry, especially Whitman's. At midnight he got into a hansom cab, and on the way to his lodgings he had an unexpected and overwhelming mystical experience. Years later he published an account of the experience written in the third person:

> All at once . . . he found himself wrapped around as it were by a flame-colored cloud. For an instant he thought of fire, some sudden conflagration in the great city; the next, he knew that the light was within himself. Directly afterwards came upon him a sense of exultation, of immense joyousness accompanied or immediately followed by an intellectual illumination quite impossible to describe. Into his brain streamed one momentary lightning-flash of the Brahmic Splendor which has ever since lightened his life; upon his heart fell one drop of Brahmic Bliss, leaving thenceforward for always an aftertaste of heaven. Among other things . . . he saw and knew that the Cosmos is not dead matter but a living Presence, that the soul of man is immortal, that the universe is so built and ordered that without any peradventure all things work together for the good of each and all, that the foundation principle of the world is what we call love and that the happiness of every one is in the long run absolutely certain.

Bucke believed that his "illumination," as he called it, was both transcendent and transhistorical, identical to the mystical experiences of sages from the Buddha to William Blake. However, Bucke's account of his illumination was clearly shaped by his wide reading and intellectual enthusiasms. For example, his references to "Brahmic Splendor" and "Brahmic Bliss" were imposed post hoc on his 1872 illumination, since Bucke did not begin reading books on Asian religion until years later. Even the knowledge he claimed to gain from the experience—"that the Cosmos is not dead matter but a living

Presence, that the soul of man is immortal, . . . that the foundation
principle of the world is what we call love"—sounds remarkably
similar, in both content and cadence, to a famous mystical passage
from Whitman's "Song of Myself":

> Swiftly arose and spread around me the peace and knowl-
> edge that pass all the argument of the earth,
> And I know that the hand of God is the promise of
> my own,
> And I know that the spirit of God is the brother of
> my own,
> And that all the men ever born are also my brothers, and
> the women my sisters and lovers,
> And that a kelson of the creation is love

Bucke would not have disputed the borrowing. *Leaves of Grass*, he
said often, was his bible.

✠ ✠ ✠

Following his mystical experience, Bucke returned to Canada determined to escape his medical practice in Sarnia. He finally succeeded
in 1876, when he was named superintendent of the newly opened
insane asylum in Hamilton, Ontario. A year later the superinten-
dency of the larger, more prestigious asylum in London, Ontario,
became vacant, and Bucke got the job. He was to remain in the post
until his death a quarter century later, after becoming one of the
most highly regarded alienists in North America. However, like
other asylum superintendents of the time, Bucke would have readily
acknowledged that he had no special training for his position. The
term *psychiatry* was not widely used in English until the twentieth
century, and there was little sense of the field as a distinct medical
specialty. In fact, the most influential British asylum superintendent
of the early nineteenth century was a former tea merchant. However,
by the midnineteenth century a medical model of insanity had been
established, and physicians had positioned themselves as the only

ones qualified to care for the insane. In the Whiggish, progressive version of the history of psychiatry, which until recently dominated the field, the medicalization of insanity was regarded as a major advance, and Bucke was seen as part of a movement of professionalization and humanization in treatment of the insane. This progressive view of Bucke's role in psychiatric history was reinforced by Walt Whitman's admiring comments in his memoir, *Specimen Days*, where he described the London Asylum as one of the "most advanced, perfected, and kindly and rationally carried on, of all its kind in America."

The reality was more complex. Certainly, treatment of the insane had changed radically in the century before Bucke took his position as superintendent. The emblematic insane asylum of the eighteenth century was London's notorious Bethlem Hospital, popularly known as Bedlam, where curious visitors could, for a fee, entertain themselves by gawking at the chained maniacs. Reaction against the degrading conditions of the bedlams across Europe led to what was known as "moral treatment": the insane were to be treated not as criminals to be locked away but as sick people who could be coaxed into health by humane treatment in a carefully controlled environment. In the first flush of enthusiasm for this new therapeutic model, institutions using moral treatment reported cure rates of more than 80 percent.

The therapeutic optimism did not last long. By midcentury asylums were filling up with difficult cases that proved resistant to moral therapy. By the century's end the typical asylum was a massive institution filled with hundreds of incurably insane people. What went wrong? In an influential account Michel Foucault argued that the asylum was intended not as a therapeutic but as a disciplinary institution, created for the surveillance and control of social deviants. However, Foucault was scarcely the first to note the asylum's therapeutic failure. As early as 1851 the Irish inspectors of lunacy concluded pessimistically that "the uniform tendency of all asylums is to degenerate from their original object, that of being hospitals for the treatment of insanity, into domiciles for incurable lunatics." In part, asylums were overwhelmed by the sheer pressure of numbers.

FIGURE 3.3. London [Ontario] Lunatic Asylum, c. 1890. Bucke was superintendent from 1877 until his death in 1901. Archives of Ontario.

In England the average asylum population rose from just more than one hundred patients in 1827 to more than one thousand by 1910, while the total number of patients in Ontario asylums increased sevenfold in the forty years after 1861. There are multiple explanations for the increase in numbers; most obviously, insane people were redistributed from families, almshouses, and jails into the new public asylums.

The London Asylum, which opened in 1871, was built to cope with the rising patient population. The largest building in western Ontario, it was a vast structure on a three-hundred-acre site, designed to hold a thousand patients; Bucke observed that it "almost reached the magnitude of a town." He began his term as the town's mayor with an optimistic platform for curing insanity by using his medical training: he would eliminate insanity among his male patients by stopping them from masturbating.

Virtually every nineteenth-century alienist agreed that masturbation was a major cause of insanity among males. In 1876, the year before Bucke came to London, Dr. Daniel Yellowlees of Glasgow reported that he had devised a method to prevent masturbation by inserting a silver wire through the foreskin. Bucke enthusiastically adopted the procedure, operating on twenty-one patients during his first months in the asylum. Unfortunately, results were discouraging. Only two patients showed any significant improvement in their mental state, and Bucke was forced to conclude that "in only a small proportion of all those cases in which masturbation exists could removal of the habit, even were this possible, be expected to be of any benefit to the patient." Bucke abandoned his medical interventions and adopted the prevailing methods of moral treatment: work, amusements, and religion.

Bucke has been hailed as a pioneer for abandoning the use of mechanical restraints in the London Asylum and ceasing to dose patients with alcohol, but in both cases he was following moral treatment tenets laid out in the early nineteenth century. In any case, by the 1880s alienists no longer thought of themselves as healers but as benign custodians. Bucke concluded that "insanity is essentially an incurable disease" and suggested that "the object of treatment in the case of insanity is not so much the cure of the disease as the rehumanization of the patient" through moral therapy. Except for a disturbing venture into attempting to treat women's insanity through gynecological surgery, undertaken in the late 1890s, Bucke made little effort to cure his insane patients after 1877. Instead, he threw his immense energy, his eccentric but powerful intellect, and his self-willed optimism not into searching for causes and cures of insanity but into interpreting and promoting Walt Whitman and *Leaves of Grass*.

✚ ✚ ✚

In his first letter to Whitman in 1870 Bucke had tentatively broached the idea of visiting the poet, but Whitman never responded. Seven years later, while on a professional trip to Philadelphia, Bucke decided to drop in unannounced. As a hero worshipper by nature, living in the great Victorian era of hero worship, Bucke came to his meeting with Whitman prepared to be overwhelmed. He was not disappointed, despite the brevity of their visit. When Bucke showed up at George Whitman's house in Camden, Walt, as was his wont, took his visitor to the Delaware River ferry and across to Philadelphia, where they rode a streetcar up Market Street before Walt went off to an appointment. Bucke later said that Whitman "only spoke to him about a hundred words altogether," yet he regarded their meeting as a turning point of his life. A week after meeting Whitman, still reeling from the encounter, Bucke wrote a long and somewhat dazed letter to Harry Forman:

> I hardly know how to tell you about W. W. If I tried to say how he impressed me you would probably put it down to exaggeration. I have never seen any man to compare with him—any man the least like him. . . . He is an average man magnified to the dimensions of a god. . . . I may say that I experienced what I have heard so much about—the extraordinary magnetism of his presence—I not only felt deeply in an indescribable way towards him—but I think that that short interview has altered the attitude of my moral nature to everything.

Bucke would return often to his first meeting with Whitman, telling the story again and again in different contexts. Bucke's letter to Forman contains all the themes that he would later emphasize. First, and most noticeably, he casts Whitman as a quasi-divine religious figure, a position from which Bucke never retreated. In fact, Bucke intensified the deification of Whitman suggested in the letter, writing later that he was certain at his first meeting with Whitman that the poet "was either actually a god or in some sense clearly and entirely preterhuman." Next, Bucke's inchoate deep feelings toward Whitman and his reference to the poet's "magnetism" suggest that Bucke's relation to Whitman, like that of Burroughs and O'Connor before him, involved an unacknowledged homoerotic attraction. Bucke reinforced this view a few years later in one of his retellings of their meeting, writing of himself in the third person that "shortly after leaving [Whitman] a state of mental exaltation set in, which he could only describe by comparing to slight intoxication by champagne, or to falling in love!" The letter's third major theme is

Bucke's personal transformation as a result of their brief encounter. Bucke despaired of conveying to Forman the impression that Whitman had made on him: "It is no use for me to try to give any idea of the man because I have no idea of him myself—I cant grasp him, I cannot take him in—he is immense." Twenty years later, revisiting the initial encounter, Bucke was similarly at a loss: "Any attempt to convey even the faintest notion upon me of that short and seemingly commonplace interview would be certainly hopeless, probably foolish. Briefly, it would be nothing more than the simple truth to state that I was, by it, lifted to and set upon a higher plane of existence, upon which I have more or less continuously lived ever since." Intoxicated by his encounter with Whitman, Bucke immediately invited the poet to visit him in Canada. Whitman declined, but Bucke persisted, and three years later the poet finally agreed. By that time Bucke's invitations had assumed a special urgency, since he had determined to write the first biography of Walt Whitman, and he needed to make an extended study of his subject.

During Walt Whitman's first decade in Camden, when he boarded with his brother, he showed an eagerness to escape George's household whenever he could, staying for weeks at a time with the Gilchrists, the Staffords, and other friends. Once he made up his mind to go to Canada, Walt exploited Bucke's hospitality to the fullest, spending four months with his Canadian friend, from June through September 1880. Whitman seems to have had the time of his life, traveling about three thousand miles altogether. With Bucke as companion, he explored the Great Lakes and the St. Lawrence River, going by boat from Lake Huron in the west to the Saguenay River in eastern Québec.

During Whitman's visit Bucke served alternately as host, researcher, and impresario. He was determined to promote Whitman's reputation in Canada; when the poet made his 1880 visit, it is likely that there was not a copy of *Leaves of Grass* to be found in any library or bookshop in the country. However, if Whitman was unread, he was not unknown; he had a reputation as an "irreligious rowdy." Bucke set to work months before Whitman's arrival, lecturing on the poet in five Ontario towns. The gist of his lecture can be discerned from a newspaper report: Bucke's strategy was to stuff the bohemian Whitman into the clothing of a respectably pious Victorian gentleman. Bucke concluded his lecture with a gushing encomium: "The distinguishing feature belonging to [Whitman], which as a key unlocks every apparent enigma about him, is his extraordinarily elevated moral nature, his exalted trust in God and his intense love for mankind." Bucke did not convince everyone. A letter to the editor of the local newspaper denounced Bucke for attempting to "dig up from the gutter a book stained with filth," and the Reverend Mr. Murray denounced Whitman from his Ontario pulpit. Bucke was elated; he wrote Whitman that the newspaper controversy meant they could sell more copies of *Leaves of Grass*.

Interest in Whitman was so strong by the time he arrived in Canada in June that both London newspapers printed lengthy articles about him the day after his arrival. Bucke had fed the reporters in advance with material favorable to Whitman, and they cooperated by taking Bucke's line. One reporter quoted Whitman as saying that the Bible was the "best of all books" and that the human body is a temple "too holy to be abused by vice and debauchery." The article concluded, "While it is not the province of the reporter to pronounce upon [Whitman's] orthodoxy, there can be no doubt that he is a reverent man, with no suggestion of irreverence or pruriency in his talk." Bucke's campaign had achieved its goal: in the eyes of Ontario's citizens Walt Whitman was no longer an irreligious debaucher but a respectable, if unorthodox, Christian gentleman.

Of course, not everyone took to Walt Whitman—Bucke had evidence of that in his own household. Both poet and promoter regarded the 1880 trip as such a success that they decided to repeat the visit the next year—a plan aborted by the opposition of Bucke's wife, Jessie, who heard about the intended return visit while taking one of her regular lengthy vacations apart from the doctor in Sarnia, Ontario. Bucke replied to Jessie's letter of protest in an initially conciliatory tone, saying that he had written to Whitman to stop him from coming, then gently chiding his wife for listening to friends in Sarnia who, Bucke believed, must have turned her against Whitman. The tone of the letter then abruptly turns chilling: "But Jessie never allow yourself to imagine for a moment that you or any of you can shake my affection for Walt Whitman—If all the world stood on one side, and Walt Whitman and general contempt on the other and I had to choose which I would take I do not think I should hesitate (I hope I should not) to choose Walt Whitman." Bucke had chosen sides, and he was determined never to retreat.

✢ ✢ ✢

The book that resulted from Whitman's visit to Canada, Bucke's *Walt Whitman* (1883), is generally referred to as a biography, but it resembles nothing readers today would call by that name. Instead, it is an eclectic collection of materials with a single goal: to portray Walt Whitman as "the Saviour, the Redeemer of the modern world." That extravagant phrase, which Bucke wanted to use as an epigraph, occurs in a letter from John Burroughs, usually the most subdued of the disciples. But Burroughs would say in a private letter things he was not willing to publish. Bucke was less restrained. His *Walt Whitman* casts the poet as a modern Christ who points the way to human salvation through evolution of the moral nature.

"Moral nature" had a special value in the Buckean lexicon. Bucke's first book was titled *Man's Moral Nature* (1879); he dedicated it to Walt Whitman, "the man who of all men past and present that I have known has the most exalted moral nature." Bucke believed that humans' moral nature—our emotional and spiritual capacities—is physiologically based and is capable of evolving. Bucke had an essentially pre-Darwinian conception of evolution; he viewed it as a process leading to a static and perfect end. Using dubious historical examples, he set out to prove that elements of hate and fear in human moral nature were becoming extinct and being replaced by love and faith. Bucke saw his book *Walt Whitman* as a sequel to *Man's Moral Nature*. His first book was on "the moral nature in the abstract," as he put it, while the goal of *Walt Whitman* was to depict an individual moral nature, "the highest that has yet appeared." Bucke believed that Whitman stood at the pinnacle of human evolution, pointing the way; the rest of humanity would catch up with him over generations.

Critical commentary on Bucke's *Walt Whitman* has focused on the role Whitman played in the book's composition, spurred by Whitman's claim to a friend that he wrote the first twenty-four pages himself. It is true that Whitman blue-penciled the book in manuscript and galleys. However, Whitman's additions to the manuscript are trivial compared to his deletions: he struck out vast tracts of prose that Bucke had lifted from *Man's Moral Nature*. Whitman was willing to let Bucke ride his evolutionary hobbyhorse through *Leaves of Grass* to some extent, but the poet had his limits. Returning Bucke's first draft, he said that the passages he had struck "would have been nuts to the caricature baboons"; he assuaged the doctor's ego by assuring him that the material was "magnificent" but belonged in *Man's Moral Nature*, not *Walt Whitman*.

Both Bucke and Whitman had a flexible sense of what belonged in *Walt Whitman*. The typical nineteenth-century biography was a "Life and Letters" hodgepodge, and Bucke's is no exception. Structurally, *Walt Whitman* is a miscellany. In its essence it is an exercise in hero worship. As a student in Europe Bucke had worshiped Auguste Comte, but Comte faded to insignificance once Bucke met Walt Whitman. Meeting him was like drinking champagne, like "falling in love!" But it was also like reading Comte. Whitman swept Bucke off his feet both emotionally and intellectually. *Walt Whitman* records Bucke's intense emotional reaction to the poet and at the same time incorporates Whitman into the complex religious-scientific theories that Bucke elaborated during his entire adult life.

The Judeo-Christian heritage that Bucke absorbed from his clergyman father asserted the idea of a perfect book, an inerrant scripture directly inspired by God. The progressive version of evolutionary theory that Bucke took from Comte and others suggested the perfectibility of humankind. Bucke united these two cultural streams in his analysis of *Leaves of Grass* and Walt Whitman. It is a commonplace in modern academic criticism of *Leaves of Grass* to talk of the persona "Walt Whitman" created by writer Walter Whitman. Bucke would have none of that. Walt Whitman on the page was identical to Whitman in person; this perfect book came from a perfect man. The man who could write *Leaves of Grass* had to be the most morally evolved person in human history, the final destination of thousands of years of human progress. Six years after meeting Whitman, Bucke was still unsure whether the poet was fully human or a god in human form. *Walt Whitman* paints a portrait of its subject that only faintly resembles twenty-first-century ideas of the poet but that perfectly matches Victorian conceptions of Jesus.

With the poet's collusion Bucke composed an account of Whitman's life that turns New York Harbor into a Sea of Galilee frequented by the saintly Carpenter of Brooklyn. Recent biographies describe the pre–*Leaves of Grass* Whitman as a conventional, politically partisan journalist, a dandy-about-town whose writing alternated between the clever and the maudlin. Bucke erased the newspaperman in favor of the carpenter—stretching the truth, since although Whitman for a time speculated in house construction in Brooklyn, there is no evidence that he ever wielded a hammer himself. Nevertheless, Bucke's Whitman is a man of the people, consorting in perfect intimacy and equality with men and women from every walk of life, absorbing into himself all of modern life, all religions, all occupations, and the best of ancient and modern learning. In short, Bucke seems to draw his portrait of the young Whitman from "Song of Myself," Whitman's autobiographical fantasia.

For his account of the older Whitman, Bucke had his own observations to draw on, including the four months that the two men spent together in Canada. However, Bucke's chapter "The Poet in 1880" is as fantastical as his rendering of the poet's early years. According to Bucke, Whitman never felt anger or fear, never complained, loved everything and everyone he encountered. All his senses were exceptionally acute—Bucke took literally the poetry's reference to the "bustle of growing wheat"—and Whitman's body exuded "an exquisite aroma of cleanliness." He was especially fond of children and, when invited to meet distinguished guests at a social occasion, preferred to go off into a corner and entertain the young ones. His only vice, according to Bucke, was reading the newspaper. The portrait that emerges is "both insipid and implausible," according to one critic. Even Whitman was taken aback. "The character you give me is not a true one in the main," he wrote Bucke. "I am by no means that benevolent, equable, happy creature you portray—but let that pass."

For Bucke's Christological interpretation of Whitman's life to be complete, the poet had to perform miracles, undergo a Passion, and be crucified. The Civil War served admirably for the first two. In Bucke's view Whitman's Civil War service as a hospital volunteer was not only admirable but literally miraculous. He wrote that Whitman possessed an "extraordinary power" that enabled him "to turn the scale in favor of life, when without him the result would have been death." But the miracles came at a cost. The Civil War was Whitman's Passion, and it left him a broken man. Whitman contracted "hospital malaria," supposedly the first illness of his life, and "never entirely recovered from [it]—and never will." According to Bucke, Whitman's 1873 stroke, which left him partially paralyzed, was a direct result of his Civil War illness.

Finally, to complete the parallel Bucke needed a crucifixion. Whitman's treatment by the critics filled the bill. Bucke incorporated a forty-four-page appendix of "contemporaneous notices" into his book, devoting a quarter of the collection to hostile reviews, from an 1855 assertion that the poet's "indecencies stink in the nostrils" to an 1881 attack on the poems as "bestial." Bucke emphasized the opposition to *Leaves of Grass* in order to support his claim of Whitman's status as Saviour and Redeemer. In Bucke's evolutionary interpretation of man's moral nature, Whitman possessed the highest "moral elevation" of any person in history, completing a lineage from the Buddha to Confucius to Zoroaster to Muhammad. According to Bucke, every person prominent for his moral elevation was also the object of hostility from his contemporaries—had been, in Bucke's words, "traduced, banished, burned, poisoned, or crucified."

Bucke's *Walt Whitman* identifies Whitman as a new Christ and treats *Leaves of Grass* as a gnostic gospel accessible only to the initiated. Bucke's two chapters titled "Analysis of the Poems" contend that the surface of the poems conceals depths of meaning from even the most intelligent of readers; Bucke promised to crack the code.

His comments on "The Ship Starting" offer a good demonstration of his methodology. This four-line poem might seem to most readers a straightforward description of an observed scene:

> Lo, the unbounded sea,
> On its breast a ship starting, spreading all sails, carrying
>   even her moonsails,
> The pennant is flying aloft as she speeds she speeds so
>   stately—below emulous waves press forward,
> They surround the ship with shining curving motions
>   and foam.

In Bucke's gnostic analysis the poem's surface meaning is irrelevant; he offers in its place the correct interpretation: "The ship is the book [*Leaves of Grass*], the ocean is the human mind. The large ship, with all sails set, starts on her voyage; as she presses through the water, the waves (the resistance the book meets) roll from her bows and down her sides. The angry, hostile criticisms and clamors are the bubbles of foam in the wake." Whitman himself was often surprised by Bucke's elaborate interpretations of his poetry. He told Horace Traubel,

> I put in almost unqualified endorsement of Dr. Bucke's book, but as to his *explication*—no, no, no—that I do not accept—for Leaves of Grass baffles me, its author, at all points of its meaning—so that things perhaps plain to Doctor are not so plain to my mind. . . . What I quarrel with is the Doctor's damned definiteness—and it is *very* damned! I often pull him up short when he is here. He is explicating this, that, the other, as if there was no doubt in the world about it. Yet *I*, the author, am in constant doubt about it.

Bucke clashed with Whitman because so much was at stake in his Christological view of the poet. He regarded *Leaves of Grass* as a collection of opaque parables, much like the Christian gospels. In Bucke's view of Christianity Jesus would have sunk into obscurity if not for the interpretive brilliance of Paul; Bucke often quoted Comte's assessment that Paul was *le vrai fondateur*—the true founder—of Christianity. Bucke believed that he could go down in history as the Canadian St. Paul to Whitman's American Christ.

By the time *Walt Whitman* was published in 1883, Bucke and Whitman had worked together on the manuscript for more than two years. Their relationship was complicated; Bucke even called it "a little embarrasing [*sic*] at times." Bucke was referring to his uncertainty about whether Whitman was human or divine, but he must have had similar uncertainties about the nature of his passionate feelings for the poet, which threatened to push beyond the boundaries of conventional nineteenth-century male friendships: Bucke wrote in *Walt Whitman* that "no description can give any idea of the extraordinary physical attractiveness of the man." Then, of course, there was Jessie Bucke's disapproval of Whitman, the difference in the two men's ages, and the hundreds of miles that separated them. Any simple friendship with Whitman was impossible, and in the five years following the publication of *Walt Whitman* the two men seem to have had relatively little contact with one another. That changed in 1888, when Bucke was visiting Whitman while on a professional trip to Philadelphia. During the night of June 3–4 Whitman suffered a series of devastating strokes. In the days that followed, everyone around Whitman believed that he was going to die. That he did not Whitman attributed to Dr. Bucke's presence: "I am quite sure—oh! I am quite sure!—Dr. Bucke this time saved my life: that if he had not been here to roll up his sleeves and stay and work and watch it would have been a final call," he told Horace Traubel shortly after the event. Given the lack of effective medical interventions for dealing with cerebral hemorrhage in the nineteenth century, it is not clear that Bucke actually aided Whitman significantly in a medical sense. But the poet was certain: Maurice Bucke had saved his life. For the next four years, until Whitman's death, he and Bucke would be closer than ever.

☩ ☩ ☩

The nature of their relationship changed significantly after Whitman's near-fatal strokes. If before they had been principally master and disciple, now they were also patient and physician. Following his stroke Whitman began writing Bucke two to three times a week; Bucke replied at least as often and sometimes wrote daily. Whitman's brief, prosaic letters usually described the weather, frequently discussed his current writing projects and publications, and always mentioned his bowel movements. Constipation was one of the most persistent side effects of Whitman's strokes, and whenever he moved his bowels, he reported to Bucke with a toddler's (not to mention an artist's) certainty that whatever he produced would be of interest to others. He told Bucke what he ate, described his many symptoms, and talked about the visits of his local physicians and the care of his live-in nurses. For his part Bucke served as a combination of physician and Dutch uncle during Whitman's last years. Bucke gave Whitman copious instructions about his health, his finances, and his publications—most of which Whitman blithely ignored.

Bucke may have been bossy, but his immense and genuine affection for Whitman shines through his letters to the poet and the other disciples. Walt Whitman was the central fact of Bucke's life after 1888, and that year he stepped up his efforts to escape from his asylum duties. As a young man Bucke had dreamed of striking it rich as a gold and silver miner. Now he was certain that he could become wealthy with the aid of his wife's brilliant but irresponsible brother, Willie Gurd. Gurd was a backyard tinkerer who in the mid-1880s invented a new water meter. He convinced his brother-in-law Maurice that the meter could make them both rich, and during the next several years Bucke poured more than $30,000 into developing the meter, producing prototypes, and promoting it. With characteristic enthusiasm and generosity Bucke promised his friends that he would make their fortunes also: Horace Traubel would be the meter company bookkeeper; Traubel's brother-in-law Thomas Harned, a Camden attorney and Whitman disciple, would do the legal work. "I have no doubt whatever that the meter is worth millions of dollars," Bucke confidently wrote Traubel in 1888. The next spring Bucke told Whitman that he was writing his final report as asylum superintendent; within a year the meter would make him a millionaire, and he could retire. Unfortunately, the next year Willie Gurd was still tinkering with the meter, and Bucke's letters predicting his imminent retirement became an annual ritual. Whitman politely wished him well but in private told Traubel that the doctor was chasing an illusion.

Bucke's friends may have thought that his obsession with the meter was foolish, but they understood his motives. Bucke desperately wanted to quit the asylum so that he could devote all his time to the "Great Cause" of Walt Whitman and *Leaves of Grass*. "Should this meter *go*," he wrote Horace Traubel, "it is my dream to devote the rest of my life . . . to the study and promulgation of the new religion." Bucke's view of Whitman as a religious founder makes his micromanaging of the poet's publications more understandable. Bucke gave Whitman detailed advice about margins, typography, and paper, in part from a bibliophile's love for books as physical objects, in part from his regard for *Leaves of Grass* as scripture. When Whitman was preparing his *Complete Poems and Prose* after his 1888 stroke, Bucke peppered him with advice and pep talks. After the ailing poet complained about delays, Bucke replied, "The 'Complete Works' takes time, a lot of time, but that is all right— *take time*—enough of it, and have it *right*—it is worth taking pains about—it will be a standard book for many a day—to many and many it will be a sacred, and altogether priceless volume—a bible of the bibles—a resumé of them all." Once the volume appeared at the end of the year, Bucke wrote ecstatically, "It is grand, grander than even I had hoped. It is the bible of the future for the next thousand years."

With the scriptural canon established, Bucke could turn his attention to other aspects of the new religion. He did not expect Whitman to survive long after the June 1888 strokes, and in the months following he fired off numerous letters to Traubel about Whitman's will. Bucke cared nothing about Whitman's money, but he was deeply anxious about control of the poet's texts. Bucke had often waded through the knee-high piles of paper scattered about Whitman's Camden bedroom, and he knew that the room contained thousands of letters and unpublished documents. These may not have been sacred scripture like *Leaves of Grass*, but control of

Whitman's papers meant the power to shape his image after his death. When Anne Gilchrist's son Herbert came to Camden from England in September 1888, Bucke assumed that Herbert was trying to grab hold of the literary executorship for himself, and Bucke enlisted Traubel to foil the Englishman's schemes. Fortunately for Bucke, when Whitman, moving in his own good time, finally got around to signing a will, he named Bucke, Traubel, and Harned as his literary executors.

Despite Bucke's certainty that Whitman could not long survive his 1888 stroke, the poet lived another four years. However, he remained in ill health throughout the period, and there were many times when it seemed he was dying. Bucke desperately wanted to be by Whitman's side at the end, and on several occasions he made the twenty-four-hour train trip from Ontario to Camden, only to find the poet rallying. The final visit occurred in December 1891. On the twenty-first Bucke received an urgent telegram from Traubel; less than forty-eight hours later he was entering the ramshackle Mickle Street house. "Maurice Bucke, Maurice Bucke, Maurice Bucke," Whitman said from his bed, "how glad I am to see you, how glad I am." His friend's arrival seemed to restore the poet, and the old man pulled through the crisis. Bucke returned to Canada, where he worked on his new book about cosmic consciousness and, as the poet declined during the early weeks of the new year, wrote Horace Traubel lengthy, frantic letters asking him to quiz Whitman about the poet's spiritual experiences. Traubel ignored the letters; Whitman could barely speak. The end came too abruptly to summon Bucke; Walt Whitman died on March 26, 1892, two months before his seventy-third birthday.

Speaking at Whitman's graveside, Bucke was astonished that he had the fortitude to address the crowd. It was Whitman's strength that buoyed him up, he concluded. Bucke pointed out that Whitman's poetry is suffused with the conviction of immortality: "Is it wonderful that I should be immortal?" Whitman asks in *Leaves of Grass*. "Every one is immortal." Whitman's personal immortality was the theme of Bucke's address at Harleigh Cemetery and the theme of his letters in the days following. "Over and over I keep saying to myself: The Christ is dead! Again we have buried the Christ!" Bucke wrote to two English disciples. "And for the time there seems to be an end of every thing. But I *know* he is not dead and I *know* that this pain will pass." If the Christ was buried, then it was up to the disciples to spread his word. Bucke's mission in life was clear. He had written Whitman a few months before the poet's death that their fates were inextricably linked. The letter was prompted by his receipt of the 1891–92 edition of *Leaves of Grass*, which Bucke predicted would be known in the future as "THE BOOK—all others will stand on a lower plane." He went on to predict his own future standing: "I am satisfied that I know something of it and of you—that is greatness enough for me—yes and greatness enough to carry my name down thro' all the ages." Bucke believed that he could go down in history as Whitman's greatest interpreter. There was no time to lose. Immediately after Whitman's death he rushed to publish a memorial volume.

The memorial book had its origins in 1888 when Bucke proposed a second, enlarged edition of his *Walt Whitman*. Whitman scotched the idea and suggested that Bucke instead bring out an "annex." During the next few years Bucke and Traubel worked on the annex in desultory fashion, collecting articles for what they conceived of from the beginning as an anthology. When Whitman died, they issued a call for further articles and hastily assembled the results. *In Re Walt Whitman* appeared a year after Whitman's death, edited by the literary executors, Bucke, Traubel, and Harned—it's not clear which of the three came up with the graceless title. They accurately described it as a "cluster of written material—abstract, descriptive, anecdotal, biographical, statistical, poetic." The volume opens with a long poem by John Addington Symonds and closes with a transcript of Whitman's funeral service; the material in between ranges from Anne Gilchrist's "A Woman's Estimate of Walt Whitman" to an interview with Whitman's brother George to the pathologist's notes from Whitman's autopsy.

The editors' intention is evident on the title page, which includes the following epigraph from Lucretius:

Now, though this great country is seen to deserve in many ways the wonder of mankind, and is held to be well worth visiting, rich in all good things, . . . yet seems it to have held within it nothing more glorious than this man, nothing more holy, marvellous and dear. The verses, too, of his godlike genius, cry with a loud voice, and set forth in such wise his glorious discoveries that he hardly seems born of mortal stock.

Bucke had intended this tribute to Empedocles of Sicily to serve as the epigraph of his 1883 biography of Whitman, but the poet rejected it. With Whitman dead Bucke resurrected the passage, which aptly introduces this more overtly hagiographic volume. In their preface the editors bluntly announce their view of Whitman: "Whitman had cosmic breadth and port. His 'Leaves' foliage the heavens. He was so complicated with all men and all phenomena that his very voice partook of the sway of elemental integrity and candor. . . . Whitman speaks in [Leaves of Grass] as would heaven, making unalterable announcements, oracular of the mysteries and powers that pervade and guide all life, all death, all purpose." The extravagance of the praise betrays Bucke as the preface's primary author. Bucke had included numerous critical attacks on Whitman in his 1883 book, but In Re is pure apotheosis. The only departure from the book's worshipful tone occurs in the interview with Whitman's brother George, who confesses that when the first edition of Leaves of Grass came out in 1855, "I saw the book—didn't read it at all—didn't think it worth reading—fingered it a little. Mother thought as I did—did not know what to make of it." The incomprehension of Whitman's family serves to set off the lavish tributes in In Re, three of which were written by Bucke.

Bucke's essay " 'Leaves of Grass' and Modern Science" builds on Anne Gilchrist's view of Whitman as the only nineteenth-century poet whose works are fully in accord with the latest scientific insights. However, Bucke characteristically goes far beyond Gilchrist and claims that Whitman had innate, perfect command of every field of knowledge. He "never writes a line or word inconsistent with any part of the truth," Bucke concludes. "His instinct is infallible;

his insight never at fault; his intuition as direct and sure as gravitation." This encomium is tame compared to those contained in "The Man Walt Whitman," another Bucke contribution to *In Re*. In this lengthy, over-the-top tribute Bucke portrays Whitman as a demigod, the ultimate and perfect product of human evolution.

"The Man Walt Whitman" might be titled "The Man Maurice Bucke," so fully does it reveal Bucke's preoccupations and psychological needs. In his professional life as physician and alienist he had been unsuccessful in his efforts to cure mental illness and had fallen into an unsatisfying role as an institutional administrator. However, in his role as author and Walt Whitman's champion, Bucke embraced a grandiose evolutionary optimism and cast Whitman as the ultimate physician, capable of healing humanity's ills. Starting from the widely conceded premise that evolution occurs "fitful[ly]," in "spurts and starts," Bucke argues that Walt Whitman was an evolutionary spurt, a model of what humans will become as they evolve over future generations. Bucke declares that Whitman was a perfect and perfectly happy man, and his perfection serves as proof that each of us has the potential to live a similarly fulfilled life. Bucke's image of Whitman enabled Bucke to construct a sorely needed and profoundly optimistic worldview. It also gave Bucke a promotion in intellectual rank. In *Man's Moral Nature* Bucke had assumed the role of liberal religious advocate. Beginning with *Walt Whitman*, he shaped a far greater role for himself as principal apostle of the religion of the future. "The Man Walt Whitman" contains Bucke's first mention of Paul, who is placed on a list of the greatest men of history. Significantly, Bucke includes Auguste Comte's description of Paul as the true founder of Christianity. In Comte's view Paul was Jesus's equal. Might history hold a similarly exalted place for Richard Maurice Bucke?

Not immediately. *In Re* appeared in a limited edition of one thousand copies and was not widely reviewed; the scant notice it attracted was scathingly hostile. One reviewer wrote that Whitman would never be embraced by the "cultivated public" so long as the poet's "fanatical devotees . . . continue to lavish their extravagant encomiums upon his faults and his virtues alike." He pronounced much of the volume "foolish" and some of it "deplorable." Horace Traubel wrote an agitated letter to Bucke, who calmed the younger man down in a remarkable letter that shows more clearly than anything else Bucke wrote his conception of Whitman's place in history— and his own:

> I am sorry the periodicals are not pleased with us but they do not make me alter my opinion as to W. W. or as to "In Re." The matter stands this way: If Walt is to go down the ages as a Sam. Johnson, as a Tennyson, as a Whittier, as a Hugo, as a Goethe, &c. &c. then we are wrong, have done wrong and have injured him—or at least ourselves. In that case people will say by & by (as so many say now): "These poor ignorant fools fell in love with a crow and made themselves believe it was an eagle." . . . But suppose Walt is really a Guatama [Gautama Buddha], a Jesus, a Zoroaster, an Isaiah? . . . How then? Consider (this is the way I put it to myself constantly)—consider if some one had put on record such details of the life and death of Guatama, of Jesus, of Dante, of "Shakespeare," of Paul and they had come down the ages safely? What would these sweet critics have said to the man or men who had done the work? How would the world at large thank the men?
>
> In my own heart *I know* that Walt will be loved because *I know* how passionately he is loved. But what do these critics know about it? For them and for 99 men out of every 100 today their view is correct, their words are true; and from their point of view and that of nearly all who buy their papers they *are right*. But that is not the last word—the day will come when we shall be right—I am sure of it and as the good Catholics say "in that faith I am firmly resolved to live and die."
>
> Have patience, dear Horace, wait till we hear what God says about it.

Bucke draws no attention to the date of his letter: December 25, 1893. Others might spend the day celebrating the birth of Jesus; Bucke preferred to spend it testifying to his own faith. In the years to come he focused his efforts on completing his magnum opus laying out the doctrines of the Whitmanite religion. Bucke believed that his book *Cosmic Consciousness* would definitively fix the place of both Walt Whitman and R. M. Bucke for generations to come.

✞ ✞ ✞

Cosmic Consciousness was not published until 1901, but the book had its origin ten years earlier, when Bucke met Edward Carpenter in England. The ostensible purpose of Bucke's 1891 English journey was to secure a British patent for Willie Gurd's meter, but his real interest lay in apostolic visits to Whitman's British disciples. In a speech to the Bolton disciples that Carpenter also attended, Bucke awkwardly laid out a new theory of Walt Whitman's poetry. "There is a quality in Whitman," he hesitatingly began, "there is a faculty which he possesses, a sense or whatever name you may give it, which is not possessed by ordinary people. It is from that faculty, that sense that the whole thing springs. . . . I want to give you some idea (I have no name for it of course) of what this faculty is." In the rest of his short address Bucke briefly and somewhat enigmatically described the "new spiritual faculty" that Whitman possessed as a "sense . . . of the reality and immortality of things." He went on to offer an evolutionary interpretation: this "new faculty is in process of being developed in the race and that faculty [is] the most important of all to us, and Whitman is the man in whom the faculty has the most complete development of any man the race has produced." The discussion after Bucke's address, as recorded in a transcript of the event carefully preserved by the Bolton disciples, reveals that most of them were baffled by his speech. However, one person present understood what Bucke was talking about even better than he did. Edward Carpenter had recently returned from India and Ceylon, where he had studied with a succession of gurus. In adapting translations of Asian texts, Carpenter had come up with a phrase that fit perfectly the faculty Bucke was describing: cosmic consciousness.

Bucke immediately adopted the term, and during the next ten years, in time snatched from his asylum duties, he worked on the manuscript of *Cosmic Consciousness*. The final product is an idiosyncratic mélange of texts: scientific charts, brief biographies, and extensive quotations from scripture and poetry that are subjected to Bucke's tortuous interpretations. Unexpectedly, the book became a worldwide best seller. It has never gone out of print and currently, more than a century after its publication, is available in seven different paperback editions in the United States and Canada.

The book begins with three chapters on the phenomenon of cosmic consciousness, all three a combination of shaky logic and ecstatic evolutionary optimism. Bucke starts by arguing that human consciousness evolved from simple consciousness—the awareness of body and the environment possessed by animals—to self-consciousness, a uniquely human property. Since evolution is ongoing, it is likely that new faculties are evolving even now, and Bucke asserts that the most significant of these is cosmic consciousness, which represents as great an advance over self-consciousness as the latter represented over simple consciousness. Bucke offers no single definition of cosmic consciousness, but the following passage is his most concise description: "[Cosmic] consciousness shows the cosmos to consist not of dead matter governed by unconscious, rigid, and unintending law; it shows it on the contrary as entirely immaterial, entirely spiritual and entirely alive; it shows that death is an absurdity; that everyone and everything has eternal life; it shows that the universe is God and that God is the universe; and that no evil ever did or ever will enter into it."

Bucke attempts to overwhelm skeptics with a flurry of scientific rationalism and elaborate charts. One of his charts prefigures the bulk of *Cosmic Consciousness*, for which his first three chapters serve as introduction: an analysis of fifty cases of cosmic consciousness, from Moses to Edward Carpenter. The chart is designed to prove two of his key contentions about cosmic consciousness. The first is that since ontogeny recapitulates phylogeny, the various human faculties appear in individuals in the same order in which they evolved in the race as a whole; thus humans gain simple consciousness almost immediately after birth and self-consciousness at the age of two or three, but cosmic consciousness does not appear until a human is thirty to forty years old. The second crucial proof of Bucke's evolutionary theory is that cases of cosmic consciousness are becoming more frequent. He offers a statistical analysis: there were only five certain cases of cosmic consciousness in the eighteen hundred years from the Buddha to Dante, but there were eight definite cases from Dante to 1901, thus demonstrating that cosmic consciousness was 4.8 times more frequent since the Middle Ages than before. However, Bucke's quasi-scientific charts and statistical analyses are no more important to his argument than are his rhetorically ecstatic forecasts of a utopian future when, thanks to inevitable evolutionary progress, every human will be cosmically conscious from birth:

> In contact with the flux of cosmic consciousness all religions known and named to-day will be melted down. The human soul will be revolutionized. . . . Religion will govern every minute of every day of all life. Churches, priests, forms, creeds, prayers, all agents, all intermediaries between the individual man and God will be permanently replaced by direct unmistakable intercourse. Sin will no longer exist nor will salvation be desired. Men will not worry about death or a future, about the kingdom of heaven, about what may come with and after the cessation of the life of the present body. Each soul will feel and know itself to be immortal, will feel and know that the entire universe with all its good and with all its beauty is for it and belongs to it forever.

Bucke's mystical, prophetic fervor would seem to set him apart from the mainstream, but for all its strange intensity *Cosmic Consciousness* is in many ways a characteristic product of nineteenth-century religious liberalism. Take, for example, the book's ecumenicism. Writing *Cosmic Consciousness* during the 1890s, Bucke could build on the tremendous interest in non-Western religions stirred by the World's Parliament of Religions in 1893. Part of the Chicago Columbian Exposition, a grandiose world's fair, the Parliament of

From Self to Cosmic Consciousness

No.	Name	Date of Birth	Age at Illumi- nation	Sex	Time of Year of Illumination	Age at Death
1	Moses	1650?		M		Old
2	Gideon	1350?		M		
3	Isaiah	770?		M		
4	Li R	604?		M		Old
5	Gautama	560?	35	M		80
6	Socrates	469?	39?	M	Summer	71?
7	Jesus	4	35	M	January?	38?
8	Paul	0	35	M		67?
9	Plotinus	204		M		66?
10	Mohammed	570	39	M	May?	62
11	Roger Bacon	1214		M		80?
12	Dante	1265	35	M	Spring	56
13	Las Casas	1474	40	M	June	92
14	John Yepes	1542	36	M	Early Summer	49
15	Francis Bacon	1561	30?	M		66
16	Behmen	1575	35	M		49
17	Pascal	1623	31½	M	November	39
18	Spinoza	1632		M		45
19	Mde. Guyon	1648	33	W	July	69
20	Swedenborg	1688	54	M		84
21	Gardiner	1688	32	M	July	58
22	Blake	1759	31	M		68
23	Balzac	1799	32	M		51
24	J. B. B.	1817	38	M		
25	Whitman	1819	34	M	June	73
26	J. B.	1821	38	M		73
27	C. P.	1822	37	M		
28	H. B.	1823		M		
29	R. R.	1830	30	M	Early Summer	69
30	E. T.	1830	30	M		
31	R. P.	1835		M		
32	J. H. J.	1837	34	M	Late Spring	
33	R. M. B.	1837	35	M	Spring	
34	T. S. R.	1840	32	M		
35	W. H. W.	1842	35	M		
36	Carpenter	1844	36	M	Spring	
37	C. M. C.	1844	49	W	September	
38	M. C. L.	1853	37	M	February	
39	J. W. W.	1853	31	M	January	
40	J. William Lloyd	1857	39	M	January	
41	P. T.	1860	35	M	May	
42	C. Y. E.	1864	31½	W	September	
43	A. J. S.	1871	24	W		

FIGURE 3.4. Chart from R. M. Bucke, *Cosmic Consciousness* (1901). The chart, which includes almost all the cases in Bucke's book, is intended to prove that cosmic consciousness almost always occurs in males between the ages of thirty to forty and that its frequency is increasing in the modern era.

Religions was the first major occasion in North America when representatives from a wide variety of Christian denominations shared a platform with Buddhists, Hindus, and other non-Western religious leaders. Historians of religion date much of modern America's fascination with Asian religions to the parliament, when charismatic figures such as Swami Vivekananda, founder of the Vedanta Society, first came to the United States. Bucke made, at best, token nods toward the East—only three of his forty cases of cosmic consciousness are non-Western—but it was enough to place him among the vanguard of religious thinkers at the time.

Cosmic Consciousness is typical not only of turn-of-the-century interest in non-Western faiths but also of the era's efforts to reconcile religion and science. Conventional Christian doctrine suffered a staggering blow from nineteenth-century discoveries in geology and biology that contradicted the biblical account of creation. Some influential Darwinists such as T. H. Huxley lined up to give another whack to what they believed to be the dying body of religion, but many intellectuals tried to find new paradigms that could accommodate both religion and science. For example, Alfred Russel Wallace, who shares credit with Charles Darwin for developing the theory of evolution by natural selection, was deeply involved in Spiritualism. In Wallace's view Spiritualist mediums were applying the same scientific methods to the immaterial realm that he had applied to natural history; he argued that Spiritualist investigation of the afterlife depended on immediate, empirical experiences that could be verified by those in attendance at a séance. The respected philosopher Paul Carus published *The Religion of Science* in 1893, which argued that scientific methods proved the immortality of the soul. Other religious thinkers applied Darwinian vocabulary to traditional Christian belief. "Is the change from the earthly to the heavenly more mysterious than the change from the aquatic to the terrestrial mode of life?" one questioned. Bucke's evolutionary theory of human consciousness fit in easily with these late Victorian efforts to reconcile science and religion.

Moreover, Bucke no doubt saw himself as a contributor to the nascent academic field of the scientific study of religion. Writing

Cosmic Consciousness in his office at the London Asylum for the Insane, Bucke worked in isolation from university-based social scientists who were in the process of wresting religion from the theological seminaries and claiming it for psychology and sociology. However, the most famous North American religious studies scholar of the era, Harvard's William James, read *Cosmic Consciousness* immediately after its publication and wrote Bucke a letter of congratulation. He also used material from the book in his Gifford Lectures at the University of Edinburgh, which were published as *The Varieties of Religious Experience* (1902). In his chapter on mysticism James quoted Bucke's account of his illumination in a hansom cab. In addition, no doubt cribbing from Bucke's chapter on Whitman, James included from "Song of Myself" the ecstatic account of the poet's union with his soul.

Cosmic Consciousness, now relegated to New Age bookstores, and *Varieties of Religious Experience*, which still holds the respectful attention of scholars, have a great deal in common. Both Bucke and James argue that all religions, no matter how seemingly different, have a common core; both believe that it is possible to identify this core by stripping away institutional accretions of dogma and ritual and focusing on individual experience; and both identify mystical illumination as the foundation of all religious experience. Bucke claims that mystical experience leads to cosmic consciousness, and he lists eleven characteristics common to individuals who attain this higher state; James writes that "personal religious experience has its root and centre in mystical states of consciousness" and gives his own four-part definition of mystical experience, which overlaps with Bucke's list.

Bucke and James can also be seen as part of a turn-of-the-century effort to masculinize American religion. Beginning in the seventeenth century, twice as many women as men attended Protestant services in the United States. The pattern was not considered a problem until the late nineteenth century, when the increasing power of corporate capitalism had so disrupted earlier patterns of ownership of farms and businesses that most American men had become wage earners with limited control over their economic lives. In response to this perceived crisis in masculine self-definition, middle-class Protestant men attempted to assert male control in the realm of religion. Religious writers of the 1880s began touting what they called "muscular Christianity," an effort to win masses of men to the church by emphasizing the masculinity of Jesus and the heroic struggles needed for the religious life. This effort climaxed with the Men and Religion Forward Movement of 1911–12, an evangelical campaign that involved more than one million men gathered under the slogan "More Men for Religion, More Religion for Men." With their focus on the comparative study of religious experience, James and Bucke were uninterested in these Protestant crusades. However, like other anxious male intellectuals of their era, they were keen to validate their masculinity and assert male authority in what was perceived as the feminized realm of religion. They accomplished these goals by applying scientific methods to the study of intensely emotional experiences and by focusing overwhelmingly on the religious experiences of men.

A modern critic has called Bucke "crudely racist and sexist." He was undoubtedly both, but the racism and sexism of *Cosmic Consciousness* are products as much of its slipshod scientific methodology as of its author's personal failings. For example, Bucke asserted that the proof of "the Aryan people's" higher standing on the evolutionary scale of consciousness was their higher incidence of insanity, since the mental faculties acquired most recently in evolutionary terms were the first to go in cases of insanity. Bucke based his conclusions on statistics of asylum populations in the United States, which showed relatively few African American inmates; it did not occur to him that racial prejudice and segregation might be responsible for keeping nonwhites out of asylums.

Similarly, Bucke believed that statistics demonstrated that women were unlikely to gain cosmic consciousness. In his first publication on cosmic consciousness, an 1893 essay, he ingenuously commented in a footnote, "I have collected so far eighteen cases [of cosmic consciousness]—all men. Why is the new sense confined to that sex? Why is it that we have no female religious founder? Great poet? Great musician? Great humorist? Great philosopher?" Among

themselves, other disciples whispered about Bucke's obtuseness regarding women. Horace Traubel wrote to J. W. Wallace, "There is
a spice of the provincial in Bucke. . . . He has not half the respect
that he should have for woman. His wife is herself narrow & dull &
he sees all women in her likeness. Walt always found his finest specimen in woman & Bucke fails altogether to see the wondrous life
that opens up through the female nature. His conception of C.C. is
limited by this fact strangely." Fanatic Whitmanite though he was,
Bucke had not fully absorbed the lessons of the master. A Whitman
notebook entry explodes Bucke's assumption that the written record
offers reliable proof about women's achievements in religion or any
other field. "Because women do not appear in history or philosophy
with anything like the same prominence as men," Whitman wrote,
"that is no reason for treating them less than men: —The great
names that we know are but the accidental scraps.—Mention to me
the twenty most majestic characters that have existed upon the earth,
and have their names recorded.—It is very well.—But for that
twenty, there are millions upon millions just as great, whose names
are unrecorded." Unlike Bucke, Whitman had no illusions about the
infallibility of the historical record.

Bucke, myopically focused on the few cases of cosmic consciousness that he had been able to find in his library and among his
acquaintances, regarded Walt Whitman as the climax of religious
evolution and the harbinger of humanity's future. He announced
early in *Cosmic Consciousness* that "Walt Whitman is the best, most
perfect, example the world has so far had of the Cosmic Sense."
His lengthy chapter on Whitman contains extensive biographical
information, largely taken from his own 1883 biography. However,
Bucke offers a crucial reinterpretation of Whitman's life. In 1883
Bucke had constructed a portrait of the young Whitman as a working-class carpenter who developed seamlessly into the poet of *Leaves
of Grass*. In contrast, *Cosmic Consciousness* emphasizes the young
Whitman as a writer of lifeless stories and essays and argues that his
career broke dramatically in two in the early 1850s: "Writings of
absolutely no value were *immediately* followed . . . by pages across
each of which in letters of ethereal fire are written the words ETER-

NAL LIFE." How, Bucke asks, did a hack writer turn into a poetic titan? The answer, of course, was the onset of cosmic consciousness.

Whitman is central to Bucke's evolutionary argument in *Cosmic Consciousness*, but it is possible to appreciate his material on mysticism without sharing his Whitmanite fervor, which seems to be the experience of most of the book's readers in the century since it was published. *Cosmic Consciousness* became a best seller not because of its promotion of Walt Whitman but because of its close correspondence with so many developments in modern American spirituality. Bucke perfectly anticipated the key characteristics of twentieth-century seeker spirituality: religious eclecticism, rejection of tradition, emphasis on individual experience, and a valorization of mystical illumination as the primary religious experience. Bucke was elated by his discovery that so many of his contemporaries had experienced cosmic consciousness; twenty-nine of his fifty cases from the last twenty-five hundred years lived in the nineteenth century. He was convinced that his research showed that, although cosmic consciousness was still extremely rare, it represented the future of human evolution. Actually, Bucke woefully misjudged the rarity of cosmic consciousness. Recent surveys reveal that 35 percent of all Americans claim to have had a mystical experience, a finding that helps to explain the book's continuing popularity. Readers who have had a mystical experience can flatter themselves with the assurance that they represent the advance guard of humanity.

Bucke's evolutionary optimism is also enormously appealing. Appearing in the guise of a scientific study of religion, *Cosmic Consciousness* is actually utopian fiction, a portrait of a perfect future world. One of religion's primary purposes is to explain and relieve suffering; Richard Maurice Bucke—orphaned and maimed before he reached adulthood, afflicted with mental illness as a young man—had experienced his full share of pain. And in December 1899, soon after he had completed the book, Bucke received a telegram from Montana, where his oldest son and namesake was working as a mining engineer. Maurice Andrews Bucke had been killed in a carriage accident shortly after his thirty-first birthday. On the anniversary of his son's death Bucke wrote a dedicatory preface to *Cosmic Con-*

sciousness, which was about to be published. Bucke addresses this moving dedication to his son: "Through the experiences which underlie this volume I have been taught, that in spite of death and the grave, although you are now beyond the range of our sight and hearing, . . . you are not dead and not really absent, but alive and well and not far from me this moment." Bucke goes on to transcend time and space, establishing an intimate connection with his dead son as he poses a series of questions: "Do you see and approve as I write these words? It may well be. Do you read from within what I am now thinking and feeling?" He echoes the words of Whitman's great poem of immortality, "Crossing Brooklyn Ferry," in which the poet similarly ignores the boundaries of life and death to address his future readers:

> We understand then do we not?
> What I promis'd without mentioning it, have you not
>   accepted?
> What the study could not teach—what the preaching
>   could not accomplish is accomplish'd, is it not?

The dedication's final words also echo the poet Bucke loved: "So long! dear boy." ("*So long!* / Remember my words, I may again return," Whitman concludes *Leaves of Grass*.)

One year after *Cosmic Consciousness* was published, Bucke attended a dinner party with friends, where he argued the case for Francis Bacon's authorship of the Shakespeare plays, one of his favorite topics, with great gusto. It was February 19, 1902, a cold and crystalline night. Riding home in his sleigh, Bucke marveled at the stars, and when he arrived at the asylum, he told Jessie that he wanted to walk outside to look at the sky. "Rising and gliding out I wander'd off by myself, / In the mystical moist night-air, and from time to time, / Look'd up in perfect silence at the stars," Walt had written. But in the cold Canadian night the doctor, who suffered from angina, had a heart attack. His family, sitting inside, heard him fall, but by the time they reached him, he was already dead.

Not long after Walt Whitman's death, Bucke had written to J. W. Wallace, "My life has been dedicated for now many years to the 'Great Cause' and what remains of it is and shall be also so dedicated. It is the one thing I care for—that I live for, and if I could in some way die for it I think my satisfaction would be complete." Was Maurice Bucke's satisfaction complete that winter night? If he did not die for the Great Cause, surely it was on his mind as he looked up in perfect silence at the stars.

CHAPTER FOUR

John Addington Symonds,
Edward Carpenter, Oscar Wilde:
Whitman and Same-Sex Passion

*Clear to me now, standards not yet published—clear to me
    that my Soul,
That the Soul of the man I speak for, feeds, rejoices only
    in comrades.*

WHAT IS THE TRUTH about Walt Whitman's sexuality? The question
has provoked embarrassment, debate, innuendo, certainty, and ag-
nosticism for a century and a half. Many nineteenth-century readers
identified the poet with the lusty braggart who boasts in *Leaves of
Grass*, "I turn the bridegroom out of bed and stay with the bride
myself, / I tighten her all night to my thighs and lips." For the most
part they responded to such lines with outrage. There are tales of
readers throwing *Leaves of Grass* into the fire in disgust, and one
review of the 1855 edition consisted of little but variations on the
phrase "a mass of stupid filth." Other readers, more sympathetic to
Whitman, thought his sexual braggadocio obscured the humanistic,
religious, and democratic strains of his poetry. They tried to convince him to tone down the sexuality—as Emerson did in a lengthy
conversation on Boston Common in 1860 when Whitman was preparing a new edition of *Leaves of Grass*—or took matters into their
own hands, as William Michael Rossetti did in his expurgated edition

of *Leaves*. A few women, notably Ellen O'Connor and Anne Gil-christ, believed they saw past the sexual swagger to the tender, passionate lover Whitman truly was and imagined themselves to be the soul mates he was seeking.

Whatever their reaction, most nineteenth-century readers, including those who knew Whitman personally, assumed that he was romantically attracted to women. His never having married made him seem all the lustier—a swaggering poet who could never settle down with one woman. Detractors like Thomas Wentworth Higginson accused him of promiscuity; apologists like R. M. Bucke countered that despite appearances, Whitman was essentially pure. Throughout his lifetime critical battle over Whitman in the United States was engaged on heterosexual terrain: Was Whitman a libertine, or a gentleman whose sexual boasts had to be understood as part of his outsized persona?

If the notion of Whitman as unquestionably heterosexual, whether profligate or restrained, dominated discussion in the nineteenth-century United States, some English readers of Whitman were already wrestling with a question that came to prominence in the United States only in the 1970s: Was Walt Whitman gay? That phrasing of the question is, of course, particular to the late twentieth century; Whitman's nineteenth-century disciples would not have recognized the term *gay* or even *homosexual*, which did not come into the English language until the 1890s. Yet even though the Victorians might have had to struggle for language with which to pose the question, no one tried harder to discern the truth of Whitman's sexual nature than John Addington Symonds.

Symonds was one of the best-known and most prolific men of letters of the Victorian era. The son of a wealthy physician in Bristol, England, he might have become a gentleman of leisure, but his large talent and even greater ambition led him to publish dozens of volumes during the three decades between his graduation from Oxford and his early death from tuberculosis. He was best known for his popular history of the Italian Renaissance, seven volumes of appealingly lush prose on the era's great artistic and political figures. He also published a celebrated two-volume survey of Greek poetry;

biographies of Michelangelo, Boccaccio, and Cellini; an introduction to Dante; numerous books about Elizabethan drama; and several volumes of poetry. Whitman was immensely flattered that among the publications of this eminent man of letters were essays testifying to his admiration of the American poet. "I consider the friendship of men like Symonds . . . a great plume in our cap—great," he told Horace Traubel. "Symonds is the quintessence of culture: he is the culture of culture of culture—the essence of an essence."

Symonds was twenty-five years old and visiting his friend Frederic Myers at Cambridge University when Myers introduced him to Whitman in 1865. Myers, one of the few Englishmen to own the 1860 edition of *Leaves of Grass*, read aloud a "Calamus" poem that concludes with a swooningly romantic vision of male comradeship, as the poet declares:

> I heed knowledge, and the grandeur of The States, and
>   the example of heroes, no more,
> I am indifferent to my own songs—I will go with him
>   I love,
> It is enough for us that we are together—We never
>   separate again.

Symonds was overwhelmed. Recently married but deeply, if confusedly, attracted to men, he obtained his own copy of *Leaves* and devoured the "Calamus" poems, writing to a friend, "It is quite indispensable that you should have this book. . . . It is not a book; . . . it is a man, miraculous in his vigour & love & omnigenuousness & omniscience & animalism & omnivorous humanity." Although it took Symonds six years to work up the nerve, he eventually wrote to Whitman, calling him "my Master" in an extraordinarily frank and inquisitive letter. Symonds begins his letter by describing the effect on him of *Leaves of Grass*: he learned "confidently to believe that the Comradeship, which I conceived as on a par with the Sexual feeling for depth & strength & purity & capability of all good, was real—not a delusion of distorted passions, a dream of the Past, a scholar's fancy—but a strong & vital bond of man to man." He continues:

Yet even then how hard I found it—brought up in English feudalism, educated at an aristocratic public School (Harrow) and an over refined University (Oxford)—to winnow from my own emotions and from my conception of the ideal friend, all husks of affections and aberrations and to be a simple human being. *You* cannot tell quite how hard this was, & how you helped me.

I have pored for continuous hours over the pages of Calamus (as I used to pore over the pages of Plato), longing to hear you speak, *burning* for a revelation of your more developed meaning, panting to ask—is this what you would indicate?— Are then the free men of your lands really so pure & loving & noble & generous & sincere? Most of all did I desire to hear from your own lips—or from your pen—some story of athletic friendship from which to learn the truth.

The hoped-for revelation was not forthcoming. Whitman responded to Symonds, but his letters, while cordial enough, were silent on the subject of athletic friendship. Symonds was undeterred, and for the next twenty years the two writers conducted one of the most celebrated cat-and-mouse games in literary history. Symonds would write a discreet but inquisitive letter on the subject of "Calamus" and male love; Whitman would ignore it; Symonds would apologize for his temerity, and Whitman would write back in a friendly tone; the cycle would be repeated.

They might have kept on indefinitely, but by 1890 Symonds was planning books on both same-sex love and Walt Whitman and felt that he had to know the truth. That August he wrote a letter that was franker about the sexual dimensions of comradeship and more pressing in its demands for a response than any he had sent before. "I want . . . to ask you a question about a very important portion of your teaching, which has puzzled a great many of your disciples and admirers," he began blandly enough but soon became more specific: "I have always felt unable to deal . . . comprehensively with your philosophy of life, because I do not even yet understand the whole drift of 'Calamus.' . . . In your conception of Comradeship, do you contemplate the possible intrusion of those semi-sexual emotions and actions which no doubt do occur between men?" It was the first direct mention of sexuality in his correspondence with Whitman. Having gone thus far, he pressed on: Surely Whitman must be aware that the Calamus poems' "enthusiasm" for comradeship was liable to encourage "ardent and *physical* intimacies" between men—the emphasis is Symonds's. "Now: it is of the utmost importance to me as your disciple, and as one who wants sooner or later to diffuse a further knowledge of your life-philosophy," he wrote, "to know what you really think about all this." Symonds posted the letter to Camden from his home in Davos, Switzerland. The reply, he knew, might take some time in coming. He was prepared to wait.

✜ ✜ ✜

Symonds was the most tenacious, but he was not the only Englishman interested in Whitman's sexuality. Thanks to the efforts of Rossetti, Gilchrist, and others, Whitman became increasingly well known in England, and by the end of the nineteenth century a small coterie of loosely affiliated male disciples had come to regard him as the modern era's great prophet of same-sex passion. Upper-middle-class members of the British intelligentsia, they were steeped in the classics, and as adolescents they pored over Plato, hungrily searching for references to male love. The all-male precincts of Oxford and Cambridge proved a congenial setting for the cult of Hellenism, and "Dorian chivalry" came into use as a high-minded description of same-sex love. Hellenism served a desperately needed purpose for men living in an era when the only terms available to describe their sexuality were loaded with religious and moral contempt: *sodomy, buggery. Greek love* was infinitely more appealing, and the Greeks offered an image of ruggedly masculine man-lovers, warriors willing to die for their beloved comrades.

These highly educated men sought out references to same-sex love not only in the Greek classics but wherever they could find them, and certain literary works came to serve as touchstones: the biblical story of David and Jonathan, the sonnets of Michelangelo and Shakespeare. All these works, however, came from centuries long past. The allure of Walt Whitman was that here was a contemporary who offered a vision of same-sex love as noble as anything to be found in the classics. The heterosexual persona that Whitman assumes in *Leaves of Grass* can be disturbingly aggressive and impersonal: "It is I, you women, I make my way, / I am stern, acrid, large, undissuadable, but I love you, / I do not hurt you any more than is necessary for you." In contrast, the tone of the "Calamus" poems is quiet, romantic, and pure.

> One flitting glimpse, caught through an interstice,
> Of a crowd of workmen and drivers in a bar-room,
>   around the stove, late of a winter night—And I unre-
>   marked seated in a corner,
> Of a youth who loves me, and whom I love, silently
>   approaching, and seating himself near, that he may
>   hold me by the hand;
> A long while, amid the noises of coming and going—of
>   drinking and oath and smutty jest,
> There we two, content, happy in being together, speaking
>   little, perhaps not a word.

Whitman's English readers thrilled to his ennobling portrayal of male love as an island of purity amid the moral filth of the larger world. Numbers of men turned to *Leaves of Grass* for solace at a time when the larger culture, had it known the truth about their affections and desires, would have labeled them monstrous and perverse. *Leaves of Grass* was so widely known among them that Eve Kosofsky Sedgwick has famously written that "Whitman—visiting Whitman, liking Whitman, giving gifts of 'Whitman'—was of course a Victorian homosexual shibboleth." She was thinking of men such as Symonds; his friends Frederic Myers and Roden Noel; Edward Carpenter; Lionel Johnson, who introduced Lord Alfred Douglas to Oscar Wilde; and Wilde himself.

Wilde said that he had been acquainted with Whitman's poetry "from the cradle"; he was, presumably, sacrificing factual accuracy for dramatic effect. His mother evidently procured a copy of the Rossetti edition soon after it was published and read it aloud to her son, who would have been fourteen at the time. When at the age of twenty-seven Wilde made his much publicized lecture tour of the United States, he declared that there was no one in America whom he desired to meet so much as Walt Whitman. Wilde made two pilgrimages to Camden during his tour and years afterward declared that "the kiss of Walt Whitman is still on my lips."

When Whitman published his volume *November Boughs* in 1888, Wilde seized the occasion to write an admiring review, published as "The Gospel according to Walt Whitman." However, Wilde's devotion pales beside that of Symonds and Edward Carpenter. Carpenter, son of a Brighton gentleman, came from the same milieu as Symonds and Wilde: an upper-middle-class family with connections to the aristocracy, a brilliant career at university, and early promise as a poet. After graduating from Cambridge, he was ordained as an Anglican priest and appointed a Cambridge fellow. Then, at the age of thirty, he abruptly resigned from the clergy, threw aside his academic career, and spent the rest of his life as a lecturer, farmer, writer, and social activist. Walt Whitman was largely responsible for the transformation. Working independently of Symonds but along parallel lines, Carpenter cast Walt Whitman as the prophet of a utopian future. *Leaves of Grass* would be the new bible, while "Calamus" would serve as a handbook of social relations. Among North American disciples—O'Connor, Burroughs, and Bucke—sexual attraction to other men, both their own and Whitman's, remained unconscious and unacknowledged. In contrast, Carpenter and Symonds were determined to put same-sex love at the center of their Whitmanesque social project.

It was an ambitious and difficult undertaking. In the past century critics have gained a vocabulary and conceptual framework for talking about Whitman's sexuality, so that, for example, a recent highly regarded biography of Whitman carries the subtitle "A Gay Life." Symonds and Carpenter were without such linguistic tools; Symonds plaintively began his major work on same-sex passion by noting that he could hardly find a name for his subject "which will not seem to soil this paper." Both men lived within a culture that considered same-sex love an abomination. They bravely used Whitman's poetry as a central element in a crusade to transform actions that their society viewed as criminal into something holy, a love sanctified by the American poet whom they regarded as a modern Christ.

☩ ☩ ☩

Our ways of classifying sexuality have today come to seem as natural and true to us as our taxonomies of species: the division between heterosexual and homosexual seems as clear as that between vertebrate and invertebrate. No matter how easily phrases like "social construction of sexuality" may roll off a twenty-first-century tongue, it is difficult to resist the idea that if earlier periods had only possessed our knowledge and vocabulary, they too would have seen the world the way we do. Earlier ways of thinking about sexuality seem odd or quaint—none more so than the Victorian. One hundred fifty years ago it never occurred to anyone to divide love into columns labeled homosexual or heterosexual. Instead, love was pure or impure, chaste or sensual.

Armed with these ideas—and little other knowledge—about human sexuality, the bright but timid fourteen-year-old John Addington Symonds entered Harrow, the elite English public school, in 1854. What he found there profoundly shocked him. According to his sexually frank memoirs, which Symonds completed at age fifty and then sealed with instructions that they were not to be opened until after his death, Harrow was a hothouse of schoolboy sex. He wrote that every good-looking boy in the school had a female nickname and was either "a public prostitute" or "some bigger fellow's 'bitch.' " The boys were quite open about their sexual activities; one could not avoid, Symonds wrote, seeing "acts of onanism, mutual masturbation, the sports of naked boys in bed together." Symonds—studious, rather priggish—never participated in the ubiquitous sexual activities; he found them vulgar and disgusting. But neither he nor his schoolmates ever called them *homosexual*—the word did not exist in the 1850s. Symonds was appalled by the lack of "refinement" and "sentiment" in the boys' conduct—the boys themselves would have admitted that their behavior was "impure"—but it would not have occurred to anyone that their acts placed them in a distinctive sexual category. Symonds hated the "crude sensuality" of his Harrow schoolmates, not their sexual object choice. In fact, by the time he entered Harrow, he rather fancied boys himself.

Symonds was eight when he began having sexual fantasies involving the sailors he saw around Bristol. By ten he liked to imagine himself as Venus in Shakespeare's *Venus and Adonis*, and he would pore for hours over the photograph of a Greek male nude statue in his father's library, even after his father inquired whether he wouldn't prefer to look at some other statue, say, a nice nymph. At Harrow he admired various handsome boys, but he was so repelled by the sexual atmosphere of the school that he never acted on his desires, never thought such yearnings could take any form other than crude schoolboy sex play. Then, in his last year at Harrow, assigned to read Plato's *Apology*, Symonds flipped through the book and happened upon the *Phaedrus* and the *Symposium*. He began reading the dialogues late one night on holiday in London; when the sun rose the next morning, he was still reading.

It was a turning point in his life. The dialogues' defense of male love as an image of the love of beauty and truth stirred him profoundly. His Harrow schoolmates' dirty games were not the only form of love between men; Plato presented a man's passion for a beautiful youth as the highest form of human relation and the path to the ideal. *I must have been a philosophical Greek lover in some previous life*, Symonds imagined. He need not consider his erotic fantasies shameful; they showed that he was cut out for a noble love as fine as anything in a chivalric romance. It was no surprise that a few weeks after his reading of Plato, home for the Easter holidays and attending services at Bristol Cathedral, he fell in love with one of the choirboys. Willie Dyer, son of a local tailor, was fourteen, four years younger than Symonds. He and Symonds met, held hands, took long walks together, occasionally kissed. It was all pure, chaste, and, to Symonds, deliriously romantic. Decades later, writing about the experience, the sophisticated poet and critic fell into the language of a tenpenny novel: "We met then on the morning of 10 April 1858. Swallows were reeling in sunlight round the tower. The clock struck. I took Willie's slender hand into my own and gazed into his large brown eyes fringed with heavy lashes." Symonds considered the experience a new birth—literally so: he frequently subtracted eighteen years from his age, using his meeting with Willie Dyer as his date of birth.

However, his excursions with Willie after graduation from Harrow were cut short by two factors: the disapproval of Dr. Symonds, to whom he had confessed his infatuation, and the opening of the academic term at Oxford. Symonds enrolled at Balliol College, where he studied under the celebrated Plato scholar Benjamin Jowett. The morally upright Jowett was unembarrassed by the passages in Plato extolling love between men; he blandly insisted that Plato was speaking metaphorically. However, Jowett's fervent Hellenism established an atmosphere favorable to those who, like Symonds, saw more than metaphor in the Platonic dialogues. Victorian Oxford proved a congenial setting for those inclined to same-sex passion. The curriculum centered on intensive study of works that celebrated male love; one's schoolmates were entirely male; and the centuries-old requirement that fellows be unmarried was still in effect, thus establishing an entirely homosocial environment. Symonds thrived at Oxford, winning the Newdigate Prize for poetry—the same prize would be awarded to Wilde a decade later—and garnering a first-class degree in "Greats," as the study of classics was known. After completing his degree, he was elected a fellow at Magdalen College.

Unfortunately, he had been unable to follow his father's advice to have nothing to do with choirboys. During his undergraduate years he exchanged letters with a lascivious classmate who had an eye for Oxford choristers. Symonds warned his classmate against seducing boys, but his letters revealed his own appreciation of male beauty. Their friendship turned sour, and the man turned some of Symonds's letters over to the Magdalen authorities. Symonds had done nothing wrong—his flirtations at Oxford were as chaste as his love affair with Willie Dyer—but an unpleasant formal inquiry was held before Symonds was exonerated. Soon after, he had a mental and physical breakdown and contracted the tuberculosis that would plague him for the next three decades. He resigned his fellowship and plunged into depression, at a loss about how to repair his life. Dr. Symonds advised his son to marry.

This time Symonds dutifully followed his father's advice. He deliberately set out to find a wife and managed to convince himself that he had fallen in love with one of the first young women he met, Catherine North, daughter of a member of Parliament with impeccable aristocratic connections. They were married shortly after Symonds's twenty-fourth birthday. After a few nights' embarrassed fumbling, Symonds found to his relief that he could consummate the marriage, though the experience brought him little pleasure. Less than a year after their 1864 wedding Catherine bore the first of their four daughters. Symonds was delighted, but the experience of fatherhood paled beside another event soon after: his discovery of *Leaves of Grass*.

The homoeroticism of the "Calamus" poems made Symonds swoon when he first heard Frederic Myers read from *Leaves of Grass* in Cambridge, and the letter Symonds wrote to a friend soon after emphasizes, in a coded way, the poems' sexual connotations: "Leaves of Grass were published in 1860, when I was just 2 years old. Is it not strange I should only have read them this last week I am now 9 years old? Providence orders things so crookedly. If I had read them then & *if* I had understood I should have been a braver better very different man now." Symonds was actually twenty-six when he wrote this letter; he was using Willie Dyer time. The emphasis on his infatuation with a choirboy shows how closely he connected *Leaves of Grass* and male love. His letter continues, "This man has said what I have burned to say; what I should have done if opinion & authority & the contamination of vile lewdness had not ended in sophisticating my moral sense & muddling my brain."

Symonds's self-laceration reveals the split—induced by the Platonic philosophical idealism that permeated Victorian education—between spirit and flesh, between his chaste and ideal love for Willie

Dyer and the "vile lewdness" of the schoolboys at Harrow and Symonds's racier acquaintances at Oxford. The attraction of Whitman was that he seemed utterly pure and uncontaminated. The "Calamus" poems are less homosexual than homoromantic—that is, they are set in an erotically charged but presexual world of tenderness and comradely kisses. Symonds, who had never visited the United States, imagined Whitman as an Adamic innocent and America as a prelapsarian Eden. In Symonds's fervidly responsive vision Whitman and the United States were free of the class system, beastly public schools, sophisticated universities—free of the entire European tradition. Whitman "begins anew with sound and primitive humanity," Symonds would write later, as if the American poet had somehow escaped human history. Symonds idealized American culture in the same way that his circle at Oxford idealized ancient Greece. "Walt Whitman is more truly Greek than any other man of modern times," he wrote in his acclaimed *Studies of the Greek Poets*, a statement that caused no little bafflement within the walls of Oxford and Cambridge. The link between Dorian Greece and Whitman's New York, as Symonds saw it, was youth and innocence. "The Greeks had no Past: . . . whereas . . . the world has now grown old," Symonds lamented; he saw Whitman and the United States as forever young.

Leaves of Grass offered Symonds a vision of innocent, guiltless male love; it offered as well a religious vision of ecstatic apprehension of the divine. Raised as an Anglican, Symonds underwent a religious crisis as a young man. Like so many of his intellectual contemporaries, he could not reconcile conventional Christian theology with the new scientific discoveries of the era. In addition, he felt excluded from a religion that railed against men like him as sodomites. Whitman solved both problems. The God of *Leaves of Grass* is not a distant creator of the universe but an immanent presence within the world. "I hear and behold God in every object," Whitman wrote—in a leaf of grass, an ant, a mouse, and, most thrillingly to Symonds, in a common workman:

[T]he expression of a well-made man appears not only in
    his face,
It is in his limbs and joints also, it is curiously in the joints
    of his hips and wrists;
It is in his walk, the carriage of his neck, the flex of his
    waist and knees—dress does not hide him;
The strong, sweet, supple quality he has, strikes through
    the cotton and flannel.
To see him pass conveys as much as the best poem,
    perhaps more;
You linger to see his back, and the back of his neck and
    shoulder-side.

In Whitman's religious vision a well-made man was no less divine
than an infant, a saint, the earth itself. Whitman "recognises divinity
in all that lives and breathes upon our planet," Symonds wrote with
relief. The poet weaved homoeroticism into the divine fabric of a
God-permeated universe, implicitly sanctioning the sexual desires
that so tormented Symonds. By the time he was thirty, Symonds
had constructed a belief system that he called "Cosmic Enthusiasm,"
a combination of immanentist theology, Whitmanism, and Hellenism. Despite its far-from-seamless fusions, the system would serve
Symonds for the rest of his life.

✠ ✠ ✠

A few months after Symonds turned thirty, his father passed away.
Symonds's mother had died when he four, and he and his father
were extremely close. Symonds had felt comfortable enough with
his father to confess his passions for men from Willie Dyer onward,
and the elder Symonds seems to have been remarkably uncensori-
ous. On the other hand, he was certain that his son's desires were
unhealthy, and it was he who had steered the young man into marriage—a relationship that had turned out to be not without love but
that left Symonds's deep reserves of passion untouched. It is surely

FIGURE 4.1. John Addington Symonds in the 1880s. University of Bristol Special Collections.

no coincidence that, a few months after his father's death, Symonds wrote his first letter to Walt Whitman. Symonds was looking for a substitute father, one who would approve of his love for other men. As a correspondent Whitman proved disappointing—he refused to give the unambiguous approval of same-sex passion that Symonds sought—but the "Calamus" sentiment, combined with an encounter at a male brothel, radically altered the course of Symonds's life.

His first visit to a brothel occurred when he was thirty-six. In his memoirs he wrote that an old acquaintance, most likely the aristocratic libertine and Whitman admirer Roden Noel, invited him to an establishment near the Royal Guardsmen's barracks at London's Regent's Park. The licentious atmosphere disgusted the sensitive Symonds, but he made an appointment for the next afternoon with a handsome young soldier who caught his eye. "For the first time in my experience I shared a bed with one so different from myself," he wrote. Their sexual encounter proved delightful to him—"I thoroughly enjoyed the close vicinity of that splendid naked piece of manhood"—but it was what followed that made the experience a turning point in Symonds's life. "I made him clothe himself, sat and smoked and talked with him, and felt, at the end of the whole transaction, that some at least of the deepest moral problems might be solved by fraternity. . . . I learned . . . that the physical appetite of one male for another may be made the foundation of a solid friendship."

Symonds viewed his encounter with the soldier through Whitmanesque glasses, writing of their "comradeship" and of the soldier's "manly and comradely attitude." In his depiction of the incident a London brothel becomes a democratic meeting ground where an upper-middle-class writer and a working-class guardsman overcome their differences in a comradeship that begins in but transcends sex. Symonds, who was nothing if not self-aware, was conscious that the encounter could be interpreted differently—as one more instance of bourgeois men's sexual exploitation of the working class, little different from the thousands of transactions between middle- or upper-class men and impoverished women and girls that took place every day in Victorian London. Was their comradeship a delusion? he asks in his memoirs. "To this hour I do not know," he answers, although he acknowledges that he would go on to repeat the experience "a hundredfold" in the years following.

Not, however, in brothels. Instead, Symonds continued his experiments in sexually charged comradeship in the unlikely setting of a Swiss health resort. In the spring of 1877 his health, always delicate, broke down completely. His doctors warned him that his tuberculosis was so advanced that he would not survive another winter in England. They recommended Egypt, with a sojourn in the Alps along the way. One of Symonds's sisters was summering in the Swiss village of Davos Platz and invited him to join her; he arrived in August, loaded down with pith helmets and books on mummies. So weakened by the journey that he was unable to walk, Symonds soon abandoned his plans to go to Egypt. He remained in Davos through the winter of 1877–78, finding the pure dry Alpine air restorative. He began spending every winter in Davos and soon decided to make it his permanent home. He built a house there, and in 1881 his entire family relocated from Bristol, England, to this isolated village in the Swiss Alps.

Symonds made the move despite resistance from his wife. Catherine Symonds, intelligent and strong willed, loved her husband despite her awareness of his attraction to men, and she saw how the Swiss climate turned him from a feeble invalid into an active man who went sledding and hiking in the intervals of his literary work. However, the long Alpine winters were tedious for her, and she was concerned that her husband's erratic schooling of their four daughters was no substitute for a proper British education. Her wit sharpened into sarcasm, and Symonds, concerned about the tensions in their relationship, wrote his old mentor Benjamin Jowett for advice. Jowett's counsel was conventionally patriarchal: with time "she will find interests in reading & drawing & in the education of the girls." John and Catherine eventually reached a modus vivendi that included, for her, reading and drawing and gardening; for him, romantic friendships with young male villagers.

During his first winter in Davos Symonds made the acquaintance of Christian Buol, a handsome young farmer. "When he came towards me, standing erect upon an empty wood-sledge, and driving four stout horses at a brisk trot down a snow slope, I seemed to see an ancient Greek of the Homeric age," Symonds wrote. As always, though, he tempered his Hellenism with a strong dose of *Leaves of Grass*. Once he and Buol had become friends, the young man invited him to a family party, which was, Symonds enthused, "like a scene out of one of Whitman's poems." Indeed, it seemed to Symonds as if rural Switzerland were founded on Whitman's "institution of the dear love of comrades." Symonds counted scores of Swiss men among his intimate acquaintances: "porters in hotels, herdsmen on the alps, masons, hunters, woodmen, guides, hotelkeepers, shopkeepers, stableboys," and so on. They did not share his "abnormal tastes," Symonds acknowledged, yet "I have invariably received from them a frank compliant correspondence when I sought it." When Symonds treated Christian Buol to a holiday in Italy, the young man "showed that he was ready, out of sympathy and liking for me, to concede many innocent delights of privacy, which cost him nothing and which filled me with ineffable satisfaction." Symonds befriended the entire Buol family, loaned them money when the family business was at risk, and gave Christian a handsome gift when the young man decided to marry.

Symonds, to his delight, found the same easy acceptance of same-sex passion in Venice, where he established an apartment in the palazzo of his friend Horatio Brown. In the spring of 1881 Symonds was smitten with a young mustachioed gondolier named Angelo Fusato. Within a short time Symonds had hired Fusato as his private gondolier, and, as with Christian Buol, Symonds befriended Fusato's family and provided him with the money to marry. Their relationship would become the most important Symonds would have in the last decade of his life. Fusato visited him in Davos and traveled with him throughout Italy. The relationship began, Symonds acknowledged, without passion on Fusato's side; the gondolier regarded the Englishman as simply one among the *stranieri* "to whose caprices he had sold his beauty." However, over the years their passion grew to become "nearly equal," Symonds thought. Near the end of his life Symonds wrote that he regarded their relationship with complete satisfaction. "Though it began in folly and crime, according to the constitution of society, it has benefited him and proved a source of comfort and instruction to myself. Had it not been for my abnormal desire," he went on in a Whitmanesque tone, "I could never have learned to know and appreciate a human being so far removed from me in position, education, national quality and physique." Symonds acknowledged that the relationship commenced on a largely economic basis, but he was certain that he and Fusato had managed to establish a democratic comradeship.

Readers of Symonds's memoirs, which were finally unsealed and published in 1984, have not been uniformly convinced that he transcended class differences in his sexual relationships. As a wealthy Englishman who spent the last sixteen years of his life in Switzerland and Italy, where poverty and social custom led many young men into sexual liaisons with rich foreigners, Symonds has been labeled a "sexual tourist"—a Victorian version of the North American and European men who spend their holidays in Southeast Asian bordellos. Eve Kosofsky Sedgwick writes that "the difference between Symonds' political ideal and the bourgeois English actuality of sexual exploitation, for cash, of proletarian men and women is narrow and arbitrary. It seems to lie mostly in the sanguine Whitmanian coloration of Symonds' rhetoric and erotic investment."

Symonds anticipated the charges that would be leveled against him. In his memoirs he insists that his relationships with the Venetian gondolier Angelo Fusato and other men went far beyond casual sexual liaisons; he helped his lovers to find jobs, befriended their families, gave them loans and gifts. Yet he is forced to acknowledge that "an opponent might observe that all this comes to money in the long run." He was well aware that two views of his sexual life were possible: his relationships with working-class men could be seen as examples of either democratic comradeship or sexual exploitation. He favored the former interpretation; critics such as Sedgwick have promoted the latter.

It may be that the best answer to any either/or question about Symonds is "both." As Jeffrey Weeks observes of Symonds and his contemporaries, "avidly exploitative sexual colonialism ... marched, point counter-point, with the dream of class reconciliation." Symonds was not politically active, but he was sympathetic to socialist aims and wrote that "the blending of Social Strata in masculine love seems to me one of its most pronounced, & socially hopeful, features. When it appears, it abolishes class distinctions. . . . If it could be acknowledged & extended, it would do very much to further the advent of the right sort of Socialism." These remarks about socialism occur in a letter to Edward Carpenter about Walt Whitman, whom Symonds always regarded as a prophet of both social democracy and same-sex passion. "I might have been a mere English gentleman, had not I read Leaves of Grass in time," he wrote to Horace Traubel. "Brought up in the purple of aristocratic school and university, provided with more money than is good for a young man, early married to a woman of noble nature & illustrious connections," as Symonds described himself, he was on his way to becoming snobbish and aloof. Reading Whitman "stripped my soul of social prejudices." In his memoirs Symonds credits Whitman with teaching him "the value of fraternity, and to appreciate the working classes. When I came to live among peasants and republicans in Switzerland, I am certain that I took up passionate relations with men in a more natural and intelligible manner—more rightly and democratically—than I should otherwise have done."

Symonds embraced Whitman's work so eagerly because the American poet provided a contemporary alternative to the dominant view of same-sex passion as degrading, morally repugnant vice. Unlike Carpenter or Wilde, Symonds internalized the larger culture's disdain for his own sexuality. In his memoirs he refers to his sexual desires as a "perversion," an "inexorable and incurable disease," a "congenital aberration of the passions which . . . has been the poison of my life." The tone of the memoirs is overwhelmingly anguished. Friends report that Symonds was wonderful company, intelligent and witty, but his self-lacerating autobiography offers not even a trace of high spirits; his most recent biographer, the first scholar to read his memoirs, titled her book *The Woeful Victorian*.

Symonds was indeed woefully torn between a Whitmanesque view of same-sex passion as natural and noble and his society's condemnation of it. At an early age he adopted Victorian society's division between pure and impure love, so that "the attractions of a dimly divine almost mystic sensuality persisted in my nature, side by side with a marked repugnance to lust in action." By his fortieth birthday his sexual liaisons with working-class men, his move to Switzerland, and his continued study of *Leaves of Grass* had led to a greater measure of self-acceptance, but Symonds still questioned whether even Whitman could lift same-sex passion "from the filth and mire of brutal appetite." Symonds never found a fully satisfactory answer. However, about the time he turned fifty, the introspective Symonds began to move beyond tortured self-examination, taking the first halting steps toward a quasi-public political activism on behalf of men like himself.

✠ ✠ ✠

Not until he turned fifty was Symonds certain that there *were* other men like himself. When he began composing his sexually candid autobiography at the age of forty-eight, he believed himself to be unique. He wrote to his friend Graham Dakyns, "I am certain that 999 men out of 1000 do not believe in the existence of a personality like mine." It was not that Symonds was unaware that other men engaged in same-sex intercourse. However, he regarded the Swiss and Italian men with whom he had sex as heterosexuals who were not averse to sleeping with a male foreigner in exchange for gifts or money. He classified men such as the aristocratic Roden Noel as voluptuaries, jaded thrill-seekers looking for novel pleasures. Symonds's close friends Graham Dakyns and Frederic Myers were not thrill seekers; still, Symonds saw them as quite different from himself, since both experienced pleasure with women as well as men, whereas Symonds was repulsed by heterosexual intercourse and gladly slept apart from his wife following the birth of their fourth child. To appear to the world a virile male yet lust after other men from childhood; to live alongside an attractive woman yet find physical contact with her nauseating—surely, Symonds thought, there was not another man in the world like him.

Then Symonds discovered the German sexologists. The first researchers to apply scientific method to the study of sexuality, these pioneering Germans collected case histories in an attempt to create a taxonomy of sexual behavior. The most prominent of the studies was Richard von Krafft-Ebing's *Psychopathia Sexualis*, which Symonds read soon after its publication in 1889; it, in turn, sent him to earlier works by Karl Heinrich Ulrichs and others. Reading the case histories collected by these researchers, Symonds realized for the first time that he was not alone. There were thousands of men like him.

His discovery of the German sexologists had a revelatory effect upon Symonds. He was particularly drawn to the work of Ulrichs. Krafft-Ebing labeled his subjects homosexual and regarded them as psychopaths who had deviated from a healthy norm. Symonds detested the term *homosexual*; Krafft-Ebing had combined a Greek and a Latin root, and the resulting hybrid affected Symonds and other classically trained Englishmen like fingernails on slate. Moreover, he rejected the idea that his condition was psychopathic. Ulrichs, in contrast, referred to the phenomenon of "sexual inversion" and labeled its practitioners "Uranians" or "Urnings," terms derived from Plato's references to Uranos in the *Symposium*. Ulrichs, who was an Urning, argued that inversion was not a moral or psychological perversion but an innate disposition. He theorized that Urnings possessed *anima muliebris in corpore virili inclusa*—a woman's soul in a man's body. Symonds embraced Ulrichs's idea that sexual inversion was innate and ignored his etiological speculations. Symonds felt himself to be fully masculine, and for him "inversion" meant only that his sexual object choice was inverted from the norm.

Since Ulrichs believed sexual inversion to be innate, he argued that the antisodomy laws that prevailed across most of Europe should be repealed. Symonds agreed. The legal situation of English inverts was particularly acute. Sodomy had long been illegal in England, but the law was virtually unenforced in the nineteenth century. Penalties were harsh, the act was difficult to prove, and juries were reluctant to convict; between 1810 and 1880 there were, on average, only thirty-nine convictions a year for sodomy in England

and Wales. However, in 1885 Henry Labouchere, a member of Parliament, inserted into the Criminal Law Amendment Act a clause making any act of "gross indecency" between two men, whether public or private, punishable with two years' hard labor. When Symonds read the German sexologists in 1890 and realized the extent of sexual inversion, he wrote Dakyns that he felt "duty bound" to agitate for a change in English law. Symonds was emboldened by Italy's recent revision of its penal code, which brought Italy's treatment of sexual acts between men in line with France's Napoleonic Code: both nations punished violence, protected minors, and provided for public decency but otherwise did not interfere with the sexual activities of consenting adults.

Symonds determined to compose an English-language equivalent of Ulrichs's studies. But in order to treat the subject thoroughly, Symonds had to know what his master, Walt Whitman, thought of same-sex passion. It was at this moment, in August 1890, that Symonds wrote his notorious letter to Whitman stating that "Calamus" seemed "calculated to encourage ardent and *physical* intimacies" between men. "What I earnestly desire to know," he continued, "is whether you are content to leave the ethical problems regarding the private behaviour of comrades toward each other, to the persons' own sense of what is right and fit. ... Will you enlighten me on this?"

Walt Whitman had a gift for ignoring questions that made him uncomfortable, could even grow irate that the queries were posed— "I'm tired of not answering questions" about *Leaves of Grass*, he once said slyly to Horace Traubel. But Whitman responded to Symonds's letter almost immediately after receiving it. After a minimum of genial preliminary chatter, he turned to Symonds's questions about "Calamus." He was, he claimed, quite dazed by their implications: "That the calamus part has even allow'd the possibility of such construction as mention'd is terrible—I am fain to hope the pages themselves are not to be even mention'd for such gratuitous and quite at the time entirely undream'd & unreck'd possibility of morbid inferences—wh' are disavow'd by me & seem damnable." After a digression about his health he casually added, "Tho' always unmarried I have had six children—two are dead—One living southern grandchild, fine boy, who writes to me occasionally. Circumstances connected with their benefit and fortune have separated me from intimate relations."

Never have two sentences spurred so many biographers to such futile investigations. Vast amounts of effort have been expended in hunting for Walt Whitman's children—to no avail. The old poet apparently invented them out of whole cloth—not a surprise when considered in the context of the letter's concluding sentence: "I see I have written with haste & too great effusion—but let it stand." Whitman was being stunningly disingenuous; the line about his haste and effusion appears in a heavily worked-over draft of the letter.

In his reply to Whitman, Symonds professed to take him at his word. You "set the matter as straight as can be," he wrote, "[and] base the doctrine of Calamus upon a foundation of granite." However, in letters to fellow Whitmanites he expressed skepticism about Whitman's denial of any physical dimension to the "Calamus" sentiments. "I exchanged some words by letter with Walt lately about his 'Calamus,' " he wrote Horace Traubel. "I do not think he quite understood what I was driving at." Undeterred by Whitman's refusal to acknowledge the sensual dimensions of comradeship, Symonds continued with his literary campaign to change public opinion and English laws relating to sexual inversion.

Between his 1890 letter to Whitman and his death early in 1893, Symonds labored on two works about same-sex passion. *Sexual Inversion*, a collaboration with the physician and writer Havelock Ellis, was not published until four years after Symonds's death, and his role in its authorship was effectively erased. Symonds's wife and his literary executor, worried about his reputation, bought up virtually the entire first edition, which had Symonds's name along with Ellis's on the title page. They persuaded Ellis to issue a second edition without Symonds's name, his contributions cryptically credited to "Z." The other book, *A Problem in Modern Ethics*, was unknown outside the circle of Symonds's acquaintances, since he had it privately printed in an edition of only fifty copies. Symonds was being discreet, yet he was also quietly courageous. When Symonds published the book in 1891, the only English-language writing on same-sex sexuality occurred in police reports, judicial proceedings, and studies of the insane; the Labouchere Amendment had recently criminalized all sexual contact between men; and his idol Walt Whitman had just declared that any inference of sexuality in his poems of male love was "damnable."

Despite the discouraging social climate Symonds persevered with his "inquiry into the phenomenon of sexual inversion," as *A Problem in Modern Ethics* is subtitled. The book is organized as a survey of modern—that is, postclassical—writing on same-sex passion. For the most part it makes for dismal reading. Symonds, a scrupulous scholar, dispassionately records the disdainful invective that permeated Western writing on the topic. Historians such as Gibbon treated the subject as repugnant; legal authorities regarded it as criminal; physicians considered it a disease. When, in his final chapter, Symonds comes to *Leaves of Grass*, it is with the amazed excitement of an explorer upon a peak in Darien. His tone changes from dry neutrality to avid enthusiasm. Whitman ignores "classical associations of corruption [and] the perplexed questions of a guilty passion doomed by law and popular antipathy to failure." He "begins anew," as if two thousand years of homophobic history had been erased. Symonds rhapsodically describes the "superb friendship" and "democratic chivalry" of the "Calamus" poems, which hold the potential to elevate same-sex love in the same way that medieval chivalry idealized love between the sexes.

Symonds composed his chapter on Whitman after their final correspondence on the subject of same-sex passion, and Symonds's enthusiasm is tempered by Whitman's letter of disavowal. Symonds glumly acknowledges that "the man who wrote 'Calamus,' and preached the gospel of comradeship, entertains feelings at least as hostile to sexual inversion as any law-abiding humdrum Anglo-Saxon could desire." Yet Symonds had not said his last word on the topic of "Calamus" love. Shortly after the poet's death in 1892, he wrote the book-length work on Walt Whitman that he had long been contemplating.

Walt Whitman: A Study was intended as a general introduction to the poet. In chapters titled "Religion," "Self," and "Democracy," Symonds offers an interpretation of *Leaves of Grass* that is familiar from earlier works by Burroughs, Gilchrist, and Bucke. Symonds minimizes the political dimension of Whitman's art or, rather, spiritualizes it, arguing that democracy and religion are identical in his work. He calls Whitman's religion "cosmic enthusiasm," Symonds's label for his own religious beliefs, which he defines as "a recognition of divinity in all things." This recognition, he argues, "is the secret of the democratic spirit. . . . Whitman regarded [democracy] not merely as a political phenomenon, but far more as a form of religious enthusiasm." Symonds offers not just analysis but testimony, movingly recording how Whitman saved him in both body and soul. Before reading Whitman, Symonds was enfeebled by invalidism, "decidedly academical, and in danger of becoming a prig." Whitman gave him a new appreciation of his body, bolstered his religious faith, and stripped him of social prejudices.

Symonds links Whitman's democratic spirit not only to religion but also to "the love of comrades," the title of one of his chapters. In this analysis of the "Calamus" poems Symonds is considerably bolder in pursuing their sexual implications than he had been in *A Problem in Modern Ethics*. He acknowledges that Whitman "never suggests that comradeship may occasion the development of physical desire." On the other hand, Symonds continues, the poet "does not in set terms condemn desires, or warn his disciples against their perils. There is indeed a distinctly sensuous side to his conception of adhesiveness." Skirting close to an admission of his own proclivities, he writes that "those unenviable mortals who are the inheritors of sexual anomalies will recognise their own emotion in Whitman's 'superb friendship, exalté, previously unknown.' " Symonds continues, "Had I not the strongest proof in Whitman's private correspondence with myself that he repudiated any such deductions from his 'Calamus,' I admit that I should have regarded them as justified; and I am not certain whether his own feelings upon this delicate topic may not have altered since the time when 'Calamus' was first composed."

Symonds's statements were the closest anyone had yet come to linking Whitman with "sexual anomalies." Symonds's tone was so discreet and his suggestions so hedged with double negatives that most readers seem to have been oblivious to his implications. However, the American disciples were outraged. William Sloane Kennedy, the Boston journalist and Whitman disciple, wrote, "We here in America were astounded that it seemed to [Symonds] necessary in his work on Walt Whitman to relieve the Calamus poems of the vilest of all possible interpretations. It was a sad revelation to us of the state of European morals, that even the ethical perfume of these noblest utterances on friendship could not save them from such a fate." Kennedy defended Whitman as if the poet were a character in a Henry James novel, his American innocence threatened by European corruption. However, a more fruitful way to understand Symonds's interpretation of "Calamus" is to consider not that Symonds went too far but that he did not go far enough.

When he wrote to Whitman in 1890, Symonds was newly embarked on his crusade on behalf of those he preferred to call Urnings. But *crusade* may be too strong a word for his tentative campaign. Symonds, emotionally close to his father, could never shake free of the moralistic censures of his father's generation. *A Problem in Modern Ethics*, Symonds's sole polemical work, is hedged with qualifiers. Sexual inversion is innate, he argues, and undeserving of prosecution, yet over and over he concedes that it is morally noxious: a "perversion of appetite," he calls it, an "abnormal instinct," an "aberration." *A Problem in Modern Ethics* follows the same strategy used today by campaigners for the legalization of heroin: the practice under discussion may be unhealthy and distasteful, but it ought not be criminal.

In his letter to Whitman Symonds wrote that any increase in "ardent and *physical* intimacies" between men caused by the "Calamus" poems "would [not] be absolutely prejudicial to Social interests." This halfhearted negative was as far as Symonds was prepared to go. Little wonder that Whitman was appalled by the letter. His "Calamus" poems were not intended to avoid prejudice to social interests; they were designed to bring American democracy to its

full glory. Symonds's highest goal in his campaign on behalf of Urnings was the right to be left alone, to be free to love in private,
unafraid of criminal prosecution. In contrast, Whitman announced
his goals for "manly love" in the fourth poem of the "Calamus"
sequence, "For You O Democracy":

> Come, I will make the continent indissoluble,
> I will make the most splendid race the sun ever
>   shone upon,
> I will make divine magnetic lands,
>   With the love of comrades,
>   With the life-long love of comrades.

Symonds believed sexual inversion to be limited to an unfortunate
minority of men. Whitman saw "Calamus" love as potential in all
men; once realized, it would bind the nation in a way that merely
political alliances never could. In his great, optimistic political essay
"Democratic Vistas," written in the depths of Grant administration
corruption, Whitman wrote, "It is to the development, identifica-
tion, and general prevalence of that fervid comradeship, (the adhesive love, at least rivaling the amative love hitherto possessing
imaginative literature, if not going beyond it,) that I look for the
counterbalance and offset of our materialistic and vulgar American
democracy, and for the spiritualization thereof." Whitman left
"adhesive love" strategically undefined, the better to amplify its
significance. Symonds, in contrast, was obsessed with definitions.
Was adhesiveness, he in essence asked Whitman, the same as sexual
inversion?

Whitman refused to be pinned down. Writing to Edward Carpenter, Symonds acknowledged as much: "I think [Whitman] was afraid
of being used to lend his influence to 'Sods.' Did not quite trust me
perhaps." *Sod*, or sodomite, is often taken as a nineteenth-century
synonym for *homosexual*, but the two terms have radically different
implications. To nineteenth-century Britons and Americans a sodomite was not a man who loved other men; rather, the term described a viciously depraved person who performed unnatural sexual
acts. More specifically, in legal terms a sodomite was one who com-

mitted anal intercourse with a man, woman, or beast. When Walt Whitman borrowed the term *adhesiveness* from phrenology to describe the love between comrades, he was not searching for a euphemism for *sodomy*; he was inventing a language to describe passionate emotions that had nothing in common with the depravity implied by the latter term. Whitman could write freely and fearlessly about adhesive love because it would not have occurred to anyone in 1860, when he published "Calamus," that the emotion had any connection with sodomitical practices.

The nineteenth-century cult of romantic love held that the highest form of relationship was the union of man and woman in marriage. Still, the ideal love between the sexes was seen as constantly under threat from physical lust, which inevitably led to some degree of tension in relations between men and women. In this atmosphere same-sex friendships offered an escape from the threat of impurity; they were understood to be located in a lust-free zone. The "Calamus" poems depended on this cultural approval of emotionally intense same-sex relations. Lines from "Calamus" that now seem highly sexual—such as "the one I love most lay sleeping by me under the same cover in the cool night, / In the stillness in the autumn moonbeams his face was inclined toward me, / And his arm lay lightly around my breast"—never raised an eyebrow in the decades after their publication, while "To a Common Prostitute," which has no directly sexual content, was frequently singled out in censorship cases involving *Leaves of Grass*. The latter poem seemed to many nineteenth-century readers to endorse impure sexuality; the former seemed to have nothing to do with sex.

"Calamus" is an inextricable mixture of sensuality and politics— the embrace of comrades in the cool night makes possible the union of democratic citizens. Symonds was thrilled by this conception, and in his most optimistic moments he saw his cross-class relationships as harbingers of a more democratic future; in his published writings, however, the most he proposed was an end to criminal sanctions. Whitman refused to be enlisted in a narrowly focused campaign on behalf of Sods, but he never repudiated his disciple John Addington Symonds. Housebound in Camden, Whitman liked to fish out old

Symonds letters from the piles of papers littering his room and have Horace Traubel read them aloud. "He is always driving at me . . . : is that what Calamus means?" Whitman said of Symonds. "It always makes me a little testy to be catechized about the Leaves." Yet even as he complained about Symonds's persistent curiosity, Whitman paid tribute to his English disciple: "Anyway, I love Symonds. Who could fail to love a man who could write such a letter?" Symonds was not the only man writing such letters. Edward Carpenter's Calamus-infused letters to Whitman began arriving in Camden soon after Symonds's.

✢ ✢ ✢

"It is just dawn," Carpenter's first letter to Walt Whitman begins, "but there is light enough to write by, and the birds in their old sweet fashion are chirping in the little College garden outside. My first knowledge of you is all entangled with that little garden." The placid, bucolic scene setting is typical of Carpenter. Symonds's letters, with their recurrent questions about the true meaning of "Calamus," reflect his anguish about his sexuality. Carpenter's initial contact with Whitman evokes his sunnier disposition, his enthusiasm for Walt Whitman, and his calm acceptance of his own sexual nature. "Yesterday there came (to mend my door) a young workman with the old divine light in his eyes . . . and perhaps, more than all, he has made me write to you," Carpenter wrote in explanation of his letter. He went on, "Because you have, as it were, given me a ground for the love of men I thank you continually in my heart. (—And others thank you though they do not say so.) For you have made men to be not ashamed of the noblest instinct of their nature. Women are beautiful; but, to some, there is that which passes the love of women."

None of the disciples was influenced more strongly by Whitman than Edward Carpenter. Whitman not only shaped Carpenter's understanding of his sexual nature but also influenced what he wrote, how he lived, even his physical appearance—like Bucke, Carpenter grew a beard and began wearing a large, soft-brimmed hat after meeting the poet. At the age of thirty-one Carpenter avowed, "I feel that my work is to carry on what you have begun. You have opened the way: my only desire is to go onward with it." The next year he made the first of two pilgrimages to Camden. By the time he was forty he had transformed himself into a writer and social activist often labeled "the English Walt Whitman."

Note, however, that he was the *English* Walt Whitman. The American Walt Whitman was fiercely individualistic, suspicious of political movements. Carpenter, in contrast, had a hand in virtually every reform movement of late Victorian England: socialism, vegetarianism, environmentalism, women's rights—he wrote, spoke, donated, and organized on behalf of them all. Including, notoriously, sex reform. Whitman's love poetry, both amative and adhesive, has a political dimension, but the poet himself always steered clear of the American "free love" movement despite attempts to enlist him in the cause. Carpenter, however, threw himself into sex reform. He believed in the connection between comrade love and political democracy that Whitman asserted in "Calamus" but went far beyond his master. Drawing, like Symonds, on the German sexologists, Carpenter argued that Urnings represented a higher stage in human evolution and were destined to lead humanity into a utopian future. The visionary Carpenter combined *Leaves of Grass* with socialism, mysticism, simple living, and what he preferred to call "homogenic love" into an optimistic program that had enormous influence in turn-of-the-century England.

✣ ✣ ✣

Edward Carpenter was born in 1844 into a life of upper-middle-class privilege in the seaside city of Brighton. His grandfather was an admiral; his father left careers in the navy and in law to live off his investments. Like the equally well-off Symonds, Carpenter was a sensitive, introspective boy. But unlike Symonds, who was traumatized by the early death of his mother and his experiences at

boarding school, the emotionally resilient Carpenter grew up surrounded by both parents and nine siblings. When it came time to
attend university, he made a conventional choice for conventional
reasons: he decided to attend Trinity Hall at Cambridge because of
its successful rowing team. At university he was indistinguishable,
for the most part, from his fellow undergraduates; his days slid by,
he remembered in his autobiography, with sports and wine parties
and boat suppers. Rather to his surprise, he found himself at the
head of his class; he had not come to Cambridge with any intellectual ambitions. With the encouragement of his tutor he took an
honors degree in mathematics and, upon graduation, received an
offer to remain at Trinity as a fellow. It was a clerical fellowship,
but Carpenter had long thought about being ordained, and in 1869
he was named a deacon, followed the next year by his ordination
as an Anglican priest.

Carpenter's father was a religious liberal and a supporter of the
Anglican priest F. D. Maurice, who was renowned as a leading pro-
ponent of Christian socialism. Raised in this progressive religious
atmosphere, Carpenter believed that the Church of England was
changing from within and that earnest, enlightened young men such
as himself could help move it forward. His optimism was checked
only slightly when the bishop called him in following his written
examination for ordination in order to correct his heretical interpretation of the story of Abraham and Isaac. Carpenter, steeped in liberal theology, had cheerfully offered the view that Abraham's intended sacrifice of Isaac was a relic of Moloch worship, and that the
voice of God commanding Abraham to substitute the ram represented the evolution of human spirituality to a higher ideal. The
bishop was incredulous: Did not Carpenter understand that the story
prefigured the sacrifice of Jesus? He and the bishop talked far into
the early morning hours of the day on which Carpenter was to be
ordained. At the end of their discussion the bishop declared that,
although he could not fully understand Carpenter's ideas, he was
sure that they were *not* the doctrine of the Church of England. The
bishop expected that the young heretic would gracefully withdraw.
Instead, Carpenter went ahead with his ordination.

He soon found himself teaching undergraduates at Trinity Hall and serving as curate at St. Edward's Church in Cambridge, whose vicar was none other than F. D. Maurice. Carpenter admired Maurice, but he became increasingly uncomfortable with clerical duties. How, he wondered, could the grand old man mount the pulpit each Sunday to conduct services for a congregation of tradespeople and shopkeepers in their sleek Sunday best who did not understand a word of doctrine and took it all "in a spirit of mere superstition"? Everything Carpenter did came to seem false to him, from reading services to uncomprehending parishioners to visiting elderly women who, when they saw the parson coming, would hastily shuffle a Bible or prayer book onto the table. Finally, he felt that he could keep up the pretense no longer, and he submitted his resignation from holy orders four years after taking his vows, thus effectively giving up his Cambridge fellowship. His university colleagues derided his scruples. The dean told him confidentially that they all knew Anglican doctrine was tomfoolery, so why make such a bother about whether one believed it or not? "You let the matter drop," he advised Carpenter, "and it will all blow over." But Carpenter felt that he had to make a radical break and find a more authentic mode of existence. In 1874, the year he turned thirty, it flashed upon him that he "must somehow go and make [his] life with the mass of the people and the manual workers." He resigned his orders, left Cambridge, and took a position as a university extension lecturer in the industrial towns of northern England.

It was at this juncture that Carpenter wrote his first letter to Walt Whitman. Like Symonds, who first wrote to Whitman shortly after his father died, Carpenter was drawn to make contact with the poet at a moment of personal crisis. He had first read Whitman six years earlier in the Rossetti edition and had thrilled to the "Calamus" poems. Like all the disciples, he had thrilled also to the individuality and self-celebration of Whitman's outsized persona and was drawn to the book's curious mixture of egotism and emotional neediness. When Whitman responded warmly to his initial letter, opening a correspondence between them, Carpenter began making plans to visit the United States. Three years after their first exchange, he crossed the Atlantic and quickly made his way to Camden.

The young Englishman presented himself at George Whitman's house on May 2, 1877. Walt's sister-in-law Louisa called out that a visitor had arrived. The poet came downstairs heavily, dragging his paralyzed leg, and warmly grasped Carpenter's hand. "What news do you bring from Britain?" he asked, and the two were soon embarked on a discussion of English politics and personalities. After a bit Whitman suggested that they go over to Philadelphia, and they took the ferry across the Delaware, then boarded a streetcar for a ride about the city. Americans did not much like to walk, Carpenter observed, and in any case Whitman's lameness meant that he had to take the trams.

Carpenter's visit to Whitman preceded Bucke's by only a few months, and the two disciples had similar first impressions of their master. Both were struck by his magnetic personality. "I was aware of a certain radiant power in him, a large benign effluence and inclusiveness, as of the sun," Carpenter later wrote. Both remarked on his friendships with working-class women and men in Philadelphia. "The men on the ferry steamer were evidently old friends," Carpenter remarked, "and when we landed on the Philadelphia side we were before long quite besieged" by Whitman's acquaintances, including "the man or woman selling fish at the corner of the street, the tramway conductor, the loafers on the pavement." Both disciples also lovingly detailed Whitman's physical appearance: "A face of majestic simple proportion, like a Greek temple," Carpenter wrote. In a letter to a friend a few days after the encounter, he was even more lavishly reverential. "The likeness to Christ is quite marked," he wrote of Whitman, and he enclosed a sketch that is remarkable for looking almost nothing like the overweight fifty-eight-year-old Walt Whitman but very much like conventional Victorian representations of a slender young Jesus.

Anne Gilchrist also thought that Whitman resembled Jesus; she and Carpenter talked about it during his visit. Whitman arranged for the young Englishman to stay at Gilchrist's house in Philadelphia for a week, and she and Carpenter became friends. They had much

FIGURE 4.2. Edward Carpenter about the time of his first pilgrimage to Camden in 1877. Edward Carpenter, *My Days and Dreams* (London: George Allen & Unwin, 1916).

FIGURE 4.3. Sketch of Walt Whitman in 1877 by Edward Carpenter. Bayley/ Whitman Collection of Ohio Wesleyan University.

in common: reading Whitman had upended their lives, sending them both across the Atlantic to encounter the master. Gilchrist's journey, of course, yielded less than she had expected, since Whitman showed no interest in taking her as his wife, as she had imagined. By the time Carpenter arrived, several months after Gilchrist had moved to Philadelphia, the poet had settled into the role of Gilchrist family friend, staying overnight for days at a time, spending long evening hours on the front stoop chatting with her and the children as the spring days lengthened and the air warmed. Carpenter, on the other hand, may well have gotten more than he hoped from his visit; it is possible that he and Whitman became lovers.

The evidence is ambiguous. Carpenter's only direct reference to intimacy with Whitman occurs in a letter he sent from Philadelphia to a friend in England. Whitman "has taken me to himself," Carpenter wrote; the phrase might mean only that Whitman had taken a liking to his handsome young disciple. However, almost fifty years later Gavin Arthur, a young American, visited the elderly Carpenter and cheekily asked if he had slept with Whitman. "Oh yes—once in a while—he regarded it as the best way to get together with another man," Carpenter supposedly replied before taking Arthur upstairs to show him how Whitman made love. There is reason to doubt Arthur's account—he wrote differing versions of his encounter with Carpenter, with the dialogue and actions varying each time. But Allen Ginsberg, who knew Gavin Arthur, believed the story and liked to place himself in a Whitmanesque lineage: he had slept with Neal Cassady, who had slept with Gavin Arthur, who had slept with Edward Carpenter, who had slept with Walt Whitman.

Certainly, Carpenter had an ex-lover's cool awareness of the multiple dimensions of Whitman's personality. Bucke never lost his initial infatuation with Whitman, never drew back from his assertion that Whitman lived on a higher, superhuman plane, unacquainted with baser emotions of anger, annoyance, or fear. Carpenter revered Whitman, but he also recognized the poet's shortcomings—his moodiness, his "omnivorous egotism," what Carpenter called his cussedness. In his book about Whitman, published after the poet's death, Carpenter listed cussedness as one of Whitman's most notable characteristics, defining it as "the contrary moods, the spirit of refusal, the wilfulness, which by their at times necessary opposition and antagonism to his ample and loving humanity formed, I believe, a great tragic element in his nature—and possibly prevented him ever being quite what is called 'happy in love affairs.'" Clearly, Carpenter had collided against the rockier aspects of Whitman's personality, yet his admiration for both the poet and his poetry never diminished. *Leaves of Grass* was "the most deliberately daring advance ever made in literature," Carpenter wrote, and he acknowledged that this challenge to the genteel literary establishment could have been made only "by one in whom the rocky elements of character were abundantly present."

Whatever happened between them, Carpenter was sufficiently buoyed by his 1877 visit to Whitman to repeat the experience seven years later. During those years, inspired by Whitman's example, Carpenter reinvented himself, turning himself from an interesting but publicly unknown figure—an ex-clergyman turned science lecturer, with a slim book of conventional poems to his credit—into "Edward Carpenter," a name that by the century's end was instantly recognizable throughout England, connoting a combination of avant-garde poetry, mystical religion, radical politics, and a host of social reforms. Between 1883 and his death in 1929 Carpenter published a best-selling collection of poems, twelve books of essays, song lyrics, translations, and dozens of pamphlets on political and social topics. He lectured across Great Britain on socialism, feminism, sex reform, colonialism, animal rights, the environment, and other socially progressive topics. To imagine Carpenter's equivalent in the American counterculture, one would have to combine Daniel Berrigan, Tom Hayden, Ram Dass, Gary Snyder, Larry Kramer, Gloria Steinem, and Wavy Gravy. And, presiding over all, the spirit of Walt Whitman.

The example of Whitman's unconventional life and art emboldened Carpenter at the beginning of the 1880s when he began reshaping his life. Following his return from the United States, he became increasingly dissatisfied with his career as a university extension lecturer, which was all too reminiscent of his hated clerical duties. He had imagined that in the industrial north of England he would be immersed in the life of the common people; instead, he found himself lecturing on abstruse topics to the uncomprehending middle class. He suffered from insomnia and psychosomatically induced eye trouble. At the age of thirty-six he resigned his position and moved to a farm, a transition spurred both by a desire for change and by falling in love.

The object of his affections was Albert Fearnehough (pronounced *Fernuff*), a Sheffield ironworker who approached Carpenter after one of his lectures and invited him to visit. Fearnehough lived with his wife and two children on a farm outside Sheffield, where he rented a cottage from his friend Charles Fox. Carpenter began spending more and more time with Fearnehough, until eventually he formed a plan: he would give up lecturing, move in with Fearnehough, and begin farming—first on Fox's farm and then, after 1883, at Millthorpe, a seven-acre property near Sheffield that Carpenter purchased with his inheritance from his parents. Living with Fearnehough and working the earth were inextricably combined for Carpenter; both were a return to nature. Carpenter viewed his new life through lenses colored by his reading of Whitman. Fearnehough "was delightful to me, as the one 'powerful uneducated' and natural person I had as yet, in all my life, met with," Carpenter wrote in his memoirs; he was quoting from *Leaves of Grass*. Influenced by Whitman, Carpenter took a highly romantic view of the working class. Fearnehough and Fox represented, Carpenter wrote, "a life close to Nature and actual materials, shrewd, strong, manly, independent, not the least polite or proper, thoroughly human and kindly, and spent for the most part in the fields and under the open sky." Fearnehough would be the first of a series of working-class lovers, the longest lasting of whom was George Merrill, who joined Carpenter at Millthorpe when Carpenter was fifty-four and Merrill twenty-nine and who stayed until Carpenter's death more than thirty years later.

"My ideal of love is a powerful, strongly built man, of my own age or rather younger—preferably of the working class," Carpenter wrote in the case history he prepared for Ellis and Symonds's *Sexual Inversion*. The statement could easily have come from Symonds. However, Carpenter's relation to the working class was significantly different from Symonds's. Carpenter lived among the working class, did similar labor—he had a stint in a carpentry shop before he took up farming—and, after hours, joined his working-class neighbors in socialist political organizations. Symonds, theoretically committed to democratic socialism, never lost his sense of noblesse oblige. "I have brought my cultured self into the sheep-cotes, have lost it or disguised it there, and have found with hinds and peasants pleasure and profit which Parnassus and the Muses could not yield me," he wrote in his autobiography, sounding, at best, as if he imagined himself living out "Lycidas"; at worst, as if he were Marie Antoinette in drag, playing the role of shepherd in an Alpine Versailles.

In contrast, Carpenter moved easily among his working-class friends. "Railway men, porters, clerks, signalmen, ironworkers, coach-builders, Sheffield cutlers, and others came within my ken, and from the first I got on excellently and felt fully at home with them," Carpenter wrote of his Sheffield days. "I felt I had come into, or at least in sight of, the world to which I belonged, and to my natural *habitat*." The testimony of Anne Gilchrist confirms Carpenter's self-assessment. "Carpenter knows intimately, goes freely among, a greater range & variety of men than any Englishman I know," she wrote Whitman after she returned to England. "He has a way of making himself thoroughly welcome by the firesides of mechanics & factory workers." Nevertheless, evidence suggests that class differences were less easily dissolved than Carpenter and Gilchrist acknowledged. George Merrill was listed as Carpenter's servant on the local tax rolls, and in the many photographs of the two men Merrill always takes a subordinate position: he leans against the upright Carpenter, stands as Carpenter and a friend sit, or, while Carpenter and middle-class friends pose in chairs, Merrill sits on the ground in front of them, tailor-fashion, looking like the group's mascot.

Carpenter and Symonds believed that they were living out the democratic vision of *Leaves of Grass*, and they were fascinated by Whitman's relationships with the streetcar conductor Peter Doyle and other working-class men. However, both *Leaves of Grass* and Whitman's friendships fit imperfectly with the deeply class-stratified European societies in which Carpenter and Symonds lived. The two English disciples grew up in privilege and attended elite universities; Walt Whitman was raised by an unsuccessful house builder and a

FIGURE 4.4. George Merrill seated in front of Edward Carpenter (center) and two friends, c. 1900. John Rylands University Library, University of Manchester.

lightly educated homemaker and ended his formal education when he was eleven. Thanks to the relatively fluid antebellum American class system, Whitman lifted himself out of the working class, yet it is not quite accurate to label his love affairs as "cross class"; men like Peter Doyle and Harry Stafford came from backgrounds almost identical to Whitman's. When he called Doyle or Stafford or Civil War soldiers *brother* or *son* or *nephew*, he was not merely using terms of endearment but suggesting that, in their backgrounds and education, these men could have been members of his own family.

No matter how fully Carpenter embraced the democratic equality of Whitman's "Calamus" poems, the Englishman was unable to eliminate entirely the divisions between him and his working-class lovers. Still, he cannot, as Symonds can, be accused of sexual tourism. Carpenter tried as hard as any person in nineteenth-century Europe to give up class privilege and share working-class life. On his farm at Millthorpe, working the land and carting vegetables into

Sheffield to sell at market, Carpenter invites comparison with Tolstoy, who adopted the dress of a serf and worked alongside peasants. Like Tolstoy, his motives were as much religious as political. About the time he began farming, Carpenter experienced a mystical illumination, an event that changed his life and radically transformed him as a writer.

His illumination occurred in 1881, when Carpenter was thirty-six, about eight years after he published his volume of conventional poems and resigned from the ministry. Bucke was so impressed by Carpenter's later accounts of the event that he included the Englishman as one of only fourteen certain cases of cosmic consciousness in history. According to Carpenter, his mother's death was the immediate stimulus, exercising "a great etherealizing influence" on him. "The *Bhagavat Gita* about the same time falling into my hands gave me a keynote. And all at once I found myself in touch with a mood of exaltation and inspiration—a kind of super-consciousness—which passed all that I had experienced before, and which immediately harmonized all these other feelings, giving to them their place, their meaning and their outlet in expression. And so it was that *Towards Democracy* came to birth."

"Towards Democracy," Carpenter's masterwork, is a lengthy free-verse poem originally published in pamphlet form in 1883; other poems were added to form a collection, also called *Towards Democracy*, that went through three editions between 1885 and 1905. If the Bhagavad Gita was the keynote for the original "Towards Democracy," "Song of Myself" was the template. Like Whitman's great spiritual epic, "Towards Democracy" presents the inspired vision of a superhuman self—congruent with rather than identical to the poet's—who is also identified with you, the reader. "Every atom belonging to me as good belongs to you," Whitman writes in the first stanza of "Song of Myself," while Carpenter states, "These things I, writing, translate for you—I wipe a mirror and place it in your hands." Just as the speaker of "Song of Myself" is able to survey the entire American continent ("I skirt sierras, my palms cover continents, / I am afoot with my vision"), the poet in "Towards Democracy" sees all of England "spread like a map below me" and catalogues the country from the Thames to the Mersey. Just as "Song of Myself" includes an ecstatic account of the poet's spiritual illumination—the great mystical-erotic encounter that begins, "I mind how once we lay, such a transparent summer morning"—"Towards Democracy" describes its narrator's mystical awakening:

> I arise out of the dewy night and shake my wings.
>
> Tears and lamentations are no more. Life and death lie stretched below me. I breathe the sweet aether blowing of the breath of God.
>
> Deep as the universe is my life—and I know it; nothing can dislodge the knowledge of it; nothing can destroy, nothing can harm me.
>
> Joy, joy arises—I arise. The sun darts overpowering piercing rays of joy through me, the night radiates it from me.
>
> I take wings through the night and pass through all the wildernesses of the worlds, and the old dark holds of tears and death—and return with laughter, laughter, laughter:
>
> Sailing through the starlit spaces on outspread wings, we two—O laughter! laughter! laughter!

"Whitman and water" was Havelock Ellis's famously dismissive reaction to his first reading of "Towards Democracy." Ellis later recanted, but his characterization has stuck. Carpenter was understandably touchy about the comparison, and in an 1894 essay about "Towards Democracy" he offered contradictory assessments of Whitman's influence. On the one hand, Whitman's influence was as pervasive as the influence of "the sun or the winds. These influences lie too far back and ramify too complexly to be traced." On the other hand, "our temperaments, standpoints, antecedents, etc., are so entirely diverse and opposite that, except for a few points, I can hardly imagine that there is much real resemblance to be traced."

Actually, there is quite a bit of real resemblance to be traced. "Towards Democracy" is a rewriting of "Song of Myself," with Whitman's singing cadences replaced by prosy short paragraphs.

Despite its shortcomings Carpenter's poem had thousands of admirers in England. Based on their testimony, many of them were drawn by its political dimensions. "Towards Democracy" spoke to the late nineteenth-century British political situation in a way that *Leaves of Grass* could not. However, "Towards Democracy" is notoriously vague about the nature of the democracy toward which it points and how it is to be achieved. Carpenter stresses individual transformation over any sort of institutional change: "Of that which exists in the Soul, political freedom and institutions of equality, and so forth, are but the shadows (necessarily thrown); and Democracy in States or Constitutions but the shadow of that which first expresses itself in the glance of the eye or the appearance of the skin." Political reform was less significant to him at the time than spiritual awareness and a celebration of the body. However, once the poem was published, Carpenter began tentatively exploring the small socialist societies that had begun to arise in the 1880s; by the end of the decade he had achieved his reputation as one of England's leading socialists.

✢ ✢ ✢

On a visit to London in 1883 Carpenter decided to drop in on a meeting of the Social Democratic Federation, or SDF. Earlier that year he had read *England for All* by H. M. Hyndman, chair of the SDF. Hyndman was a colorful eccentric, a wealthy Marxist who delighted in wearing his silk top hat and frock coat to address radical meetings. Karl Marx had little patience for Hyndman, who had managed to write a book about socialism without once mentioning Marx's name. But Hyndman had accurately gauged his British audience: he offered his readers a political program seemingly untainted by any whiff of continental radicalism. Over the next few years Carpenter worked closely with the SDF. However, he also joined political organizations that were seemingly at odds with the Marxist-in-all-but-name federation, such as the utopian Fellowship of the New Life and William Morris's Socialist League. Carpenter was

cheerfully indiscriminate in his political activities: he single-hand-
edly funded an SDF journal, worked the land alongside members of
one of John Ruskin's back-to-the-medieval-future guilds, served as
character witness for an anarchist charged in a bomb-making plot,
and lectured to George Bernard Shaw at a Fabian Society meeting.
When an anarchist scolded Carpenter in print for supporting the
Fabians and trade unionists, he wrote his critic a good-humored
reply: "Certainly, Comrade Creaghe, I stick up for the Fabians and
the Trade Unions just as I do for the Anarchists. . . . We are all
travelling along the same road. Why should we be snarling at one
another's heels?" Comrade Creaghe was most likely unconvinced
by Carpenter's political ecumenicism; certainly, Bernard Shaw disagreed. When Carpenter invited Shaw to contribute to a volume of
essays, the Fabian playwright responded with an essay that ridiculed
"the cherished illusion that all Socialists are agreed in principle
though they may differ as to tactics."

Carpenter never pulled back from his eclectic, big-tent approach
to socialism. He differed from Bernard Shaw and Comrade Creaghe
not simply in their varying approaches to politics but in their clash-
ing definitions of politics itself. To Shaw and Creaghe politics and
tactics were indistinguishable, and it was nonsense to say that there
was no difference between the Fabian interest in infiltrating the constitutional parliamentary system and the anarchist commitment to
the violent revolutionary overthrow of the state. Carpenter, on the
other hand, was uninterested in tactics. Politics to him was fundamentally an individual and emotional phenomenon, consisting of a
belief in human equality and the conviction that social arrangements
should reflect that equality. The point of socialist political activity
was to make socialists—in other words, politics was all about conversion. For Carpenter socialism was not so much a matter of political ideology as of religious belief.

Carpenter saw the individual's conversion to the religion of socialism as a necessary step on the path to the transformation of society as a whole. Socialism was one element in the grand millennial
vision that he championed in essays such as "Civilisation: Its Cause
and Cure." Carpenter regarded modern civilization—which he de-

fined as the system of private property and ruling-class governance—as a disease that required the dual treatments of socialism and a return to nature. In the conclusion to "Civilisation," originally given as a lecture to the Fabian Society, Carpenter painted an ecstatic picture of a future Eden, a time when humanity would strip off all the husks of civilization: government, institutional religion, houses, and clothing. "On the high tops once more gathering," he wrote, humanity "will celebrate with naked dances the glory of the human form and the great processions of the stars." The cure for civilization was the simultaneous "establishment of a socialistic and communal life on a vast scale" and "a move towards Nature and Savagery." Carpenter's speech to the Fabians prompted Bernard Shaw to refer to him from then on as "the Noble Savage." Shaw's scorn was matched by Hyndman's; the latter said that he did not want the socialist movement to be "a depository of old cranks, humanitarians, vegetarians, anti-vivisectionists, arty-crafties and all the rest of them." Carpenter was unfazed by the criticism and ridicule. To the end of his life he linked socialism to simple living, the liberation of women, and Whitmanesque love of comrades.

"What made me cling to [*Leaves of Grass*] from the beginning," Carpenter wrote in his autobiography, "was largely the poems which celebrate comradeship." As Symonds had done, Carpenter set *Leaves of Grass* in the place on his bookshelf formerly reserved for Plato. American comradeship shouldered aside Greek love; reading Whitman made Carpenter realize that "there had been something wanting" in the Greeks. Yet if Carpenter's initial reaction to *Leaves of Grass* recalls Symonds's, Carpenter also had much in common with Bucke. Carpenter too saw Whitman as the greatest example in history of cosmic consciousness; Bucke borrowed the term from Carpenter, who had first used it in writing about Asian religions. In his book *Days with Walt Whitman* Carpenter insisted on the importance of Whitman's midlife "illumination," or mystical experience: " 'Leaves of Grass,' of course, would not have been written without it; it runs behind every page—'the vision and the faculty divine.' " He called Whitman the prophet of a new era, the latest in a lineage of great spiritual teachers reaching from the Buddha to Jesus to St.

Francis. Like Bucke, Carpenter printed passages from *Leaves of Grass* alongside excerpts from the Upanishads, the Bhagavad Gita, the Tao-te ching, and the Gospels.

Like both Bucke and Gilchrist, Carpenter also embraced Whitman's evolutionary optimism, the poet's belief that evolution was not a morally blind biological force but a divine instrument leading inevitably toward the good. Whitman, Carpenter, and the other disciples preferred Lamarck to Darwin because the French scientist gave a role to desire in evolution. The force of will—in animals and, preeminently, in humans—could drive changes to species. Carpenter detested the social Darwinism of the late nineteenth century because it implied an amoral law of change, with the strong inevitably triumphing over the weak. He promoted "social Lamarckism," the notion that the desire for justice and democracy could determine the future structure of society.

Along with this optimistic sense of evolution Carpenter, like Symonds, took from Whitman the belief that comradeship, love between men, could play a key role in the evolution of humankind. Symonds speculated that the "Calamus" sentiment might inspire "a new Chivalry," a force for good equivalent to the medieval codes of chivalry that, in his view, had elevated the status of women. Yet in the same letter to Whitman in which he expressed his hope for the future, Symonds timidly suggested that the expression of same-sex passion would not be "absolutely prejudicial to Social interests." Carpenter was not so faint-hearted. Following his reading of the German sexologists in the early 1890s, he produced a series of works in which he argued that Urnings could serve as pathfinders on the way to a democratic socialist millennium.

Like Symonds, Carpenter embraced the German sex researchers' theories that sexual inversion was innate. Symonds went on to suggest that since Urnings' temperament was inborn, laws prohibiting sexual contact between men should be repealed. Carpenter agreed, but, going far beyond Symonds, he argued that Urnings had a special role to play in humanity's social evolution. Building on Ulrichs's belief that Urnings possessed a female soul in a male body, Carpenter developed a theory that both male and female inverts constituted what he called the "intermediate sex." He drew on anthropological studies of the era in theorizing that members of the intermediate sex had made possible all human progress to date. In primitive societies ordinary men were warriors and hunters, while women were absorbed in domestic labor. Intermediate men, whose temperaments were marked by feminine elements, had little interest in fighting or hunting; intermediate women, more masculine than their peers, were not drawn to the domestic. Instead, intermediate types turned to other activities: scientific experimentation, religious speculation, and music and dancing, thus becoming the healers, priests, and artists of early human history.

In contemporary society, Carpenter suggested, intermediate types maintained a special role as religious leaders, artists, and educators. However, they were poised to play an even greater role in the future. Capitalism had exaggerated sexual difference, Carpenter argued, so that men had become obsessed with property and ownership, while women, economically dependent on men, had sacrificed individuality and independence. Consequently, the two sexes had become essentially estranged from one another, "wont to congregate in separate herds, and talk languages each unintelligible to the other." Given this gender segregation in Victorian society, Carpenter believed that members of the intermediate sex had a role to play in bringing men and women together on a basis of greater equality. With their temperamental mix of the masculine and feminine, they had "a special work to do as reconcilers and interpreters of the two sexes to each other." Carpenter suggested that male Urnings combined men's strength of purpose with women's emotional sensitivity. As he wrote in his poem "O Child of Uranus":

> Thy Woman-soul within a Man's form dwelling
> (Was Adam perchance like this, ere Eve from his side was drawn?)
> So gentle, gracious, dignified, complete,
> With man's strength to perform, and pride to suffer without sign,
> And feminine sensitiveness to the last fibre of being;

Strange twice-born, having entrance to both worlds—
Loved, loved by either sex,
And free of all their lore!

Free of the conventional limitations of both men and women, having entrance to the emotional worlds of each, intermediate types were poised to help end sexual inequality in society. They also had a crucial part to play, Carpenter argued, in ending economic inequality. "Eros is a great leveller," he wrote. Drawing on his own relationships with Albert Fearnehough, George Merrill, and other men, Carpenter remarked that "it is noticeable how often Uranians of good position and breeding are drawn to rougher types, as of manual workers, and frequently very permanent alliances grow up in this way." These cross-class love affairs suggested, he went on, that "the Uranian spirit may lead to something like a general enthusiasm of Humanity, and that the Uranian people may be destined to form the advance guard of that great movement which will one day transform the common life by substituting the bond of personal affection and compassion for the monetary, legal and other external ties which now control and confine society."

In this movement toward a millennial future in which the state would wither away, to be replaced by voluntary bonds of affection, Uranian artists had a special role to play, and none more than Walt Whitman. "Thousands of people date from their first reading" of Whitman's poems "*a new era in their lives*," Carpenter emphasized in a study of Whitman's "sex-psychology." "Thousands date from the reading of them a new inspiration and an extraordinary access of vitality carrying their activities and energies into new channels. How *far* this process may go we hardly yet know, but that it is one of the factors of future evolution we can hardly doubt. I mean that the loves of men towards each other—and similarly the loves of women for each other—may become factors of future human evolution just as necessary and well-recognised as the ordinary loves which lead to the birth of children and the propagation of the race." In Carpenter's Lamarckian vision of the future Whitmanesque same-sex desire would drive biological and social change, resulting in a more androgynous (that is, more loving and less acquisitive) male and a similarly more androgynous (that is, stronger and more independent) female.

At the same time as he celebrated androgyny as the key to a more humane future, Carpenter relied on conventional Victorian ideas about sexual difference. "Anything effeminate in a man . . . repels me very decisively," Carpenter wrote in his autobiographical case history for Ellis and Symonds's *Sexual Inversion*. Part of Walt Whitman's appeal for Carpenter, Symonds, and other man-loving Englishmen of the period was his rugged American masculinity. Struggling to establish a masculine identity in a culture that offered no conceptual space for them, these men were attracted by the "Calamus" poems' positive portrayal of the manly love of comrades. During the 1890s, when Symonds began work on *Sexual Inversion* and Carpenter composed *The Intermediate Sex*, vigorous conceptual battles were being waged about the newly identified figure of the homosexual. With the exception of Ulrichs, Continental sex researchers identified homosexuality as pathological. The Labouchere Amendment to British criminal law in 1885 had raised public consciousness of same-sex passion by labeling any sexual contact between men as "gross indecency" liable to criminal prosecution. And residents of London and other large cities were increasingly aware of the subculture of "fairies," effeminate men given to dressing in women's clothing. In this highly charged atmosphere Carpenter and Symonds offered Walt Whitman as a model of a fully masculine man-loving man, a poet for whom comradeship and democracy were inextricably linked. Casting their lot with Whitman, they tried to promote a model of male sexual inversion that rejected any association with pathology or effeminacy and was instead linked with conventional masculinity and cross-class solidarity.

There was an urgency to their efforts, since both were well aware that a competing model of the man-loving man was gaining attention in England—one based on aestheticism and elitism and embodied in the spectacular figure of Oscar Wilde. Following Wilde's arrest and imprisonment in 1895 on charges of gross indecency, the association between an elite, effeminate style and homosexuality became so strong that Edward Carpenter's call for an alternative model was, for a time, literally silenced. Immediately following the Wilde trials, Carpenter's publisher, Fisher Unwin, reneged on an agreement to publish *Love's Coming-of-Age*, a book of sex-reform essays, and, for good measure, booted *Towards Democracy* off his list, returning the entire stock of two thousand unsold volumes to Carpenter. From the moment of Wilde's arrest, Carpenter wrote in his autobiography, "a sheer panic prevailed over *all* questions of sex, and especially of course questions of the Intermediate Sex." So strong was the social outrage aroused by the Wilde trials that even twenty years later, in his 1916 autobiography, Carpenter felt compelled to distance himself from the notorious aesthete by adding in a footnote that he had never met Oscar Wilde. Yet if Carpenter preferred to ignore Wilde, and the Wildean model of the male homosexual, in favor of Whitmanesque comradeship, Carpenter was surely aware that, a few years after his first pilgrimage to Camden, Wilde had also journeyed to New Jersey in order to embrace, figuratively and literally, the good gray poet.

✠ ✠ ✠

At the time of his 1882 American tour, Oscar Fingal O'Flahertie Wills Wilde was twenty-seven years old and had published nothing but one slim volume of poems. Yet such was his genius for self-promotion that he was already a trans-Atlantic celebrity. Wilde had so successfully established himself as the high priest of the aesthetic movement that, when Gilbert and Sullivan satirized the movement in their 1881 operetta *Patience*, they based Bunthorne, a leading character, on Wilde. Everyone recognized the similarities—the long hair, the flamboyant clothing, the paradoxical pronouncements on art and life. When Gilbert and Sullivan's producer, Richard D'Oyly Carte, decided to bring *Patience* to New York, he shrewdly calculated that a simultaneous lecture tour by Wilde could increase the audiences for *Patience*. D'Oyly Carte proposed the venture to the young poet, who readily agreed. Wilde landed in New York in early

January 1882, grandly announcing to the customs agent that he had nothing to declare but his genius.

Wilde lectured in New York on the English Renaissance, one of his two topics; the other was "The House Beautiful." Like Whitman, he was not a commanding public speaker—both men tended to fall into a monotone—but he was nonetheless well received, even if not quite to the extent that Wilde claimed. His New York audience was "larger and more wonderful than even Dickens had," he wrote to a friend in England, and he boasted that he had to employ several secretaries. One wrote autographs all day—he later, Wilde claimed, was hospitalized with writer's cramp—another did nothing but receive bouquets of flowers, and a third "whose hair resembles mine is obliged to send off locks of his own hair to the myriad maidens of the city, and so is rapidly becoming bald." Wilde slyly added, "Loving virtuous obscurity as much as I do, you can judge how much I dislike this lionizing."

His next stop was Philadelphia. "I do so hope to meet Mr. Whitman," he declared to a reporter. Once in Philadelphia Wilde demonstrated the sincerity of his desire by persuading his host, J. M. Stoddart, the American publisher of the Savoyard operas, to arrange a meeting. On January 18, 1882, Wilde presented himself at the door of George and Louisa Whitman's home.

The meeting of Wilde and Whitman was the subject of intense interest on the part of journalists and the public. If relatively few Americans had read either's poetry, almost everyone was familiar with the public personas of both men. They seemed diametrically opposed. The *Philadelphia Press* played up their differences in its headline about their encounter: "The Aesthetic Singer Visits the Good Gray Poet." Wilde, the Aesthetic Singer, was notorious for his elaborate witticisms and hyper-refined dress; Whitman, the Good Gray Poet, retained his reputation as a "rough," a plainspoken, simply attired, working-class figure. The two seemed to have no more in common than a peacock and a tomcat.

Contrary to expectations, the meeting of the two men was a huge success. Wilde stayed more than two hours. They began talking in the parlor, where Whitman offered his guest a bottle of his sister-in-law's homemade elderberry wine, then repaired upstairs to his study, where, as Whitman said, they could be on "thee and thou" terms. "I shall call you 'Oscar,' " the old poet said. "I like that so much," Oscar replied, laying a hand on Walt's knee. Whitman was in correspondence with many English poets and critics, and Wilde was famously well connected, so the two men discussed their mutual acquaintances and talked about art and the reading public. "We had a very happy time together," Whitman said later. On his way back to Philadelphia from Camden, Wilde was unwontedly silent. When Stoddart, attempting to get a conversation going, joked that Louisa Whitman's elderberry wine must have been hard to get down, Wilde abandoned his customary flippancy: "If it had been vinegar I should have drunk it all the same, for I have an admiration for that man which I can hardly express." Writing to "My Dear Dear Walt" several weeks later, Wilde said, "Before I leave America I must see you again—there is no one in this wide great world of America whom I love and honour so much." He made a second pilgrimage to Camden that spring.

Whitman was well aware of the astonishment with which his friendship with Wilde was greeted. Several years after their meeting he said to Horace Traubel with a touch of belligerence, "I have been told a thousand times what Wilde is but I do not see why Wilde is not what he is and I am not what I am with both of us friends according each other a mutual respect." Actually, their differences may be a large part of what drew the men to one another. In their statements to the press at the time of their first meeting, each was able to give the other exactly what he needed. Wilde tried to burnish the reputation of a poet who was still regarded as scandalous in his native country. He told a reporter that Whitman was "the grandest man I have ever seen, the simplest, most natural, and strongest character I have ever met in my life." And he linked Whitman, whose verse was considered crude and unartistic by most Americans, with the European high art tradition. "I admire him intensely," Wilde said of Whitman. "Dante Rossetti, Swinburne, William Morris and I often discuss him. There is something so Greek and sane about his poetry; it is so universal, so comprehensive. It has all the pantheism of Goethe and Schiller." Whitman repaid the compliment not by praising Wilde's verse, which it is doubtful he had read, but by associating the young aesthete with Whitman's own plainspoken, virile persona. "I think him genuine, honest, and manly," he told a reporter, then repeated: "He is so frank, and outspoken, and manly."

Oscar gave Walt class; Walt gave him manliness. From the beginning of his career, Wilde had delighted in transgressing gender boundaries. Photographs from his American tour show him wearing the velvet knee breeches, black silk hose, and patent leather pumps with bows in which he frequently appeared onstage. A cartoon published soon after his arrival in the United States emphasizes Wilde's effeminacy: a backwoodsman accompanied by an American eagle looks suspiciously at the British aesthete who, clad in breeches and pumps, seems lost in rapture over a sunflower. American audiences clearly regarded Wilde as effete. However, it is important to note that they did not consider him to be homosexual.

Their assumption of Wilde's sexual conventionality had several sources. Most obviously, the category of the homosexual had not yet entered the English language or the Anglo-American consciousness in the 1880s. Just as important, at the time there was no obvious link between effeminacy and sexuality. From the Renaissance until the twentieth century, effeminacy of the Wildean sort was associated with the well-established English role of the dandy. The Restoration rake, for example, was often portrayed as feminine in his clothing and mannerisms, but his sexuality was not questioned; the effeminate seducer was a stock character in English literature. Drawing on the long tradition of the English dandy, Wilde could establish his opposition to the conventional, black-suited Victorian bourgeois male without anyone's questioning his sexuality—including, it seems likely, Oscar Wilde himself.

Wilde's biographers think it probable that when he visited the United States in 1882, he had no sexual experience with men. That would not occur for another four years, after he had married and fathered two children. Unlike Symonds and Carpenter, Wilde seems to have readily met conventional sexual expectations in his teens and twenties, even as he dressed in an affected manner, concerned him-

FIGURE 4.5. Oscar Wilde in 1882 during his American tour. Library of Congress, Prints and Photographs Division.

FIGURE 4.6. Brother Jonathan—the iconic American—and the American eagle gaze warily at Oscar Wilde. Caricature by Arthur Bryan in the *Entr'acte*, January 21, 1882.

self with traditionally feminine areas such as home decoration, and expressed his admiration for male beauty. His American audiences may have laughed at his effeminacy but not at his sexuality. He was mocked at his Boston lecture by a group of Harvard students who minced down the aisle and into the front rows wearing a parody of Wildean costume and carrying flowers. Yet shortly before Wilde went to Boston, a group of young New York club men invited him on an expedition to sample the city's bordellos, an invitation he apparently accepted.

Sexuality has become so strong a marker of identity in the twenty-first century that it seems natural to class Walt Whitman and Oscar Wilde together as homosexuals. Yet at the time they met, both men would have protested any such label. Whitman believed that "Calamus" love was a potential within every person, not a special category of identity. For his part Wilde evidently had little experience of same-sex passion at the time, and throughout his career he resisted sexual theorizing. In contrast to Symonds and Carpenter, who were drawn to *Leaves of Grass* by the "Calamus" poems, Wilde never made any reference to Whitman's poems of manly love. Instead, he emphasized Whitman's religious significance; Wilde's one essay on Whitman is "The Gospel according to Walt Whitman." A review of Whitman's 1888 volume *November Boughs*, the essay is not the unqualified rave that its title might lead one to expect. In his opening Wilde locates himself between Whitman's "eloquent admirers" and "noisy detractors," promising a "saner view." This view is that while Whitman's verse itself may be lacking—Wilde implicitly deplores its formlessness—the poet is to be admired as a prophet. "He is the herald to a new era," Wilde writes and adds that Whitman is "a factor in the heroic and spiritual evolution of the human being." Devoid of cleverness or wordplay, Wilde's "Gospel" reveals his interest in a Whitmanesque spirituality. It foreshadows the lengthy, brilliant, and serious essay about the heroic and spiritual evolution of the human being that he would publish two years later, "The Soul of Man under Socialism."

"The Soul of Man" reveals a Victorian optimism akin to Carpenter's, a belief in a new era of human transformation made possible by the abolition of private property. Yet Wilde's vision of socialism is ultimately quite different from that of Carpenter, who saw socialism as a means to replace individualism with cross-class solidarity. Wilde, in contrast, favored socialism because he believed that it would promote individualism. "The chief advantage . . . of Socialism," he provocatively begins his essay, is that "it would relieve us from that sordid necessity of living for others." He dismisses the sober reflections of socialists like Carpenter as "sickly cant about duty" and "hideous cant about self-sacrifice." The primary aim of life, Wilde argues, is to allow the self, in all its glory, to blossom. "With the abolition of private property," he writes, "we shall have true beautiful, healthy Individualism. Nobody will waste his life in accumulating things, and the symbols for things. One will live."

For Wilde the political was always personal. Socialism was a way of not being bourgeois. So was having sex with men. Once Wilde, in his thirties, began physical relations with other men, he saw his sexual preferences as a way of distinguishing himself from the masses and asserting his individuality. Wilde regarded his sexuality as a mark of distinction, one more way—along with long hair, flamboyant clothing, and witty epigrams—of setting himself above the philistines.

His love for men led to heavily encoded works such as *The Picture of Dorian Gray* (1891), which conceals its characters' homoeroticism in clouds of ambiguous verbiage. It is clear from contemporary reviews and articles that most readers in the early 1890s were oblivious to the same-sex desires and behaviors of the novel's principal male characters. The novel was intended to be fully accessible only to a textual and sexual elite, who would have recognized the work's homoerotic undertones from the moment that Lord Henry Wotton is introduced as he lounges on a divan of Persian saddlebags, smoking opium-tainted cigarettes and admiring the painter Basil Hallward's portrait of Dorian Gray, a young man of "extraordinary personal beauty." In contrast, Whitman celebrates the love of comrades as openly as he celebrates the self. The "Calamus" poems are remarkably frank about the details of love between men: "The one I love most lay sleeping by me under the same cover in the cool night,

... / And his arm lay lightly around my breast," Whitman writes. He can be so explicit in part because, in the absence of a concept of homosexuality, his work could be read in the tradition of friendship poetry; in part because, as other "Calamus" poems make clear, the intense equality of private intimacy is linked to the public, political equality of democracy. "The special meaning of the 'Calamus' cluster," Whitman wrote in his 1876 preface, "mainly resides in its political significance." A few years earlier he had written in "Democratic Vistas" that "democracy infers such loving comradeship, as its most inevitable twin or counterpart, without which it will be incomplete, in vain, and incapable of perpetuating itself." Wilde believed that his sexuality placed him among an elite; Whitman imagined that the manly love of comrades could unite the entire American nation.

Following Wilde's imprisonment for gross indecency in 1895, he began including references to "Uranian love" in his letters, borrowing the term popularized by Symonds and Carpenter. It is possible to see *Uranian love* as a synonym of Whitman's phrenological term *adhesiveness*, one of many linguistic variants in the era before the love that dare not speak its name was labeled homosexuality. However, in important ways all three English disciples' versions of same-sex love differed fundamentally from Whitman's. Wilde's version—effeminate, elite, and individualistic—was obviously distinct. Symonds, for all his talk of the union of sexual inverts across class lines, thought of sexual behavior as primarily a private matter that should be tolerated by the state. Only Carpenter agreed with Whitman that the love of men for one another could be a positive political force, an integral part of a more democratic future. Yet even Carpenter seems politically timid in comparison to Whitman. Carpenter's theory of the intermediate sex depended on biologically based ideas about difference, the notion that sexual inversion was innate. Urnings had a crucial role to play in social evolution, he suggested, and the homogenic sentiment might become more widely diffused, but Carpenter's ideas were rooted in a rigid taxonomy of inborn sexual characteristics. Whitman, in contrast, was not trying to differentiate a special category of men in his "Calamus" poems; he was identifying a capacity for love that existed in every person:

To the East and to the West,
To the man of the Seaside State and of Pennsylvania,
To the Kanadian of the north, to the Southerner I love,
These with perfect trust to depict you as myself, the
    germs are in all men,
I believe the main purport of these States is to found a
    superb friendship, exaltè, previously unknown,
Because I perceive it waits, and has been always waiting,
    latent in all men.

The word *latent* may mislead post-Freudian readers. Whitman was not suggesting that all men were repressing a supposedly shameful tendency; rather, he was celebrating the seeds of a politically powerful democratic affection that existed within every person and that only needed encouragement to blossom. Whitman's poems of adhesiveness were intended not to set a few men apart but to bring all Americans together.

It is this inclusiveness that has made arguments about Whitman's sexuality so intense. When Oscar Wilde said, years after his visit to the United States, that the kiss of Walt Whitman was still on his lips, he was claiming an artistic consecration, a mark of special favor. Symonds and Carpenter used Whitman to defend the rights of a persecuted minority, to suggest that same-sex passion was natural and innate in a certain portion of the population. But Walt Whitman refused to consider himself as special or different. He was not a minority but a kosmos. In depicting himself he was depicting *you*, any reader, every reader—the germs of adhesive love are in *all* people. It is a message that remains more radical and unsettling than any that Symonds, Carpenter, or Wilde—for all their transgressive courage—ever offered.

CHAPTER FIVE

J. W. Wallace and the Eagle Street College: "Blazing More Fervidly Than Any"

God bless the Church & branch of the Church (with candelabras blazing more fervidly than any) that is planted & grown in Bolton.

ON A SPRING EVENING IN 1887 Dr. John Johnston and J. W. Wallace of Bolton, England, labored together over a letter to Walt Whitman, who was about to celebrate his sixty-eighth birthday. "Dear Walt," they began boldly—then, appalled at their temerity, hastened to explain: "In no less familiar or colder terms *can* we bring ourselves to address you, the most loved of friends, though such a salutation from strangers to anyone but yourself would seem an impertinence." The two young men went on to introduce themselves in similarly awkward, earnest terms: Johnston was a physician who had been delivered from "soul-benumbing scepticism" by Whitman's verse, Wallace an architect's assistant who regarded *Leaves of Grass* as a "Gospel, bringing glad tidings of great joy." Posting their letter to Camden, they were not certain they would receive a reply, but to their delight Whitman wrote each a brief note in return. Whitman did not respond to every letter from readers; he tossed requests for autographs into the fire after thriftily saving any stamps enclosed. But he was always stirred by letters from young men declaring their love and allegiance. "Avowal letters," Whitman called them, and such letters always received a brief acknowledgment. It is likely that he would have replied to Johnston and Wallace's heartfelt avowal letter in any case, but the two friends assured a response by enclosing a ten-pound note as a birthday present. The parsimonious poet never declined a gift of cash, and he gratefully acknowledged both their generous present and their "good affectionate letter."

Whitman could not have foreseen the relationship that would develop from this opening exchange. During the next few years Wallace, Johnston, and the Eagle Street College—Johnston's playful name for a small group of friends who met weekly at Wallace's house—became the center of Whitmanism in Great Britain. R. M. Bucke and Edward Carpenter visited Bolton; John Burroughs, John Addington Symonds, and Horace Traubel corresponded with Wallace and Johnston; and eminent political activists and leaders paid tribute to the college's fervent espousal of the Whitman gospel. The college's improbable rise to prominence came about, everyone agreed, because of J. W. Wallace. He was an unlikely leader: unprepossessing in appearance, with myopic eyes distorted behind thick spectacles, a throat condition that left his voice soft and husky, and a manner so self-effacing and diffident that he could scarcely order for himself in a restaurant. Yet for a few heady years it seemed that the Eagle Street College might play a central role in transforming Great Britain into a socialist utopia suffused with the liberal spirituality and democratic comradeship that Wallace and company found in *Leaves of Grass*.

‡ ‡ ‡

By the time James William Wallace was born in 1853, the international textile trade had turned Bolton, about twelve miles from Manchester, into an industrial center. The town had so many mills crowded into it that on the infrequent "smoke holidays," when factories shut down, families would walk about and marvel at the views of the nearby Lancashire hills, normally invisible through the smog. Wallace was born in the Haulgh, a working-class district of soot-begrimed attached brick houses; with one exception he never trav-

FIGURE 5.1. J. W. Wallace c. 1887, when he first wrote to Whitman. Bolton Central Library.

eled more than a few dozen miles from his birthplace. He was an only child, never married, and lived with his parents on Eagle Street for much of his adult life. He left school at fourteen to work in a Bolton architect's office and stayed with the firm until his retirement forty-five years later. The facts of his biography suggest a life as colorless and constrained as the blueprints he spent his days producing. Yet his death in 1926 occasioned a flood of affectionate testimonials—two published biographies, numerous lengthy speeches written out and carefully preserved, and letters from eminent public figures, including Ramsay MacDonald, the prime minister. Wallace's friends repeatedly spoke of a man with an extraordinarily attractive personality and a rare gift for friendship. He was utterly selfless, they said, a saint and a mystic—a St. Francis of the industrial North, a Boddhisatva in a business suit.

They agreed that Wallace's mysticism dated from his mother's death in 1885, when he was thirty-one. Wallace and his mother were unusually close. His father, a millwright, was frequently away from home, fitting out mills as far away as Russia. Mrs. Wallace, crippled by rheumatism, depended heavily on her son; each night he carried her up narrow stairs to her bedroom. A warm-hearted, uncomplaining woman, she never told her son about the cancer that was destroying her organs; he found out one morning when she was unable to rise from bed. The ten days that followed were the most wrenching of Wallace's life. He spent every moment possible with his mother, doing his best to make her comfortable. His father was in Bolton, doctors and nurses looked in regularly, but Wallace, fittingly, was alone with his mother at the moment she died—the moment also of Wallace's "New Birth."

His friend Fred Wild called it that. Wild, a cotton waste dealer who had known Wallace since boyhood, said that everyone could see the transformation in Wallace after his mother's death. "It was not that his character was in any way changed," Wild said, "nor that his mode of speech or his daily action were in any way altered." Rather, "it was in the heart of him that the great change was." Externally, things continued as before. Wallace remained at home with his father, walked each day the few blocks to his job at the architectural firm. "But there it was," Wild said—the fact of Wallace's "Illumination." It showed in "a steady calmness and air of peace with him. His thoughts and actions were all for the help of others." The death of his mother precipitated a crisis that Wallace, a spiritual seeker, interpreted in religious terms. At the moment of her death, he wrote, "It seemed to me . . . that I stood in the very presence of the Infinite Love and felt it through my being." From that moment on Wallace embarked on a profound, if vaguely defined, spiritual quest.

The details of Wallace's spiritual journey are unique, but in many ways he is broadly representative of his lower-middle-class peers. The British lower middle class was largely a creation of the nineteenth century. When Wallace entered the workforce in the 1860s, the vast majority of English families—about three-quarters—were considered working class. At the lower end of that class were malnourished families in urban slums; at the upper were skilled workers such as Wallace's father, who could afford to buy an attached house and to send his children to the local grammar school. Members of the working class had no hope of entering the British upper class and little chance of rising into the middle class, which, defined at the time as those earning more than three hundred pounds a year, constituted fewer than 2 percent of the population. However, working-class children like Wallace who showed a talent for studies could move into the lower middle class. Great Britain had long had a petty bourgeoisie of shopkeepers and small businesspeople. In the nineteenth century those traditional members of the lower middle class were joined by increasing numbers of white-collar salaried workers—schoolteachers, managers, and, most notably, clerks, who served the rapidly expanding fields of government and industry.

The Victorian lower middle class was notoriously conservative, obsessed with status, clinging to respectability on an income little greater than that of skilled workers. Unlike the upper class, members of the lower middle class generally were religious nonconformists, attending the Protestant chapels that proliferated in Great Britain during the nineteenth century. Unlike the working class, they dressed respectably, kept out of pubs, and for the most part voted

Tory. Determined to rise in the world, they supervised their children's studies and filled their savings accounts.

Yet out of this unpromising milieu came many of the era's political and cultural radicals. The lower middle class's emphasis on self-improvement encouraged intellectual independence, and its religious seriousness could spur social conscience. Wallace, typically, was raised as a Presbyterian and remained active in the church through his teens. Then he, like thousands of other educated Britons, came across the works of Charles Darwin. "Darwinism demolished for me the Biblical account of creation, the authority of the Bible and the account it gives of the origin of evil and the fall of man," he wrote. With that, "the whole theological superstructure" toppled.

The conventional understanding of the era is that once Darwinism demolished religious orthodoxy, the way was cleared for modern secular culture, with the gospel of upward mobility filling the void. Although that was true for many, thousands of young people like Wallace rejected the dominant values of modern culture: career success, competition, materialism, and the nuclear family. Moreover, although they rebelled against the narrow orthodoxy of the Protestant homes in which they were raised, they also turned against the secularism prevalent in Victorian intellectual life. It was largely members of the lower middle class who filled the new religious movements that blossomed across the late nineteenth-century British landscape: New Thought, Theosophy, Spiritualism, Ethical Culture—a smorgasbord of beliefs available for the sampling.

Frequently drawing upon Christian religious forms but rejecting creedal orthodoxy, these religious movements appealed to young adults adrift in a rapidly changing culture. Modern secular culture appeared to them soulless, yet traditional churches seemed burdened by cumbersome institutional hierarchies, outmoded liturgies, and centuries-old dogma at odds with contemporary science. In contrast, the new metaphysical religions welcomed religious seekers. They provided an instant community for lower-middle-class individuals who were alienated from their families and without the forms of support available to those both above and below them on the socioeconomic scale—the economic security enjoyed by the middle and upper classes; the trade unions, social organizations, and neighborhood pubs that served the working class.

Living in the industrial North, particularly fertile soil for new religious movements, Wallace would have breathed the atmosphere of alternative religious fervor, preparing him for his mystical illumination at his mother's death. From that moment he was looking for a personal connection to a spiritual guide. Across England small groups of spiritual seekers had attached themselves to contemporary prophet-artists: Tolstoyans in Purleigh, Ruskinians in Liverpool. When Walt Whitman responded to Wallace and Johnston's birthday letter, the Bolton Whitmanites were born.

✠ ✠ ✠

With the earnestness typical of his class, after Wallace left grammar school he frequently gathered with friends to discuss books and ideas. For years he regarded Carlyle and Emerson as his masters. Both writers had enormous cultural prestige in Victorian England as prophets who railed against the age's materialism. Wallace regarded both as spiritual teachers also. "Each believed in his own way in a divine purpose," Wallace wrote in a memoir, "Emerson with genial and growing optimism, Carlyle with an accompanying Hebraic sense of the mystery and terror of evil." However, both writers died in the early 1880s, a few years before Wallace's mystical illumination. Searching for a spiritual guide after his mother's death, he turned to the writer often regarded as Carlyle's heir: John Ruskin. Now best known for the art criticism he published early in his career, in the late nineteenth century Ruskin was revered as a social critic who attacked industrial capitalism and, drawing upon the religious fervor of his evangelical upbringing, preached the dignity and sanctity of the common man. One year after his mother's death, Wallace reached out to Ruskin, sending him a birthday greeting. "Dear Sir," he began. "I trust you will pardon me—though a total stranger— for presuming to add my congratulations and best wishes to those which you will receive along with this, and briefly expressing the love and gratitude which . . . I owe you. . . . I . . . am coming with growing force to recognize you as my master." Wallace optimistically posted the letter to Ruskin's home in the Lake District, then waited for a reply. Nothing. He could not have known that by his sixty-seventh birthday, Ruskin had fallen into severe mental illness and was in the grip of agonies that the proffered discipleship of a Bolton architect's assistant could do nothing to relieve.

The resilient Wallace quickly shifted his attention elsewhere. Not long before, he had read *Leaves of Grass* for the first time. Thanks to the efforts of William Michael Rossetti, Anne Gilchrist, Symonds, Carpenter, and others, by the 1880s Whitman was as well known in England among the educated classes as he was in the United States. It was inevitable that Wallace, as an admirer of Emerson's, would be led to Whitman at some point. When Wallace picked up *Leaves of Grass* after his mother's death, Whitman's faith in immortality proved immensely reassuring. "The smallest sprout shows there is really no death," Whitman writes in "Song of Myself":

> And if ever there was it led forward life, and does not
>   wait at the end to arrest it,
> And ceas'd the moment life appear'd.
> All goes onward and outward, nothing collapses,
> And to die is different from what any one supposed,
>   and luckier.

Three months after writing to Ruskin, Wallace decided to devote an evening's discussion to Whitman and invited an acquaintance to join the three men who were regulars at his Eagle Street house: his boyhood friend Fred Wild; William Pimblett, who was a journalist; and Wentworth Dixon, a lawyer's clerk. "Fred Wild, Pimblett, and Dixon have been in the habit of coming to our house on Monday evenings for reading and discussion," Wallace wrote in late May 1886. "Next Monday is Whitman's birthday, so I proposed having a 'Whitman evening' and shall be glad if you will join us." The recipient of his letter was thirty-two-year-old John Johnston, who had come to Bolton ten years earlier from his native Scotland.

Wallace could not have chosen a more appropriate person. Like him, Johnston was an earnest spiritual seeker and an admirer of Carlyle. The energetic young general practitioner was already a prominent figure in Bolton, frequently seen making house calls on a three-wheeled cycle. A civic-minded person, he volunteered in the local ambulance corps and held multiple medical-related public appointments. In addition, he was an enthusiastic amateur poet who delighted in writing humorous poems and song lyrics in Scots and Lancashire dialects. The combination of Johnston's high spirits and Wallace's sweet-tempered charisma quickly drew additional young men to the Monday evening gatherings at Wallace's home. Johnston dubbed the group the Eagle Street College and celebrated Wallace and "the boys" in a dialect poem:

> In a quare little house in a quare little sthrate
> There's a quare little room, about twelve fut be eight,
> An 'tis there that the 'rale dacint boys' congregate
> Wid the Masther ov Aigle Sthrate Collidge.
>> Och boys! He's the Phelosipher!
>> He is the wan for the knowledge!
>> He's as good as he's clever
>> An' we'll stick forever
>> To the Masther ov Aigle Sthrate Collidge!

Johnston, like so many Victorians, was a natural hero worshiper. He idolized Wallace, and within months after meeting him, Johnston idolized the Masther's new spiritual guide: Walt Whitman.

In May 1887, one year after his invitation to the Monday evening gathering on Eagle Street, Johnston enthusiastically joined his new friend in writing their joint birthday letter to Whitman. Thrilled by Whitman's response to this initial letter, Johnston and Wallace sent birthday greetings each of the next three years. Whitman replied only once, in 1889, but the two Bolton enthusiasts were undeterred. When Johnston was advised to take a sea voyage for his health, he decided to make a Whitman pilgrimage. He wrote Whitman a letter informing the poet of his intention, then sailed for Philadelphia in July 1890. The moment he arrived, he took the ferry to Camden.

When Johnston knocked at the door of 328 Mickle Street and was shown upstairs to Whitman's large, cluttered bedroom, the poet greeted him with banalities about the weather and an old man's mild confusion: "So you've been travelling about our States, have you?" Whitman inquired. When Johnston replied that he had just that day landed in Philadelphia, Whitman gracefully covered his tracks: "Ah, I am confounding you with another friend of mine." The two spoke for more than an hour, discussing mutual acquaintances in the United States and Great Britain and talking about the Eagle Street College. As Virginia Woolf put it in a review of Johnston's memoir of his visit, the elderly man whom Johnston encountered had "much more likeness to a retired farmer who spends his time in gossip with passers-by than to a poet with a message." The ordinariness of their conversation did not discourage Johnston. The open-hearted, emotionally effusive young physician had come to America prepared to be overwhelmed, and in his eyes Whitman's simplicity in conversation served to set off the poet's "Jove-like . . . majesty." Johnston left their first encounter exhilarated, convinced that he had been "face to face with the living embodiment of all that was good, noble and lovable in humanity."

Johnston spent two more days in Camden, followed by pilgrimages to other Whitman sites: his Long Island birthplace, his youthful haunts in Brooklyn, and his disciple John Burroughs's Hudson Valley farm. When Johnston returned to England, he privately published an account of his visit, a pamphlet that, like so many of the disciples' writings, is as much hagiography as memoir. Like O'Connor, Burroughs, Bucke, and Carpenter, Johnston wrote in profuse detail about the poet's physical appearance, devoting several pages to "the irresistible magnetism of his sweet, aromatic presence." Convinced of the significance of his encounter with the man whom he and Wallace regarded as a modern messiah, Johnston recorded in painstaking detail the hours he spent in Whitman's presence, at times adopting biblical cadences, as if conscious that he was composing a gospel: "I bade him good-night," he wrote of parting from Whitman on the first day of his visit, "and went to my hotel, pondering deeply on many things, and marvelling at the wondrous magnetic attraction this man had for me—for I felt I could stay with him for ever."

When Whitman received a copy of Johnston's pamphlet, he called it "fearfully eulogistic." Nevertheless, he was flattered by Johnston's devotion and asked the doctor to send copies of the pamphlet to friends and relatives in the United States and Europe. Johnston's visit cemented the relationship between Whitman and the Eagle Street College, and Whitman began writing the members brief letters at least once a week, frequently more often. Wallace and Johnston responded with a flood of letters and gifts. "What staunch tender fellows those Englishmen are!" Whitman wrote to Bucke. "I doubt if ever a fellow had such a splendid emotional send-back response as I have had f'm those Lancashire chaps under the lead of Dr. J. & J.W.W.—it cheers and nourishes my very heart." "It surprises me a bit that you should be so taken with these Bolton folks," sniffed Herbert Gilchrist on one of his visits to Whitman. "They're not famous in England at all." Whitman roared back at him: "It surprises you, does it, Herbert? Well: I've had my belly full of famous people! Thank God they're just nobody at all, like all the people who are worth while!" Whitman, always receptive to young male disciples, responded to the Bolton nobodies' lavish professions of love and devotion. The Englishmen, for their part, found in *Leaves of Grass* a gospel perfectly suited to their circumstances in both form and content.

As Andrew Elfenbein has pointed out, *Leaves of Grass*, like Edward Carpenter's *Towards Democracy*, is written in a "middle style" that is "poetical enough to signal elevated utterance but prose-like enough to detach itself from the pressured artifice of Victorian poets like D. G. Rossetti or Tennyson." The style appealed to lower-middle-class readers who were intellectually ambitious yet lacked the intense grounding in the classics common to Rossetti, Tennyson, and their middle- and upper-class audience. In addition, for all Whitman's celebration of the common worker, his poetry was not read by the working class of either North America or Great Britain. A taste for Whitman allowed one both to declare sympathy for democracy and to distinguish oneself from those lower on the social

FIGURE 5.2. Walt Whitman photographed by John Johnston during his 1890 pilgrimage to Camden. Bayley/Whitman Collection of Ohio Wesleyan University.

scale. As Elfenbein says, *Leaves of Grass* nicely avoided "both the elitism of established Victorian writers and the vulgarity of traditional labor lyrics."

Whitman's verse form was perfectly suited for the clerks and minor professionals of the Eagle Street College. In addition, they were attracted by his religious message. All the men of the college were spiritual seekers, and their Monday evening conversations resembled a Unitarian discussion group, with earnest debate on topics such as the immortality of the soul. Early in the group's history Wallace lectured to them on the religious dimensions of *Leaves of Grass*. He argued that Whitman's purpose was to liberate the true, spiritual self from the inferior self by which it is encumbered, making "the divine pride of man in himself the radical foundation of the new religion." Wallace, mindful of the need to bring along slowly the members of the college less devoted to Whitman than were Johnston and he, acknowledged that this individualistic doctrine might sound cold in comparison to the comforting conventional belief in God as "the father, ever . . . helpful to his children." Wallace went on to explain Whitman's immanentist theology: the poet recognizes God "in all the experiences of life, and in all the shows of this wonderful universe. [God] is not a far distant ruler, but a spirit ever speaking to our spirits. The world is *not* made up of dead lifeless matter . . . but is itself spiritual, supernatural and miraculous." ("Why, who makes much of a miracle?" Whitman wrote in an early poem. "As to me I know of nothing else but miracles.")

Wallace was attracted to both the individualistic religious message of *Leaves of Grass* and its fervent gospel of comradeship. He saw the college's spiritual earnestness and the men's affection for one another as inextricably intertwined. There were times, he wrote, when their discussions of religion and philosophy "led us, by imperceptible stages, to a deepened intimacy, in which the inmost quests and experiences of the soul were freely expressed, and each grew conscious of our essential unity, as of a larger self which included us all." All the men of the college experienced this sense of unity, frequently declaring their love for one another in fervent terms.

Even Johnston's humorous songs were often love lyrics in essence, as in this tribute to Wallace on his birthday:

> Braw chiefs who dae haud WALLACE dear,
> Gude freens than wham nane love him mair,
> Welcome gie him, fealty swear,
>   On this auspicious day.
> Now's the day and now's the hour
> We honour pay the Man whase power
> Unites us a' the warld ower,
>   In chains o' Love for aye.

The Scots dialect does not disguise the song's remarkably open declarations of affection. "The College Battle Song," plus numerous other songs and poems and letters by members of the Eagle Street College, constitute a collective mash note to J. W. Wallace.

The college challenges stereotypes of Victorian masculinity, the common view that late nineteenth-century Englishmen were reserved and unexpressive. The men of the college were remarkably free in declaring their love for one another. Wallace had bound them in chains of love, they sang, and Wallace responded fervidly: "I . . . shall think of you constantly," he wrote to Johnston the evening before the doctor departed for America. The doctor was journeying to see Walt, who made possible the emotional expressiveness of the Eagle Street group. Whitman offered them a model of male affection, and their allegiance to Whitman provided the Bolton group a haven within Victorian culture, a cultural safe space in which they could freely express their love for one another. "This little band o' brithers true's defiant o' assault," Johnston wrote in one of his college songs, "For isna ilka member o't 'sealed o' the tribe o' Walt'?"

To be sealed of the tribe of Walt was to be a member of a subculture that gave the same value to intense male friendships that the larger culture gave to heterosexual courtship and marriage. The men of the college seized on the Whitmanesque ideal of comradeship and waved the word like a banner. Whitman gave them a large and sacred purpose. They were not simply a group of friends meeting weekly for cocoa and discussion but the vanguard of an army dedicated to establishing "the institution of the dear love of comrades." Wallace appropriated these words from Whitman in describing how he and Johnston gave Fred Wild a copy of *Leaves of Grass* inscribed with a verse from "Calamus": "With the love of comrades / With the lifelong love of comrades." By providing the men of the Eagle Street College a ready-made language to express their love, as well as suitable tokens of affection—Wallace ordered direct from Camden multiple copies of a pocket *Leaves of Grass*—Whitman made possible the creation of a male "world of love and ritual."

The phrase comes from a classic essay by Carroll Smith-Rosenberg on nineteenth-century women's intimate friendships. Only recently have historians noted that at least some Victorian men were able to shape similar worlds for themselves. Many friendships among the members of the Eagle Street College preceded Wallace and Johnston's discovery of *Leaves of Grass*, but Whitman provided the language and rituals that enabled them to draw together with a closeness unusual among men of the era. One college member wrote a song to the tune of "Auld Lang Syne" that reveals the uses they made of Whitman:

> O manly love of comrades!
> Cease not until life ends!
> In Whitman's name we plight our troth,
> And swear we'll aye be friends.

Whitman's name enabled the college men to pledge their love for one another in vows that mimicked a wedding ceremony but that were nevertheless "manly." The college members extended the loving fellowship of their meetings by writing up reports of the events, having them printed, and then giving them to one another as keepsakes, invariably signed "with love." Walter Hawkins, who joined the college during the 1890s and chronicled many of its meetings, noted how rare such demonstrations of male friendship were in the culture at large. He wrote that the Whitmanites' celebrations were marked by "a freedom of expression, a genuine outspokenness, which is as delightful as it is uncommon." They pledged their "loving fellowship" to one another without "false shame," enabled to do so "in keeping with Walt's own utterances respecting comradeship."

When an American Whitmanite visited Bolton, Wentworth Dixon wrote a tribute that combined "Calamus" with Gilbert and Sullivan's "Titwillow" song from *The Mikado*:

> Institutions of dear love of comrades to found,
>   We are ready, quite "ready, aye ready,"
> With bands of affection to bind the world round,
>   We are ready, quite "ready, aye ready."
> To stamp out class feeling, war, bitterness, strife,
>   To establish full freedom, abundance of life,
> To make brotherhoods of friends universally rife,
>   Be ready, quite "ready, aye ready."

Dixon's lyrics reveal the college's simultaneously serious and playful approach to Whitmanesque comradeship. The lyrics suggested that institutions of the "dear love of comrades" had the potential to transform global society at the same time as they provided the men of the college with an excuse to sing a humorous song that drew them closer to their visitor and to one another.

Dixon's lighthearted appropriation of "Calamus" signals the college's distance from Symonds's and Carpenter's interpretations of Whitman. Symonds wished to use "Calamus" on behalf of his campaign for legal tolerance of sexual inversion; Carpenter theorized that Whitman and other sexually "intermediate types" represented the evolutionary advance guard of humanity. In contrast, the men of the Eagle Street College saw comrade love as a powerful but unproblematic sentiment that had nothing to do with sex. At one of the college's Whitman birthday celebrations, Wallace delivered a lengthy address on the "Calamus" poems that is remarkable for its complete obliviousness to their erotic dimensions. Near the end of his talk he quoted the conclusion to a poem in which Whitman says that he will give the calamus root "only to them that love as I myself am capable of loving." The line has become a touchstone for gay critics who argue that Whitman virtually outs himself here by proclaiming that the root meaning of "Calamus" is evident only to same-sex lovers. However, Wallace blithely sidestepped any sexual connotation. Whitman is referring, he said, to those who love "with complete self-abandonment." Wallace thus transformed what might be read as sexual innuendo into a signifier of spiritual depths.

It would be easy to argue that Wallace was simply repressing the erotic dimensions of the college men's intense friendships, but that would be as misleading as to insist that homoerotic elements were completely absent. As Smith-Rosenberg notes of women's friendships during this era, applying modern binary views of love and sexuality—people are either straight or gay; relations are either physical or not—distorts the more flexible notions prevalent in the nineteenth century. She argues that as paradoxical as it may seem to modern minds, many friendships in this era were "*both sensual and platonic.*"

Wallace and Johnston prove her point. The emotional intensity of their friendship is revealed in the letters and gifts they exchanged, their effusive proclamations of love. That their intimacy had a sensual dimension is evident from Johnston's diary, in which he casually notes that after a college meeting Wallace stayed behind, and "we had a right good talk together before we went to bed—and after too (for we slept together, my wife being away)." It's important to remember that during the Anglo-American nineteenth century, sharing a bed did not necessarily have any sexual connotation. Boys frequently grew up sharing a bed with a brother, and bed sharing, even with strangers, was common in inns and lodging houses; Abraham Lincoln, for example, shared a bed with his landlord Joshua Speed after arriving in Springfield, Illinois, as a young lawyer. John Burroughs occasionally shared a bed with Walt Whitman in Civil War–era Washington, but it is unlikely that they had sexual relations. Nevertheless, there was an affectionate sensuality in all these relationships: between Lincoln and Speed, Burroughs and Whitman, and Wallace and Johnston.

Wallace and Johnston sharply distinguished the physically and emotionally demonstrative friendships within the Eagle Street College from the emerging category of "sexual inversion" promoted by John Addington Symonds, with whom they began corresponding in the early 1890s. Describing a letter from Symonds to Wallace on the topic of sexual inversion and the "Calamus" poems, Johnston wrote in his diary, "This . . . to me is one of the most damnably atrocious suggestions conceivable. . . . To speak of 'sexual inversion' as being implied seems to me nothing short of a gross insult to Walt himself. Surely Symonds cannot be serious in that odious suggestion!" Wallace reacted to the same letter more in sorrow than in anger. He told a friend that he had replied to Symonds with a sixteen-page letter: "It seems curious to me that it should fall to my lot to explain to him what 'the drift' of Calamus is and to show how ungrounded are the fears which he entertains of one direction of its possible influence. Is it not a striking illustration of the sophistication and stunting effect of what is called 'literary culture' that Symonds . . . should be so much at sea in dealing with the fresh natural emotions expressed in 'Calamus' and well enough known to simple and unlettered people?"

Johnston and Wallace reacted strongly to Symonds's suggestion of a link between "Calamus" and sexual inversion. Yet as Harry Cocks has pointed out, their disavowal of Symonds's homoerotic interpretation served to enable romantic friendships among the men of the Eagle Street College, acting "to remove the taint of corruption from any association with Whitman [and] licensing their own comradeship by displacing any possible homoerotic desire into a distant and abject realm of moral corruption and disease." With Symonds relegated to the realm of overly sophisticated Continental literary culture, Johnston and Wallace were able to develop strong ties to Edward Carpenter, who at the time was much less insistent about pressing his own "homogenic" interpretation of Whitman. Johnston and Wallace met Carpenter in 1891, when he visited Bolton. A year later Carpenter invited the two friends to stay at his Millthorpe farm. Wallace, then and afterward, was almost comically resistant to viewing Carpenter as having any association with sexual inversion. In notes of his visit Wallace described how pleasant it was "to see how naturally and simply Carpenter and George Hukin intertwined arms round each other's waists like boys or lovers." Other evidence suggests that Carpenter and Hukin almost certainly were lovers, but to Wallace sexual love between the men remained only a figure of speech, as innocent as the suggestion that they acted like boys.

Johnston's position as a married man perhaps served psychologically to help him distance himself from any personal connection to sexual inversion, even though he acknowledged in his diary that he was "intensely interested" in the subject. The other college men were also married, except for Wallace. Wallace's biography seems to fit classic Freudian conceptions of homosexual development: raised in a family where the father was often absent, his "tastes and pursuits [making him] more a 'home bird' than most young men," he was unusually close to his mother. However, there is no evidence that Wallace ever had sexual relations with either men or women; he seems to have channeled his sexual energy into intense friendships with dozens of people of both sexes. In 1891, the year after Johnston's pilgrimage to Camden, Wallace added to his wide network of friends the eminent Canadian Whitmanite R. M. Bucke.

✢ ✢ ✢

In the summer of 1891 Bucke sailed for England with two purposes in mind: to secure British patents for the water meter he was developing and to serve as a roaming Whitman ambassador. When he wrote Wallace and Johnston that he would visit Bolton after landing in Liverpool, the two friends were nervously aflutter. Bucke's visit came at an emotionally charged moment for the Eagle Street College. Following Johnston's 1890 visit to Whitman and the poet's frequent correspondence with the Bolton disciples in the months following, the college increasingly assumed the character of a Whitmanite church. When attendance flagged for a period, Wallace wrote a lengthy epistle to the group, emphasizing the members' special status as Whitman's chosen apostles in England. "Since Christ died . . . no greater spiritual force has appeared on earth than is incarnated in Walt Whitman," he wrote. "I ask you—are we not—as members of a Society dear to *him*, as friends of *his*, . . . as objects of his paternal interest and affection—*bound*—by all the answering and responding affection and reverence . . . of which we are capable, to maintain and develop our College, and the spirit of 'comradeship' which binds it together? To this end we must all work and definitely consecrate ourselves." Wallace noted that "Churches and Chapels have lost their attractions" for the members of the College; he offered Whitmanism as a substitute. "Let us make our little *College* a church! a church where, without formulas or ritual, with honest freedom of opinion and speech, we may nevertheless meet 'in His name.'" Wallace's version of Whitmanism appealed to adherents because, like many new religious movements, it was perfectly poised between radical rejection of existing religious institutions and comforting embrace of familiar forms: *Leaves of Grass* was a gospel, the college served as a church, and Whitman himself was parallel to Christ.

Wallace communicated his religiously charged sense of events in a letter to Whitman shortly before Bucke's arrival, writing that the doctor's visit would be "a consecration of the life you have lived—an apostolic visit to the small church planted here." Whitman was flattered by Wallace's praise, and he fanned the flames of his English disciples' devotion: "God bless the Church & branch of the Church (with candelabras blazing more fervidly than any) that is planted & grown in Bolton," he responded to Wallace. With Whitman's blessing ringing in their ears, Wallace and Johnston met Bucke at his disembarkment and escorted him to Johnston's house, where a dozen members of the Eagle Street College were waiting. The men treated their guest to dinner, toasts, and a song that began:

> Comrade-stranger, glad we greet you.
> One and all are pleased to meet you,
> Cordial friendship here shall heat you,
>   Whilst with us you stay.
> Friend of Walt! Be that the token,
> That enough our hearts to open,
> Though no other word be spoken
>   Friends are we alway.

"Most of the evening I laughed and the rest of it I could have cried their warm-hearted friendship for you and for me was so manifest and so touching," Bucke wrote to Whitman. In a letter to Horace Traubel written the same day, Bucke was more ebullient: "I was very greatly gratified to find that they realize the magnitude of this Whitman business just as fully as we do—nothing that I said of the meaning and probable future of Whitmanism (and I spoke out pretty plainly) staggered them at all—they had thought it all before; and I tell you, Horace, I am more than ever . . . convinced that we are right at the centre of the largest thing of these late centuries." Bucke was drawing grand conclusions from a gathering of a dozen Lancashire friends, but Wallace and Johnston shared his faith in the future of Whitmanism. Bucke urged Wallace to return to America with him in order to meet Whitman. The men of the college immediately collected the funds to pay for Wallace's trip, but their shy, diffident master could not make up his mind to go. Finally, just before Bucke was scheduled to depart, Wallace agreed. When Bucke returned to Bolton before sailing from Liverpool, bringing Edward Carpenter along with him, the college members threw a grand farewell dinner for Wallace and their guests.

It was at this August 1891 dinner that Bucke made his speech trying out ideas for what later, thanks to Carpenter, he would call cosmic consciousness. The speech was greeted with loud applause from those assembled, but the discussion afterward—as recorded in a lovingly preserved transcript—reveals that most members of the college were there because of their affection for Wallace rather than their comprehension of Whitman's poetry. "Walt Whitman has hitherto eluded me," acknowledged Samuel Hodgkinson, a hosiery manufacturer, "but one may hope in the light of Dr. Bucke's speech to again tackle *Leaves of Grass*." He soon shifted to more comfortable ground. "One great benefit I have most indisputably derived from Whitman is the love of brotherhood and camaraderie. . . . If this is practical Whitman it is a great and noble thing." Joining in a ritual of brotherhood, the college members then sang a series of songs specially written for the occasion. The farewell to Wallace had the following chorus:

FIGURE 5.3. The Eagle Street College, August 1891. Wallace (left) and Bucke are seated. Johnston is standing behind Bucke's left shoulder; behind Johnston, with hats on, are Fred Wild (left) and Edward Carpenter. Bolton Central Library.

> Cheer! Boys, Cheer! With voices loud and frantic!
> Cheer! Boys, Cheer! Till roof and rafters ring!
> For our beloved Master is going to cross th'Atlantic
> To visit dear old Whitman, boys, our Comrade and
>   our King.

The song reveals Wallace's centrality to the group and Whitman's dual role as one of the boys and a distant, majestic presence only dimly comprehended by some members.

With the boys' songs still in their ears, Bucke and Wallace sailed from Liverpool. Like Johnston, Wallace headed to Camden immediately after landing. "Well, you've come to be disillusioned, have you?" Walt teased him as they shook hands in greeting. "Indeed, I *was* a little disillusioned," Wallace acknowledged in his memoir of his visit. However, his initial disappointment soon wore off, and his memoir is even more fearfully eulogistic than Johnston's. "I shall

FIGURE 5.4. J. W. Wallace and R. M. Bucke, August 1891. Bolton Central Library.

never forget the noble and pensive majesty of [Whitman's] appearance," Wallace writes. "His expression was . . . that of one who is visibly clothed with immortality, sharing to the full the limitations of our mortal life and yet ranging in worlds beyond our ken."

Unlike Johnston, who spent only three days in Camden, Wallace remained for three weeks, visiting Whitman daily. Horace Traubel described him on their first meeting as "tall, slender, with a good head and fine mouth—eyes losing much expression by their defect—a good hand—nervous manner—voice quite weak." Wallace was personally unprepossessing, yet his emotional warmth drew people to him. By the time he left Camden he had so endeared himself to Horace and Anne Traubel that they named their son, born the next year, after him. Whitman also was drawn to the emotionally demonstrative Englishman, and he was flattered by the devotion of the Bolton "branch church," as he liked to call it. Yet at the same time he was uneasy with the more extreme demonstrations of the college's religious fervor. "Wallace seems disposed to worship 'Leaves of Grass'—to see it as the summing up," Whitman said at the time of Wallace's visit. He and Johnston "say too much about me as a man—are too extravagant. . . . In earlier ages, Wallace would have made a follower of Jesus—a saint—a disciple!"

"My visit to Camden has only confirmed and deepened my previous reverence" for Whitman, Wallace wrote afterward. When Whitman died soon after Wallace's return to England, he was prepared to demonstrate how apt was the poet's assessment of Wallace as a would-be saint and disciple. Four days after Whitman's death Wallace gathered the college for a memorial meeting that had the tone of an Easter celebration; it was as if the rock had already rolled from the entrance to the tomb. "What I think we all ought to feel," Wallace told the group, "is that the change at death so far from severing him from us, brings him closer to us." He went on, "It is impossible . . . to escape a feeling . . . that he is nearer to us now than he has ever been before. Hitherto he has been removed by a distance of 3000 miles. . . . Now, I doubt not he knows us each one better than we know ourselves. Not only that but his love for us is as great as ever." The excitable Bucke made Wallace's implicit comparison of Whitman and Jesus explicit in the letter Bucke sent to Bolton after Whitman's funeral: "Over and over I keep saying to myself: The Christ is dead! Again we have buried the Christ! And for the time there seems to be an end of every thing. But I *know* he is not dead and I *know* that this pain will pass."

With the Christ buried a sacred charge was laid upon his disciples. "It seems to me that we ought to feel . . . a new call to duty," Wallace said in his address immediately following Whitman's death. It took Wallace some time to work out what that duty might be. In the college's early days the Whitmanesque spirit of comradeship that infused their meetings had been an end in itself. With Whitman's death Wallace became convinced that the members had a greater mission. At the celebration of Whitman's birthday in 1893, the year after his death, Wallace was still struggling to define the nature of their charge. He began by saying that "Walt Whitman's work has descended to us; . . . he has bequeathed to us . . . tremendous and important duties that we have not yet begun to realize." Wallace's articulation of those duties was vague but emotionally stirring: "We are summoned to an active sustained war, a war for the great idea—that of perfect, free individuals." What was clear in Wallace's address was that Whitman was as important a figure in human history as Jesus. Walt came, Wallace said, "that we might have life and have it more abundantly, he too has given us a gospel of glad tidings and comfort and hope and joy, he too has given us a message which is specially precious to the outcast and lowest classes, he too is a Prince of Peace."

Wallace's estimate of Walt Whitman and of the college's duties was extravagant, but it was shared by some outsiders. Katharine St. John Conway, a celebrated socialist orator and a friend of Wallace's, sent a letter to be read aloud at the same meeting at which Wallace described Whitman as a Prince of Peace. "As I understand it," she wrote, "like the disciples of old, you are meeting together after the 'Death' of him you know as your leader, that you may strengthen each other's faith in his gospel . . . and learn together how best to send it forth to the nations." Conway's greeting implied that the small band of the faithful in Bolton, like the twelve disciples of the earlier prophet, could make Whitmanism a worldwide religious movement. However, Wallace and the college struggled with how best to disseminate Walt's gospel. As Max Weber pointed out, the sort of charismatic authority possessed by a prophet like Jesus is inherently unstable, and after the prophet's death his disciples are inevitably thrown into turmoil. How can they turn a religious movement that was centered on one magnetic individual into an enduring institution? Early Christianity brilliantly solved this dilemma through a church structure that combined hierarchical bureaucracy (through the system of papal and episcopal authority) with charismatic authority (through the sacrament of the mass). Wallace and his circle, at Whitman's death, were left with only one frail institutional structure on which to build: their annual celebration of Whitman's birthday.

Two years before Whitman's death Wallace had left the house on Eagle Street, where he had lived all his life, for Anderton, a Lancashire village several miles outside Bolton. His move disrupted the college's Monday night gatherings. The annual celebration of Whitman's May 31 birthday became the only regular gathering, and these meetings were devoted more to cementing friendships than to propagating the gospel. Typically, these birthday celebrations began with a group photograph. The many surviving examples show the disciples gathered around a Whitman shrine, a table covered with relics that Wallace and Johnston had reverently assembled: books, letters, photographs, a lock of hair, leaves of grass taken from outside Whitman's birthplace—even Whitman's canary, which on its death had been stuffed, mounted, and sent to England. Once photographs had been taken, it was time for tea, followed by a reading of letters and salutations from distant Whitmanites. After the salutations Wallace would read from Whitman's work and deliver an address—the evening's sermon. His address was followed by a toast to Whitman that, in Wallace's hands, became a spiritually charged sacrament. Each member of the college drank from a specially inscribed loving cup that had been sent to Bolton by an American disciple. One of the group described the significance of the moment: "At a Whitman Birthday Celebration when J. W. Wallace read . . . something from 'Leaves of Grass,' when the very living spirit of Whitman seemed to leap lucent from the page, and the event was a pentecostal experience for those whose blessed privilege it was to be present, and when Wallace raised his glass in his hand and we all stood and copied the gesture while he exclaimed 'Here's to you Walt,' then the very air of the room seemed charged with holy influences." The Whitman birthday celebrations served perfectly the purposes of religious ritual: to unite the community of believers and to strengthen their faith. What they could not accomplish was to disseminate Walt's gospel beyond the small circle of the college. After Whitman's death Wallace began searching for other ways to spread the good news. Like his new friend Edward Carpenter, he found what seemed to be the answer in England's growing socialist movement.

‡‡‡

Living in Lancashire, Wallace was at the epicenter of the "ethical socialism" movement. Largely indifferent to orthodox Marxism, ethical socialists were much more heavily indebted to Thomas Carlyle

FIGURE 5.5. The Eagle Street College at the 1907 Whitman birthday celebration. Wentworth Dixon is on the far left, Fred Wild third from left, Wallace second from right with his arm around Johnston. Note the shrine with copies of *Leaves of Grass* and photographs of Whitman. Bolton Central Library.

and John Ruskin. Like Marx, these great Victorian moralists detested modern industrial capitalist society, but whereas Marx looked forward to a dictatorship of the proletariat, they looked back to an idealized precapitalist past of independent farmers and artisans. Ruskin's disciple William Morris joined his master's interest in handicrafts to political action, and in 1885 Morris helped to found the Socialist League, one of a number of ethical socialist organizations that flourished during the next fifteen years.

Ethical socialism was particularly powerful in Lancashire and Yorkshire. Not coincidentally, these northern industrial provinces were centers of nonconformist Protestantism. Both working- and lower-middle-class residents were comfortable with the evangelical emphasis on personal transformation as the basis of social renewal, and the socialist movement in these areas put less stress on changing institutions than on winning individual converts to socialism. Marx saw economics as the base on which superstructures of culture and consciousness depended; ethical socialists were convinced that consciousness itself was the base. Ethical socialism was as much a religious as a political movement, and its exponents were clear about where their priorities lay. "It is of much more importance to teach and live socialism than it is to elect socialist representatives," a leading socialist wrote in Robert Blatchford's *Clarion*, the era's largest-circulation socialist journal. "A million theoretical socialists are of less real and ultimate value than one earnest soul whose socialism is the expression of his heart's religion and life." Even Keir Hardie, the first socialist member of Parliament, said that socialism had come "to resuscitate the Christianity of Christ" and that it was simply "the embodiment of Christianity in our industrial system."

Along with Wallace's friend Katharine Conway and her husband, Bruce Glasier, Hardie was one of the founders of the Independent Labour Party, or ILP. The river of twentieth-century English socialism was fed by multiple streams, including the Fabianism of London intellectuals and the Marxism of H. M. Hyndman and the Social Democratic Federation, but the spiritually imbued socialism of Edward Carpenter and the ILP was a major source. Wallace was closely involved with the ILP from its beginning in 1892–93 and was president of his local chapter. "I have been dosing [Lancashire socialists] with Walt," he proudly announced to Traubel.

When the ILP held a national conference in Bolton, Wallace dosed the entire assembly with Walt. Nothing reveals English socialists' openness to religiously inflected rhetoric more clearly than their invitation to Wallace to speak at this major political gathering. He began by minimizing the importance of politics and elevating morality, quoting Whitman: "*Produce great persons and the rest follows.*" Wallace went on to hold Whitman up as the ideal democratic citizen. In the remainder of his address—or, more accurately, his sermon—Wallace preached that the first characteristic of the "Democratic Ideal" was a Whitmanesque pride in oneself. "But pride," he cautioned, "in the *deeper* self which is superior to meanness or vanity—which is essentially the same in all—the personal *soul*, which tallies all nature and all humanity and is of like nature with God himself." He concluded, "This . . . is the ideal which I offer to you, which I have learned from my master Walt Whitman," then read Whitman's "Pioneers! O Pioneers!" a poem that, with its stirring evocation of a vaguely envisioned future, circulated widely among English socialists.

ILP leader Keir Hardie agreed with Wallace's moral and religious interpretation of socialism and his Whitmanesque certainty that if great people are produced, the rest follows. Hardie himself said that "the chief aim of a Socialist organization [is] surely to make Socialists," not to concern itself with elections or legislation. However, when at Wallace's prodding Hardie read *Leaves of Grass* and "Democratic Vistas," he remained unimpressed. He wrote to Wallace that there was nothing in Whitman that had not already been said by Carlyle and Burns. However, afraid that his sardonic view of Whitman might offend his friend, Hardie backpedaled: "It may be however that there are hidden meanings which I failed to grasp and I am always very willing to learn. I do not write in any deprecatory spirit of either your hero or his writings. . . . I will . . . return to his books with a new zest, and doubtless will find that something which has hitherto eluded me but which must be there to have fired men like yourself and Dr. Johnston into such enthusiasm." Hardie eventually came round, later listing Whitman among the great "teachers and prophets of the nineteenth century"—along with Carlyle, Mazzini, Ruskin, Tennyson, and Morris—who elevated "the spiritual side of man's being" and prevented the labor movement from foundering on "the rocks of materialism."

Despite Walt Whitman's own indifference to the socialist movement of his time, Wallace was successful in turning the American poet into a patron saint of British socialism—literally so: Wallace wrote a biography of Whitman for the monthly "Calendar of Socialist Saints" feature of the *Young Socialist* magazine. Wallace's efforts were aided by the influential John Trevor, founder of the Labour Church. Trevor came to Manchester in 1890 as a newly minted Unitarian minister but left his congregation within a year to establish the first Labour Church. The Labour Church drew its membership primarily from lower-middle-class and working-class churchgoers put off by conventional churches' hostility to the labor movement. Its First Principle, as formulated by Trevor, was that "the Labour Movement is a Religious Movement." Its leaders emphasized that social and economic justice depended on personal transformation, an idea appealing to the many congregants who had grown up in evangelical households. Thanks to Trevor's energy and a widespread cultural receptiveness to the union of religion and socialism, Labour churches quickly multiplied, especially in the north of England; by 1895 there were about fifty congregations. Services typically included socialist hymns, such as Edward Carpenter's popular "England, Arise"; sermons by local or visiting speakers—Carpenter, Hardie, and Bruce and Katharine Glasier were all big draws; and readings of poems, often by Whitman.

Trevor tirelessly promoted Whitman, whom he described as "nearer to God than any man on earth." Trevor and Wallace were successful in dosing the socialist movement with Walt Whitman, but Wallace had more difficulty dosing the Eagle Street College with socialism. His involvement in the labor movement made some of the members uneasy, and he acknowledged their discomfort in an 1893 address. "I am very well aware," he began, "that our discussions of 'Socialism' lately have been distasteful to some of our members, who are now rather hanging back in doubt as to where we are going." Wallace urged them to ignore their differences on economic questions and to focus on the principles central to the college: comradeship, spirituality, and Walt Whitman. Democracy, Wallace argued, was inevitably spreading in England; the only question was whether it would be "wise and religious." Warming to his theme, Wallace pulled out all the rhetorical stops, offering an emotionally vivid portrait of the college's special role in England's future: "*We* are the heaven-appointed preachers to the Democracy of England! *We* stand in the closest relation to Walt Whitman—the divinely inspired prophet of World-Democracy. To *us* the leaders of the English Democracy will look more and more for Spiritual food and sustenance." His rhetoric at white heat, he went on to claim, "It has already begun!—already one or two of their number recognise our mission and function." Wallace failed to win over everyone in the college; the members decided that although as individuals they were free to join the Labour Church or another organization, they would not commit the college to any collective action.

Wallace was undeterred. During the early 1890s he became increasingly convinced that his connection to Walt Whitman and his friendships with Carpenter, Trevor, and the ILP leadership gave him and the college a unique role in the nation's political and spiritual future. "More and more I see," he wrote Traubel, "how great a work there is to do—and for *me* especially in Walt's cause in England. I am coming more and more into personal contact with the leaders of English Democracy and I *long* to supply what I perceive them to hungrily demand, the comradeship of a disciple of Walt's who, with loving hands, might lead them, and the multitudes they influence, to the saviour who can alone supply their immense spiritual needs." Wallace was living in heady times. The socialist movement was growing rapidly, and he was receiving impassioned daily letters from Traubel, who was convinced that his Camden-based Walt Whitman Fellowship was on the verge of becoming a vast international movement.

However, Traubel's dreams never materialized, and in the late 1890s Great Britain's ethical socialist movement began to decline. For the parliamentary election of 1895, the Independent Labour Party put up twenty-eight candidates, every one of whom was defeated—including Keir Hardie, the sole labor representative in Parliament. Beatrice Webb called it "the most expensive funeral since Napoleon." The ILP leadership regrouped; it seemed the party must make a choice between the strategy of "making socialists"—that is, winning converts to the cause—and winning elections. The leaders chose the latter, and the ILP began to place less stress on its socialist identity, to form alliances with trade unions, and to focus its resources on political organizing. The strategy paid off when, ten years later, thirty labor candidates were elected to Parliament and the modern Labour Party was effectively launched.

The changed environment afforded little place for J. W. Wallace—or Walt Whitman. Once the ILP turned its attention to the trade unions, the Labour Church declined dramatically. The more

politically minded members found the church an increasingly unlikely means for realizing socialism in Great Britain; the more religiously minded became disillusioned with a political movement that
seemed increasingly uninterested in spiritual values. Once John
Trevor resigned from the Labour Church in 1900, the movement
was effectively finished. Still, Wallace maintained his faith in the
necessity of a spiritually imbued democracy even as he recognized
that he had little role to play in an ILP that was focused on electoral
success. He told Carpenter that while he "accepted and rejoiced in
the Socialistic spirit," he was uninterested in socialism as a theory
of government. Wallace's hopes that the Eagle Street College might
serve as the spiritual beacon of English democracy gradually unrav-
eled as the century wound down. By 1898 he could not summon the
energy to write his annual greeting to American Whitmanites on
the poet's birthday. "Alas for our College!" he wrote instead to
Traubel. "It is very small nowadays."

Paradoxically, at the same time as Wallace was forced to acknowledge that the college could have little national effect, its annual
Whitman birthday celebrations became more fervent and better attended. Men too young to have attended the meetings on Eagle
Street were attracted to the college by Wallace's personality and the
emotional intimacy of their gatherings. Walter Hawkins, who became the group's chronicler, emphasized the spirit of comrade love
in his reports of their annual meetings. He wrote that at the conclusion of the 1901 Whitman birthday celebration, " 'Eyes looked love
to eyes that spake again,' and the little band separated. Each carried
with him thoughts deep and tender, each went forth into the world
stronger to grapple with its problems and perplexities; each felt the
bond of comradeship drawn tighter round his heart." Some years
later he wrote of the atmosphere of reverence, sympathy, and affection that pervaded the meetings: "It is under the spell of such
spiritual enthusiasm that great deeds have been accomplished and
great movements inaugurated." The comment recalls Wallace's millennial enthusiasm of the mid-1890s, when he believed that the college could play a central role in transforming English democracy.
However, Hawkins continued, "Whether great results, as men count

greatness, spring from such gatherings or not, true it undoubtedly is that each soul there present is filled with a deeper, truer joy, and a more intense longing for closer communion with comrades, and surely this is enough." The Eagle Street College, once the beacon of English democracy, had diminished to a cozy comradely glow.

Plagued by poor health and deteriorating eyesight, Wallace retired from the architectural firm of Bradshaw and Gass at the age of fifty-nine. Katharine Conway Glasier led an effort to raise funds so that he could live comfortably, and his home in the village of Anderton became a socialist retreat where itinerant lecturers and activists recuperated under the tender ministrations of "Uncle Wallace," as the younger generation called him. By the time of the centennial of Whitman's birth in 1919, Wallace, then sixty-five years old, still clung to his belief in Whitman's prophetic power, but he acknowledged that his dream of a Whitman-inspired millennium would not be realized until far into the future. In an article for a Labour Party newspaper, Wallace wrote that Whitman's fame and influence "are as yet little more than at the beginning of their growth, and it will take a much longer period in the future to fully realise the significance of his advent and the importance of his influence in relation to the new era yet to dawn upon the world." He insisted that Whitman "was in the line of succession with the greatest religious founders [of] the past" and was the pioneer of a "new order—the era of true Democracy," but he declined to speculate when the new era might arrive.

For all his grand dreams of the future Wallace never ceased to treasure the intimate comradeship of the college, the fellowship of men gathered to pledge their hearts not just to Walt but to one another. He began the 1925 birthday celebration by lamenting the absence of Johnston, who for the first time in forty years was not present—some months before, he had been paralyzed by a stroke. Wallace used the occasion to testify to his undimmed love for Johnston and for his dead master, Walt Whitman. "I myself have for half my life believed [Whitman] to be the greatest, most significant, and most prophetic figure that has appeared in literature since the beginning of the Christian era," he told those gathered around him.

His tribute to Walt Whitman was to be his last testament. Seven months later J. W. Wallace died of a ruptured appendix at the age of seventy-two. In their numerous memorial speeches and essays, his friends marveled that this supremely modest man attracted so many people into his circle, including celebrated authors and political figures. What was it, wondered William Broadhurst, who had met Wallace at the Bolton Labour Church in the 1890s, that "distinguished him from all other men I have ever met?" It was, Broadhurst decided, his *utter unconsciousness of self.* In Wallace "self consciousness was lost, submerged in the all-pervading universal self or soul of created things. He was essentially, but unconsciously, a mystic. The one reality for him of which he was as fully cognizant as of his identity, was the eternal onward march of souls, toward he knew not what, but it was towards something supremely grand." Like Anne Gilchrist and the other disciples, J. W. Wallace was certain that the universe was going somewhere. Walt Whitman, they were convinced, pointed the way.

CHAPTER SIX

Horace Traubel and
the Walt Whitman Fellowship:
The Gospel according to Horace

I call to the world to distrust the accounts of my friends, but
*   listen to my enemies, as I myself do,*
I charge you forever reject those who would expound me, for
*   I cannot expound myself,*
I charge that there be no theory or school founded out of me,
I charge you to leave all free, as I have left all free.

HORACE TRAUBEL WAS DETERMINED to live until May 31, 1919. The year before, he had suffered a serious stroke, and for the first time since 1889, when he had organized a seventieth birthday party for the ailing poet, he had missed the annual Walt Whitman birthday celebration. This year, the hundredth anniversary of Whitman's birth, Traubel would not be deterred. At the beginning of May he moved in with friends in New York City so that if he had another stroke or a heart attack hit him again—he'd had a few during the last five years—he would not be stuck in Camden as he had been the year before. As it turned out, there was no need to worry. He was fine on the thirty-first, able to walk into the Hotel Brevoort in Greenwich Village. He used a cane now, dragging his paralyzed left leg behind him, but that only emphasized his connection to Whitman, who had also used a cane after a midlife stroke. Otherwise, there was little physical resemblance between the two men. Walt had been a big man, more than six feet tall, whereas Traubel was barely five and a half feet, with noticeably short legs; he liked to joke that he was part dachshund. But he was a strikingly handsome man, with a moustache and a full head of tousled white hair; both women and men would follow him with their eyes when he walked down the street, dressed in stylishly bohemian fashion with a flowing tie and no overcoat, no matter what the weather.

More than two hundred people were gathered at the Brevoort for the Walt Whitman Fellowship dinner, many drawn there as much by Traubel as by Whitman. Traubel had been known as Whitman's errand boy when Walt was alive, but now Horace Traubel was a figure in his own right, a poet and writer with three books to his credit and a large network of friends among cultural and political radicals. The artist John Sloan spoke at the Brevoort, and Emma Goldman and Eugene Debs would have sent greetings, as usual, had they not been in prison for their opposition to the world war. Helen Keller was there, invited by Traubel, with whom she had a long-standing epistolary friendship based on their mutual interest in socialist causes. When it was Keller's turn to speak, she altered the course of the evening's river of tributes. Others might praise Walt Whitman, but she would honor Horace Traubel. "The truth is, I love Horace Traubel," Keller said. "We all love [him]," she continued, her effusive tribute climaxing in a comparison of Traubel to Christ: "Indeed, there is something of the Savior about his interest in human beings, and his sympathy with their struggles." Keller was widely regarded as a secular saint for her brilliant achievements despite deafness and blindness, and she willingly assumed priestly authority to bless Traubel, a fellow radical. Emboldened by her example, another member of the audience suggested that everyone rise to their feet in honor of Horace Traubel. The older Whitmanites, those who had known the poet personally, looked on with dismay as Walt was forgotten and the two hundred men and women in the Brevoort ballroom gave a standing ovation to Horace Traubel.

"He had a lot of fool friends that tried to make him believe that he was a greater man than Whitman," wrote Traubel's brother-in-law and fellow Whitman executor, Thomas Harned, thinking no doubt of the annual Horace Traubel dinners organized by a band of socialists during the last few years of his life. Remembering how Traubel would print the fulsome tributes delivered at these dinners in his monthly journal, the *Conservator*, Harned added, "As to Horace it was a case of 'Barkis is willin'.'" But no man deserves to have the final verdict on him delivered by his brother-in-law. And even Harned acknowledged that Traubel "was always true to Whitman." Never truer than in the final months of Horace's life, when he husbanded the scarce energy supplied by his fatally weakened heart to revisit, over and over, his relationship with Walt. For his entire adult life he had been a prodigiously productive writer, but now he wrote solely about the years with Whitman in Camden. "Dear Walt," he wrote in one of his last poems, "I think myself back to my young days with you: / I'm overwhelmed by memories of an unforgettable past." Traubel held on with all his dying strength to his memories of Whitman, his most precious possession: "They cant rob me of my past: it's mine: all mine."

✣ ✣ ✣

Horace Traubel's unforgettable past began in 1873 when Walt Whitman, hobbled by a stroke and emotionally devastated by his mother's death, left Washington, D.C., in order to accept his brother George's offer of a room in his home on Stevens Street in Camden. Soon after he arrived, the fifty-four-year-old poet became friendly with one of the neighborhood boys, Horace Traubel, an energetic and outgoing teenager who enjoyed chatting with Whitman during time off from his job in a newspaper print shop. At fifteen Traubel had already been out of school for three years when he met the poet, but he adored reading, and he would engage Whitman in lengthy, intense front-stoop conversations about literature. Traubel's father, Maurice, a German-Jewish immigrant, was a commercial lithographer with artistic inclinations. Like his wife, Katherine Grunder, who had been raised in a Protestant family in Philadelphia, Maurice Traubel was a freethinker who encouraged his son's friendship with

Whitman, despite some neighbors' prejudices against the poet as a dangerous radical, the author of a nasty book. For his part Whitman was delighted with his young friend. Isolated and melancholy during his early years in Camden, he found that Horace acted as a tonic. "Horace, you were a mere boy [when] we met," Whitman recalled years later. "Not so often as now—not so intimately: but I remember you so well: you were so slim, so upright, so sort of electrically buoyant. You were like medicine to me—better than medicine: don't you recall those days? down on Stevens Street, out front there, under the trees? You would come along, I would be sitting there: we would have our chats."

Bright, energetic, and restless, Traubel was promoted to foreman of the newspaper print shop when he was only sixteen, but he soon left to work in his father's lithography shop, then took a position as a factory paymaster, which left him time to work as Philadelphia correspondent for a Boston newspaper. Yet none of these jobs fully engaged his intellect and ambitions. Finally, late in his twenties he hit upon his vocation: he would become Walt Whitman's biographer.

During the 1880s, after George Whitman moved out of Camden to the countryside and Walt bought his own house on Mickle Street, Traubel began visiting the poet daily. Whitman, in his sixties and in worsening health, depended on others for help. He had invited Mary Davis, a widow in the neighborhood, to live rent free in his house, and the motherly Davis looked after his meals and the housekeeping. But Whitman needed a literary secretary to aid in his ongoing project of publishing ever-expanding editions of his poetry and prose. Horace Traubel, writer and former printer, was the ideal person for the job. He began stopping by Whitman's Mickle Street house every evening after work. Often there were proofs to be delivered, letters and packages to be mailed; just as often the two men would simply sit and chat. Whitman was grateful for both the assistance and the audience; he had grown more garrulous with age, liked to reminisce about old letters that he happened across in his paper-strewn room. Horace Traubel proved a good listener and an energetic assistant. "You have saved my books," Whitman told him one evening. "I could not do these books without assistance. Of all the people I have known or know you are the most fitted to help me just now. You know books, writers, printing office customs—best of all you know *me*—my ways and what I need to be humored in."

Traubel filled a vital role for the old poet, but theirs was not simply a friendship of convenience. Whitman genuinely loved the young man. "Come, kiss me for good night," he urged Traubel one evening, taking his hand and pressing it fervently. "I am in luck. Are you? I guess God just sent us for each other." Another evening he held Traubel's hand and mused, "I feel somehow as if you had consecrated yourself to me. That entails something on my part: I feel somehow as if I was consecrated to you. Well—we will work out the rest of my life-job together." Then he took Traubel's face between his hands, drew the young man toward him, and kissed him. There is nothing to suggest that the relationship between Whitman and Traubel was ever a sexual one, yet there was clearly an erotic charge between the two men, just as there was in Whitman's relationships with William O'Connor, John Burroughs, and R. M. Bucke. At the same time Whitman's kisses were also religious, a form of anointment, as his mention of consecration suggests. Traubel was the youngest member of the Whitman circle and the sole person in the group committed to daily ministrations to the master. In response Whitman acknowledged Horace Traubel's status as first among his disciples. "There is a sort of apostolic succession in [our partnership]," he told Traubel, "a laying on of hands."

We know the relationship between Whitman and Traubel in such detail because in March 1888 Traubel began recording their daily conversations. After leaving his job, Traubel would drop by Mickle Street for anywhere from a few minutes to an hour or more. He generally did not take notes during his visits but later, at home, would write a summary, recording Whitman's memorable remarks and transcribing any letters that the poet had him read aloud. Whitman was aware of Traubel's project, and he regularly fed the young man letters and manuscripts as they floated to the surface of the clutter in his large second-floor bedroom. Traubel had a gift for remembering conversation, and his record of Whitman's speech is consistent, convincing, and completely in accord with interviews and memoirs of the poet. Traubel wrote, on average, one to two thousand words a day; in the course of four years, until Whitman's death in March 1892, the record grew to almost two million words. After Whitman's death Traubel determined to publish every word, but while he was alive he succeeded in issuing only three volumes, which cover ten months of Whitman's life. The next six volumes appeared sporadically, the last two not published until 1996, nearly eighty years after Traubel's death.

Later in his life Traubel developed a considerable ego; Tom Harned liked to recall the remark of his mother, who declared Horace the most conceited man she had ever known. But Traubel is almost invisible throughout the nine volumes of *With Walt Whitman in Camden*, an ideal interlocutor, waiting in silence for Whitman to finish a thought, asking leading questions, occasionally making a saucy remark to stir the old man up. Traubel's record is so detailed and his devotion to Whitman so apparent that it comes as a shock when, in volume 5, he makes his first reference to his outside employment, casually mentioning that a friend came by the bank to join him before they went to visit Whitman. Some months after beginning the record of his visits to Whitman, Traubel took a position as clerk at the Farmers and Mechanics Bank in Philadelphia, a ferry ride away from his Camden home. The salary was presumably a step up from that for his factory paymaster position, but he now had a significant commute to and from his full-time job. In addition, he increased his visits to Whitman, frequently stopping by after breakfast as well as in the evening. At the same time Traubel was a member of one civic club in Philadelphia and secretary-treasurer of another; helped to found a branch of the Ethical Culture Society and served as its secretary and treasurer; founded, edited, and published a monthly magazine; supervised Whitman's numerous publications; and wrote twenty to forty letters every day to Whitman's friends and supporters, keeping them abreast of the poet's activities. An acquaintance described Traubel as "lethally industrious"; he seems to have been referring to the effect of this activity not on Traubel himself but on those who tried to keep up with him.

FIGURE 6.1. Horace Traubel about age thirty, when he began writing *With Walt Whitman in Camden*. Bolton Central Library.

Traubel's most significant public initiative after beginning *With Walt Whitman in Camden* was founding the *Conservator*, a monthly magazine. Traubel's title was puckishly misleading; the *Conservator* was not a right-wing political journal but a liberal religious publication. Like all the disciples, Traubel was a spiritual seeker, but whereas the others promoted a highly individualistic, anti-institutional spirituality, he had a mania for organizing. When he founded the *Conservator* in 1890, he envisioned it as the instrument for uniting the Philadelphia area's liberal religious societies. "To bring Unitarian, Hebrew, Quaker, Ethical, together—this is our purpose," he wrote in one of the first issues. The four sects he named were all shaped by the liberal religious movements of the late nineteenth century, the efforts to reconcile premodern religions with post-Darwinian science and democratic political theory. Traubel was connected to Unitarianism, long a home of religious liberals, through his brother-in-law Tom Harned and through John H. Clifford, minister at the Germantown Unitarian church outside Philadelphia and a Whitman disciple who frequently quoted the poet in his sermons. By "Hebrew" he meant Reform Judaism. Philadelphia's Quakers by and large stayed apart from ecumenical efforts, but a minority recognized that their centuries-old doctrine of the Inner Light— the divine presence within every individual—was congruent with religious liberalism. As for "Ethical" religion, Traubel was referring to the Society for Ethical Culture, a new religious movement that consumed much of his energy not devoted to Whitman.

Traubel was a founding member of the Philadelphia Society for Ethical Culture, established in 1885. The Ethical Culture movement had begun a decade before when Felix Adler, a brilliant young rabbi and the heir apparent to New York City's largest Reform synagogue, shocked his father's congregation with a radical sermon that simultaneously terminated his rabbinical career and launched a new religious movement. Adler shared the universalist impulse of other religious liberals, the belief that all religions share a common core of immanentist theology and ethical moral code. Ethical Culture originally attracted Reform Jews, but disaffected Unitarians soon joined Adler's movement, which rejected traditional Judaism and Christianity in favor of a spiritually tinged ethical humanism. When an Adler protégé and former Unitarian came from New York to Philadelphia to found a chapter, Traubel—son of a nonpracticing Jew and a nonbelieving Christian—quickly found a home in Ethical Culture.

However, the ambitious Traubel became restless within the confines of the Ethical Culture Society and founded the *Conservator* as a vehicle for what he imagined might be a Philadelphia-area meta-church—what he called a "Liberal Conference"—uniting the various liberal religious bodies. At its beginning, the magazine was an eight-page journal with Page One devoted to Traubel's "Collect," a collection of disconnected paragraphs featuring his reflections on religion and other topics; three pages of short signed essays, generally extracts from lectures by Unitarian ministers and Ethical Culture leaders; the "Budget," with three pages of reports from various liberal churches; and one page of ads from Philadelphia merchants. Traubel's efforts to unite the churches soon faltered; barely a year after he began publishing the *Conservator*, subscribers began dropping away. Traubel soon gave up his idea of uniting Philadelphia's liberal churches and in 1892 turned the *Conservator* into an unofficial voice of the national Ethical Culture movement. The magazine flourished under its new mission. It added a part-time staff of four and expanded from eight to sixteen monthly pages, filled with reports from Ethical Culture branches across the country and essays by the movement's prominent figures. Its readership was no longer regional but national, as reflected in the ads, which now featured books and magazines rather than Philadelphia merchants.

At the same time as he was pouring energy into the *Conservator*, Traubel continued writing two dozen or more letters a day to Whitman's friends, giving them details of the ailing poet's health and activities. One of his most ambitious Whitmanite projects was the celebration of the poet's seventieth birthday in May 1889. The event was an effort by Traubel and the other organizers to demonstrate that this prophet was not without honor in his own country. They put together a guest list of notable Camden residents—some of whom had never read a word of *Leaves of Grass*—and invited birthday greetings from every writer in the United States and Europe who they thought might send a word favorable to Whitman. The organizers then cajoled Whitman's Philadelphia publisher into issuing the record of the affair as *Camden's Compliment to Walt Whitman*. Traubel apparently considered the event a great success, although in his eulogistic introduction to *Camden's Compliment* he acknowledged that a gathering of New Jersey burghers in evening wear might not fully capture the spirit animating *Leaves of Grass*. "The unconstraint and felicity of the event was from beginning to end as generous as the spirit of the man it was aimed to celebrate," he wrote, "except for the absence of women and of the distinctly mechanical classes." The exceptions were large ones. Whitman was realistic enough to accept the absence of working-class men; he knew that *Leaves of Grass* had attracted artists and intellectuals, not the heroic artisan readers he had originally imagined. However, he was not pleased by the exclusion of women. It seems "entirely out of place," he told Traubel, "inconsistent with my best-held convictions, as expressed from the start, which would include women equally with men." Still, Whitman, who downed a bottle of champagne as he listened to the eulogistic speeches, left the event feeling, he said, "gloriously well and sassy." As tributes poured in during the days before the event from those who could not attend, he had said meditatively to Traubel, "Isn't it wonderful, Horace, how the best of us like to be flattered? I am quite surprised at myself more than often."

Traubel was careful to include women in future birthday celebrations, among them, Anne Montgomerie. He had met Montgomerie a few years before at the factory where he was paymaster and she worked as a supervisor. Their courtship was conducted under the approving gaze of Walt Whitman, who was immensely fond of Montgomerie and delighted in playing the role of a grizzled Cupid. When Whitman proved too ill to leave his house on their wedding day in May 1891, the entire party crammed into his bedroom. The Unitarian minister John Clifford conducted the service as the old poet sat propped up in bed, occasionally interjecting comments as

Clifford read poems by Whitman and Emerson. The newlyweds delayed their honeymoon—a visit to Bucke in Canada—in order to attend Whitman's seventy-second birthday celebration.

Whitman remained too feeble to leave his house, and his seventy-second birthday was celebrated in his Mickle Street parlor, with thirty-two guests crowded into the small space. Daniel Brinton, a University of Pennsylvania professor who served as master of ceremonies, read aloud greetings from absent disciples, including the excitable William Sloane Kennedy. Kennedy praised *Leaves of Grass* as "the Bible of the Nineteenth Century" and touted its superiority to the earlier scripture, predicting that Whitman's "new gospel" would eventually supplant Christianity. Kennedy's contribution was the most overtly religious, but the entire event was reverential. Bucke came down from Canada, John Addington Symonds wrote an effusive tribute, and John Johnston sent his newly published account of his pilgrimage to Camden the previous year. Most of the thirty-two guests spoke in praise of Whitman. Traubel, however, did not speak. When called upon, he demurred: "No, I must be excused. I feel myself in the midst of a battle of which I may some time have something to say. My turn has not come. When the battle is over, then I may write of it."

Traubel's sense of mission as standardbearer of the Whitmanite cause is obvious. However, his comment is ambiguous in one sense. Would the end of the battle be the widespread acceptance of Whitman as a poet-prophet, or would it be Whitman's death? No one had thought Whitman would still be alive to celebrate his seventy-second birthday. Following Whitman's series of massive strokes in June 1888, Bucke was certain that he could not last long and wrote multiple letters to Traubel about the poet's funeral. Bucke wanted to wrest control of the funeral away from Whitman's brother George, who, Bucke was certain, would want a conventional Protestant service, but the doctor was at a loss as to what the alternative should be. "I cannot get this funeral business out of my head and cannot see my way to a solution of the difficulty," he wrote Traubel late in 1888. "To take the body of W. W. to the grave, bury and come away as if we had buried a criminal or an animal and were on the whole a little ashamed of the transaction! To have some clergy-man read his verses and say his prayers over the grave and stultify W's whole life and our convictions and professions. How can we accept either of these?" Bucke continued to stew for the next three and a half years; Whitman surprised everyone by continuing to live, his every swing of health recorded by Traubel.

In December 1891, seven months after his seventy-second birth-day, Whitman contracted pneumonia, and it seemed the end was near. Bucke came down from Canada, and he and Traubel once again made funeral plans. Once again, however, the old man rallied, although he remained bedridden and in terrible pain. Traubel in-creased his visits to Mickle Street to two or three a day, scribbling lengthy accounts of them at night and firing off dozens of letters and telegrams daily to disciples in the United States and England. Whitman remained lucid despite his pain, and he frequently ex-pressed his love and gratitude to Traubel. He would hold Traubel's hand as they talked, whispering, "Dear dear boy!" For years he had acknowledged Traubel's role as his biographer; now, near death, he pressed on Traubel his duties as keeper of the Whitman flame: "Keep an eye out for all our affairs: it all devolves upon you now. . . . I depend upon you: you are more than my right arm."

Stirred by Whitman's affection and trust, fired by Bucke's convic-tion that they were "right at the centre of the largest thing of these late centuries," Traubel was in an emotionally heightened state throughout the early months of 1892 as Whitman's health declined. "Dear Walt, you do not realize what you have been to us!" he whispered one evening in March as he prepared to leave. "Nor you what you have been to me!" Walt whispered back, as Horace wiped away tears. Three weeks later Traubel hurried to Mickle Street from a long day at the bank to find Tom Harned waiting for him in the hallway. "Walt is dying," Harned said. "It is nearly over." Traubel took Whitman's hand and held it for the next half hour as Whitman's breathing diminished. At last Harned murmured, "It is done." Traubel felt transfigured: "I laid his hand quietly down—something in my heart seemed to snap and that moment commenced my new life—a luminous conviction lifting me with him into the eternal."

The funeral came off as Bucke and Traubel wanted, although they had a close call when Louisa Whitman, George's wife, engaged a minister to conduct the services. "My God! It was like to wreck us all! . . . and dear old Walt would be outraged!" Bucke exclaimed to Traubel. Instead, Robert Ingersoll, a celebrity orator and Whitman admirer known as "the Great Agnostic," delivered the principal address. Ingersoll was more a religious liberal than a materialist, and he praised Whitman for his "gospel of humanity." He was preceded by the Philadelphia poet Francis Howard Williams, who highlighted the cosmopolitan spirituality of Whitman and the disciples by reading quotations from Jewish, Christian, Confucian, Buddhist, Islamic, and Hindu scriptures.

John Burroughs attended the funeral, though he declined to speak. Burroughs mistrusted Bucke and Traubel, thinking them excessive in their praise of Whitman. However, just before the coffin was closed for the journey from Mickle Street to Harleigh Cemetery, Burroughs went with Traubel into the parlor where the gaunt body of their master lay. In a moment of reconciliation Whitman's oldest living disciple and his youngest held hands and gazed into the open coffin. "As we stood there together," Traubel reflected, "I heard the lid drop, the door closed, the face forever shut out, the new life begun."

✠ ✠ ✠

Horace Traubel began the new life by founding a Whitmanite organization. At the 1892 observance of Whitman's birthday, two months after the poet's death, Traubel established the Walt Whitman Reunion. Even as he did so, he acknowledged the inherent contradiction of forming a Whitmanite church. Like all the disciples, he knew by heart the lines from *Leaves of Grass*: "I charge that there be no theory or school founded out of me, / I charge you to leave all free, as I have left all free." "This is not to create a new institution," Traubel insisted as he created the new institution. "It is only for brotherliness and understanding." Immediately afterward he wrote another disciple, "We must always adopt Walt, *leaving all free as he left all free*—but we must *cohere* and make the world see our brother-hood and the great soul and eternal principle, announced through him as in no other, for which we stand." Traubel's insistent underlin-ings emphasize the tension he felt between Whitmanesque freedom and organizational cohesion: How was he to honor both?

To his credit Traubel struggled mightily with this question. How-ever, in the period following Whitman's death, he increasingly came to feel that he had a unique mission to spread the poet's gospel. After all, had not Walt himself spoken of an "apostolic succession"? J. W. Wallace fanned Traubel's sense of calling: "*You* are the natural centre of our comradeship and succeed to Walt's position," he wrote a few weeks after Whitman's death. Succeeding to Walt's position was a heady prospect for the thirty-three-year-old Traubel but one he was not unwilling to grasp. His 1894 poem "Succession" reveals his sense of destiny:

O my dead comrade—my great dead!
. . .
I sat by your bedside, I held your hand:
Once you opened your eyes: O look of recognition!
    O look of bestowal!
From you to me then passed the commission of the
    future,
. . .
Entered, shone upon me and out of me, the power of the
    spring, the seed of the rose and the wheat,
As of father to son, as of brother to brother, as of god
    to god!
O my great dead!
You had not gone, you had stayed—in my heart, in
    my veins,
Reaching through me, through others through me,
    through all at last, our brothers,
A hand to the future.

The year after Whitman's death Traubel, who had previously written conventional rhymed poetry, abruptly shifted to a Whitmanesque style. "Succession" reveals that he assumed Whitman's mantle along with his manner, believing that he had a sacred deathbed commission to shape the future.

The same year that he wrote "Succession," Traubel decided to transform the small and loosely organized Walt Whitman Reunion into a more formal and vastly more ambitious organization, the Walt Whitman Fellowship: International (Horace Traubel, secretary-treasurer). Traubel launched the fellowship at the 1894 Whitman birthday dinner. He drew up a constitution, convinced the widely respected professor Daniel Brinton to serve as president, named six distinguished Whitmanites—including the highly reluctant John Burroughs—as vice presidents, and appointed a ten-person council. The organization gained more than one hundred members in its first year and soon established branches in Philadelphia, New York, Boston, Knoxville, and Chicago. However, as the organization's full title reveals, Traubel's plans extended beyond the United States. "I look to see [the fellowship] become a big thing—extending the globe across," he wrote early in 1894.

At the same time as he was laying plans for the Walt Whitman Fellowship: International, Traubel was engaged in struggles with the leadership of the Society for Ethical Culture. From the moment that Traubel abandoned his efforts to form a Philadelphia alliance of liberal religions and began filling the *Conservator* with Ethical Culture news and features, his relationship with the society's leadership had been rocky. Traubel had a pugnacious streak—Tom Harned said that "Horace is apt to call a person a God Damn fool or worse, if something is said touching some of his vagaries"—and Traubel occasionally used his "Collect," his long front-page editorial, to attack Ethical Culture leaders with whom he disagreed. Following a stormy public confrontation with the head of the Philadelphia branch in early 1894, Traubel resigned from the society. Within months he turned the *Conservator* from an Ethical Culture organ into a highly individualistic mélange that combined commentary on Traubel's political and social interests with detailed coverage of the newly founded Walt Whitman Fellowship: International.

Traubel's hopes for making the international dimension of the fellowship a reality lay principally with the Eagle Street College. Remarkably, the omnipresent Traubel never met John Johnston when the latter visited Camden in 1890. However, when J. W. Wallace made his pilgrimage the next year, Traubel arranged for the leader of the Bolton church to stay with him and his new bride, Anne Montgomerie. The three young people struck up an intense friendship during Wallace's weeks in Camden, and when he returned to England he became a daily recipient of Traubel epistles, letters that combined news of Whitman with effusive declarations of love. When the Traubels' second child was born in 1893, they named him Wallace. Initially embarrassed by this tribute, Traubel's friend soon began signing his letters "Uncle Wallace," but he remained unable to match Traubel's prodigious epistolary output. "What an ardent indefatigable fellow you are!" Wallace wrote. "I simply *cannot* keep pace with you!" Nevertheless, in the two years following Whitman's death, Wallace sent more than two hundred letters to Traubel, filled with news of the Eagle Street College and professions of affection. Nothing clouded the two men's deep friendship until early 1894, when Traubel began organizing the Walt Whitman Fellowship: International.

Traubel first floated the idea at a Whitmanite dinner in January. The next day he wrote Wallace an enthusiastic account of the event: "The dinner was moved by a beautiful spirit. . . . The world wears a new color. The tender atmosphere of that hour will remain to sweeten every future year. We thought of you all and toasted you." However, the dinner was not all sentimental toasts; Traubel used the occasion to lay out his plans for an international organization and told Wallace, "We shall look to you to work up the English branches." In the weeks following, Traubel burbled about the fellowship in his daily letters, while Wallace politely ignored the subject. Finally, Traubel sent an uncharacteristically brief letter, devoid of his usual salutation to "Dearest Wallace":

> Consider well this—refer it to the College:
>
> 1st, Will you form a branch, connected with our Whitman league?
>
> 2nd, Will you fellows there in Bolton, you leading, conduct the British work of organizing?
>
> Weigh this well. Send any suggestions you consider vital. The ship will be afloat before another month. Headquarters will be here, with us. In some way this must be held the center from which the spokes diverge.

This clumsy, peremptory letter reveals an autocratic streak in Traubel. Wallace's response was remarkably mild: "Our College is one thing—a definite Whitman Society to which all would be invited is another."

For all their personal affection for one another and their mutual desire to spread the gospel of Whitmanism, Traubel and Wallace had incompatible visions of the future. Traubel wanted to establish an international Whitmanite institution, with Camden as its Rome and himself as pope. Wallace prized the Eagle Street College—the small group of friends meeting weekly for cocoa and conversation, their affection for Whitman deepening their bonds to one another. During the next few months the two men maintained a cordial tone in their letters, largely because Wallace continued to ignore his friend's frequent requests to organize English branches of the fellowship, all the while assuring Traubel of his affection. In midsummer Traubel chided him: "We are all somewhat surprised here that no memberships for the Fellowship have so far come from Bolton. . . . Why do you not send on your [membership] cards?" Traubel had only fifty-nine members at that point, wanted to reach one hundred, and was determined that Wallace should help him meet his goal. Wallace replied with a stern letter that revealed the steely side of this amiable Englishman: he told Traubel that the fellowship's two-dollar dues requirement was unacceptable because it would bar from membership some of the Eagle Street College boys who were in modest circumstances. Traubel shot back that the provision as to the dues was unalterable.

Throughout this period Traubel kept up his daily letters to Wallace, and in many ways the relationship seemed unimpaired. But Traubel's mania for organizing and his imperious manner had driven a wedge between the two friends. Both protested that their love was unaltered, but within a year the frequency of letters on both sides dropped dramatically. By autumn 1895 Wallace was lamenting that weeks passed without word from Traubel, while Traubel complained, "Your old familiar letters are now almost far lost in history." The two men maintained a cordial but sporadic correspondence that increased suddenly in 1898 when Wallace Traubel contracted scarlet fever. J. W. Wallace's namesake died on February 27, five months before the child's fifth birthday. In the aftermath the two men renewed their endearments: "I think of you every day and every hour I live," wrote Traubel. "No hour is so crowded but I can find room for you in it." However, it was clear to Traubel that the Whitman Fellowship would be international in name only. As the nineteenth century gave way to the twentieth, the Eagle Street College and the Walt Whitman Fellowship took parallel but separate paths.

✢ ✢ ✢

The clash with Wallace over the Whitman Fellowship shook Traubel deeply and led him to question his organizational ambitions. During the course of the 1890s he increasingly favored individualism over institutions. In 1896 he amended the fellowship's constitution, eliminating the dues and establishing a membership card that read simply, "I announce myself to be a member of the Walt Whitman Fellowship: International." A few years later he began printing at the top of the fellowship's official stationery these lines from Whitman's "Myself and Mine":

I call to the world to distrust the accounts of my friends,
   but listen to my enemies, as I myself do,
I charge you forever reject those who would expound
   me, for I cannot expound myself,
I charge that there be no theory or school founded out
   of me,
I charge you to leave all free, as I have left all free.

Traubel's change of heart may have been congruent with Whitman's message, but it was fatal for the growth of the Whitman Fellowship. Meetings fell off from several a year in each of several cities to an annual Whitman birthday celebration in New York and one in Chicago. The elimination of dues left the fellowship chronically underfunded. Traubel published fifteen issues of the *Walt Whitman Fellowship Papers* in its first year, 1894–95, but by 1899 the *Fellowship Papers* had been reduced to three thin issues a year: a list of the officers, a report of the annual meeting in New York, and an announcement of the upcoming meeting.

By the end of his life Traubel was claiming the fellowship's institutional failure as a sign of its Whitmanesque success. For the 1919 Whitman centenary he wrote a long article for the *Philadelphia Press* that focused on Whitman's resistance to being commemorated and included such sentiments from Walt as, "I hope to God there'll never be Walt Whitman societies. Societies are a disease." Rather proudly, Traubel noted that the annual birthday dinner in New York was all that was left of formerly active branches in New York, Boston, and Philadelphia. "We've always regarded Walt's prohibitions, the same as if he were here and able to defend himself. . . . We've never violated them." Traubel was in effect rewriting the fellowship's early history and erasing his own early ambitions for it, when he imagined that it might extend across the globe.

Traubel's early ambitions seem less implausible given that he had participated in the founding and flowering of the Ethical Culture movement in Philadelphia. In addition, he had observed from a distance the spectacular success of two other religious movements founded in the nineteenth-century United States, Mormonism and

Christian Science. Each originally began as a small circle of disciples around a charismatic prophet who produced a scripture as eccentric and powerful—if not as artful—as *Leaves of Grass*. However, there were crucial differences between Mormonism and Christian Science and the nascent religious movement of Whitmanism. Both Mormonism and Christian Science are what sociologists call absolutist religious movements, their absolutism expressed in both cognitive and institutional terms. That is, the sacred books of both movements claim to offer unique theologies, while membership in the group demands conformity to church doctrine in matters ranging from dress and diet to family structure and medical decisions. The Whitman Fellowship's failure to thrive reflects both the rejection of absolutism in *Leaves of Grass* ("You shall no longer take things at second or third hand," Whitman writes in "Song of Myself," "You shall not look through my eyes either, nor take things from me, / You shall listen to all sides and filter them from your self") and the disciples' democratic values.

If Whitman's emphasis on individual autonomy and the disciples' suspicion of authority lessened organizational cohesion, these qualities also attracted to the fellowship a remarkable variety of cultural radicals. The self-educated Traubel possessed a curious mind and wide interests, and like Edward Carpenter in England he had a finger in virtually every radical movement of his era. Following Traubel's break with the Ethical Culture Society in 1894, he opened the *Conservator* to a range of contributors from the cultural and political left, many of whom began attending the Whitman Fellowship's annual birthday dinner. Whitman, who at the beginning of his career envisioned himself as the poet of the American masses, was embraced after his death by middle-class radicals who read *Leaves of Grass* as a countercultural manifesto, a source of alternative models of spirituality, politics, sexuality, and gender identity.

These radical interpretations of *Leaves of Grass* began before Whitman's death, and no revisionist interpreter was more avid than Traubel himself. By the age of thirty, when he began recording his conversations with Whitman, Traubel was absorbed by the left-wing politics of his era. He was not a member of a socialist party, but he was fascinated by socialist ideas and was convinced that Whitman was, without knowing it, a protosocialist. Repeatedly during the four years of his daily visits to Whitman, Traubel would attempt to lead the poet to endorse socialism. Whitman was always generous in acknowledging that *Leaves of Grass* had a life of its own, that others might find in his creation meanings he had not intended. After reading an article entitled "Walt Whitman as Socialist Poet" that Traubel brought to his attention, Whitman acknowledged, "I find I'm a good deal more of a socialist than I thought I was." Yet when Traubel would press him about the socialists' political program, Whitman always refused to commit himself: "Of that I'm not so sure," he told Traubel. "I rather rebel. I am with them in the result—that's about all I can say." Born only ten years after the end of the Jefferson administration, to the end of his life Whitman held fast to the Jeffersonian ideal of the yeoman farmer, the notion that American democracy was to be ensured by broadly diffused ownership of land and property. When Traubel pressed the poet to define his economic goal, he finally offered, "I look forward to a world of small owners."

"Or maybe no owners at all," Traubel suggested. "Don't you think that would be best?"

"I don't know: I haven't thought it out," Whitman acknowledged. "It *sounds* best: could it *be* best?"

Traubel recognized Whitman's deep-seated antipathy to what he called his young friend's "fierce agitations," but the younger man never stopped pushing the old poet to declare himself a socialist. Gently chiding Traubel at one point, Whitman revealed his suspicion of all political activism: "It is queer, how the whole world is crazy with the notion that one book, one ism . . . is to save things. . . . I would not go across the room to change the course of the stream—not a step: in due time, under the right conditions, the stream will fix its own bed anew as it has in the past—no hand, yours or mine, being needed to force it."

Traubel clearly enjoyed these irresolvable debates about politics, liked playing the young radical to Whitman's aging Whig. Yet he shared Whitman's doubts that one "ism" could save the world, doubts he articulated in his correspondence with Wallace, who by the early 1890s had moved beyond an interest in socialist ideas toward commitment to the socialist political program of Keir Hardie and the Independent Labour Party. Aware of his friend's growing involvement, Traubel wrote Wallace in 1892, "I want you to tell me sometime how you look on the Socialistic movement." As for himself, "I am an individualist. I would not make more of the state but less. There seems a need that we should go alone and have freedom first of all." Freedom and individualism were Traubel's bywords for most of the 1890s, and he told Wallace that he was more "anarchist than socialist." Yet by the end of his life Traubel was hailed as "the premier socialist of the day" and "the leading writer in this country, if not in the world, whose work is completely saturated with Socialism and, indeed, grows exclusively out of Socialism." How was a man who expressed such skepticism about socialist politics transformed into one of the leading socialists of his era?

The answer lies partly in changes in Horace Traubel, even more in changes within American socialism. When Traubel was taunting Whitman during the 1880s, socialism was associated with European immigrants who had been born into a sharply stratified, immutable class system and reared on Karl Marx. Americans regarded socialism as a foreign import, at odds with America's democratic traditions and more flexible class structure. By the turn of the century this perception had changed, and during the next two decades a hearty socialist movement and culture flourished in the United States, reaching its zenith in 1912, when more than twelve hundred socialists were elected to public office in the United States, the leading socialist magazine had 750,000 subscribers, and the Socialist Party candidate for president gained nearly one million votes, 6 percent of the total. Much of the movement's success can be ascribed to its five-time presidential candidate, Eugene Victor Debs.

Born three years before Traubel, Debs also left school at an early age—in Debs's case, to work on the railroad. By the age of twenty he had become a union official; before he was forty he was founding president of the American Railway Union and leader of the bitter 1894 Pullman strike. His role in the strike and his heroic reaction to the prison sentence he incurred made him a national figure, and when Debs announced his conversion to socialism in 1897, he brought thousands of Americans along with him. Horace Traubel was one of them.

The socialism championed by Debs and Traubel in the early twentieth century was very different from the closely reasoned dialectical materialism of Marx and Engels. Debs repeatedly cited as his models Jesus Christ, Thomas Jefferson, Abraham Lincoln, and Walt Whitman. The notion of a dictatorship of the proletariat was anathema to Debs; his ideal was a rose-colored version of the antebellum Terre Haute of his childhood, a classless, democratic small town. The Debses were not churchgoers, but Gene Debs absorbed the evangelical Protestant fervor of his midwestern youth, and Debsian socialism was a religious crusade. One of the keys to Debs's success was that he enabled Americans disenchanted with traditional religion to transfer their millennial aspirations from individual salvation to the transformation of society. European socialism may have been linked to atheism, but Debs cited Jesus so often that his audiences might well have assumed that Christ had been a member of the Nazareth branch of the Socialist Party.

Debs's references to Jesus were salted throughout speeches that frequently lasted one to two hours, deeply emotional addresses that brought his audiences to a wildly fevered state. Debs's socialism was lyrical and sentimental, his talks and articles full of over-the-top rhetorical flourishes, as in this 1900 article: "The skies of the East are even now aglow with the dawn; its coming is heralded by the dispelling of shadows, of darkness and gloom. From the first tremulous scintillation that gilds the horizon to the sublime march to meridian splendor, the light increases till in mighty flood it pours upon the world." A Debs biographer comments that this passage reveals how he "too often descended to depths of excessively flowery language and sloppy sentimentalism." The criticism suggests that Debs was unaware of what he was doing, that if he had only reined in his purple prose the United States might now have a socialist government. But this attack misunderstands the nature of Debs's appeal and imposes contemporary tastes on a different era. Horace Traubel would have applauded Debs's frequent ascent to the heights of flowery language and sublime sentimentalism, nowhere more so than in letters to his friends.

"Way down here on the rim of the Pacific your message reached me," Debs wrote in a 1909 letter from California, "and it is sweeter to me than the fragrance of the orange blossoms. Well do I know that I can never get beyond the bounds of your love—a love as broad and bounteous as the azure skies above—and in that love I'm rich beyond all earthly riches." The recipient of his effusions was Horace Traubel. It is not clear exactly when Debs and Traubel first met, but by 1901 they were sending heartfelt declarations of devotion to one another. "My heart opens to receive your message as the rosebud opens to receive the sunshine and flowers," Debs began one letter to Traubel; another opens, "Sweet as the fragrance of violets is your message of devotion to me and my heart turns to you as the flower does to greet the sunrise." After the turn of the century Debs and socialism assumed for Traubel the role that J. W. Wallace and the Whitman Fellowship had played briefly in the 1890s. Traubel and Debs participated in a male world of love and ritual that rivaled the intense bonding among the men of the Eagle Street College. The Debs biographer Nick Salvatore has noted that Traubel was only one among many male recipients of letters from Debs filled with images of flowers and professions of love. One of Debs's central goals was to redefine American manhood and dethrone the self-made independent businessman as the paragon of manliness. His rhetoric offered an alternative model of masculinity, one based on love and mutually dependent comradeship—themes perfectly congruent with Walt Whitman's poetry.

Debs began sending greetings to the annual Whitman Fellowship dinners soon after meeting Traubel. His 1905 greeting is typical: "When the . . . Whitman Fellowship assembles, though far away, I shall be there in heart and soul, and share with you in all the delights of the joyous occasion. 'The dear love of comrades' will pervade the gathering and make it holy, and the hands of dear old Walt will be raised above it in benediction." Debs's brief greeting combines all the central themes of early twentieth-century socialism: comradeship, sentiment, and religion. From the turn of the century until his death, Traubel blended Debs and Whitman in a political program that was eccentric yet powerfully appealing to large numbers of Americans.

Horace Traubel may have been hailed as one of the great socialists of his era, but he had remarkably little to do with socialist politics in the conventional sense of the term. Debs founded the Socialist Party in 1901 and turned it into one of the most successful third parties in American history, but there is no evidence that Traubel had any involvement in the party beyond voting for his friend Gene Debs every four years. Traubel's socialism was intellectual and emotional rather than politically activist, and his interest was in winning souls, not elections. Traubel functioned as a propagandist—or, more accurately, an evangelist—using the *Conservator* to spread the gospel of Whitmanesque socialism.

After Traubel's break with the Society for Ethical Culture in 1894, the *Conservator* functioned for a time as a Whitmanite journal, with reports on the Walt Whitman Fellowship, reprints of newspaper and magazine discussions of Whitman, and poems by Traubel and others in the Whitman style. At the turn into the twentieth century the journal's tone began to change. Without losing its emphasis on Whitman-related matters, the *Conservator* began to give more attention to economics. Traubel's "Collect" was originally a miscellany of news and observations about Ethical Culture, liberal religion, and Walt Whitman. By 1901 it had become a lengthy essay that was frequently devoted to attacking prominent capitalists: In successive issues early that year he excoriated Andrew Carnegie and J. Pierpont Morgan. The next year he devoted a "Collect" to George Baer, a more obscure but, for Traubel, much more significant target. Baer, president of the Reading Coal & Iron Company, was also a director of the Farmers and Mechanics Bank of Philadelphia, where Traubel had managed to hold on to his job as a clerk for thirteen years despite conducting much of his voluminous correspondence on company time. The bank's remarkably tolerant managers did not fire Traubel for his attack on Baer, but they invoked a hitherto ignored regulation stipulating that employees could not conduct an outside business. Traubel could keep his position, but he would have to give up the *Conservator*. He quit his job instead, and in 1902 forty-three-year-old Horace Traubel, husband and father of a ten-year-old daughter, determined to emulate Walt Whitman: he would earn a living, however precarious, with his pen.

✢ ✢ ✢

Quitting his job at the bank enabled Traubel to enjoy the bohemian lifestyle that Whitman had sampled for a brief period in New York City before the Civil War, when he wrote freelance journalism and frequented Pfaff's saloon, a gathering place for writers and theater people. Freed from the bank's regular schedule, Traubel would rise at ten in the morning and take the ferry to Philadelphia, where a friend had donated office space for the *Conservator*. He would work on the *Conservator* and his other writing projects, then spend the evening and night-time hours with his large network of friends. He presided over an informal group of writers and artists, known as the "Pepper Pot Club," who met for long, talkative dinners at an inexpensive Philadelphia restaurant. Casual customers would stare at the group of eight to a dozen men and women, yelling and thumping on the table as they discussed a vast range of topics that typically included, according to one participant, "Christian Science, anarchism, vaccination and vivisection, literature, drama, art, labor and capital, prohibition and women's suffrage." When not knocking back chicken sandwiches and bad coffee, Traubel was a familiar figure at plays, concerts, baseball games, and prizefights in Philadelphia. He attended virtually every Philadelphia Symphony concert—more than forty-six hundred concerts, he claimed—saw his favorite actor, Edwin Booth, in more than three hundred plays, and was a regular in the Philadelphia Athletics' bleachers, renowned for his "bellowing pair of leather lungs." He generally did not return to Camden until well after midnight, at which point he would read until dawn and then go to bed—he needed only four or five hours' sleep.

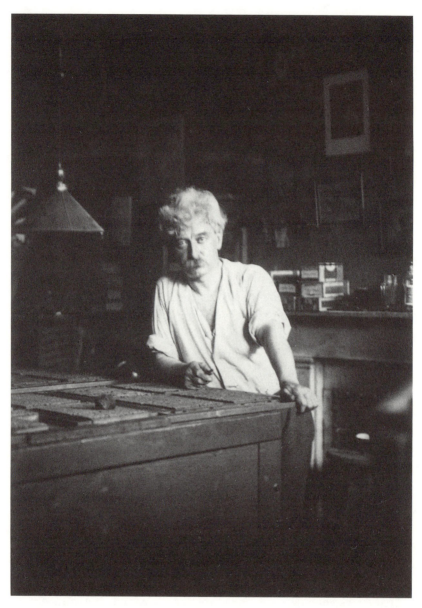

FIGURE 6.2. Horace Traubel at the *Conservator* printing press, c. 1905. Bolton Central Library.

Tom Harned, a successful lawyer, was appalled by his brother-in-law's bohemian lifestyle. "His *family* ties were very slender," Harned observed. Nevertheless, Traubel's wife, Anne, was devoted to her husband, to Walt Whitman, and to the *Conservator*. Beginning in 1898, she was listed on the *Conservator*'s masthead as associate editor, a role that continued for the next twenty-one years. "In truth," said a close friend of the Traubels, "she lived to see her husband's life work on Whitman recognized by the world." One of Horace's bohemian friends offered a sympathetic portrait of Anne based on his attendance at their weekly open house on Sunday, when guests would come to play the piano, sing, talk, and argue. "The hours flew fast," he recalled. "Presently Mrs. Traubel was missed, and we knew that she had gone to superintend the preparation of supper for which every one hoped he would be bidden to remain. Bidden or unbidden, every one stayed as a matter of course, and Mrs. Traubel's larder always appeared to have the best qualities of the widow's cruse, though the poor lady could never be sure in advance whether four or fourteen would sit down to supper. Hospitality of the best sort was Horace Traubel's sole dissipation."

Traubel's critics, of whom there were many, would have argued that his writing was a much more significant and egregious dissipation. After leaving the bank in 1902, Traubel began contributing to the socialist weekly the *Worker* in addition to editing the *Conservator*; he quickly developed the eccentric style and subject matter that would distinguish his writing for the remainder of his career. For the next two decades, aside from his writing about Whitman, he focused almost entirely on the twin themes of love and the people, repeating the two terms in endless variations throughout hundreds of poems and essays.

Yet in Traubel's case it is misleading to talk of poems and essays as separate genres. Traubel's writing after 1902 is all one massive prose poem. *Chants Communal* was his first effort to win a wider audience for his new style. Published in 1904, *Chants Communal* collected forty of his pieces for the *Worker*. "And the Heart of the Matter Is Heart" is typical. Its final paragraph begins:

I repeat myself? So I do. But the evil, too, repeats itself. As long as the evil repeats itself I will repeat myself. Let evil go where it may I will follow it. I will make evil uncomfortable to evil. I will harry it until it can stand my whip no longer. I will not use the weapon of evil against evil. I will use the weapon of good. But the weapon of good is not the easiest to bear. It is the hardest to bear. I concede nothing. Let defeat concede. Are you too timid to assert your whole case? I will assert it for you. I contend for my whole case. Not half my heart. All my heart. It is the case of the heart. I say it over and over again. The heart. The heart. The inexorable claims of the heart. The world belongs to the heart. The heart of the matter is the heart.

Traubel's lyrical socialist style was emotional, abstract, and repetitious. It was also invitingly easy to parody, and critics responded to the publication of *Chants Communal* with numerous takeoffs. "Time was when Traubel sounded the note individualistic," one wrote. "Vaguely, perhaps. With the air of mysticism. For Traubel is a mystic. He has said so. From mysticism to sentimentalism. The road is short. It is soon traveled. Traubel has traveled it." Ernest Crosby, an occasional contributor to the *Conservator*, wrote, "Traubel chants. Traubel trebles and warbles. Traubel sings a lone song. Traubel plays a lone hand. Traubel takes your best and goes it alone. Traubel is a monopolist in chants. Traubel needs competition. Compete! Learn to chant like Traubel. Let Traubel learn what it feels like to listen to his chants. Rub it in. Hard. Let us all learn to warble and traubel."

Yet if some found Traubel's writing risible, others regarded his as a valiant radical voice. "Every page of [*Chants Communal*] is up to a high water mark of inspiration," Gene Debs wrote. "It is a book that sheds light and radiance and ought to have a million circulation." The book had far less than a million circulation, but it went into a second edition and was praised by Clarence Darrow, Jack London, and scores of less prominent socialists. Emma Goldman subscribed to the *Conservator* and wrote Traubel, "I can say without flattery of all the papers in the English language I read, I enjoy the Conservator most." Goldman would have found in the *Conservator* poems by Traubel with titles such as "I Love to Go among My Dear Comrades the People" and "The People Are the Masters of Life." The latter begins:

> The people are the masters of life: the people, the people!
> So I go about in the streets of cities singing with glad
>   assurance, the people, the people!—
> Needing no reasons for my great joy beyond the reasons
>   in my own heart,
> Not asserting myself in dubious words, not being afraid,
> Letting the dissenters and scorners have their unhindered
>   way with themselves,
> I for my part figuring life out into magnificent totals
>   of love.

The style of this poem is recognizably Whitmanesque, but as many reviewers of Traubel's collection of poems *Optimos* (1910) noted, his poetry is uniformly exhortatory in tone and relentlessly abstract. H. L. Mencken called the poems "dishwatery imitations of Walt Whitman" and closed his review with a command: "Away with such stuff!" However, a significant number of socialist readers argued that Traubel was not Whitman's imitator but a successor who had surpassed his master. The generous Gene Debs led the way. "Although a loyal disciple and devotee of Walt Whitman, from whom he undoubtedly caught his earliest and deepest inspiration, he goes far beyond his revered master," Debs wrote of Traubel. "He not only brings the old Prophet of Democracy up to date but he traverses untrodden fields and explores new realms in quest of the truth." Three prominent socialists wrote books about Traubel, and all suggested that he would ultimately be regarded as a more complete poet than Whitman because his work "contains the spiritual force augmented by the economic fact," as one said.

The comment may seem strange, since "economic fact"—not to mention political fact or any concrete reference to contemporary events—is conspicuously missing from Traubel's later writing.

What it offers instead is abundant and prolix pronouncements about love, as Traubel acknowledged in a poem that begins, "I'm just talking all the time about love." He continues, "I try sometimes to talk of other things but I come back to love: / To my simple love for men and women, to my love for you, to my love for life: / Not caring at all what may be said of me because of it, coming back to love." Not unjustly, one reviewer of *Optimos* dubbed Traubel "the platitudinarian." That his work was taken seriously by so many socialists shows the millennial strain in the movement, the eagerness to envision a utopia brought about by the power of love. What may seem the worst feature of Traubel's writing, its repetitiveness, may well have been responsible for its success among socialists: his incantatory chants about love and the people perhaps served to numb the anger and anxieties of early twentieth-century middle-class leftists— their anger at social injustice in the heyday of laissez-faire capitalism and their anxieties at the class violence associated with the labor and anarchist movements.

Adam Shatz has called the decades following the end of Reconstruction "America's forgotten civil war," an era of such violence between capital and labor that it pushed even mainstream figures like the novelist William Dean Howells toward socialism. Howells's radicalism was sparked by the Haymarket affair of 1886, when a bomb was thrown at a Chicago labor rally, killing seven police and injuring sixty-seven others; in response, authorities arrested eight anarchists, some of whom had not even been present at the rally, and executed four of them. The Haymarket riot was only one among many bloody clashes between capital and labor near the turn of the century, such as the Homestead strike of 1892, when the United States Steel Corporation hired Pinkerton thugs to attack striking workers; the Pullman strike of 1894, which was broken by federal troops with drawn bayonets; and the attempted assassination of the businessman Henry Clay Frick by Emma Goldman's lover Alexander Berkman. It seemed to many Americans of the era that the nation was on the verge of a bloody class war. While the government responded with judicial and military repression, leftist intellectuals such as Howells sought to sidestep conflict by imagining utopian alternatives. Howells wrote a series of earnest utopian novels that were overshadowed by Edward Bellamy's hugely popular *Looking Backward* (1888), a portrait of a socialist future that spawned a short-lived political movement. Debsian socialists rejected Howells's and Bellamy's authoritarian models and instead embraced the democratic, if vague, utopianism offered by Horace Traubel.

Middle-class socialists' eagerness for nonviolent democratic alternatives to the current brutalities of capitalist repression and the potential violence of Marxist revolution explains their attraction to both Traubel and Whitman. After the turn of the century the Walt Whitman Fellowship's annual birthday dinners became a haven for socialists. Older disciples such as Burroughs and Harned were dismayed; Harned complained that the fellowship had become dominated by "socialists, anarchists, [and] cranks" and that "Traubel has worked the socialistic racket, much to my exclusion and disgust." Harned preferred the religious emphasis of the fellowship's early years. However, despite his brother-in-law's claims, Traubel never turned the Walt Whitman Fellowship into a purely political gathering. Throughout its existence the fellowship mixed political and religious perspectives on Whitman. Its eclecticism is nicely illustrated in the program for its eighteenth annual meeting in 1911; among the speeches were both "What Walt Whitman Means to a Revolutionist" and "The Spiritual and Religious Significance of Whitman."

During the first two decades of the twentieth century, a fertile period for both political radicalism and cultural experimentation in the United States, the Whitman Fellowship and the *Conservator* were havens for those interested in blending spirituality, politics, and bohemianism. Traubel himself was an avid cultural experimenter, and for several years he participated in an effort to transform society through a return to precapitalist modes of production. Shortly after quitting his job at the bank, he helped to found Rose Valley, a utopian arts and crafts community near Philadelphia.

The American arts and crafts movement took its lead from William Morris, the English artist and social visionary. Today Morris is remembered primarily as an interior designer, a nineteenth-century Ralph Lauren whose fabric and wallpaper designs are still marketed in upscale retail outlets. However, Morris saw his design work as part of his socialist politics. Influenced by John Ruskin's studies of medievalism, Morris believed that among the most pernicious of modern capitalism's effects was its focus on mass production and the accompanying dismissal of traditional craftsmanship. In protest against the factory system he established workshops where craftsmen could discover the joys of unalienated labor through centuries-old production techniques.

In the United States Morris's arts and crafts ideology was frequently depoliticized. Traditional crafts such as pot throwing or furniture making, which Morris saw as the basis for a regenerated society, became pastimes for middle-class hobbyists, and arts and crafts products were seen as one more commodity in the marketplace. However, a limited number of Americans recognized the political dimensions of arts and crafts, and Horace Traubel was among their leaders. Traubel came to the arts and crafts movement in 1903, when the Philadelphia architect Will Price enlisted him in a plan to purchase an abandoned mill village on Ridley Creek outside Philadelphia and turn it into an arts and crafts community. Price and his business partner Hawley McLanahan recognized that propaganda was as vital to their project as wood lathes and potter's wheels, and they convinced Traubel to edit the *Artsman*, printed by hand at the site. Traubel's distinctive contribution was to unite Morris-derived politics with Whitman-inspired spirituality. At Rose Valley, Traubel predicted in the *Artsman*, shops would be temples and labor would be worship. In language that might have been lifted from Whitman's poem "A Song for Occupations" Traubel wrote, "I can see God in the honest joint of a chair. I can see God woven in tapestries and beaten in brasses and bound in the covers of books." Traubel featured in every issue of the *Artsman* what he called "Rose Valley Scriptures," quotations from writers whom he considered to be the spiritual forebears of the arts and crafts movement—Walt Whitman, of course, prominent among them.

Whitman might have been surprised at finding himself in such company, since one of the central features of his poetry is its celebration of material progress. His "Song of the Exposition," written to commemorate a New York industrial trade show, claims that his muse is undismayed "by thud of machinery and shrill steam-whistle." He says further of her, "Bluff'd not a bit by drain-pipe, gasometers, artificial fertilizers, / Smiling and pleas'd with palpable intent to stay, / She's here, install'd among the kitchen ware!" Traubel excluded "Song of the Exposition" from the Rose Valley Scriptures and focused on passages from *Leaves of Grass* more in keeping with arts and crafts ideals. He succeeded in establishing Whitman as a patron saint of arts and crafts, but he and the other Rose Valley founders were less successful in keeping their venture afloat. Rose Valley folded in 1907, four years after it began. Traubel was left with a handsome new arts and crafts design for the *Conservator* and an undiminished enthusiasm for other progressive causes.

Among the many campaigns he supported was black Americans' struggle for civil rights. His *Conservator* reviews of books by African Americans reveal someone unusually willing to condemn white racism and question white privilege. "If you are a white American you grow grave when you think of the serious negro problem that you have on your hands," he wrote in a review of W.E.B. DuBois's *The Souls of Black Folk*. "But if you happen to be a negro or half negro or colored anyhow you are grave because you have a white problem on your hands." When Traubel visited Atlanta in 1899 and expressed his wish to meet DuBois, his hosts advised him to wait until the last day of his two-week visit so as not to alienate white Atlantans; Traubel pointedly ignored their advice and immediately sought out DuBois. He also befriended the novelist Charles W. Chesnutt, who wrote him in 1903, "If present tendencies continue much longer, the colored people of this nation are likely to need friends and it is quite clear that they can count you among them." Moreover, the Walt Whitman Fellowship was integrated almost from its beginning. Traubel invited Kelly Miller, an African American dean at Howard University, to address the fellowship's second annual meeting and later appointed him a fellowship director.

Traubel's antiracism can arguably be seen as an extension of his master's doctrines. Racial equality is at the center of Whitman's poetic project: grass grows "among black folks as among white," he writes in the opening pages of his pre–Civil War first edition, and he goes on to describe the beauty of black as well as white bodies and to narrate a powerful, if invented, tale of aiding a runaway slave. However, a decade before the first *Leaves of Grass* the young Walter Whitman wrote newspaper editorials that use the defense of white labor as the primary objection to slavery, while the old poet in Camden talked about the "nigger question" in terms to gladden the heart of any white supremacist. Kelly Miller may have heard rumors about Walt Whitman's attitudes toward blacks, since he asked rhetorically in his 1895 fellowship address, "What did [Whitman] do practically in his lifetime for the negro?" He answered his own question: "Beyond the fact that he imbibed the anti-slavery sentiment of his environments, and that this sentiment distills throughout 'Leaves of Grass,' I do not know. Nor does it matter in the least." Miller was more interested in how Whitman rejected the virtually universal portrayals of blacks as either buffoons or victims and invited them, along with all humankind, to celebrate the beauty of their bodies and the dignity of the self.

Given Traubel's defenses of black dignity in the *Conservator*, Miller may have decided that the disciple's contradictory attitudes toward race mattered as little as the master's. Like many white socialists in the early twentieth century, Traubel supported racial equality but insisted that the civil rights movement had to take a backseat to socialism. In his generally sympathetic review of *The Souls of Black Folk*, he chided DuBois for not recognizing that the key to solving the race problem was to embrace "the economic radicalisms that are becoming increasingly prevalent in the north." Traubel was echoing his friend Debs, who insisted that the Socialist Party must "receive the Negro and all other races upon absolutely equal terms" but also believed that there was "no 'Negro problem' apart from the general labor problem."

The Whitman Fellowship's record on the "woman question" was as contradictory as its stance toward the "Negro problem." In many ways the fellowship served as a model of gender equality at the turn of the century. Following the all-male 1889 Camden birthday tribute to Whitman, when the poet himself complained about the exclusion of women, Traubel worked conscientiously to include women in the Whitman circle. Thirty percent of the original fellowship members were women, and women were always represented among its leadership. The high proportion of female members seems the result of a spontaneous response to Whitman's poetry among turn-of-the-century feminists.

Anne Gilchrist was a precursor of the many feminists who responded passionately to *Leaves of Grass*. Thirty years after Gilchrist's "A Woman's Estimate of Walt Whitman," Helena Born, an Englishwoman who emigrated to the United States and joined the Boston branch of the Whitman Fellowship, wrote "Whitman's Ideal Democracy," a rousing celebration of the poet's commitment to women's equality. Mabel MacCoy Irwin, a New York City fellowship member, published a longer, even more extravagant tribute, *Whitman: The Poet-Liberator of Woman*. The radical feminist Charlotte Perkins Gilman regularly attended the Whitman Fellowship meetings along with Emma Goldman. All responded both to Whitman's political claims on women's behalf ("I say it is as great to be a woman as to be a man") and his positive depiction of women's sexuality ("Without shame the woman I like knows and avows [the deliciousness of her sex]").

At the same time other women in the Whitman Fellowship felt it important to point out the poet's limitations. In a powerful feminist analysis Helen Abbot Michael, a member of the Boston fellowship, concluded that "after all Whitman has said on woman there remains a feeling of dissatisfaction. Woman in many characters accompanies the poet, but there comes a moment in the life of his poems when his path seems to diverge from her. He goes on his way to heights and out-reaching vistas alone." Michael's essay appeared in *Poet-Lore*, a journal edited by Charlotte Porter and Helen A. Clarke. At Traubel's urging, Porter had agreed to serve as president of the Boston Whitman Fellowship, but the same year that she assumed the office, she and Clarke, who lived together, published an essay pointing out that "in all [Whitman's] singing of comradeship and friendship he makes no direct reference to comradeship between women, which is fast becoming one of the most marked characteristics of modern civilization." Porter and Clarke refused to ignore

Whitman's shortcomings as an advocate of gender equality, and they were equally demanding of Traubel. When he failed to invite any women to present papers at the 1897 fellowship meeting, Clarke wrote a letter chastising him for the omission and also for expecting her and Porter to share a single ballot in the election of the fellowship's officers. "Why is it that when women are in charge they always give [men] such a fair representation, but if men are in charge they overlook women if they possibly can?" she asked Traubel. Later she acknowledged that he was "among the few men whose attitude toward women" was generally "just and true" and even supplied an excuse for his lapses: they were "not so much intentional as the result of a carelessness men sometimes manifest through an unconscious inherited bias."

Through his work with the Whitman Fellowship and the *Conservator*, Traubel became immersed, much sooner than most Americans, in a modern world where all that had seemed solid melted into air. The women and men in his circle questioned everything: religion, politics, gender roles, marriage, the family, and sexuality. Like Whitman himself, Traubel was never directly involved in the sex-reform and free-love movements of his era, but his *Conservator* writings subtly supported the free-love ideology of early twentieth-century sex radicals. "Is love an affair you can settle with the marriage bed?" he asked rhetorically in a 1904 article. "Love cannot be honest and be confined. Love is always an overflow. No enfranchised man could contain his love. Or bestow it all upon any other individual." Anne Traubel, associate editor of the *Conservator*, must have read this essay. Did she know upon whom her husband bestowed his overflowing love? If so, she never gave any indication. It was not until long after her death that scholars found the letters documenting Horace Traubel's lengthy and passionate love affair with a fellow Whitman disciple.

✠ ✠ ✠

Gustave Percival Wiksell was a Boston dentist who joined the local branch of the Walt Whitman Fellowship soon after it was founded.

He quickly became a stalwart of the Boston group and an officer in the national organization; by 1903 he was president of the Whitman Fellowship, an office he held for the rest of the group's existence. Traubel and Wiksell became acquainted in 1894; within a few years they were lovers.

Of course, one has to be careful about asserting that men of a century ago were lovers in our sense of the term, particularly men involved in the Whitman Fellowship. One of the attractions of Whitmanism in both England and the United States was that it provided a culturally safe space for men to declare their love for one another. "Be you my lover," Traubel wrote Wallace near the beginning of their friendship, and his correspondence with Debs was full of passionate declarations of love on both sides: "It would be impossible for one human being to love another more than I love you," Debs wrote Traubel in 1910. It is unlikely that Traubel ever had a physical love affair with either Wallace or Debs; rather, these men were immersed in a Whitman-sanctioned discourse of male love that, even during the decade after the Oscar Wilde trials, allowed them to express their affection for one another without sexual implications.

However, Traubel's letters to Wiksell move beyond comradeship into physically explicit expressions of desire. "I dream of . . . the little bed in your paradise and the two arms of a brother that accept me in their divine partnership," Traubel wrote shortly before a trip to Boston. After his visit he wrote longingly, "I sit here and write you a letter. It is not a pen that is writing. It is the lips that you have kissed. It is the body that you have traversed over and over with your consecrating palm. Do you not feel that body? Do you not feel the return?" These and other letters leave little doubt that the two men had a sexual love affair, an affair that seems to have been remarkably guilt free. Wiksell's letters to Traubel refer to his own wife and child and mix heavy-breathing passion with cheery greetings to "Annie and Gertrude."

The complete lack of furtiveness or shame in the Traubel-Wiksell correspondence is particularly striking given Traubel's angry response to John Addington Symonds's suggestions that Whitman's

"Calamus" poems encouraged "ardent and *physical* intimacies" between men. After Whitman's death Symonds began querying other Whitmanites, including J. W. Wallace, for confirmation of his theories. When Wallace told Traubel about Symonds's inquiry, Traubel replied vehemently: "Homosexuality is disease—it is muck and rot—it is decay and muck—and Walt uttered the master-cries of health, of salvation, and purity, of growth and beauty." Traubel's response has an edge of hysterical defensiveness, though at the time he was newly married and years away from his affair with Wiksell. By the time the affair began, he had put any defensiveness aside, and his correspondence with Wiksell reveals how both men found a sanction for their passion in a heavily religious discourse that combined Walt Whitman, Christianity, and Eastern religion.

The Traubel letters, with their talk of a "divine" partnership and a "consecrating" palm, reveal how the two men mingled the erotic and the religious, interpreting their love affair in spiritual terms. The Christmas season seemed to bring their eroticized spirituality to its height. "Oh darling my brother I hold your hands in mine," Wiksell wrote in December 1901. "I kiss you and thank God for you. You are one of God's ties to hold me to the holy things of love." Traubel wrote on December 25, 1903, "When it is Christmas and I think of Christ I find it natural and easy to think of you. When Christ is present to me you also are present to me. You have done the work of Christ, and that is better than to wear his name. . . . I send you a kiss for this sacred day." Neither Traubel nor Wiksell identified himself as Christian—that is, they did not "wear [Christ's] name"—but they borrowed Christian terminology as a sanction for their affair.

They also borrowed from the language of Theosophy. There was an overlap in membership between the Walt Whitman Fellowship and the Theosophical Society, and although Wiksell and Traubel were no more formally Theosophist than they were Christian, they were influenced by Theosophy's eclectic appropriations of Eastern religion. Wiksell wrote Traubel after a visit, "When I left you on the train . . . I had no feeling of loss as we often feel when one we love goes away. I did not have any feeling of separation. Your visit was a bodily one—spiritually we are never separated. 'Kill out all sense of separateness' is one of the laws of yoga. This will be the real heaven when all men have become one and there are no separate persons in the world. My lips to yours dear one." Wiksell and Traubel interpreted their lovemaking as a physical demonstration of mystical human union.

However, Theosophical interpretations of their love were much less frequent than their invocations of Walt Whitman. After 1903 the two men almost always inscribed their love letters on official stationery of the Walt Whitman Fellowship, which listed their names below Whitman's: Wiksell as president and Traubel as secretary-treasurer. Walt Whitman literally enclosed their relationship, and they referred constantly to Whitman and *Leaves of Grass*. Traubel's connection to Whitman was important for Wiksell, who had never met Whitman personally. "In you I find alive so much of our dear friend Walt," he wrote Traubel early in their relationship. When the first volume of *With Walt Whitman in Camden* appeared in 1906, Wiksell's indirect connection to Whitman seemed to intensify enormously: "I feel now as though I know as much about him as you yourself and have kissed his bearded lips. Through you I arrive at kinship with the divine compassionate man." The "divine" Whitman's poetry provided a spiritualized sanction for their love affair.

It is not clear how long their physical affair lasted, but Wiksell and Traubel remained close friends until the latter's death. The last piece in the final issue of the *Conservator* is a Wiksell prose poem that asserts Whitman's religious significance: "If all the theologies . . . were to sink in the quicksands . . . out of Leaves of Grass would come the flowers of worship satisfying the soul, and forms and ceremonies to meet the use of temples and groves in the religious expression of vital events. . . . Leaves of Grass—biography of a man—is the biography of God." Whitmanism offered Wiksell and Traubel a way to sanctify their love during the opening years of the twentieth century, the decades when same-sex passion was being turned into the supposedly deviant sexual category of homosexuality. Their identities as members of the Whitman Fellowship enabled them to turn their backs on the emerging psychiatric-legal understanding of male love and locate their passion within a religious framework that borrowed terms from Christianity, Theosophy, and, above all, *Leaves of Grass.*

✢✢✢

Traubel saw less of Wiksell—and of everyone else, for that matter—after 1914, when a bout of rheumatic fever left him with a seriously weakened heart. He had his first heart attack in 1917 and several more in the months following. The social circle of this formerly vibrant, gregarious man contracted to a few intimates, including David Karsner, editor of a socialist newspaper in New York. In the spring of 1919 Traubel left Camden, for what he probably sensed would be the last time, to stay with Karsner in New York City, where Traubel could see his new grandson and be on hand for the Whitman centennial celebration in May. Karsner occupied two floors of an East Side brownstone with his wife, Rose, and daughter, Walta Whitman. As Eugene Debs's biographer, Karsner had obtained the table that Debs used in prison following the Pullman strike, and Karsner arranged for Traubel to work there. The table was at a window overlooking the East River, and as Traubel gazed at the water he thought about Walt. For most of his career, after the brief, heady period in the mid-1850s when Ralph Waldo Emerson had endorsed *Leaves of Grass*, Whitman had emphasized his personal poverty and the general neglect of his work. Traubel continued the martyrdom theme in the *Conservator*, devoting substantial portions of many issues to reprinting attacks on *Leaves of Grass* and the Whitman Fellowship. But as the one-hundredth anniversary of Whitman's birth approached, Traubel was inclined to declare victory. "I say, Walt, dear Walt," he wrote in his final poem:

> Ain't it funny, considering the light way they used to
>   dismiss you, how they have to eat their words?
> They were always so sure you'd come to nothing—that
>   their universities and editorial chairs comprised all
>   heaven and earth:

How they passed you by without a word or with con-
   temptuous words or foul epithets:
We've come upon a milder period, Walt: This year they
   are saying kind things of you in choruses:
And those of us who were with you when you were out-
   lawed are almost fashionable, so great is the demand
   for us.

"Walt, I could go on all day in this style," he wrote near the poem's
end, striking fear into readers' hearts—not even the most devoted
Whitmanite could wish this prosy, repetitious poem to be any
longer. "Traubel was born with every gift except the blue pen-
cil," a reviewer of one of his books wrote; Traubel would not
have disputed the judgment. Unlike Whitman, who obsessively
worked over his poems, frequently trying out multiple variations
of a single phrase, Traubel never revised. He was a believer in what
spiritualists called "automatic writing." Early in his career as editor
of the *Conservator*, he bragged that he had composed a fifty-page
essay in only two hours: "Thinking comes easy. I dip my pen in
the ink and let the rest take care of itself. There is a self back of
one's formal self which uses the external agents as *media* only. It is
a mediumistic trait. I seem to have it in abundance and it quickly
facilitates my labor."

Traubel's dual interests in mediumistic traits and Walt Whitman
were shared by many in his circle but by no one more fervently than
Flora MacDonald Denison. Traubel met her on one of his many
trips to Toronto, where he stayed with his old friends Mildred and
Frank Bain, wealthy socialists and Whitmanites who had started a
Toronto branch of the Whitman Fellowship. Denison, nine years
younger than Traubel, had discovered Whitman as a young woman
and integrated *Leaves of Grass* into the eccentric and powerful political and religious program that absorbed her energies as an adult.
Denison was best known in Canada as a founder of the nation's
foremost women's suffrage organization and its leader from 1911 to
1914. During those years she wrote a weekly column for a Toronto
newspaper with the Whitmanesque title "The Open Road Towards

Democracy." Her devotion to Whitman, democracy, and women's suffrage was matched by her passion for other causes, including socialism, Spiritualism, and Theosophy.

In 1916 Denison took time from her feminist and socialist political activities to attend to a property she had bought some years before: Bon Echo, a rambling lodge on the shores of Lake Mazinaw in Ontario. She determined to turn it into a combination summer hotel and spiritual community dedicated to the ideals of Walt Whitman, and she began publishing the *Sunset of Bon Echo*, a sporadically appearing journal with contributions from eminent Whitmanites such as Traubel, Harned, and her close friend and sister Spiritualist-suffragist Charlotte Perkins Gilman.

Early in 1919, Denison attended a Toronto séance at which a medium summoned the spirit of Walt Whitman. Whitman communicated with the group by ouija board, and Denison printed his lengthy address in *Sunset of Bon Echo*. Whitman had evidently been reading his friend Bucke's book in the spirit world, since most of his message dealt with cosmic consciousness, a subject he had resolutely avoided while alive. The séance confirmed Denison's decision to dedicate a massive granite outcropping on Lake Mazinaw—two miles long and nearly four hundred feet high—to Whitman. When she told Traubel about her plans, he decided to travel to Canada for the dedication.

On May 31, 1919, Traubel basked in the adulation of the large group of socialists, Spiritualists, and other radicals who had come to the Hotel Brevoort in Greenwich Village to pay tribute to both Walt Whitman and the dying Horace Traubel. Once the centennial celebration was over, he was determined to move on to Canada. Doctors told Anne that Horace might not survive the trip, but he probably would not die on the train. His friend Frank Bain came from Toronto to New York to escort Horace and Anne to Ontario. Just before they reached Montreal, Traubel had another heart attack. They paused briefly, then pushed on to Bon Echo.

At Bon Echo Traubel was surrounded by friends who had come for the Canadian Whitman Fellowship's centennial celebration. He seemed to rally in their presence and three weeks after his arrival decided he was strong enough to make the trip by boat to dedicate "Old Walt," as Denison had dubbed the giant rock cliff. On August 25 two men carried Traubel's wheelchair onto the dock, where a party of fifteen embarked across the lake in canoes and rowboats. Once they reached the rock, they maneuvered the rowboat carrying the Traubels and Denison into position so that Horace and Denison could perform the simple dedication ceremony: simultaneously, they placed their hands on the granite and uttered the words "Old Walt." Immediately both Horace and Anne broke into sobs, while the others respectfully observed the affecting scene.

Three days later Horace began having visions. With his mind running on his days with Whitman ever since the birthday celebration in New York, his emotions heightened by the dedication ceremony, and his receptiveness quickened by his association with Denison and her Spiritualist friends, it is not surprising that Traubel started to see Walt Whitman in the Canadian wilderness. Three days after the dedication, as he sat at sunset gazing at "Old Walt" across the lake, he rapped his cane on the floor to summon Flora Denison. She came running, fearing the worst, and found him radiant. "Look, look, Flora; quick, quick, he is going."

"What, where, Horace, I do not see anyone."

"Why just over the Rock Walt appeared, head and shoulders and hat on, in a golden glory—brilliant and splendid. He reassured me, beckoned to me, and spoke to me. I heard his voice but did not understand all he said, only 'Come on.'"

Traubel would live only eleven more days. During that time Anne bustled about him, loving and attentive, feeding her husband's insatiable ego: "You're triumphant, Horace, you've affected the ages, no regrets, Horace, no regrets." Walt was present to Horace as well. "Come on, come on," Horace heard him saying.

On September 8, 1919, Traubel came on. His funeral three days later was scheduled to take place at a Unitarian church in New York. As the mourners started to assemble and the hearse carrying Traubel's remains turned onto the street in front of the church, the chancel suddenly burst into flames, and the crowd fled through dense smoke. No one was injured, and on the spot it was decided to move the ceremony to People's House, a nearby socialist club. "He burned the church down before he'd be taken into it," one of the mourners remarked. "The church burned down before it would have him in it," his companion replied. Percival Wiksell led the services for his old friend, quoting poems by Whitman and Traubel.

Following the ceremony, the hearse made its way to Camden. The next day a small group gathered in Harleigh Cemetery, not far from Whitman's tomb. As he requested, Horace Traubel was buried close to Walt. At the end all the "isms" seemed less important to him than the simple fact of the years of friendship with the old man he loved. "Oh! those blessed old times, Walt!" Traubel wrote in his last poem. "They're sacreder to me than the scriptures of races: / They're the scriptures of our two personal souls made one in a single supreme vision." As J. W. Wallace said, Horace had been the disciple whom Walt loved best. Now, as Traubel had envisioned, he and Walt would be one, as immortal as leaves of grass.

AFTERWORD

Failing to fetch me at first keep encouraged,
Missing me one place search another,
I stop somewhere waiting for you.

HORACE TRAUBEL'S DEATH changed everything for the American Whitmanites. The *Conservator* folded immediately. For years it had been a one-man, money-losing operation, and none of Traubel's friends was foolish enough to take it on. The 1919 centennial celebration of Whitman's birthday also proved to be the final gathering of the Walt Whitman Fellowship: International. Absent Traubel's organizational zeal, the group dwindled into an association dedicated to preserving Whitman's Mickle Street house. The disciples, those who had been in Whitman's charismatic presence, were dying off. John Burroughs published a final, fervid essay on Whitman the year after Traubel's death, insisting to the end that Whitman was a "seer and philosopher," not a mere poet, and that *Leaves of Grass* was not a collection of poems but "an inspired utterance." A year later Burroughs himself died at eighty-three.

In England J. W. Wallace carried on the Eagle Street College's annual Whitman birthday celebrations until his death in 1926. By that point John Johnston was bedridden, felled by a stroke; he died one year after Wallace. After their deaths the Lancashire birthday celebrations continued, carried on by younger men and women who had been drawn to the group by their friendships with Wallace and Johnston. Inevitably, however, the religious fervor that the group's founders brought to *Leaves of Grass* faded. The next generation admired Whitman but saw him as a poet, not a prophet.

Yet even as the disciples' religiously inspired organizations dissolved, Whitman's reputation rose. The earliest disciples, starting with William O'Connor, were intent on rescuing Whitman from, on the one hand, utter obscurity and, on the other, from charges of incoherence and obscenity. Thanks in great part to their efforts, Whitman's fame spread rapidly, so that by the time of his death in 1892 he was perhaps the most widely known U.S. poet in both North America and Great Britain. However, notoriety need not imply acceptance; opinion of Whitman's merits was radically divided. The disciples regarded him as the greatest figure in history; hostile critics saw him as an untalented poseur who had foisted his tedious verse and prophetic aspirations upon the credulous. One turn-of-the-century critic judiciously called Whitman "the best loved and best hated of modern poets."

Whitman remained a controversial figure throughout the 1890s, but during the first years of the new century his reputation as a great American poet began to solidify. The appearance of Bliss Perry's *Walt Whitman* in 1906 proved a decisive event. The bare facts of the book's publication reveal the shift in Whitman's reputation: The volume was part of Houghton Mifflin's prestigious "American Men of Letters" series, and its author was editor of the *Atlantic Monthly*, a former professor of English at Williams and Princeton, and the newly appointed holder of the Harvard professorship formerly filled by Henry Wadsworth Longfellow and James Russell Lowell. Twenty-four years earlier *Leaves of Grass* had been banned in Boston; now the New England literary establishment was canonizing Whitman. Perry took for granted Whitman's importance as a poet, and he acknowledged the religious dimensions of *Leaves of Grass*, calling Whitman a mystic and, à la R. M. Bucke, juxtaposing passages from "Song of Myself" and the Bhagavad Gita. Perry concluded the book by stating that "no American poet seems more sure to be read . . . after one hundred or five hundred years."

The disciples were furious. Traubel commenced an attack on Perry in the pages of the *Conservator* that lasted for more than a year, until the appearance of the book's second edition unleashed a new pack of critical articles by Traubel and others. In part, the disciples' hostility was provoked by what they saw as factual errors, such as Perry's assertions that Whitman was unreliable with money. More significantly, they resented Perry's condescension toward them. He referred disparagingly to the Whitman "cult" and the cultists who had enveloped Whitman in a "Camden apotheosis," and he dismissed the disciples as "hot little prophets," a clever label that was picked up by other writers and recycled innumerable times. Most of all, though, the disciples resented Perry's book because he regarded Walt Whitman as only a poet. In his conclusion Perry acknowledged that "in certain moods" one might regard Whitman primarily as a seer and prophet. But then, as if shaking off an hallucination, he asserted that in one's more rational moments one saw Whitman as an artist. In that case one had to conclude that, for all his brute strength, Whitman never reached the artistry of, say, Keats.

"Perry's point of view is always literary before it is human," Traubel wrote in one of his *Conservator* articles. The disciples' attacks on Perry were so vehement and sustained because they recognized that this well-written biography by a major critic was likely to be widely read and regarded as definitive—as it proved to be. Traubel and the disciples resented Perry's judicious on-the-one-hand-on-the-other-hand evaluation of Whitman and the critic's judgment that only a few poems in *Leaves of Grass* would live. The disciples responded to Perry as if their beloved master were being taken away from them. They were right.

Perry's book coincided with the institutionalization of American literature as a field of academic study. When departments of English were first established in American colleges during the second half of the nineteenth century, they were restricted to the study of the British classics, from *Beowulf* through Milton. Gradually, more recent British literature entered the curriculum, but it was not until the end of the century that the first courses in American literature were offered. These courses were widely regarded as a radical innovation, and instructors had to choose their subject matter carefully. Oscar Lovell Triggs, a young instructor at the University of Chicago and an enthusiastic participant in the local Whitman Fellowship, was dismissed from the university for including Whitman in his courses during the 1890s. Ten years later Perry's book served to nudge Whitman into the emerging American literary canon. The disciples sensed, correctly, that the imprimatur of this esteemed Harvard professor meant both literary immortality for Walt Whitman and the death of *Leaves of Grass* as they knew it. They read *Leaves of Grass* as scripture, an inspired book meant to be absorbed as a transformative whole. The professors, they knew, would select individual poems from an anthology and teach Whitman alongside Bryant and Whittier and Longfellow, reducing the eagle to a songbird.

By 1919, the year of both Traubel's death and the centennial of Whitman's birth, American literature had become firmly established in the curriculum of U.S. schools and colleges. The patriotic fervor following the Bolshevik Revolution and World War I spurred the demand for courses that could serve nationalist ends, and *Leaves of Grass*—or at least parts of it—fit easily into a master narrative of the growth of American democracy. Teachers set aside long, spiritually fervid poems such as "Song of Myself" or "Crossing Brooklyn Ferry" in favor of brief democratic chants such as "I Hear America Singing" and the perennially popular "O Captain! My Captain!" Meanwhile, critics were drawn to the formal intricacies of poems such as "When Lilacs Last in the Dooryard Bloom'd," Whitman's elegy for Abraham Lincoln, and "Out of the Cradle Endlessly Rocking," his account of the birth of his poetic vocation—poems that invited comparison not to the Bible and the Bhagavad Gita but to such poetic classics as Milton's *Lycidas*, Tennyson's *In Memoriam*, and Shelley's "To a Skylark." Almost all of the hundreds of newspaper and magazine articles published about the 1919 centennial of Whitman's birth acclaimed *Leaves of Grass* as a work of genius, but they also used the occasion to denounce what they saw as the excesses of the disciples. The *Chicago Evening Post* summed up the situation as follows: "[The disciples] imagine that no one honors [Whitman] except themselves. Whereas the fact is that all good judges have long since given Whitman his due. . . . That Whitman was not a mystical savior or avatar of some new dispensation is a statement that in some quarters needs to be insisted upon."

The death of Traubel, the disciples' principal polemicist, only months after the Whitman centennial signaled the end of the pitched battles between the disciples and mainstream critics. By 1950 Charles Willard, a professor of English, could note with satisfaction in his history of Whitman's American reception that "the last of the band who knew [Whitman] personally, loved him, and believed him the founder of the religion of the future" was gone, and discussion of the poet was firmly established on the plane of "sane and traditional literary criticism." However, Willard oversimplified the history of Whitman's reception, casting it as an agon between crackpot disciples and rational academics. Although academic critics may have downplayed the mystical, prophetic dimensions of Whitman's poetry, Malcolm Cowley reached hundreds of thousands of readers with his introduction to a 1959 paperback edition of *Leaves of Grass* in which he argued that "Song of Myself" should be read as one of the great inspired prophetic works of world literature; it was Cowley's edition of the *Leaves* that I read in New York during the 1970s and that brought to a boil my own religious appreciation of *Leaves of Grass*. Cowley was not alone in his view of Whitman as a spiritual genius. Appreciation of Whitman as the prophet of a spiritualized democracy did not die with Traubel but continued to thrive outside the academy throughout the twentieth century. In the 1930s, for example, Mike Gold called Whitman the "heroic spiritual grandfather" of his generation of radical writers and activists and encouraged the young Woody Guthrie to read *Leaves of Grass*. A decade later Langston Hughes edited a collection of Whitman's poetry for the leftist International Publishers, writing in his introduction that Whitman was a "cosmic" poet of democracy. This image of Whitman as the avatar of a spiritualized democracy was recently revived by Richard Rorty in his powerful polemic *Achieving Our Country*, which links Whitman and John Dewey as prophets of the American civic religion.

If Rorty can be seen as Horace Traubel's heir in his portrayal of a Whitman who is equal parts prophet and democrat, other writers have grasped for Bucke's position as explicator of Whitman's mysticism. Will Hayes, a renegade Unitarian minister in Chatham, England, published *Walt Whitman: The Prophet of the New Era* in 1921;

its first two chapter titles—"The Christ of Our Age" and "The Carpenter of Brooklyn"—provide a good sense of its contents. More recently, Gary David Comstock, Protestant chaplain at Wesleyan University, provided the introduction for the Whitman volume in the SkyLight Paths "Mystic Poets" series; Whitman was the fourth in the series, which began with Hafiz, Tagore, and Hopkins.

The Hayes and Comstock volumes were issued by respected publishers, but there is also a long tradition of self-published books about Whitman and spirituality. These range from Dilys Gold's endearingly eccentric *A Marriage of True Minds*, which records an elderly English widow's ouija-board conversations with Walt Whitman's spirit self, to Philip Akers's philosophically grandiose *The Principle of Life: A New Concept of Reality Based on Walt Whitman's "Leaves of Grass"* to Gregory Leifel's novel *The Day I Met Walt Whitman*, an artful first-person narrative of a young man who, like John Burroughs, sees Whitman as the singer of a spiritualized apprehension of the natural world and who encounters the mystically revivified poet on a walk through an Illinois nature preserve.

The Internet has radically expanded the opportunities for readers interested in Whitman and spirituality to publish their views. One of the longest-running and most extensive Whitman sites is LeavesofGrass.org. Despite its official-sounding name, the Web site is a one-man show created by Mitchell Gould, a freelance multimedia designer who works out of his studio—he calls it "Paumanok West"—in Portland, Oregon. Gould is simultaneously a gay rights activist, Quaker, and self-described "public historian," and his Web site features his extensive research into the nineteenth-century intersections of gay history and liberal American religion. He is convinced that the origins of *Leaves of Grass* can best be understood by tracing the connections between nineteenth-century maritime culture, where gay relationships flourished, and Quakerism. He sees the links among sailors, gay lovers, and Quakers as the foundation of *Leaves of Grass*, and he has unearthed hundreds of examples of Whitman's connections to all three groups.

I talked with Gould by telephone about his interest in Whitman, which recently led him to write and perform a Whitman monologue,

"I Call to Mankind." So far Gould has performed it three times for various Quaker audiences. "It's the culmination of my fourteen years of work trying to connect Walt's voice back to the Quakers," he told me. Gould had been browsing through *Leaves of Grass* for years, but in 1992 everything suddenly fell into place. That year he read Jonathan Ned Katz's *Gay American History*, which revealed the extent of gay relationships among both sailors and Quakers in the nineteenth-century United States, and Gould began reading Whitman biographies, which explained Whitman's connections to Quakers: the poet's maternal grandmother was a Friend, and as a boy he heard the great Quaker liberal Elias Hicks preach. "I had been skating on the surface of *Leaves of Grass*," Gould recalls, "then in '92 the ice cracked and I was immersed." He began attending the local Friends meeting and soon became a "convinced Friend," as Quakers term converts.

As I listened to Gould, I felt as if I were speaking with an American Edward Carpenter—earnest, reasonable, and impassioned about Whitman's intertwined gospel of spirituality and sexuality. Gould told me that when he testified at public hearings in Portland regarding gay marriage, he had been inspired by Whitman. "The reason people want to destroy my relationship with my partner, Roger," Gould testified, "is that they think they are doing God's will. In fact, the relationship of a man to the man he loves, or of a woman to the woman she loves, is sacred." That, he explained to me, "is ultimately what Walt Whitman is all about. The most important message of *Leaves of Grass* is that man's love for man or woman's love for woman is a path to God. In the middle of the nineteenth century who else, besides Walt Whitman, was going to make that case?"

✝ ✝ ✝

Neil Richardson isn't convinced that man's love for man is Whitman's central message. In fact, he argues that Whitman wasn't gay, a point he made at length several years ago when he found himself talking to Allen Ginsberg at a party following a poetry reading in Washington, D.C. Ginsberg enjoyed the argument with Richard-

son—a handsome, athletic guy who once played professional soccer—and wound up grabbing him and kissing him on the mouth.
"If I'm right," Ginsberg told him, "you just kissed a man who kissed
a man who kissed a man who slept with Walt Whitman."

Richardson told me about his encounter with Ginsberg over lunch
at an outdoor cafe near Washington's Dupont Circle. We had just
come from a "Walt Whitman Meditation" led by Richardson at the
nearby Quaker meetinghouse. Richardson is not a Quaker, but he's
a deeply spiritual person with an eclectic religious practice that
began as a teenager when he taught himself to meditate from articles
in *Rolling Stone*. At about the same time he encountered *Leaves of
Grass* in the public library. "I was overwhelmed," he recalls. "It
completely changed my life." *Leaves of Grass* became Richardson's
companion as he pursued extensive travels and an unconventional
career following his graduation from college. He played soccer,
worked construction, hiked from Texas to Panama, explored the
Amazon, and received a master's degree in international affairs from
Georgetown. The degree led to a variety of jobs in community organizing: training election observers in Ghana, working as a consul-
tant, and serving as deputy director for neighborhood action in the
office of the mayor of Washington, D.C.

This last job enabled Richardson to unite his dual passions for
political change and for Walt Whitman. "I see *Leaves of Grass* as
political as well as spiritual," Richardson told me. "It's a call to
revolution in spirit and in politics. However, it's not about politics
in the sense of voting but of being a citizen. And being a citizen is
connecting to your fellow man and fellow woman." Working in the
mayor's office, he organized the world's largest town meeting: four
thousand Washington residents turned out to talk about revitalizing
their neighborhoods. "Walt Whitman was my inspiration for that
meeting," Richardson said. "I even got the mayor quoting Whitman. Whenever I talked to reporters, I'd say that it was inspired by
a former D.C. resident, Walt Whitman."

As he worked in community organizing, Richardson was deepening his connections to Whitman. He visited the Library of Congress
regularly to read through Whitman manuscripts, and he began going

to Camden once or twice a year to collect trash around Whitman's tomb in Harleigh Cemetery, then to lie on the grass nearby. Reading through the six-volume edition of Whitman's notebooks, he stumbled across an extraordinary passage written shortly after the poet first published *Leaves of Grass*:

> Abstract yourself from this book,—realize where you are at present located,—the point you stand, that is now to you the centre of all.—Look up, overhead,—think of space stretching out—think of all the unnumbered orbs wheeling safely there. . . . Spend some minutes faithfully in this exercise.—Then again realize yourself upon the earth, at the particular point you now occupy—Which way stretches the north, and what countries, seas, &c? Which way the south?—which way the East? Which way the west?—Seize these firmly with your mind—pass freely over immense distances,—fix definitely (turn your face a moment thither) the directions, and the idea of the distances, of separate sections of your own country— also of England, the Mediterranean sea, Cape Horn, the North Pole, and such like distinct places.

The passage resembles instructions for meditation from a variety of esoteric religious traditions; Richardson believes it provides evidence of Whitman's own meditation practice. "If we can establish that Whitman had a meditation practice," he explained to me over lunch, "that establishes meditation as an American tradition. If we can get it out that this great American meditated, we can get more people sitting, which could only make better citizens, better communities, and maybe better national policies."

When the Washington Friends of Walt Whitman put out a call for events to celebrate the 150th anniversary of *Leaves of Grass* in 2005, Richardson volunteered to lead a Whitman Meditation. Sixteen people gathered in the parlor of the Quaker meetinghouse on a Saturday morning in April: a couple of members of the Friends of Whitman, staffers at the Library of Congress, and a variety of people of different ages who had read about the event in a *Washington Post* article. After introductions those assembled settled into their chairs and closed their eyes while Richardson read aloud the instructions for meditation from Whitman's notebook, followed by passages from *Leaves of Grass*. Once the thirty-minute guided meditation was over, members of the group talked enthusiastically. Few in the room knew Whitman well, but they were familiar with a variety of religious traditions, and they commented excitedly on how *Leaves of Grass* reminded them of Sufism or Lakota spirituality or yoga or Quakerism or Unitarianism. People were particularly struck by a brief passage from "Song of Myself" that Richardson had recited; they asked him to read it twice more:

> There was never any more inception than there is now,
> Nor any more youth or age than there is now,
> And will never be any more perfection than there is now,
> Nor any more heaven or hell than there is now.

"It's a prayer," one woman commented.

Neil Richardson was pleased with the meditation session, which had introduced a few more people to the transformative spiritual dimensions of *Leaves of Grass*. He had tried to publicize his view of Whitman through the *Walt Whitman Quarterly Review*, but his essay was rejected. "Yeah, the academics shot me down," he said ruefully. "In turning him into a great poet, they've lost sight of his spiritual dimension." The heart of Richardson's essay was a revision of Bucke. "Cosmic consciousness is a great way of understanding Whitman," Richardson told me, "but there's something off about Bucke's conception of it. He believed that once a century or so lightning would strike from the heavens and single out one person to be the channel of the divine. I think that's elitist. We don't have to wait for a lightning bolt. We can access the enlightened state through meditation, and Walt Whitman proves that. Whitman *democratized* spirituality."

✝ ✝ ✝

The people who gathered for Neil Richardson's meditation were all comfortable exploring an overtly religious approach to Whitman's poems. Washington, D.C., has a large population of people interested in eclectic spirituality, and Richardson told me that he turned away another dozen people who wanted to attend the session. Small towns are less likely to have a concentration of spiritual seekers who are also interested in nineteenth-century poetry. Yet I came across two small towns that hold annual celebrations of Walt Whitman's birthday, gatherings that are not explicitly religious but that offer ordinary readers an opportunity to testify to the power of Whitman's verse.

Conroe, Texas, does not seem, at first glance, a promising spot for poetry. A small town in the East Texas plains north of Houston, it reached its peak in the early twentieth century when it was designated county seat, and the massive Montgomery County Courthouse was built downtown. Low-slung brick buildings from the same era surround the courthouse, their stepped pediments echoing the wooden facades of the frontier-era constructions they replaced. They house law offices, bail bondsmen, private investigators, and a surprising number of old-fashioned barber shops—clearly, Conroe is a town where a fair proportion of the male citizens still prefer their hair cut short, clean on the neck, and high above the ears.

The Texas Arts Venue is directly across the street from the courthouse. A landlord who couldn't find a commercial tenant donated the space to the county arts council, and now art exhibits and concerts and plays take place in the back room, a large, pleasant space with a high pressed-tin ceiling. Every May 31 a dozen or so people gather to celebrate Walt Whitman's birthday. The event was initiated by Dave Parsons, a poet who teaches at the local community college. He's a sophisticated poet, author of an award-winning book, and at the same time a good ol' boy, a Texas native with a deep drawl and a southwesterner's immediate, uncomplicated friendliness. Parsons kicked off the 2005 Whitman birthday celebration by inviting members of the audience to come up and read Whitman poems that matter to them, and a half-dozen people took him up on the offer, introducing themselves with their first names. Alicia talked about the unreality of war in the age of television, how insulated she felt from the death and suffering in Iraq, then read three short

"Drum-Taps" poems. George, a physician, read two excerpts from *Specimen Days* about Civil War hospitals. "I don't know any other writing," he said, "that's so realistic and matter-of-fact about what goes on in a hospital." Dereseé, mother of a toddler, talked about her daughter's joyousness, her intense, ongoing wonder at the novelty of experience. "A walk to the playground can be the peak of her life," she said, and then she read "There Was a Child Went Forth" ("There was a child went forth every day, / And the first object he look'd upon, that object he became"). Nobody talked about Whitman as a spiritual teacher, but they all expressed a deep personal connection to his poetry. They had come to otherwise deserted downtown Conroe on a weeknight not for aesthetic pleasure—or not only for that—but for the chance to testify to this poetry's meaning in their own lives. When Cliff read aloud, he chose "Crossing Brooklyn Ferry" because, he said, "I like the way Whitman is talking directly to *me*."

That sense of Whitman's presence is also strong at the annual Whitman birthday celebration in Lancashire, England. Younger members of the Eagle Street College continued the Whitman celebrations until the 1950s, a quarter-century after Wallace's and Johnston's deaths, but with the demise of the second generation, the gatherings sputtered out. The group's copious records, as well as Whitman's canary, stuffed and preserved under glass, remained untouched in the Bolton library until the 1980s when Paul Salveson, who was conducting research for his doctoral dissertation on Lancashire dialect poetry, happened across Johnston's poems. Fascinated, he plunged into the Eagle Street archives, eventually publishing an essay about the group. Salveson acknowledged Wallace and Johnston's spiritual approach to Whitman, but as a member of the local Socialist Club Salveson was more interested in their political involvement. A community activist, he decided to revive the local tradition, and in 1984, one hundred years after Wallace invited a few friends to join him in his sitting room to talk about *Leaves of Grass*, Salveson organized a revival of the Lancashire Whitman birthday celebrations, an annual event now in its third decade.

I timed a research trip to Bolton to coincide with the May event. Some years ago Salveson moved from Bolton to Yorkshire, so much of the organizing for the Whitman birthday celebration now falls to Jacqueline Dagnall, a Socialist Club stalwart. Dagnall picked me up in central Bolton at midday on a beautiful Saturday, a bit late—she'd been in the countryside gathering lilacs. She gunned her aging Nissan up the motorway leading out of Bolton and turned off at Barrow Bridge, a picturesque nineteenth-century mill village with a public park where the mill once stood, the workers' housing now occupied by affluent professionals who commute to Manchester. Two dozen people had assembled at Barrow Bridge, and everyone chatted as they cut lilac blossoms from the branches Dagnall had gathered and pinned them to their shirts—a nod to the nineteenth-century Bolton disciples, who sported lilacs on their lapels at Whitman celebrations. After posing for a photograph, the group walked through Barrow Bridge and onto a footpath leading into the Lancashire hills.

After a half hour's hike the group reached the crest of a hill overlooking Walker Fold, a country house where the Eagle Street College occasionally gathered. Everyone flopped onto the lush meadow grass, and Don Lee, a long-time Socialist Club member, stood downhill from the group to act as master of ceremonies. A large, diverse, multiracial group had gathered, with old leftists, young parents with children, and a sprinkling of first-timers who had heard about the gathering and decided to come out for a ramble on this fine spring day.

Following introductions, Dagnall removed the bubble wrap from a loving cup made by one of Whitman's American disciples and presented to Wallace and Johnston: a large, eccentrically designed three-handled ceramic mug with a pewter rim. The Bolton library loans the cup from its archives each year for this event. Someone poured in a bottle of Spanish red wine, and the cup was passed round the circle in a high-spirited secular sacrament, with everyone taking a drink and making jocular toasts—"I'm proud to be part of this eccentric radical tradition," said one man—as the children swooped in and out of the group, laughing, grabbing handfuls of grass to throw at one another.

Once the cup had made its way round the circle, it was time for readings from *Leaves of Grass*. A friend who had attended this Lancashire celebration years ago told me that I'd be expected to read a poem—"They love to hear Whitman read with an American accent." Sure enough, I was invited to go first, and I read from "Song of the Open Road," a paean to nature that seemed perfect for this outdoor setting: "Afoot and light-hearted I take to the open road, / Healthy, free, the world before me, / The long brown path before me leading wherever I choose." As I recited this ecstatic poem to the group strewn about the hillside, the wind threatening to obliterate the words unless I delivered them at full volume, I understood fully for the first time Whitman's insistence that his poetry should be read in the open air.

Salveson read next, an excerpt from "Song of the Broad-Axe" that begins, "The place where a great city stands is not the place of stretch'd wharves, docks, manufactures, deposits of produce merely." The passage goes on to claim that a great city stands "Where the men and women think lightly of the laws, / Where the slave ceases, and the master of slaves ceases, / Where the populace rise at once against the never-ending audacity of elected persons, ... / Where the citizen is always the head and ideal, and President, Mayor, Governor and what not, are agents for pay." It was a perfect choice for a Socialist Club event, a reminder of Whitman's fiercely democratic instincts, his insistence on the supremacy and ultimate worth of individuals in an age of laissez-faire capitalism.

After a few additional readings—like a Quaker meeting, people rose and spoke as the spirit moved them—Don Lee ended the program with a love song to the earth from "Song of Myself," a passage ending, "Prodigal, you have given me love—therefore I to you give love! O unspeakable passionate love!" We stood, brushed the grass from our clothes, and began walking. After an hour's hike we reached our destination: a sixteenth-century farmhouse where we gathered in a low-ceilinged, rough-beamed room off the kitchen for a proper English tea. Later, sated with scones and jam and clotted cream, we said our good-byes, some setting off through the farm's meadows to catch the bus to Manchester, others circling back to parked cars.

✢✢✢

The Lancashire Whitman celebration is unique, a product of the English fondness for the outdoors, intense interest in local traditions, the continuity of a democratic socialist tradition, and an openness to Whitman's prophetic dimensions. However, both in Lancashire and elsewhere I kept encountering individuals who consider Whitman to be an inspired mystic as much as a poet. One Sunday in Bolton I attended services at the Bank Street Unitarian Chapel, where the Eagle Street College used to meet occasionally. Tony McNeile, the minister, included a reading from "Song of Myself" in the service, and in his sermon he told the congregation, "The whole world is the temple of the spirit, and it is only our poets who can tell us this truth. Walt Whitman reminds us that there is a spirit deep within everyone." Afterward I met with McNeile in his office in the chapel, a beautiful, high-ceilinged late Victorian building. He picked up a copy of *Leaves of Grass* from his cluttered desk and told me, "I use this often in readings." McNeile was only vaguely familiar with Whitman before he came to Bolton in 1993, but soon after his arrival he learned about the Eagle Street College and participated in one of the Lancashire birthday celebrations. He started using Whitman in church services, "even though some of the older parishioners say to me, 'But that's not poetry!' " McNeile went on, "Still, Whitman strikes a chord in people. He says, 'To me every hour of the light and dark is a miracle.' What he does is to take the everyday and to recognize not so much God, as people used to think of God, but divinity and spirituality in everything."

McNeile, who's well versed in Bolton history, talked about what the town was like in the nineteenth century when the Eagle Street College began. "Conditions were very bad: unemployment, terrible working conditions in mills, the entire town covered in dense smoke year-round. People needed a vision of something better, they needed to be freed, and I think the Whitmanites represented that. Since coming here I've been caught up in that liberating aspect of Whitman. I like to think that we're keeping the spirit of the Whitmanites alive."

There must be hundreds of Unitarian ministers besides Tony McNeile who slip Walt Whitman into their sermons and thousands of individuals who read *Leaves of Grass* as part of their spiritual practice. After an essay I wrote about Horace Traubel was published online, I received e-mails from a wide variety of Whitmanites, including Fred Strohm, a software engineer in Southern California who's writing a book about Whitman as one of four "spiritual heroes" of the nineteenth century, along with Swami Vivekananda, Leo Tolstoy, and José Martí; Cary Bayer, a workshop leader and life coach in Florida whose master's thesis at Maharishi International University was titled "Walt Whitman: Poet for the Age of Enlightenment"; and Bruce Noll, a lecturer in education at the University of New Mexico who sees his one-man show based on *Leaves of Grass* as a form of evangelism and who wrote me, "Spirituality pervades *Leaves of Grass*. It's not uncommon for some members of my audiences to tell me after my performance that they felt as if they had been in church."

Strohm, Bayer, and Noll are all located toward the left of the American political, religious, and cultural spectrum, where it's not surprising to find people interested in Whitmanesque spirituality. Yet perhaps the most fervent, articulate Whitmanite I encountered is a Republican lawyer and accountant who served as New Jersey secretary of commerce during the administration of Christine Todd Whitman. I met Gualberto Medina several years ago when he delivered the opening remarks at a Whitman conference sponsored by Rutgers University in Camden. It was a major event, drawing Whitman scholars from around the country, and Medina was there in his role as secretary of commerce. I don't think any of us in the audience expected anything more than a perfunctory greeting and some boilerplate remarks about Whitman, Camden, and the great state of New Jersey. Instead, Medina began by talking about his parents, who were immigrants from Latin America. "Growing up in Camden," he said, "I could not avoid experiencing the powerful pull that Walt Whitman exerted on my life. There were my parents speaking to me of Whitman in hushed tones, not as if he were the epic poet of democracy but as if he were an Old Testament prophet. And they were right: he was a prophet." Medina went on to say that, as a student at Rutgers, he read "When Lilacs Last in the Dooryard Bloom'd." "I can divide my life into two periods: the time before I read it and the time after." He told about running, as a young man, through the trails of Harleigh Cemetery: "Whenever I ran there I would recite parts of *Leaves of Grass* to myself and sense Whitman's mystical presence and feel somehow united with the voluptuous, cool breath'd earth upon which I ran; the earth of the slumbering and liquid trees; the earth of departed sunsets; the earth of the vitre-ous pour of the moon; the far-swooping elbow'd earth; the rich, apple-blossom'd earth." When Medina sat down, those of us in the audience looked in disbelief at one another: *Wow! Who* is *this guy?* I introduced myself to Medina at the reception afterward, and we arranged to talk further about Whitman.

We met at the Department of Commerce in Trenton. His office took up much of the top floor of a glass-sheathed skyscraper, with a spectacular view of the Delaware River as it flowed south toward Camden. Medina, a big man in his forties, had his dark hair slicked back and wore an expensive tailored suit. He'd recently returned from a trade mission to Latin America—standard fare for a state secretary of commerce. But he was eager to talk about a less conven-tional part of the mission: a symposium he helped to organize at the University of Chile on Neruda, Borges, and Whitman. "Poetry brings people together in much more profound ways than trade alone can," he told me. An open, enthusiastic person, Medina quickly warmed to the topic. "There is a strong current that runs in the caverns of our beings and unites us across the divides of culture and race—the collective unconscious, to use Jung's term. The great poets are in touch with the unconscious—Whitman more than most. Walt Whitman is going to be a more effective ambassador than Madeleine Albright in the long run, because people react more sin-cerely and instinctively to our great literary figures."

Medina got his awestruck view of Whitman from his parents, who were not well educated but who shared the reverence for poets that is common across Latin America. "When my parents spoke about Whitman's house, which was not far from ours, it was as if they were speaking about a temple of worship, the home of a great prophet. They had a real clear understanding of what prophecy truly is—the prophecy of the Old Testament. What is a prophet but a person who brings us to a closer understanding of God? And that's what Whitman does."

I asked him about reading "When Lilacs Last in the Dooryard Bloom'd" for the first time, the experience that he said divided his life in two. "Before that," he told me, "I used to experience literature on a cognitive level. But Whitman was trying to move you spiritually and emotionally in a way that other artists didn't—or couldn't. Reading 'Lilacs,' I felt transported. It was a mystical experience, the kind that the Spanish mystics write about when they speak of God as their lover. I realized that the role of the artist is greater than entertainment. When I read Whitman, I feel a closeness to the eternal, a kinship with God."

✣ ✣ ✣

Gualberto Medina no doubt speaks for thousands of readers whose spiritual lives have been shaped by *Leaves of Grass*. Like Medina, these readers do not have institutional ambitions for a Whitmanesque religion "extending the globe across," as Traubel wrote to Wallace in a heady moment during the 1890s. Never having been in Whitman's magnetic presence, they do not imagine, as did Bucke, that he possessed suprahuman faculties. Conscious of the continuing strength of organized Christianity a century and a half after Darwin, they do not suppose that Whitman will supersede Jesus, as O'Connor, Burroughs, and Gilchrist did. Instead, *Leaves of Grass* forms one element of these readers' eclectic, individualized spirituality—a spirituality sometimes grounded in a liberal religious tradition, such as Quakerism or Unitarianism, but just as often self-constructed.

What would Walt Whitman think of his reception by spiritual seekers in the twenty-first century? During his lifetime he swung between grandiose ambitions—such as the plans for the "Great Construction of the New Bible" that he confided to his notebook in 1857—and a more modest appraisal of his accomplishments. Chatting with Horace Traubel one evening in 1888, he pulled out an old letter from Moncure Conway, a Unitarian minister and Whitman admirer. Conway concluded his letter by saying that *Leaves of Grass* "is to me the more I read it (as I do daily) the Genesis of an American Bible." When Traubel commented on the phrase, Whitman replied, "Conway, you will notice, does not call the Leaves a new Bible but the Genesis of a new Bible. That's more like sense than to make monopolistic claims." Religious liberals, both in the nineteenth century and today, tend to be skeptical of absolutist claims—aversion to dogma is what makes them liberals. For many, *Leaves of Grass* serves as one book of an eclectic, personal bible, taking its place alongside such works as the Hebrew scriptures, the New Testament, the Bhagavad Gita, the Dhammapada, Emerson's essays, and William Blake's poetry. They love *Leaves* for its message, which they see as congruent with that of other spiritual texts, and for its artistry.

In that sense the disciples and their twenty-first-century heirs may not be so different from other readers of *Leaves of Grass*. Few claim that Whitman's spiritual messages are unique. His themes—the divine equality of all women and men, the sacredness of nature and the material world, the holiness of the body and sexual desire— appear in countless works. Rather, they find, as Emerson did, that *Leaves of Grass* contains "incomparable things said incomparably well." They thrill to the image of a man talking to his soul in poetry as lushly sensual as that in the biblical "Song of Songs":

> Loafe with me on the grass, loose the stop from your
>   throat,
> Not words, not music or rhyme I want, not custom or
>   lecture, not even the best,
> Only the lull I like, the hum of your valvèd voice.

They respond to both the nature mysticism and the carefully crafted imagery in a passage such as this from "Song of Myself":

> I depart as air, I shake my white locks at the runaway
>   sun,
> I effuse my flesh in eddies, and drift it in lacy jags.
> I bequeath myself to the dirt to grow from the grass
>   I love,
> If you want me again look for me under your boot-soles.

They find that *Leaves of Grass* offers both gorgeous language and deep wisdom. You could argue that anyone who responds deeply to Whitman's poetry feels the same.

At an academic conference several years ago I listened to a speaker, a distinguished professor of English, who had just published a highly regarded book on Whitman. Before he began his talk he said, "There are many different ways of expressing our love for Walt Whitman. Mine happens to be historical scholarship." It was the first time I'd ever heard the word *love* used this way at a scholarly conference. More than any other poet, I think, Whitman evokes not just admiration but love. The disciples felt that love in the *Leaves*, they sought it from the man, and although things did not always turn out as they expected, none of them was entirely disappointed. "I love you," Whitman says in the final lines of *Leaves of Grass*, just before he craftily disappears. The disciples responded, each in his or her own way.

More than one hundred years after Whitman's death, few readers are inclined to worship Walt in the same way as the nineteenth-century disciples. Yet these generous, eccentric, brilliant women and men demonstrate a way of reading *Leaves of Grass* that acknowledges the aesthetic achievements of Whitman's verse while also finding in it a modern, inclusive spirituality that reaches across the divides of gender, race, and sexual orientation. The disciples, long dismissed as cranks, offer a model for interpreting *Leaves of Grass* that can be as powerful and potentially transformative in our moment as it was in theirs.

NOTES

Frequently Cited Sources

Bolton   Bolton (England) Central Library.

Corr.   *The Correspondence of Walt Whitman*, ed. Edwin Haviland Miller, 6 vols. (New York: New York University Press, 1961–77).

CPCP   Walt Whitman, *Complete Poetry and Collected Prose*, ed. Justin Kaplan (New York: Library of America, 1982).

Feinberg   Charles Feinberg Collection, Library of Congress, Washington, DC.

HHG   Herbert Harlakenden Gilchrist, *Anne Gilchrist: Her Life and Writings* (London: T. Fisher Unwin, 1887).

In Re   *In Re Walt Whitman*, ed. Horace L. Traubel, Richard Maurice Bucke, and Thomas B. Harned, (Philadelphia: David McKay, 1893).

NUPM   Walt Whitman, *Notebooks and Unpublished Prose Manuscripts*, ed. Edward F. Grier, 6 vols. (New York: New York University Press, 1984).

Rylands   John Rylands University Library, Manchester, England.

TC   Horace and Anne Montgomerie Traubel Collection, Library of Congress.

WWC   Horace Traubel, *With Walt Whitman in Camden*, 9 vols. (various publishers, 1906–96).

WWQR   Walt Whitman Quarterly Review

A Note on Citations from Leaves of Grass

Leaves of Grass has a complicated textual history, with several editions in Whitman's lifetime. Whenever possible, I have quoted from the widely available Library of America hardbound edition of *Complete Poetry and Collected Prose* (1982), which includes both the 1855 first edition and the 1891–92 "deathbed" edition and is cited as *CPCP*. Unless otherwise indicated, I quote from the deathbed edition. When it

is important to quote a poem as one of the early disciples would have first encoun-
tered it, I use the abbreviations *LG 1860* to indicate the third edition of *Leaves of Grass* (Boston: Thayer and Eldridge) and *LG 1867* to indicate the fourth, self-published edition. All these editions, as well as a wealth of other material related to Whitman and the disciples, are available online at the Walt Whitman Archive, edited by Ed Folsom and Kenneth M. Price, www.whitmanarchive.org.

INTRODUCTION

Page

1   **"Have you reckon'd":** "Song of Myself," *CPCP* 189.

3   **"Swiftly arose":** "Song of Myself" (1855), *CPCP* 30–31. Cowley's essay is found in the 1855 edition of *Leaves of Grass* published by Viking in 1959 and reprinted by Viking and then by Penguin many times. Note that the four-dot ellipsis is original to the 1855 edition. Whitman used this invented punctuation mark freely in his first edition, then abandoned it in subsequent editions. When I omit material within a quotation from the 1855 edition—but only from that edition—I enclose my ellipsis in brackets.

   "Why should I wish to see God": "Song of Myself" (1855), *CPCP* 85.

   "Folks expect of the poet": Preface to the 1855 edition of *Leaves of Grass*, *CPCP* 10.

   "I swear I see now": "To Think of Time" (1855), *CPCP* 106.

4   **recent work in religious studies:** I have benefited particularly from Leigh Eric Schmidt, *Restless Souls: The Making of American Spirituality* (New York: HarperSanFrancisco, 2005) and from Jeffrey J. Kripal, who argues in *Esalen: America and the Religion of No Religion* (Chicago: University of Chicago Press, 2007) that the Esalen Institute in Big Sur is an heir of the democratic mystical humanism articulated by Emerson, Thoreau, and, above all, Walt Whitman. See also Catharine L. Albanese, *American Spiritualities* (Bloomington: Indiana University Press, 2001).

   The transcendentalists surrounding Emerson were the nation's first spiritual seekers: Leigh Schmidt convincingly makes this argument in his introduction to *Restless Souls*, distinguishing what he calls "seeker spirituality" from Puritan religion and Enlightenment deism.

   "*Leaves of Grass* is primarily a gospel": John Burroughs, "Walt Whitman and His Recent Critics," in *In Re*, 102.

5   **"minstrels and edifiers":** John Burroughs, *Whitman: A Study* (1896; Boston: Houghton Mifflin, 1904), 22.

     "Whitman means a life": Ibid., 223.

     "essential unity": Ibid., 87.

     "a religion to live by": Thomas B. Harned, "Whitman and the Future," *Conservator* 6 (June 1895): 54.

     "Someone was here": *WWC* 1:128.

     "When I commenced": "Preface, 1872," *CPCP* 1002–3.

     "No one will get at my verses": "A Backward Glance o'er Travel'd Roads," *CPCP* 671.

6   **puzzle:** Paul Zweig, *Walt Whitman: The Making of the Poet* (New York: Basic Books, 1984), 15.

     "Dear Walt": *WWC* 6:369.

     "will further the knowledge": Walter Grünzweig, " 'Collaborators in the Great Cause of Liberty and Fellowship': Whitmania as an Intercultural Phenomenon," *WWQR* 5 (1988): 21.

     "Whitman's magnetic quality": William Sloane Kennedy, *Reminiscences of Walt Whitman* (London: Alexander Gardner, 1896), 109.

7   **"superb calm character":** *NUPM* 2:889.

     "personal magnetism": Richard Maurice Bucke, *Walt Whitman* (Philadelphia: David McKay, 1883), 52.

     "I am by no means": *Corr.* 3:266.

     "You all overrate me": Ibid., 5:237.

8   **"Hark close, and still":** "From Pent-up Aching Rivers," *LG 1867,* 97.

9   **"Do you suppose":** *WWC* 7:397.

     "crisis of faith": See Paul A. Carter, *The Spiritual Crisis of the Gilded Age* (DeKalb: Northern Illinois University Press, 1971); Richard J. Helmstadter and Bernard Lightman, eds., *Victorian Faith in Crisis* (Basingstoke, UK: Macmillan, 1990); Hugh McLeod, *Religion and Society in England, 1850–1914* (London: Macmillan, 1996), 169–224; and Frank M. Turner, *Contesting Cultural Authority: Essays in Victorian Intellectual Life* (Cambridge: Cambridge University Press, 1993). On the secularization thesis see Steve Bruce, ed., *Religion and Modernization* (Oxford: Oxford University Press, 1992).

10   **"Magnifying and applying come I":** "Song of Myself," *CPCP* 233.

11   **the poet-prophet remains alive in non-Western cultures:** See Carmine Sarracino, "Redrawing Whitman's Circle," *WWQR* 14 (1996–97): 113–27.

11 **the notion of Whitman as a religious prophet is seldom discussed by scholars:** The work of David Kuebrich is a notable exception; see *Minor Prophecy: Walt Whitman's New American Religion* (Bloomington: Indiana University Press, 1989) and "Religion and the Poet-Prophet," in Donald D. Kummings, ed., *A Companion to Walt Whitman* (Oxford: Blackwell, 2006), 197–215. Kuebrich, who takes a primarily phenomenological approach to Whitman and religion, mentions the disciples only briefly. The other major study of Whitman and religion is George B. Hutchinson, *The Ecstatic Whitman: Literary Shamanism and the Crisis of the Union* (Columbus: Ohio State University Press, 1986), which analyzes Whitman's poetry as a shamanic performance intended to heal the American nation. V. K. Chari, *Whitman in the Light of Vedantic Mysticism* (Lincoln: University of Nebraska Press, 1964), and O. K. Nambiar, *Walt Whitman and Yoga* (Bangalore, India: Jeevan, 1966), analyze Whitman's poetry in the context of Indian religion; David S. Reynolds places *Leaves of Grass* in the context of nineteenth-century American religion in *Walt Whitman's America: A Cultural Biography* (New York: Alfred A. Knopf, 1995), 251–78; and D. J. Moores explores what he calls Whitman's "cosmic mystical rhetoric" in *Mystical Discourse in Wordsworth and Whitman* (Leuven, Belgium: Peters, 2006). I have also benefited from Herbert J. Levine, " 'Song of Myself' as Whitman's American Bible," *Modern Language Quarterly* 48 (1987): 145–61, and James E. Miller Jr., Karl Shapiro, and Bernice Slote, *Start with the Sun: Studies in Cosmic Poetry* (Lincoln: University of Nebraska Press, 1960). M. Jimmie Killingsworth traces the history of religious approaches to Whitman in *The Growth of* Leaves of Grass: *The Organic Tradition in Whitman Studies* (Columbia, SC: Camden House, 1993), 85–101. The only general studies of the Whitman disciples are Charles B. Willard's condescending chapter on the American "Whitman Enthusiasts" in *Whitman's American Fame* (Providence: Brown University, 1950) and Harold Blodgett's more nuanced treatment of the British disciples in *Walt Whitman in England* (Ithaca: Cornell University Press, 1934). See also two recent doctoral dissertations: Steven Jay Marsden, " 'Hot Little Prophets': Reading, Mysticism, and Walt Whitman's Disciples" (Texas A&M University, 2004), and John Tessitore, "Whitmania: The Poetics of Free Religion" (Boston University, 2006).

12 **"What do you suppose":** "Laws for Creations," *CPCP* 512.
"I claim everything for religion": *WWC* 1:10.

13 **Michael Warner:** Michael Warner, introduction to *The Portable Walt Whitman* (New York: Penguin, 2003), xxi.

a long tradition of scoffing: See, for example, Bliss Perry, *Walt Whitman* (Boston: Houghton Mifflin, 1906), 286; and Gay Wilson Allen, *Walt Whitman as Man, Poet, and Legend* (Carbondale: Southern Illinois University Press, 1961), 107–8.

CHAPTER ONE

WILLIAM O'CONNOR AND JOHN BURROUGHS

14 **"No one will get at my verses":** "A Backward Glance o'er Travel'd Roads," *CPCP* 671.

In the summer of 1857: In my accounts of Whitman's life I have relied not only on his correspondence and other primary materials but on four invaluable biographical works: Gay Wilson Allen, *The Solitary Singer* (New York: New York University Press, 1967); Justin Kaplan, *Walt Whitman: A Life* (New York: Simon and Schuster, 1980); Joann P. Krieg, *A Whitman Chronology* (Iowa City: University of Iowa Press, 1998); and Jerome Loving, *Walt Whitman: The Song of Himself* (Berkeley: University of California Press, 1999).

"Dear Sir": R. W. Emerson, "Letter to Walt Whitman," *CPCP* 1326.

15 **"Here are thirty-two Poems":** "Letter to Ralph Waldo Emerson," *CPCP* 1326–27.

16 **"*The Great Construction* of the *New Bible*":** *NUPM* 1:353.

" 'Leaves of Grass'—Bible of the New Religion": Walt Whitman, *Notes and Fragments Left by Walt Whitman*, edited by Richard Maurice Bucke (London, Ontario: A. Talbot, 1899), 55.

Leaves of Grass was only one among numerous new bibles: See Lawrence Buell, *New England Literary Culture: From Revolution through Renaissance* (Cambridge: Cambridge University Press, 1986), 166–90; W. C. Harris, *E Pluribus Unum: Nineteenth-Century Literature and the Constitutional Paradox* (Iowa City: University of Iowa Press, 2005), 71–109; and Carl T. Jackson, *The Oriental Religions and American Thought: Nineteenth-Century Explorations* (Westport, CT: Greenwood, 1981), 45–140.

17 **"The priest departs":** "Democratic Vistas," *CPCP* 932.

"Make your own Bible": Ralph Waldo Emerson, *The Journals and Miscellaneous Notebooks*, edited by William H. Gilman et al., 16 vols. (Cambridge: Harvard University Press, 1960–1982), 5:186.

17   **"Hebrew and Greek scriptures"**: Emerson, "An Address," *The Selected Writings of Ralph Waldo Emerson*, edited by Brooks Atkinson (New York: Modern Library, 1968), 84, 81.

    "Slough": *NUPM* 1:405.

    "Dear Sir": Allen, *Solitary Singer*, 236.

18   **"I too, following many"**: "Proto-Leaf," *LG 1860*, 11, 13.

    "I celebrate myself": "Song of Myself" (1855), *CPCP* 27.

19   **"I am the man"**: "Song of Myself," *CPCP* 225.

    "In all people I see myself": Ibid., *CPCP* 206.

    John Updike: John Updike, "Whitman's Egotheism," *Hugging the Shore* (New York: Alfred A. Knopf, 1983), 106–17.

    "Divine am I inside and out": "Song of Myself," *CPCP* 211.

    "Did you suppose": Preface to the 1855 edition of *Leaves of Grass*, *CPCP* 14, 16.

    "is miracle enough": "Song of Myself," *CPCP* 217.

    "The pismire is equally perfect": Ibid.

    "If the body were not the soul": "I Sing the Body Electric," *CPCP* 250, 256.

20   **"If I worship one thing"**: "Song of Myself," *CPCP* 211.

    "ecclesiasticism" and "feudalism": "Democratic Vistas," *CPCP* 935.

    "Really what has America to do": *NUPM* 6:2095, 2091–92.

    "the divine pride of man in himself": "Democratic Vistas," *CPCP* 980.

    "Nothing, not God": "Song of Myself," *CPCP* 244.

    "Bibles may convey": "Democratic Vistas," *CPCP* 965.

21   **"Not that half only"**: Ibid., 949.

    "programme of chants": "Proto-Leaf," *LG 1860*, 7, 13, 12, 16.

22   **"New York stagnation"**: *Corr.* 1:61.

23   **"I never before had my feelings"**: Ibid., 1:76.

    "Mother, I have real pride": Ibid., 1:115–16.

    "champion": Robert Scholnick, "The Selling of the 'Author's Edition': Whitman, O'Connor, and the *West Jersey Press* Affair," *Walt Whitman Review* 23 (1977): 20. The major studies of O'Connor are Florence Bernstein Freedman, *William Douglas O'Connor: Walt Whitman's Chosen Knight* (Athens: Ohio University Press, 1985); and Jerome Loving, *Walt Whitman's Champion: William Douglas O'Connor* (College Station: Texas A&M University Press, 1978). See also the account of the relationships among William O'Connor, Nelly O'Connor, and Whitman in David Cavitch, *My Soul and I: The Inner Life of Walt Whitman* (Boston: Beacon, 1985), 170–85.

25 **"The great Walt is very grand"**: Loving, *Walt Whitman's Champion*, 37.

"instant on both sides": *WWC* 3:78.

"the most attractive man I had ever met": Freedman, *William Douglas O'Connor*, 352.

"erotics of discipleship": Robert K. Nelson and Kenneth M. Price, "Debating Manliness: Thomas Wentworth Higginson, William Sloane Kennedy, and the Question of Whitman," *American Literature* 73 (2001): 498.

"striking masculine beauty": Willliam Douglas O'Connor, "The Good Gray Poet: A Vindication," reprinted in Loving, *Walt Whitman's Champion*, 157.

"I must say I like them": Edward Carpenter, *Days with Walt Whitman* (New York: Macmillan, 1906), 37.

"I can never forget their kindness": *Corr.* 1:108.

26 **"The O'Connor home was my home"**: *WWC* 3:525.

"a caged tiger": Loving, *Walt Whitman's Champion*, 144.

27 **"Dear Walt"**: Freedman, *William Douglas O'Connor*, 146.

"I have missed you terribly": Ibid., 152.

28 **"My very dear friend"**: Ibid., 246.

"Many a soldier's kiss": "The Wound-Dresser," *CPCP* 445.

29 **"My dearest comrade"**: *Corr.* 1:107.

"Since coming here": Charley Shively, *Calamus Lovers: Walt Whitman's Working-Class Camerados* (San Francisco: Gay Sunshine Press, 1987), 81.

"It was a lonely night": Martin G. Murray, " 'Pete the Great': A Biography of Peter Doyle," *WWQR* 12 (1994): 13. On Doyle and Whitman see also Jonathan Ned Katz, *Love Stories: Sex between Men before Homosexuality* (Chicago: University of Chicago Press, 2001), 165–77; and Gary Schmidgall, *Walt Whitman: A Gay Life* (New York: E. P. Dutton, 1997), 206–14.

30 **"Always preserve a kind spirit"**: *NUPM* 2:887–89.

"Pete, there was something in that hour": *Corr.* 2:101.

32 **"the rules of decorum"**: Loving, *Walt Whitman's Champion*, 57.

"To a Common Prostitute": *LG 1860*, 399.

"forbidden voices": "Song of Myself," *LG 1860*, 55.

33 **"terrific outburst"**: Clara Barrus, *Whitman and Burroughs, Comrades* (Boston: Houghton Mifflin, 1931), 28.

"Let us repair": H. L. Mencken, *Prejudices: First Series* (New York: Alfred A. Knopf, 1919), 249–50.

"the grandest gentleman": O'Connor, "Good Gray Poet," 162, 191, 196, 203.

34 **"William's onslaught is terrifying"**: *WWC* 2:240.

34   **"a battle-ship"**: Ibid., 1:54.

"the devotees of a castrated literature": O'Connor, "Good Gray Poet," 195.

35   **"the love passing the love of women"**: William O'Connor, "The Carpenter," *Putnam's Magazine* (January 1868): 71, 77. Despite the date, the story appeared well before Christmas 1867; it was reviewed in the December 12, 1867, issue of *The Nation*.

36   **"the grand incarnation"**: Loving, *Walt Whitman's Champion*, 88.

"different and more subtle": O'Connor to Bucke, June 10, 1882, Feinberg.

"were in the habit": Barrus, *Whitman and Burroughs*, 96.

37   **"a knight of chivalric ages"**: *WWC* 8:352, 3:351, 3:352, 4:90, 5:166.

38   **"John and William are very different men"**: Ibid., 2:171. Edward J. Renehan, *John Burroughs: An American Naturalist* (Post Mills, VT: Chelsea Green, 1992), is the most recent biography. James Perrin Warren discusses the Whitman-Burroughs relationship in *John Burroughs and the Place of Nature* (Athens: University of Georgia Press, 2006), 42–72.

"Have you ever heard": John Burroughs, "The Return of the Birds," *Wake-Robin* (1871; Boston: Houghton Mifflin, 1904), 17.

39   **"Audubon of prose"**: Renehan, *John Burroughs*, 77.

"I read him in a sort of ecstasy": Clara Barrus, *The Life and Letters of John Burroughs* (Boston: Houghton Mifflin, 1925), 1:41.

"scribbling": Renehan, *John Burroughs*, 47, 43, 55, 56, 52.

42   **"Walt, here's the young man"**: Barrus, *Whitman and Burroughs*, 7.

"such a handsome body": Ibid., 17, 13.

"voracious": Renehan, *John Burroughs*, 77. Renehan repeats the phrase in "Comrades: Scenes from the Friendship of John Burroughs and Walt Whitman," in Charlotte Zoë Walker, ed., *Sharp Eyes: John Burroughs and American Nature Writing* (Syracuse: Syracuse University Press, 2000), 66.

"is by far the wisest man": Barrus, *Whitman and Burroughs*, 17.

43   **"Whatever else"**: John Burroughs, "The Poet of the Cosmos," *Accepting the Universe* (1920; New York: Wm. H. Wise, 1924), 317.

"a larger": John Burroughs, *Whitman: A Study* (1896; Boston: Houghton Mifflin, 1904), 6.

"absolute nature": Ibid., 191.

"gospel of nature": John Burroughs, "The Gospel of Nature," *Time and Change* (Boston: Houghton Mifflin, 1912), 243–73.

"irrational and puerile": Burroughs, "Soundings," *Accepting the Universe*, 263.

"the man Emerson invoked": Burroughs, *Whitman: A Study*, 100.

"spiritual catastrophe": Renehan, *John Burroughs*, 3.

43   **"Amid the decay"**: Burroughs, "The Faith of a Naturalist," *Accepting the Universe*, 116.

44   **"Under the influence"**: Burroughs, "Manifold Nature," *Accepting the Universe*, 20–21.

    "I find": "Song of Myself," *CPCP* 217.

    "the most religious book": John Burroughs, *Notes on Walt Whitman as Poet and Person* (New York: American News, 1867), 72.

    "primarily a gospel": John Burroughs, "Walt Whitman and His Recent Critics," in *In Re*, 102.

    "the old religion": Burroughs, *Whitman: A Study*, 290–91.

    "a great & astounding": Burroughs to Bucke, December 31, 1880, Feinberg.

45   **"The coffee would boil"**: Renehan, *John Burroughs*, 78.

    "suicidal": Barrus, *Whitman and Burroughs*, 49.

    "wantonness": Renehan, *John Burroughs*, 77.

    "It is a feast": Barrus, *Whitman and Burroughs*, 160.

46   **"incredible and exhaustless"**: Burroughs, *Notes on Walt Whitman*, 13.

    "In History": Ibid., 3.

    "I look upon him": Burroughs, "Poet of the Cosmos," 316.

47   **"I hope"**: John Burroughs, preface to *Birds and Poets* (1877; Boston: Houghton Mifflin, 1905), v.

    "in the Virgilian": Burroughs, "The Flight of the Eagle," *Birds and Poets*, 260, 215, 219.

    "They cut up like two boys": Barrus, *Whitman and Burroughs*, 164.

    "honeysuckle": "Happiness and Raspberries," *Specimen Days*, *CPCP* 820.

48   **"that half-dead place"**: J. Johnston and J. W. Wallace, *Visits to Walt Whitman in 1890–1891* (London: George Allen and Unwin, 1917), 78.

    "presence and companionship": Barrus, *Whitman and Burroughs*, 245.

    "For years and years": *WWC* 2:35.

    "had not grown cold": Barrus, *Whitman and Burroughs*, 342.

    "are too boisterously radical": *WWC* 2:35.

49   **"Walt, I keep your birthday"**: Horace L. Traubel, "Round Table with Walt Whitman," in *In Re*, 304, 305.

    "Walt on the bed": Renehan, *John Burroughs*, 185.

    "I am fairly well these days": Barrus, *Whitman and Burroughs*, 299.

    "is not a poet": Burroughs, *Whitman: A Study*, 225.

50   **"I am too jealous"**: Burroughs to Bucke, undated [June 1895], Feinberg.

    "I do not like it": Burroughs to Traubel, October 24, 1893, TC.

    "a great religious teacher and prophet": Burroughs, *Whitman: A Study*, 225, 223.

CHAPTER TWO
ANNE GILCHRIST

51 **"Are you":** "Are you the New Person Drawn Toward me?" *LG 1867*, 129.

52 **"I had not dreamed":** Anne Gilchrist, "A Woman's Estimate of Walt Whitman" (1870), as reprinted in HHG, where it is retitled "An Englishwoman's Estimate of Walt Whitman," 289.

"Dear Friend": Thomas B. Harned, ed., *The Letters of Anne Gilchrist and Walt Whitman*, (New York: Doubleday, Page, 1918), 58, 63, 66.

"I am not insensible": Ibid., 67.

The background of Anne Burrows Gilchrist: The principal source for information on Anne Gilchrist's life is Marion Walker Alcaro, *Walt Whitman's Mrs. G* (Cranbury, NJ: Associated University Press, 1991). For more recent analyses of the Gilchrist-Whitman relationship see Suzanne Ashworth, "Lover, Mother, Reader: The Epistolary Courtship of Walt Whitman," *Nineteenth-Century Contexts* 26 (2004): 173–97; Max Cavitch, "Audience Terminable and Interminable: Anne Gilchrist, Walt Whitman, and the Achievement of Disinhibited Reading," *Victorian Poetry* 43 (2005): 249–61; and Steve Marsden, " 'A Woman Waits for Me': Anne Gilchrist's Reading of *Leaves of Grass*," *WWQR* 23 (2006): 95–125.

54 **"Rhoda and I":** HHG 23.

"I feel deeply grateful": Ibid., 25–27.

"as a wife should love": Harned, *Letters of Anne Gilchrist and Walt Whitman*, 58.

"hateful, bitter humiliation": Gilchrist, "A Woman's Estimate," 299–300.

apartheid: Barbara Taylor, *Eve and the New Jerusalem: Socialism and Feminism in the Nineteenth Century* (New York: Pantheon, 1983), 264. On women's sexuality in Victorian Great Britain see also Lucy Bland, *Banishing the Beast: Sexuality and the Early Feminists* (New York: New Press, 1995); Margaret Jackson, *The Real Facts of Life: Feminism and the Politics of Sexuality, c. 1850–1940* (London: Taylor and Francis, 1994); Sheila Jeffreys, *The Spinster and Her Enemies: Feminism and Sexuality, 1880–1930* (London: Pandora, 1985); Susan Kingsley Kent, *Sex and Suffrage in Britain, 1860–1914* (Princeton: Princeton University Press, 1987); Philippa Levine, *Feminist Lives in Victorian England: Private Roles and Public Commitment* (Oxford: Basil Blackwell, 1990); Janet Horowitz Murray, *Strong-Minded Women and Other Lost Voices from Nineteenth-Century England* (New York: Pantheon, 1982) ; and Jeffrey Weeks, *Sex, Politics, and Society: The Regulation of Sexuality since 1800*, 2nd ed. (New York: Longman, 1989).

55 **"As a general rule"**: Murray, *Strong-Minded Women*, 128. Carl Degler notes that Acton's book was "one of the most widely quoted sexual-advice books in the English-speaking world" but argues that his view was more "an ideology seeking to be established than the prevalent view or practice of even middle-class women" (Degler, "What Ought to Be and What Was: Women's Sexuality in the Nineteenth Century," *American Historical Review* 79 [1974]: 1467–90). See also Nancy F. Cott, "Passionlessness: An Interpretation of Victorian Sexual Ideology, 1790–1850," *Signs* 4 (1978): 219–36; and Elizabeth K. Helsinger, Robin L. Sheets, and William Veeder, eds., *The Woman Question: Society and Literature in Britain and America, 1837–1883*, vol. 2, *Social Issues* (New York: Garland, 1983), 58–75.

"dark and gloomy": Harned, *Letters of Anne Gilchrist and Walt Whitman*, 59.

56 **"I dare not advise"**: HHG 55.

"Can you conveniently": Ibid., 80.

57 **Even Wordsworth**: Anne Gilchrist, "The Indestructibility of Force," *Macmillan's Magazine* 6 (August 1862): 344.

58 **"skin, and bury herself alive"**: HHG 115.

"Walt Whitman, an American": "Song of Myself" (1855), *CPCP* 50.

"I celebrate myself": Ibid., *CPCP* 27, 88.

60 **"Camerado, this is no book"**: "So Long!" *CPCP* 611.

"Come closer to me": "To Workingmen," *LG 1867*, 239.

61 **"not been so happy"**: Harold Blodgett, *Walt Whitman in England* (Ithaca: Cornell University Press, 1934), 19.

Rossetti . . . initially toyed with the idea: *Corr.* 1:352.

He would change nothing: *WWC* 3:303–4.

Rossetti claimed that he had refused: HHG 178.

Rossetti omitted words: Blodgett, *Walt Whitman in England*, 30.

"gross" and "crude": Whitman, *Poems by Walt Whitman*, edited by William Michael Rossetti (London: John Camden Hotten, 1868), 4.

62 **"spell-bound"**: HHG 177.

"bluntness" and "directness": Ibid., 178.

"Hark close": "From Pent-up Aching Rivers," *LG 1867*, 97, 95.

63 **"[L]ove-flesh swelling"**: "I Sing the Body Electric," *LG 1867*, 102.

"Without shame": "A Woman Waits for Me," *LG 1867*, 108.

Sherry Ceniza: Sherry Ceniza, *Walt Whitman and Nineteenth-Century Women Reformers* (Tuscaloosa: University of Alabama Press, 1998).

"I am the poet of the woman": "Song of Myself" (1855), *CPCP* 46.

63   **"They are not one jot less":** "A Woman Waits for Me," *LG 1867*, 108–9. On Whitman and women see Ceniza, *Walt Whitman and Nineteenth-Century Women Reformers*; Betsy Erkkila, *Whitman the Political Poet* (New York: Oxford University Press, 1989); Jerome Loving, "Whitman's Idea of Women," in Geoffrey M. Sill, ed., *Walt Whitman of Mickle Street* (Knoxville: University of Tennessee Press, 1994), 151–67; and Vivian R. Pollak, *The Erotic Whitman* (Berkeley: University of California Press, 2000), 172–93.

64   **"I had not dreamed":** Gilchrist, "A Woman's Estimate," 289.

    "the cause": William Michael Rossetti, *Letters of William Michael Rossetti concerning Whitman, Blake, and Shelley to Anne Gilchrist and Her Son Herbert Gilchrist*, edited by Clarence Gohdes and Paul Franklin Baum (Durham: Duke University Press, 1934), 37.

    "make a clean breast of it": Ibid., 29–30.

    "an outrage upon decency": Richard Maurice Bucke, *Walt Whitman* (Philadelphia: David McKay, 1883), 215.

65   **"acceptance from a woman":** HHG 189.

    "astounding invention": Ibid.

    "fullest, farthest-reaching": Gilchrist, "A Woman's Estimate," 287–88.

66   **"If the thing":** Ibid., 297–98, 300, 288.

    "Whitman is, I believe": HHG 203–4.

    "Here at last": Edward Carpenter, *Days with Walt Whitman* (New York: Macmillan, 1906), 16.

    "the same radiant glowing consciousness": HHG 205.

67   **"Christ's beautiful life and teaching":** Ibid.

    "there is a range of considerations": Ibid., 208.

    "had hitherto received": Corr. 2:91.

    "That Lady": Ibid., 2:98.

68   **"I whisper":** "To You," *CPCP* 375.

    "Among the men and women": "Among the Multitude," *LG 1867*, 143.

69   **"exhaustion of the nervous energy":** HHG 210.

    "the lady": Corr. 2:131.

    Rossetti replied affirmatively: Rossetti, *Letters of William Michael Rossetti*, 79–80.

    "Dear Friend": Harned, *Letters of Anne Gilchrist and Walt Whitman*, 58–64.

70   **"Dear Friend, I wrote you":** Ibid., 65–66.

71   **"muscular throat":** Justin Kaplan, *Walt Whitman: A Life* (New York: Simon and Schuster, 1980), 216.

71 **"unspeakably delicious":** Jerome Loving, *Walt Whitman: The Song of Himself* (Berkeley: University of California Press, 1999), 206; Kaplan, *Walt Whitman*, 217.

"Know Walt Whitman": *WWC* 4:312–13.

72 **"? insane asylum":** Ibid., 4:312.

"I have been waiting": *Corr.* 2:140.

"Ah, that word 'enough' ": Harned, *Letters of Anne Gilchrist and Walt Whitman*, 70.

73 **"Dear friend, let me warn you":** *Corr.* 2:140.

"I will not write": Harned, *Letters of Anne Gilchrist and Walt Whitman*, 79–80.

"please . . . be indulgent": Ibid., 120.

"I am sure": Ibid., 81.

"taken from my finger": *Corr.* 2:235.

74 **"the great dark cloud":** Ibid., 2:242.

"inexpressibly beloved": Ibid., 2:234.

"Do not think me": Harned, *Letters of Anne Gilchrist and Walt Whitman*, 139, 141.

"My dearest friend": *Corr.* 3:31.

75 **"Yesterday *was* a day":** Harned, *Letters of Anne Gilchrist and Walt Whitman*, 147.

"*I want to hear about Mrs. Gilchrist*": *Corr.* 3:60.

76 **"O, I could not live":** Harned, *Letters of Anne Gilchrist and Walt Whitman*, 78.

"Walt came over every evening": Clara Barrus, *Whitman and Burroughs, Comrades* (Boston: Houghton Mifflin, 1931), 138.

77 **"Herbert, see about the stove":** *Corr.* 3:74.

"George believes in pipes": *WWC* 1:227.

"I don't know a soul": *Corr.* 2:245.

"I am very comfortable": Ibid., 2:248.

"I have been over here": Ibid., 3:74.

"Our greatest pleasure": HHG 229.

78 **"I have that sort of feeling":** *WWC* 1:218.

"my noblest woman-friend": "Going Somewhere," *CPCP* 627.

"She was more": *WWC* 2:292.

"I am not sure": Barrus, *Whitman and Burroughs*, 152.

"She was *all* courage": *WWC* 5:13, 2:268, 2:292.

"Never saw Walt": Barrus, *Whitman and Burroughs*, 160.

79 **Carpenter left a record:** Carpenter, *Days with Walt Whitman*, 16–17.

79 **"It is all very pleasant":** *Corr.* 3:86.

"a rosy woman": Barrus, *Whitman and Burroughs*, 138.

"There are two grown daughters": *Corr.* 3:88.

The few British women physicians had all studied abroad: Catriona Blake, *The Charge of the Parasols: Women's Entry to the Medical Profession* (London: Women's Press, 1990). On the history of women physicians in the United States, see Ruth J. Abram, *"Send Us a Lady Physician": Women Doctors in America, 1835–1920* (New York: W. W. Norton, 1985); Regina Morantz-Sanchez, *Sympathy and Science: Women Physicians in American Medicine* (New York: Oxford University Press, 1985); and Mary Roth Walsh, *"Doctors Wanted: No Women Need Apply": Sexual Barriers in the Medical Profession, 1835–1975* (New Haven: Yale University Press, 1977).

81 **"greeted by yells":** Clara Marshall, *The Woman's Medical College of Pennsylvania: An Historical Outline* (Philadelphia: P. Blakiston, 1897), 19–20.

"out of respect": Ibid., 21.

"all they could rightly understand": Harned, *Letters of Anne Gilchrist and Walt Whitman*, 63.

82 **"We were all gathered":** Alcaro, *Walt Whitman's Mrs. G*, 174.

"There have always appeared": Grace Gilchrist Frend to J. W. Wallace, February 2, 1919, Rylands.

"loving admiration": Harned, *Letters of Anne Gilchrist and Walt Whitman*, 105.

83 **"prophet's chamber":** Carpenter, *Days with Walt Whitman*, 17.

"I will have to *controol*": *Corr.* 3:5.

84 **"Herbret cut me pretty hard":** Ibid., 3:92.

86 **"big cheap house in Brooklyn":** Ibid., 3:148.

87 **in a letter to Whitman:** Ibid., 3:178.

"You would not want me to live": Alcaro, *Walt Whitman's Mrs. G*, 211.

88 **"Many hearts mourn her":** Ibid., 212.

"The story of Mary Lamb's life": Anne Gilchrist, *Mary Lamb* (Boston: Roberts Brothers, 1883), 1.

"I . . . hope . . . that before long": HHG 268.

89 **"put my heart":** Ibid., 270

"what we thought": Anne Gilchrist, "A Confession of Faith" (1885), reprinted in Harned, *Letters of Anne Gilchrist and Walt Whitman*, 30.

90 **"Hurrah for positive Science!":** "Song of Myself," *CPCP* 210.

"going somewhere!": Gilchrist, "A Confession of Faith," 33, 41, 31.

"Fifteen years ago": Gilchrist, "A Confession of Faith," 26.

90   **"Why! who makes much of a miracle?":** Ibid., 30.

91   **"has infused himself into words":** Ibid., 47–48.

      "I could not get my Whitman article": Barrus, *Whitman and Burroughs,* 150–51.

92   **"I am seeing a good deal":** Harned, *Letters of Anne Gilchrist and Walt Whitman,* 234.

      "Mother is very sickly": *Corr.* 3:408.

      "Her condition is critical": Ibid.

      "I . . . cannot but trust": Ibid., 3:411.

93   **"Dear Herbert":** Ibid., 3:412–13.

      "My science-friend": "Going Somewhere," *CPCP* 627.

94   **"one of the great pioneers":** Alcaro, *Walt Whitman's Mrs. G,* 23.

      "banishing the beast": Bland, *Banishing the Beast.* See also the works cited earlier by Jackson, Jeffreys, Kent, Levine, and Weeks. On the New Woman of the 1890s see Angelique Richardson and Chris Willis, eds., *The New Woman in Fiction and in Fact* (New York: Palgrave, 2001).

      "conscious of her own": Murray, *Strong-Minded Women,* 11.

95   **"Without shame":** "A Woman Waits for Me," *CPCP* 259.

      "These beautiful, despised poems": Gilchrist, "A Woman's Estimate," 300.

      "Wives and mothers will learn": Ibid., 302.

96   **"No man ever lived":** Ceniza, *Walt Whitman and Nineteenth-Century Women Reformers,* 239–40.

      "Touch me": "As Adam Early in the Morning," *CPCP* 267.

      "Sometimes I think": Ceniza, *Walt Whitman and Nineteenth-Century Women Reformers,* 238–39.

      "pathetic Victorian lady": *Corr.* 5:6.

      "Whoever takes up": HHG 206, 204.

CHAPTER THREE

R. M. BUCKE

97   **"I, too, following many":** "Starting from Paumanok," *CPCP* 180.

      the speeches they gathered to hear: Titles come from vols. 1 (1894) and 2 (1895) of *Proceedings of the American Medico-Psychological Association.*

98   **"The simple truth":** R. M. Bucke, "Cosmic Consciousness," *Proceedings of the American Medico-Psychological Association* 1 (1894): 327. Bucke's address was reprinted in the *Conservator* 5 (1894): 37–39, 51–54, which noted that it was read before both the Medico-Psychological Association and the Philadelphia Theosophical Society.

98   **"It was an experience":** William Osler, quoted in Philip W. Leon, *Walt Whitman and Sir William Osler* (Toronto: ECW Press, 1995), 23.

99   **"a god":** Artem Lozynsky, *Richard Maurice Bucke, Medical Mystic: Letters of Dr. Bucke to Walt Whitman and His Friends* (Detroit: Wayne State University Press, 1977), 46.

    "Whitman lived in an upper spiritual stratum": R. M. Bucke, "Portraits of Walt Whitman," *New England Magazine* n.s. 20 (1899): 41.

    "the Cause": See, for example, Lozynsky, *Richard Maurice Bucke, Medical Mystic*, 152, and Bucke to Horace Traubel, November 14, 1892, TC.

    Horatio Walpole Bucke: The major sources of information about Bucke's family and early life are James H. Coyne, *Richard Maurice Bucke: A Sketch* (Toronto: Henry S. Saunders, 1923), and Peter A. Rechnitzer, *R. M. Bucke: Journey to Cosmic Consciousness* (Markham, Ontario: Fitzhenry and Whiteside, 1994).

102   **"in some respects":** Richard Maurice Bucke, *Cosmic Consciousness: A Study in the Evolution of the Human Mind* (1901; New York: Penguin Arkana, 1991), 8.

103   **Gold Canyon:** The primary source for Bucke's Western adventure is his article "Twenty-Five Years Ago," *Overland Monthly* 1 (2nd series; 1883): 553–60. The account in Leon, *Walt Whitman and Sir William Osler*, 40–42, draws on a wide range of sources.

104   **"the nature of life":** R. Maurice Bucke, *The Correlation of the Vital and Physical Forces* (Montreal, 1862), 1. S.E.D. Shortt offers a detailed analysis of Bucke's thesis; see *Victorian Lunacy: Richard M. Bucke and the Practice of Late Nineteenth-Century Psychiatry* (Cambridge: Cambridge University Press, 1986), 66–71.

    "one passionate note": Bucke, *Cosmic Consciousness*, 9.

    Bucke defiantly wrote "Universalist": Shortt, *Victorian Lunacy*, 64. For brief histories of Universalism, see Shortt, 64–66, and Catherine L. Albanese, *America: Religions and Religion*, 3rd ed. (Belmont, CA: Wadsworth, 1999), 127–28.

105   **"I love the Doctor":** *WWC* 4:233.

    "comprehend[s] human life": Auguste Comte, *Auguste Comte and Positivism: The Essential Writings*, edited by Gertrud Lenzer (New York: Harper and Row, 1975), 320. Other useful introductions to Comte are W. M. Simon, *European Positivism in the Nineteenth Century* (Ithaca: Cornell University Press, 1963), and Arline Reilein Standley, *Auguste Comte* (Boston: Twayne, 1981).

106   **"My life":** Rechnitzer, *R. M. Bucke: Journey*, 52.

106 **"violent attack[s] of nervous depression"**: Shortt, *Victorian Lunacy*, 22. In *Man's Moral Nature* (New York: G. P. Putnam, 1879), Bucke describes one of his panic attacks, attributing it to an unnamed "highly intellectual medical man" (98).

"My health has completely broken": Lozynsky, *Richard Maurice Bucke, Medical Mystic*, 27.

"Here is a man": Ibid., 26.

he wrote Whitman a respectful "Dear Sir" letter: Ibid., 43–44.

107 **"All at once"**: Bucke, *Cosmic Consciousness*, 9–10.

108 **"Swiftly arose and spread around me"**: "Song of Myself," *CPCP* 192.

109 **"most advanced"**: *Specimen Days, CPCP* 879. Recent overviews of the history of psychiatry include Gerald N. Grob, *The Mad among Us: A History of the Care of America's Mentally Ill* (Cambridge: Harvard University Press, 1994); Roy Porter, *Madness: A Brief History* (New York: Oxford University Press, 2002); and Edward Shorter, *A History of Psychiatry: From the Era of the Asylum to the Age of Prozac* (New York: John Wiley, 1997).

institutions using moral treatment reported cure rates of more than 80 percent: Grob, *Mad among Us*, 99.

Michel Foucault: Michel Foucault, *Madness and Civilization: A History of Insanity in the Age of Reason* (New York: Pantheon, 1965).

"the uniform tendency of all asylums": Porter, *Madness*, 120.

110 **the average asylum population**: Shorter, *A History of Psychiatry*, 46–47; Shortt, *Victorian Lunacy*, 26, 39.

"almost reached the magnitude": Shortt, *Victorian Lunacy*, 29.

Virtually every nineteenth-century alienist agreed: See E. H. Hare, "Masturbatory Insanity: The History of an Idea," *Journal of Mental Science* 108 (1962): 2–25; and Michael Bliss, " 'Pure Books on Avoided Subjects': Pre-Freudian Sexual Ideas in Canada," in S. E. D. Shortt, ed., *Medicine in Canadian Society: Historical Perspectives* (Montreal: McGill-Queen's University Press, 1981), 266.

111 **"in only a small proportion"**: Shortt, *Victorian Lunacy*, 127.

"insanity is essentially an incurable disease": Shortt, *Victorian Lunacy*, 127.

"the object of treatment": Ramsay Cook, *The Regenerators: Social Criticism in Late Victorian English Canada* (Toronto: University of Toronto Press, 1985), 95.

attempting to treat women's insanity: Shortt, *Victorian Lunacy*, 142–59. For a discussion that places Bucke's treatment of his female patients in a broad context, see Wendy Mitchinson, *The Nature of Their Bodies:*

Women and Their Doctors in Victorian Canada (Toronto: University of Toronto Press, 1991), 312–55.

112   **"only spoke to him":** Richard Maurice Bucke, *Walt Whitman* (Philadelphia: David McKay, 1883), 50. Bucke repeats the phrase in *Cosmic Consciousness*, 217. He describes the meeting as "the turning point of my life" in "Memories of Walt Whitman," *Walt Whitman Fellowship Papers*, no. 6 (September 1894): 38.

"I hardly know": Lozynsky, *Richard Maurice Bucke, Medical Mystic*, 46.

"was either actually a god": Bucke, "Memories of Walt Whitman," 38.

Bucke's relation to Whitman . . . involved an unacknowledged homoerotic attraction: See Richard Cavell and Peter Dickinson, "Bucke, Whitman, and the Cross-Border Homosocial," *American Review of Canadian Studies* 26 (1996): 425–48.

"shortly after leaving": Bucke, *Walt Whitman*, 50.

113   **"It is of no use":** Lozynsky, *Richard Maurice Bucke, Medical Mystic*, 46.

"Any attempt to convey": Walt Whitman, *Calamus: A Series of Letters Written during the Years 1868–1880. By Walt Whitman to a Young Friend (Peter Doyle)*, edited by Richard Maurice Bucke (Boston: Small, Maynard, 1897), 12.

"irreligious rowdy": Cyril Greenland and Robert Colombo, *Walt Whitman's Canada* (Willowdale, Ontario: Hounslow, 1992), 3. Greenland and Colombo's collection reprints many primary sources concerning Whitman's visit to Canada. Whitman's account of his visit is contained in *Specimen Days*, *CPCP* 877–79.

114   **"The distinguishing feature":** Greenland and Colombo, *Walt Whitman's Canada*, 5.

"dig up from the gutter": Ibid., 6–7.

he wrote Whitman that the newspaper controversy: Bucke, *The Letters of Dr. Richard Maurice Bucke to Walt Whitman*, ed. Artem Lozynsky (Detroit: Wayne State UP, 1977), 7 (hereafter cited as *Bucke-Whitman Letters*).

"best of all books": Greenland and Colombo, *Walt Whitman's Canada*, 10.

"But Jessie": Lozynsky, *Richard Maurice Bucke, Medical Mystic*, 78.

115   **"the Saviour":** John Burroughs to Bucke, January 25, 1880, Feinberg.

"the man who of all men": Bucke, *Man's Moral Nature*, v.

"the moral nature in the abstract": Bucke, *Walt Whitman*, 8.

116   **Whitman's claim . . . that he wrote:** Edward Carpenter, *Days with Walt Whitman* (New York: Macmillan,, 1906), 37. Readers can evaluate Whitman's role in the composition of *Walt Whitman* for themselves with the

aid of Harold Jaffe, "R. M. Bucke's *Walt Whitman*" (Ph.D. diss., New York University, 1968); and Stephen Railton, *Walt Whitman's Autograph Revision of the Analysis of Leaves of Grass (For Dr. R. M. Bucke's Walt Whitman)* (New York: New York University Press, 1974).

116 **"would have been nuts"**: *Corr.* 3:267.

117 **Six years after meeting Whitman, Bucke was still unsure:** Lozynsky, *Richard Maurice Bucke, Medical Mystic*, 70.

"bustle of growing wheat": "Song of Myself," *CPCP* 214; Bucke, *Walt Whitman*, 49, 51.

"both insipid and implausible": Lozynsky, *Richard Maurice Bucke, Medical Mystic*, 61.

118 **"The character you give me"**: *Corr.* 3:266.

"extraordinary power": Bucke, *Walt Whitman*, 35, 40.

"indecencies stink": Ibid., 196, 228, 178, 180.

119 **"Lo, the unbounded sea"**: "The Ship Starting," *CPCP* 173–74.

"The ship is the book": Bucke, *Walt Whitman*, 158.

"I put in almost unqualified endorsement": *WWC* 8:320, 524.

le vrai fondateur: See, for example, *In Re*, 57.

120 **"a little embarrasing"**: Lozynsky, *Richard Maurice Bucke, Medical Mystic*, 70.

"no description": Bucke, *Walt Whitman*, 49.

"I am quite sure": *WWC* 1:385.

121 **"I have no doubt"**: Bucke to Traubel, September 17, 1888, Feinberg.

122 **"Great Cause"**: Lozynsky, *Richard Maurice Bucke, Medical Mystic*, 185.

"Should this meter *go*": Ibid., 114.

"The 'Complete Works' takes time": Bucke, *Bucke-Whitman Letters*, 74.

"It is grand": Lozynsky, *Richard Maurice Bucke, Medical Mystic*, 119.

123 **"Maurice Bucke, Maurice Bucke, Maurice Bucke"**: R. M. Bucke, "Memories of Walt Whitman: 2," *Walt Whitman Fellowship Papers*, no. 10 (May 1897): 36.

Speaking at Whitman's graveside: *In Re*, 446.

"Is it wonderful": "Who Learns My Lesson Complete?" *CPCP* 518.

"Over and over": Lozynsky, *Richard Maurice Bucke, Medical Mystic*, 184.

124 **"THE BOOK"**: Bucke, *Bucke-Whitman Letters*, 264.

"annex": *Corr.* 4:215.

"cluster of written material": *In Re*, vi.

125 **"Now, though this great country"**: Ibid., iii, vi, 35.

"never writes a line": Ibid., 251.

126 **"fitful[ly]"**: Ibid., 62.

126   **"cultivated public":** William Morton Payne, "Whitmania," *Dial* 15 (1893): 390.

127   **"I am sorry":** Bucke to Traubel, December 25, 1895, TC.

128   **"There is a quality":** "College Farewell to R. M. Bucke and J. W. Wallace," August 24, 1891, Rylands. A member of the Bolton group recorded this event in shorthand and then made a typed transcript, which Leon reprints in *Walt Whitman and Sir William Osler*, 131–35.

　　　cosmic consciousness: Carpenter first used the phrase in print in *From Adam's Peak to Elephanta* (London: George Allen, 1892). On Bucke's debt to Carpenter see Paul Marshall, *Mystical Encounters with the Natural World* (Oxford: Oxford University Press, 2005), 111–29; and Lorna Weir, "Cosmic Consciousness and the Love of Comrades: Contacts between R. M. Bucke and Edward Carpenter," *Journal of Canadian Studies* 30 (Summer 1995): 39–57.

129   **"[Cosmic] consciousness shows the cosmos":** Bucke, *Cosmic Consciousness*, 17.

130   **"In contact with the flux":** Ibid., 5.

132   **Historians of religion:** See Richard Hughes Seagher, *The World's Parliament of Religions: The East/West Encounter, Chicago, 1893* (Bloomington: Indiana University Press, 1995), and Eric J. Ziolkowski, ed., *A Museum of Faiths: Histories and Legacies of the 1893 World's Parliament of Religions* (Atlanta: Scholars Press, 1993).

　　　Alfred Russel Wallace: See Frank Miller Turner, *Between Science and Religion: The Reaction to Scientific Naturalism in Late Victorian England* (New Haven: Yale University Press, 1974), 68–103.

　　　"Is the change": Paul A. Carter, *The Spiritual Crisis of the Gilded Age* (DeKalb: Northern Illinois University Press, 1971), 97.

133   **"personal religious experience":** William James, *The Varieties of Religious Experience* (1902; Cambridge: Harvard University Press, 1985), 301.

134   **"muscular Christianity":** See Gail Bederman, " 'The Women Have Had Charge of the Church Work Long Enough': The Men and Religion Forward Movement of 1911–12 and the Masculinization of Middle-Class Protestantism," *American Quarterly* 41 (1989): 432–65; Denise Lardner Carmody and John Tully Carmody, *The Republic of Many Mansions: Foundations of American Religious Thought* (New York: Paragon House, 1990), 164–67; Michael Kimmel, *Manhood in America: A Cultural History* (New York: Free Press, 1996), 175–81; and Clifford Putney, *Muscular Christianity: Manhood and Sports in Protestant America, 1880–1920* (Cambridge: Harvard University Press, 2001).

134   **"crudely racist and sexist"**: Weir, "Cosmic Consciousness and the Love of Comrades," 45.

    "the Aryan people's": Bucke, *Cosmic Consciousness*, 58.

    "I have collected": *In Re*, 331.

135   **"There is a spice"**: Traubel to Wallace, October 26, 1893, Bolton.

    "Because women do not appear": Walt Whitman, *Daybooks and Notebooks*, edited by William White (New York: New York University Press, 1977), 3:772–73.

    "Walt Whitman is the best": Bucke, *Cosmic Consciousness*, 225, 226.

136   **surveys reveal that 35 percent of all Americans**: Andrew Greeley, *Sociology and Religion* (New York: HarperCollins, 1995), 152.

137   **"Through the experiences"**: Bucke, *Cosmic Consciousness*, n.p.

    "We understand then": "Crossing Brooklyn Ferry," *CPCP* 312.

    "So long!": "So Long!" *CPCP* 612.

    "Rising and gliding out": "When I Heard the Learn'd Astronomer," *CPCP* 410.

    heart attack: His family believed that Bucke had slipped on a patch of ice and fallen, hitting his head, and this explanation of his death appeared in all biographies before Rechnitzer's. Rechnitzer, a physician, argues that a concussion was unlikely to cause immediate death and that the circumstances suggest a heart attack.

    "My life has been dedicated": Lozynsky, *Richard Maurice Bucke, Medical Mystic*, 185.

CHAPTER FOUR
JOHN ADDINGTON SYMONDS, EDWARD CARPENTER, OSCAR WILDE

139   **"Clear to me now"**: "Calamus 1" ["In Paths Untrodden"], *LG 1860*, 341.

    "I turn the bridegroom": "Song of Myself," *CPCP* 224.

    "a mass of stupid filth": [Rufus W. Griswold], *Criterion*, November 10, 1855, in Kenneth M. Price, ed., *Walt Whitman: The Contemporary Reviews* (New York: Cambridge University Press, 1996), 26.

141   **"I consider the friendship"**: *WWC* 7:457.

    "I heed knowledge": "Calamus 8" ["Long I thought that knowledge alone would suffice me"], *LG 1860*, 354–55.

    "It is quite indispensable": John Addington Symonds, *The Letters of John Addington Symonds*, edited by Herbert M. Schueller and Robert L. Peters (Detroit: Wayne State University Press, 1969), 1:696.

    "my Master": Ibid., 2:202.

142 **"I want . . . to ask you a question":** Ibid., 3:483.

143 **"Dorian chivalry":** See Linda Dowling, *Hellenism and Homosexuality in Victorian Oxford* (Ithaca: Cornell University Press, 1994), and Peter Gay, *The Tender Passion* (New York: Oxford University Press, 1986), 237–49.

144 **"It is I, you women":** "A Woman Waits for Me," *CPCP* 259.

"One flitting glimpse": "Calamus 29" ["A Glimpse"], *LG 1860*, 371.

"Whitman—visiting Whitman": Eve Kosofsky Sedgwick, *Between Men: English Literature and Male Homosocial Desire* (New York: Columbia University Press, 1985), 28. I am deeply indebted to Sedgwick's analysis of Whitman and his English homosexual readers. Other general introductions to the topic are Jonathan Katz, *Gay American History* (New York: Thomas Y. Crowell, 1976), 337–65; William Pannapacker, *Revised Lives: Walt Whitman and Nineteenth-Century Authorship* (New York: Routledge, 2004), 105–27; Kenneth M. Price, *To Walt Whitman, America* (Chapel Hill: University of North Carolina Press, 2004), 56–69; and Gregory Woods, " 'Still on My Lips': Walt Whitman in Britain," in Robert K. Martin, ed., *The Continuing Presence of Walt Whitman: The Life after the Life* (Iowa City: University of Iowa Press, 1992), 129–40.

"from the cradle": E. H. Mikhail, ed., *Oscar Wilde: Interviews and Recollections* (New York: Barnes and Noble, 1979), 47.

145 **"the kiss of Walt Whitman":** Richard Ellmann, *Oscar Wilde* (New York: Alfred A. Knopf, 1988), 171.

"A Gay Life": Gary Schmidgall, *Walt Whitman: A Gay Life* (New York: E. P. Dutton, 1997).

"which will not seem to soil": John Addington Symonds, *A Problem in Modern Ethics* (1891; London, 1896), 3.

146 **love was pure or impure:** See Jonathan Ned Katz, *Love Stories: Sex between Men before Homosexuality* (Chicago: University of Chicago Press, 2001). The principal source of biographical information on Symonds is Phyllis Grosskurth, *The Woeful Victorian: A Biography of John Addington Symonds* (New York: Holt, Rinehart and Winston, 1964).

"a public prostitute": John Addington Symonds, *The Memoirs of John Addington Symonds*, edited by Phyllis Grosskurth (New York: Random House, 1984), 94, 96.

147 *I must have been a philosophical Greek lover:* Symonds, *Memoirs*, 99.

148 **"We met then":** Ibid., 104.

149 **"Leaves of Grass were published in 1860":** Symonds, *Letters*, 1:696.

150 **"begins anew":** Symonds, *A Problem in Modern Ethics*, 125.

150 **"Walt Whitman is more truly Greek":** John Addington Symonds, *Studies of the Greek Poets* (London: Smith, Elder, 1873), 422, 398.

Symonds underwent a religious crisis: See Symonds, *Memoirs*, 242–52. See also Howard J. Booth, "Male Sexuality, Religion and the Problem of Action: John Addington Symonds on Arthur Hugh Clough," in Andrew Bradstock et al., eds., *Masculinity and Spirituality in Victorian Culture* (New York: St. Martin's, 2000), 116–33. On the larger Victorian crisis of faith, see Hugh McLeod, *Religion and Society in England, 1850–1914* (London: Macmillan, 1996), 169–224; and Frank M. Turner, *Contesting Cultural Authority: Essays in Victorian Intellectual Life* (Cambridge: Cambridge University Press, 1993).

"I hear and behold God": "Song of Myself," *CPCP* 244.

151 **"[T]he expression of a well-made man":** "I Sing the Body Electric," quoted in John Addington Symonds, *Walt Whitman: A Study* (London: John C. Nimmo, 1893), 91.

"recognises divinity": Symonds, *Walt Whitman: A Study*, 90.

"Cosmic Enthusiasm": Symonds, *Memoirs*, 245ff.

153 **"For the first time":** Ibid., 253, 254.

154 **"she will find interests":** Grosskurth, *Woeful Victorian*, 197.

"When he came towards me": Symonds, *Memoirs*, 263.

155 **"institution of the dear love of comrades":** "I Hear It Was Charged against Me," *CPCP* 281.

"porters in hotels": Symonds, *Memoirs*, 267, 265.

"to whose caprices": Ibid., 275.

"nearly equal": Havelock Ellis and John Addington Symonds, *Sexual Inversion* (1897; New York: Arno, 1975), 62.

"Though it began": Symonds, *Memoirs*, 276.

156 **"sexual tourist":** John Pemble, *John Addington Symonds: Culture and the Demon Desire* (New York: St. Martin's, 2000), xi.

"the difference": Sedgwick, *Between Men*, 210.

"an opponent might observe": Symonds, *Memoirs*, 279.

"avidly exploitative sexual colonialism": Jeffrey Weeks, *Coming Out: Homosexual Politics in Britain, from the Nineteenth Century to the Present* (London: Quartet Books, 1977), 44.

157 **"the blending of Social Strata":** Symonds, *Letters*, 3:809.

"I might have been": Ibid., 3:667.

"the value of fraternity": Symonds, *Memoirs*, 191.

"perversion": Ibid., 281, 190.

158 **"the attractions":** Ibid., 62.

158 **"from the filth":** Symonds, *Walt Whitman: A Study*, 76.

"I am certain": Symonds, *Letters*, 3:364.

159 **the German sexologists:** Brief introductions to the nineteenth-century European sexologists include Joseph Bristow, *Sexuality* (London: Routledge, 1997), 12–61; Gay, *Tender Passion*, 219–37; David F. Greenberg, *The Construction of Homosexuality* (Chicago: University of Chicago Press, 1988), 397–433; and Jeffrey Weeks, *Sex, Politics, and Society: The Regulation of Sexuality since 1800*, 2nd ed. (New York: Longman, 1989), 141–59.

convictions . . . for sodomy in England and Wales: Graham Robb, *Strangers: Homosexual Love in the Nineteenth Century* (New York: W. W. Norton, 2004), 272–73.

160 **"duty bound":** Symonds, *Letters*, 3:548. On the Labouchere Amendment see Weeks, *Coming Out*, 11–22.

"I'm tired": *WWC* 1:204.

"That the calamus part": *Corr.* 5:72–73.

161 **"set the matter":** Symonds, *Letters*, 3:493.

"I exchanged some words": Ibid., 3:533.

162 **"classical associations of corruption":** Symonds, *A Problem in Modern Ethics*, 124, 122, 119.

163 **"cosmic enthusiasm":** Symonds, *Walt Whitman: A Study*, 33, 19, 95, 157, 72, 75–76.

164 **"We here in America":** William Sloane Kennedy, *Reminiscences of Walt Whitman* (London: Alexander Gardner, 1896), vii.

Symonds . . . did not go far enough: See the interpretations of the Symonds-Whitman correspondence in Betsy Erkkila, "Whitman and the Homosexual Republic," in Ed Folsom, ed., *Walt Whitman: The Centennial Essays* (Iowa City: University of Iowa Press, 1994), 153–71; Katz, *Love Stories*, 235–45, 257–87; Robert K. Martin, "Whitman and the Politics of Identity," in Folsom, *Walt Whitman: The Centennial Essays*, 172–81; and Michael Moon, *Disseminating Whitman: Revision and Corporeality in Leaves of Grass* (Cambridge: Harvard University Press, 1991), 11–14.

"perversion of appetite": Symonds, *A Problem in Modern Ethics*, 1, 85, 125.

165 **"For You O Democracy":** "For You O Democracy," *CPCP* 272.

"It is to the development": "Democratic Vistas," *CPCP* 981–82.

"I think [Whitman] was afraid": Symonds, *Letters*, 3:808. On nineteenth-century attitudes toward sodomy see Katz, *Love Stories*, 60–76. Michael Lynch discusses Whitman's use of phrenological terms in " 'Here Is Adhesiveness': From Friendship to Homosexuality," *Victorian Studies* 29 (1985): 67–96.

166 **"the one I love most"**: "When I Heard at the Close of the Day," *CPCP* 277.

167 **"He is always driving"**: *WWC* 1:73, 203, 204.

"It is just dawn": Ibid., 1:158, 160.

168 **"I feel that my work"**: Ibid., 3:416.

169 **his days slid by**: Edward Carpenter, *My Days and Dreams* (London: George Allen and Unwin, 1916), 47. Aside from his autobiography, the major source of information on Carpenter's life is Chushichi Tsuzuki, *Edward Carpenter, 1844–1929: Prophet of Human Fellowship* (Cambridge: Cambridge University Press, 1980).

170 **"in a spirit"**: Carpenter, *My Days and Dreams*, 58, 74, 77.

171 **"What news"**: Edward Carpenter, *Days with Walt Whitman* (New York: Macmillan, 1906), 4.

"I was aware": Ibid., 6–8.

"the likeness to Christ": Gay Wilson Allen, *Walt Whitman as Man, Poet, and Legend* (Carbondale: Southern Illinois University Press, 1961), 156. For comments on the sketch see Allen, 257, and Randall Waldron, "Whitman as the Nazarene: An Unpublished Drawing," *WWQR* 7 (1990): 192–93.

174 **"has taken me to himself"**: Allen, *Walt Whitman as Man, Poet, and Legend*, 158.

"Oh yes—once in a while": Katz, *Love Stories*, 324. Katz (321–29) offers a fully documented analysis of Gavin Arthur's multiple accounts of his visit to Carpenter. See also Martin G. Murray, "Walt Whitman, Edward Carpenter, Gavin Arthur, and *The Circle of Sex*," *WWQR* 22 (2005): 194–98.

"omnivorous egotism": Carpenter, *Days with Walt Whitman*, 32, 47, 54.

175 **Carpenter reinvented himself**: My comparison of Carpenter and the American counterculture was stimulated by Martin Green, *Prophets of a New Age: The Politics of Hope from the Eighteenth through the Twenty-first Centuries* (New York: Scribner's, 1992).

176 **"was delightful to me, as the one 'powerful uneducated' "**: Carpenter, *My Days and Dreams*, 103. The phrase "powerful uneducated persons" is from the preface to the 1855 edition of *Leaves of Grass* (*CPCP* 11).

"a life close to Nature": Carpenter, *My Days and Dreams*, 104.

"My ideal of love": Ellis and Symonds, *Sexual Inversion*, 47.

177 **"I have brought my cultured self"**: Symonds, *Memoirs*, 75.

"Railway men": Carpenter, *My Days and Dreams*, 102.

"Carpenter knows intimately": Thomas B. Harned, ed., *The Letters of Anne Gilchrist and Walt Whitman* (New York: Doubleday, Page, 1918), 191.

177   **Merrill always takes a subordinate position:** See William Pannapacker's analysis of the Carpenter-Merrill relationship in *Revised Lives*, 123–24.

179   **"a great etherealizing influence":** Carpenter, *My Days and Dreams*, 106.
"Every atom": "Song of Myself," *CPCP* 188.
"These things I, writing": Edward Carpenter, "Towards Democracy," in *Towards Democracy* (1905; New York: Mitchell Kennerley, 1922), 3.
"I skirt sierras": "Song of Myself," *CPCP* 219, 192.
"spread like a map": Carpenter, *Towards Democracy*, 51, 4.

180   **"Whitman and water":** Gilbert Beith, ed., *Edward Carpenter: In Appreciation* (London: George Allen and Unwin, 1931), 47.
"the sun or the winds": Edward Carpenter, "A Note on 'Towards Democracy,'" *Towards Democracy*, xxiv. See the extended comparisons of Carpenter's and Whitman's poetry in Andrew Elfenbein, "Whitman, Democracy, and the English Clerisy," *Nineteenth-Century Literature* 56 (2001): 76–104; and M. Wynn Thomas, *Transatlantic Connections: Whitman U.S., Whitman U.K.* (Iowa City: University of Iowa Press, 2005), 161–91.

181   **"Of that which exists":** Carpenter, *Towards Democracy*, 22.

182   **"Certainly, Comrade Creaghe":** Tsuzuki, *Edward Carpenter*, 97–98.
"the cherished illusion": Ibid., 119.

183   **"On the high tops":** Edward Carpenter, *Civilisation: Its Cause and Cure* (1889; New York: Scribner's, 1921), 57, 60. For the context of Carpenter's socialist politics see Stanley Pierson, *British Socialists: The Journey from Fantasy to Politics* (Cambridge: Harvard University Press, 1979), as well as Mark Bevir, "British Socialism and American Romanticism," *English Historical Review* 110 (1995): 878–901; Susan Budd, *Varieties of Unbelief: Atheists and Agnostics in English Society, 1850–1960* (London: Heinemann, 1977), 64–76, 207–14; Henry Pelling, *The Origins of the Labour Party*, 2nd ed. (Oxford: Oxford University Press, 1965); and Stephen Yeo, "A New Life: The Religion of Socialism in Britain, 1883–1896," *History Workshop* 4 (1977): 5–56.

183   **"the Noble Savage":** G. B. Shaw, *Sixteen Self Sketches* (London: Constable, 1949), 67.
"a depository of old cranks": Weeks, *Sex, Politics, and Society*, 170.
"What made me cling": Carpenter, *My Days and Dreams*, 65.
Bucke borrowed the term from Carpenter: See Paul Marshall, *Mystical Encounters with the Natural World* (Oxford: Oxford University Press, 2005), 111–29; and Lorna Weir, "Cosmic Consciousness and the Love of Comrades: Contacts between R. M. Bucke and Edward Carpenter," *Journal of Canadian Studies* 30 (Summer 1995): 39–57.

183 **"illumination"**: Carpenter, *Days with Walt Whitman*, 60.

184 **"social Lamarckism"**: See Edward Carpenter, "Exfoliation: Lamarck *versus* Darwin," in *Civilisation*, 161–84.

"a new Chivalry": Symonds, *Letters*, 3:483.

185 **"intermediate sex"**: See *The Intermediate Sex* and *Intermediate Types among Primitive Folk*, both of which are included, along with *Love's Coming-of-Age*, in *Sex*, vol. 1 of Carpenter's *Selected Writings*, edited by David Fernbach and Noël Grieg (London: GMP, 1984).

"wont to congregate": Carpenter, *Sex*, 117.

"a special work": Ibid., 188.

"O Child of Uranus": Carpenter, *Towards Democracy*, 387.

186 **"Eros is a great leveller"**: Carpenter, *Sex*, 237–38.

"Thousands of people": Edward Carpenter, *Some Friends of Walt Whitman: A Study in Sex-Psychology* (London: British Society for the Study of Sex Psychology, 1924), 16.

187 **Carpenter relied on conventional Victorian ideas about sexual difference**: See Sheila Rowbotham and Jeffrey Weeks, *Socialism and the New Life: The Personal and Sexual Politics of Edward Carpenter and Havelock Ellis* (London: Pluto Press, 1977), 92–99; Sedgwick, *Between Men*, 201–17; Elaine Showalter, *Sexual Anarchy: Gender and Culture at the Fin de Siècle* (New York: Viking, 1990), 172–74; and Beverly Thiele, "Coming-of-Age: Edward Carpenter on Sex and Reproduction," in Tony Brown, ed., *Edward Carpenter and Late Victorian Radicalism* (London: Frank Cass, 1990), 100–25.

"Anything effeminate": Ellis and Symonds, *Sexual Inversion*, 47.

188 **"a sheer panic"**: Carpenter, *My Days and Dreams*, 196.

189 **"larger and more wonderful"**: Ellmann, *Oscar Wilde*, 167. Additional accounts of the Wilde-Whitman relationship are found in Joann P. Krieg, *Whitman and the Irish* (Iowa City: University of Iowa Press, 2000), 163–81; and Schmidgall, *Walt Whitman: A Gay Life*, 283–337.

"I do so hope": Mikhail, *Oscar Wilde: Interviews and Recollections*, 45.

"The Aesthetic Singer Visits the Good Gray Poet": *Philadelphia Press*, January 19, 1882, 8, reprinted in Mikhail, *Oscar Wilde: Interviews and Recollections*, 46–48.

190 **"thee and thou"**: Mikhail, *Oscar Wilde: Interviews and Recollections*, 46–47.

"If it had been vinegar": Ellmann, *Oscar Wilde*, 170.

"My Dear Dear Walt": Oscar Wilde, *The Letters of Oscar Wilde*, edited by Rupert Hart-Davis (New York: Harcourt Brace, 1962), 99–100.

"I have been told": *WWC* 2:287.

190   **"the grandest man":** Ellmann, *Oscar Wilde*, 170.

       "I admire him intensely": Mikhail, *Oscar Wilde: Interviews and Recollections*, 45.

191   **"I think him genuine":** Ibid., 46–47.

       link between effeminacy and sexuality: My argument has been greatly influenced by Alan Sinfield, *The Wilde Century: Effeminacy, Oscar Wilde, and the Queer Moment* (New York: Columbia University Press, 1994). See also Joseph Bristow, *Effeminate England: Homoerotic Writing after 1885* (Buckingham, UK: Open University Press, 1995), 1–54.

194   **"eloquent admirers":** Oscar Wilde, "The Gospel according to Walt Whitman," in Richard Ellmann, ed., *The Artist as Critic: Critical Writings of Oscar Wilde* (New York: Random House, 1969), 121, 125.

195   **"The chief advantage":** Oscar Wilde, "The Soul of Man under Socialism," in Ellmann, *Artist as Critic*, 255, 284, 262.

       "extraordinary personal beauty": Oscar Wilde, *The Picture of Dorian Gray* (Oxford: Oxford University Press, 1974), 1.

196   **"The special meaning:** "Preface, 1876," *CPCP* 1011.

       "democracy infers": "Democratic Vistas," *CPCP* 982.

       "Uranian love": Ellmann, *Oscar Wilde*, 570.

197   **"To the East and to the West":** "To the East and to the West," *CPCP* 285.

CHAPTER FIVE

J. W. WALLACE AND THE EAGLE STREET COLLEGE

198   **"God bless the Church":** *Corr.* 5:231.

       "Dear Walt": Johnston and Wallace to Whitman, May 1887, copy in Rylands.

       "Avowal letters": *WWC* 3:525.

199   **"good affectionate letter":** *Corr.* 4:95.

       James William Wallace: The published biographies of Wallace are Caroline A. Eccles, *James William Wallace: An English Comrade of Walt Whitman* (London: C. W. Daniel, 1937), and Marie Louise Herdman, *J. W. Wallace: An English Friend of Walt Whitman* (privately printed pamphlet, n.d.). The principal studies of the Eagle Street College are Harold Blodgett, *Walt Whitman in England* (Ithaca: Cornell University Press, 1934), 211–15; Harry Cocks, "*Calamus* in Bolton: Spirituality and Homosexual Desire in Late Victorian England," *Gender and History* 13 (2001): 191–223; Joann P. Krieg, "Without Walt Whitman in Camden," *WWQR* 14 (1996–1997): 85–112; Carolyn Masel, "Poet of Comrades:

Walt Whitman and the Bolton Whitman Fellowship," in Janet Beer and Bridget Bennett, eds., *Special Relationships: Anglo-American Affinities and Antagonisms, 1854–1936* (Manchester: Manchester University Press, 2002), 110–38; and Paul Salveson, "Loving Comrades: Lancashire's Links to Walt Whitman," *WWQR* 14 (1996–1997): 57–84. Volumes 8 and 9 of Horace Traubel's *WWC* contain extensive discussion of Wallace. The Bolton and Rylands libraries have thousands of unpublished letters and documents by and about Wallace and other members of the Eagle Street College.

201   **"New Birth":** Fred Wild, "Sketch of Life of J. W. Wallace of Bolton," Rylands.

202   **"It seemed to me":** J. W. Wallace, "Address to the College," January 20, 1890, Bolton. R. M. Bucke reprints this document in *Cosmic Consciousness* (1901; New York: Penguin Arkana, 1991), 332–42, where Wallace is identified as "J.W.W."

the middle class . . . constituted fewer than 2 percent of the population: Harold Perkin, *The Rise of Professional Society* (London: Routledge, 1989), 29. On the lower middle class, see Perkin, 27–115, and Geoffrey Crossick, *The Lower Middle Class in Britain, 1870–1914* (London: Croom Helm, 1977).

203   **"Darwinism demolished":** Bucke, *Cosmic Consciousness*, 334.

204   **"Each believed":** Ibid., 335.

"Dear Sir": Wallace to John Ruskin, February 7, 1886, draft letter, Bolton.

205   **"The smallest sprout":** "Song of Myself," *CPCP* 194.

"Fred Wild": Wallace to John Johnston, May 28, 1886, Bolton.

206   **"In a quare little house":** J. Johnston, "The 'Masther' of Eagle Street College," 1889, Bolton.

207   **"So you've been travelling":** J. Johnston and J. W. Wallace, *Visits to Walt Whitman in 1890–91* (London: George Allen and Unwin, 1917), 32. This volume collects Johnston's privately printed *Visit to Walt Whitman* (1890), which was reprinted by the Labour Press of Manchester in 1898, with Wallace's notes of his 1891 visit and other valuable material on Whitman and the Eagle Street College.

"much more likeness": Virginia Woolf, "Visits to Walt Whitman," in *The Essays of Virginia Woolf*, edited by Andrew McNeille (New York: Harcourt Brace, 1986), 2:206.

"Jove-like . . . majesty": Johnston and Wallace, *Visits to Walt Whitman*, 86, 35.

"the irresistible magnetism": Ibid., 34, 51.

208 **"fearfully eulogistic"**: *Corr.* 5:127.

"What staunch tender fellows": Ibid., 5:218.

"It surprises me": Horace Traubel, "Visits to Walt Whitman," *Conservator* 28 (1918): 188.

"middle style": Andrew Elfenbein, "Whitman, Democracy, and the English Clerisy," *Nineteenth-Century Literature* 56 (2001): 92–93, 100.

210 **"the divine pride of man"**: J. W. Wallace, untitled address to the college, May 30, 1888, Bolton.

"Why, who makes much of a miracle?" "Miracles," *CPCP* 513.

"led us": Johnston and Wallace, *Visits to Walt Whitman*, 19.

211 **"Braw chiefs"**: J. Johnston, "The College Battle Song," August 12, 1889, Rylands.

"I . . . shall think of you constantly": Wallace to Johnston, July 1, 1890, Bolton.

"This little band o' brithers": J. Johnston, "A College Song," April 10, 1891, Bolton.

212 **"the institution of the dear love of comrades"**: Wallace to Whitman, January 9, 1891, Feinberg. This phrase is from "I Hear It Was Charged against Me," *CPCP* 281; the verse that follows is from "For You O Democracy," *CPCP* 272.

"world of love and ritual": Carroll Smith-Rosenberg, "The Female World of Love and Ritual," *Disorderly Conduct* (New York: Oxford University Press, 1986), 53–76. Historians who have applied Smith-Rosenberg's concept to nineteenth-century men include Caleb Crain, *American Sympathy* (New Haven: Yale University Press, 2001); and Donald Yacovone, "Abolitionists and the 'Language of Fraternal Love,' " in Mark C. Carnes and Clyde Griffen, eds., *Meanings for Manhood* (Chicago: University of Chicago Press, 1990), 85–95.

"O manly love of comrades!" "In Merrie England," *Camden (New Jersey) Post*, September 5, 1891.

"a freedom of expression": W. T. Hawkins, "In Memory of Walt Whitman," *Annandale (Scotland) Observer*, June 14, 1901.

213 **"Institutions of dear love of comrades"**: Wentworth Dixon, "The College to John H. Johnston," June 23, 1894, Bolton.

"only to them that love": "These I Singing in Spring," *CPCP* 273. Wallace's address is "The 'Calamus' Poems in 'Leaves of Grass,' " May 31, 1920, Rylands.

214 **"*both* sensual and platonic"**: Smith-Rosenberg, "Female World of Love and Ritual," 55, emphasis added.

214 **"we had a right good talk"**: J. Johnston diary, October 5, 1901, Bolton.

215 **"This . . . to me"**: Ibid., December 25, 1892, Bolton.

"It seems curious to me": Wallace to Horace Traubel, January 1, 1893, TC.

"to remove the taint": Cocks, *Calamus in Bolton*," 203.

"to see how naturally": J. W. Wallace, "Notes of Visit to Ed. Carpenter, Aug. 13–15, 1892," Bolton.

216 **"intensely interested"**: Salveson, "Loving Comrades," 78.

"tastes and pursuits": Wallace, "Address to the College," January 20, 1890.

"Since Christ died": Wallace to R. K. Greenhalgh, December 3, 1890, Bolton.

217 **"a consecration"**: Wallace to Whitman, July 10, 1891, Feinberg.

"Comrade-stranger": Artem Lozynsky, *Richard Maurice Bucke, Medical Mystic: Letters of Dr. Bucke to Walt Whitman and His Friends* (Detroit: Wayne State University Press, 1977), 152–53.

218 **"Most of the evening"**: Ibid., 151–52.

"I was very greatly gratified": Ibid., 154.

"Walt Whitman has hitherto": "College Farewell to R. M. Bucke and J. W. Wallace," August 24, 1891, Rylands.

219 **"Well, you've come to be disillusioned"**: Johnston and Wallace, *Visits to Walt Whitman*, 90, 91, 98.

220 **"tall, slender"**: *WWC* 8:481–82.

"branch church": Ibid., 372.

"Wallace seems disposed": Ibid., 351, 370–71.

221 **"My visit to Camden"**: Ibid., 9:236.

"What I think": J. W. Wallace, untitled address to the college, March 30, 1892, Bolton.

"Over and over": Lozynsky, *Richard Maurice Bucke, Medical Mystic*, 184.

"It seems to me": Wallace, untitled address to the college, March 30, 1892.

"Walt Whitman's work": J. W. Wallace, "Walt Whitman's Birthday," May 31, 1893, Bolton.

222 **"As I understand it"**: Katharine Conway to Eagle Street College, May 1893, Bolton.

Max Weber: Max Weber, *The Sociology of Religion* (1922; Boston: Beacon, 1963).

223 **"At a Whitman Birthday Celebration"**: William Broadhurst, "Notes of an Address Delivered before the Whitman Fellowship," December 6, 1930, Rylands.

225 **"It is of much more importance"**: Stephen Yeo, "A New Life: The Religion of Socialism in Britain, 1883–1896," *History Workshop* 4 (1977): 51. Yeo's essay provides a broad introduction to ethical socialism. See also Stanley Pierson, *British Socialists: The Journey from Fantasy to Politics* (Cambridge: Harvard University Press, 1979), and Pierson, *Marxism and the Origins of British Socialism* (Ithaca: Cornell University Press, 1973), 140–73.

"to resuscitate the Christianity of Christ": Pierson, *Marxism and the Origins of British Socialism*, 202; Henry Pelling, *The Origins of the Labour Party, 1880–1900*, 2nd ed. (Oxford: Oxford University Press, 1965), 140.

"I have been dosing": Wallace to Traubel, March 26, 1895, TC.

"*Produce great persons and the rest follows*": J. W. Wallace, "Paper Read before an ILP Conference at Bolton," May 26, 1894, Bolton. The quotation is from "By Blue Ontario's Shore," *CPCP* 470.

226 **"the chief aim of a Socialist organization"**: Pierson, *Marxism and the Origins of British Socialism*, 253.

"It may be however": J. Kier Hardie to Wallace, December 27, 1892, Bolton.

"teachers and prophets": Pelling, *Origins of the Labour Party*, 140.

227 **"the Labour Movement is a Religious Movement"**: Ibid., 135. On the Labour Church, see also Mark Bevir, "Labour Churches and Ethical Socialism," *History Today* (April 1997): 50–55; and Stanley Pierson, "John Trevor and the Labor Church Movement in England, 1891–1900," *Church History* 29 (1960): 463–78.

"nearer to God": Pierson, "John Trevor," 471.

"I am very well aware": J. W. Wallace to the college, January 6, 1893, Rylands.

228 **"More and more I see"**: Wallace to Traubel, March 23, 1893, TC.

"the most expensive funeral": Keith Laybourn, *The Rise of Socialism in Britain, c. 1881–1951* (Stroud, UK: Sutton, 1997), 50.

229 **"accepted and rejoiced"**: Wallace, "Notes of Visit to Ed. Carpenter."

"Alas for our College!": Wallace to Traubel, May 31, 1898, TC.

"Eyes looked love": Hawkins, "In Memory of Walt Whitman."

"It is under the spell": W. T. Hawkins, "Walt Whitman's Birthday Anniversary," *Annandale Observer*, June 15, 1906.

230 **"are as yet little more"**: J. W. Wallace, "The Walt Whitman Centennial: The Man and His Message," *Labour Leader*, May 29, 1919.

"I myself": J. W. Wallace, "If Walt Whitman Came to Walker Fold," May 30, 1925, Bolton.

231 **"distinguished him"**: Broadhurst, "Notes of an Address."

CHAPTER SIX

HORACE TRAUBEL AND THE WHITMAN FELLOWSHIP

232 **"I call to the world":** "Myself and Mine," *CPCP* 380.

Horace Traubel was determined: This account of the 1919 Whitman
Fellowship dinner is largely drawn from David Karsner, *Horace Traubel:
His Life and Work* (New York: Egmont Arens, 1919), 21–27. Aside from
Karsner, the principal biographical source is Donald Richard Stoddard,
"Horace Traubel: A Critical Biography" (Ph.D. diss., University of
Pennsylvania, 1970). Ed Folsom's introduction to volume 9 of *With Walt
Whitman in Camden* serves as the best concise biography (Oregon
House, CA: W. L. Bentley, 1996), xiii–xxiii.

233 **"The truth is":** Helen Keller, "Horace Traubel," *Conservator* 30 (May
1919): 45.

"He had a lot of fool friends": Thomas Harned to J. W. Wallace,
August 28, 1920, Bolton.

234 **"Dear Walt":** Horace Traubel, "As I Sit at Karsners' Front Window,"
Conservator 30 (May 1919): 37–38.

235 **"Horace, you were a mere boy":** *WWC* 3:407.

"You have saved my books": Ibid., 1:187.

236 **"Come, kiss me for good night":** Ibid., 2:82.

"I feel somehow": Ibid., 1:207.

**There is nothing to suggest that the relationship . . . was ever a sex-
ual one:** See Gary Schmidgall's discussions of the Whitman-Traubel
relationship in *Walt Whitman: A Gay Life* (New York: E. P. Dutton,
1997), 225–50; and his introduction to Horace Traubel, *Intimate with
Walt: Selections from Whitman's Conversations with Horace Traubel, 1888–
1892* (Iowa City: University of Iowa Press, 2001), a volume of selections
from *With Walt Whitman in Camden*.

"There is a sort of apostolic succession": *WWC* 4:394.

237 **Harned liked to recall:** Harned to Wallace, n.d. [c. 1919], Bolton.

his first reference to his outside employment: *WWC* 5:246.

"lethally industrious": Michael Monahan, "Smothering Walt," *Conservator* 27 (July–August 1916): 70.

239 **"To bring Unitarian":** Horace Traubel, "Collect," *Conservator* 1 (February 1891): 89. An overview of the *Conservator* and a generous selection
from its contents can be found in Gary Schmidgall, ed., *Conserving Walt
Whitman's Fame: Selections from Horace Traubel's* Conservator, *1890–
1919* (Iowa City: University of Iowa Press, 2006).

239   **Felix Adler:** See Horace L. Freiss, *Felix Adler and Ethical Culture* (New York: Columbia University Press, 1981) and Howard B. Radest, *Toward Common Ground: The Story of the Ethical Societies in the United States* (New York: Ungar, 1969).

240   **"Liberal Conference":** Traubel, "Collect," *Conservator* 1 (February 1891): 89.

241   **"The unconstraint and felicity":** Horace L. Traubel, *Camden's Compliment to Walt Whitman* (Philadelphia: David McKay, 1889), 16.
      "entirely out of place": *WWC* 5:218.
      "gloriously well and sassy": Ibid., 250.
      "Isn't it wonderful": Ibid., 218.

242   **"the Bible of the Nineteenth Century":** Horace L. Traubel, "Round Table with Walt Whitman," in *In Re* 309–10.
      "No, I must be excused": Ibid., 321.
      "I cannot get this funeral business": Artem Lozynsky, *Richard Maurice Bucke, Medical Mystic: Letters of Dr. Bucke to Walt Whitman and His Friends* (Detroit: Wayne State University Press, 1977), 117.

243   **"Dear dear boy!":** *WWC* 9:313.
      "Keep an eye out": Ibid., 395.
      "right at the centre": Lozynsky, *Richard Maurice Bucke, Medical Mystic*, 154.
      "Dear Walt": *WWC* 9:518.
      "Walt is dying": Ibid., 598, 600.

244   **"My God!":** Ibid., 9:609.
      "gospel of humanity": Horace L. Traubel, "At the Graveside of Walt Whitman," in *In Re* 451.
      "As we stood there": *WWC* 9:622.
      "This is not to create": Horace Traubel, "Walt Whitman's Birthday, May 31st," *Conservator* 3 (July 1892): 35.

245   **"We must always adopt Walt":** Traubel to Wallace, June 14, 1892, Rylands.
      "*You* are the natural centre": Wallace to Traubel, April 26, 1892, TC.
      "O my dead comrade": Horace Traubel, "Succession," *Conservator* 5 (June 1894): 57.

246   **"I look to see":** Traubel to Wallace, February 12, 1894, Bolton.
      "Horace is apt": Harned to Wallace, n.d., Bolton.

247   **"What an ardent":** Wallace to Traubel, May 16, 1892, TC.
      "The dinner was moved": Traubel to Wallace, January 28, 1894, Bolton.

248   **"Consider well this":** Traubel to Wallace, March 1, 1894, Bolton.

248   **"Our College is one thing":** Wallace to Traubel, March 15, 1894, TC.

"We are all": Traubel to Wallace, July 14, 1894, Bolton.

249   **Traubel's mania for organizing:** For an alternative interpretation of the Traubel-Wallace relationship, see Joann P. Krieg, "Without Walt Whitman in Camden," *WWQR* 14 (1996–97): 85–112.

"Your old familiar letters": Traubel to Wallace, November 3,1894, Bolton.

"I think of you": Traubel to Wallace, February 20, 1900, Bolton.

250   **"I hope to God":** Horace Traubel, "What Walt Whitman Thought of Whitman Celebrations," *Philadelphia Press Sunday Magazine*, May 4, 1919, 6.

251   **absolutist religious movements:** James Davison Hunter, "The New Religions: Demodernization and the Protest against Modernity," in Lorne L. Dawson, ed., *Cults in Context: Readings in the Study of New Religious Movements* (New Brunswick, NJ: Transaction, 1998), 105–18.

"You shall no longer": "Song of Myself," *CPCP* 189–90.

252   **"I find I'm a good deal more":** *WWC* 2:4.

"Of that I'm not so sure": Ibid., 1:222.

"I look forward": Ibid., 3:315.

"fierce agitations": Ibid., 481.

"It is queer": Ibid., 4:429.

253   **"I want you":** Traubel to Wallace, November 19, 1892, Bolton.

"anarchist than socialist": Traubel to Wallace, April 5, 1893, Bolton.

"the premier socialist": Eugene V. Debs, "Whitman and Traubel," *Conservator* 28 (July 1917): 77; William English Walling, *Whitman and Traubel* (New York: Albert and Charles Boni, 1916), 40.

changes within American socialism: On American socialism during Traubel's lifetime see Paul Buhle, *Marxism in the United States*, rev. ed. (London: Verso, 1991), 1–120; Robert J. Fitrakis, *The Idea of Democratic Socialism in America and the Decline of the Socialist Party* (New York: Garland, 1993), 3–131; and Irving Howe, *Socialism and America* (New York: Harcourt Brace Jovanovich, 1985), 3–48. On Eugene V. Debs see Nick Salvatore, *Eugene V. Debs: Citizen and Socialist* (Urbana: University of Illinois Press, 1982). Bryan K. Garman analyzes the relationships among Debs, Traubel, Whitman, and socialism in *A Race of Singers: Whitman's Working-Class Hero from Guthrie to Springsteen* (Chapel Hill: University of North Carolina Press, 2000), 1–78.

254   **"The skies of the East":** Harold W. Currie, *Eugene V. Debs* (Boston: Twayne, 1976), 54.

"too often descended": Ibid.

255 **"Way down here"**: Debs to Traubel, November 27, 1909, TC.

"My heart opens": Debs to Traubel, December 6, 1909, and April 25, 1910, TC.

Nick Salvatore has noted: Salvatore, *Eugene V. Debs: Citizen and Socialist*, 63–64, 88–89.

"When the . . . Whitman Fellowship": Eugene V. Debs, *Conservator* 16 (June 1905): 56.

257 **"Christian Science"**: Karsner, *Horace Traubel: His Life and Work*, 91.

"bellowing pair": Stoddard, "Horace Traubel: A Critical Biography," 105.

259 **"His *family* ties"**: Harned to Wallace, August 28, 1920, Bolton.

"In truth": Stoddard, "Horace Traubel: A Critical Biography," 39.

"The hours flew fast": Ibid., 109–10.

260 **"I repeat myself?"**: Horace Traubel, *Chants Communal* (1904; New York: Albert and Charles Boni, 1914), 95.

"Time was": Clarence Swartz, "Chants Communal," *Conservator* 15 (February 1905): 189.

"Traubel chants": Ernest Crosby, "Chants Communal," *Conservator* 16 (April 1905): 29.

"Every page": Eugene V. Debs, "Chants Communal," *Conservator* 16 (April 1905): 29.

"I can say": Emma Goldman to Traubel, February 19, 1902, TC.

261 **"The people are the masters of life"**: Horace Traubel, *Optimos* (New York: B. W. Huebsch, 1910), 281.

"dishwatery imitations": H. L. Mencken, "Optimos," *Conservator* 22 (August 1911): 87.

"Although a loyal disciple": Debs, foreword to Walling, *Whitman and Traubel*.

"contains the spiritual": Karsner, *Horace Traubel: His Life and Work*, 108. The same opinion is advanced by Mildred Bain, *Horace Traubel* (New York: Albert and Charles Boni, 1913) and by Walling, *Whitman and Traubel*.

262 **"I'm just talking all the time"**: Traubel, *Optimos*, 232.

"the platitudinarian": Willard Wright, "Whitman Imitations," *Conservator* 22 (November 1911): 136.

"America's forgotten civil war": Adam Shatz, "The Prophet of Terre Haute," *New York Times Book Review*, September 26, 1999, 22.

263 **"socialists, anarchists, [and] cranks"**: Harned to Wallace, n.d., Bolton.

"Traubel has worked": Harned is quoted in Clara Barrus, *Whitman and Burroughs, Comrades* (Boston: Houghton Mifflin, 1931), 360.

263   **The American arts and crafts movement:** Wendy Kaplan, *"The Art That Is Life"*: *The Arts and Crafts Movement in America, 1875–1920* (Boston: Museum of Fine Arts, 1987), offers a through introduction. Eileen Boris, *Art and Labor: Ruskin, Morris, and the Craftsman Ideal in America* (Philadelphia: Temple University Press, 1986), and T. J. Jackson Lears, *No Place of Grace: Antimodernism and the Transformation of American Culture, 1880–1920* (New York: Pantheon, 1981), discuss Rose Valley in the course of interpretations of the movement.

264   **"I can see God":** Horace Traubel, "Rose Valley in General," *Artsman* 1 (October 1903): 25.

265   **"by thud of machinery":** "Song of the Exposition," *CPCP* 343.

"If you are a white American": Horace Traubel, "The Souls of Black Folk," *Conservator* 14 (May 1903): 43.

"If present tendencies": Charles W. Chesnutt to Traubel, July 3, 1903, TC.

"among black folks": "Song of Myself" (1855), *CPCP* 31.

266   **"nigger question":** *WWC* 6:323.

"What did [Whitman] do": Kelly Miller, "What Walt Whitman Means to the Negro," *Conservator* 6 (July 1895): 72. See George B. Hutchinson, "Whitman and the Black Poet: Kelly Miller's Speech to the Walt Whitman Fellowship," *American Literature* 61 (1989): 46–58.

"the economic radicalisms": Traubel, "Souls of Black Folk," 44.

"receive the Negro": Fitrakis, *Idea of Democratic Socialism*, 82.

"no 'Negro problem' ": Howe, *Socialism and America*, 21.

267   **"Whitman's Ideal Democracy":** Helena Born, *Whitman's Ideal Democracy and Other Writings* (Boston: Everett Press, 1902).

Mabel MacCoy Irwin: Mabel MacCoy Irwin, *Whitman: The Poet-Liberator of Woman* (New York, 1905).

"I say it is as great": "Song of Myself," *CPCP* 207.

"Without shame": "A Woman Waits for Me," *CPCP* 259.

"after all Whitman has said": Helen Abbot Michael, "Woman and Freedom in Whitman," *Poet-Lore* 9 (1897): 235.

"in all [Whitman's] singing": Helen Clarke and Charlotte Endymion Porter, "A Short Reading Course in Whitman," *Poet-Lore* 6 (1894): 645.

268   **"Why is it":** Helen Clarke to Traubel, May 5, 1897, TC.

"among the few men": Clarke to Traubel, August 1897, TC.

"Is love an affair": Traubel, "Collect," *Conservator* 15 (April 1904): 19.

269   **"Be you my lover":** Traubel to Wallace, January 19, 1893, Bolton.

"It would be impossible": Debs to Traubel, April 12, 1910, TC.

269   **"I dream of":** Traubel to Gustave Percival Wiksell, January 3, 1904, G. Percival Wiksell Collection, Library of Congress.

      "I sit here": Traubel to Wiksell, May 12, 1904, Wiksell Collection.

      "Annie and Gertrude": Wiksell to Traubel, December 30, 1901, TC.

270   **"ardent and *physical* intimacies":** John Addington Symonds, *The Letters of John Addington Symonds*, edited by Herbert M. Schueller and Robert L. Peters (Detroit: Wayne State University Press, 1969), 3:483.

      "Homosexuality is disease": Traubel to Wallace, January 10, 1893, Bolton.

      "Oh darling my brother": Wiksell to Traubel, December 30, 1901, TC.

      "When it is Christmas": Traubel to Wiksell, December 25, 1903, Wiksell Collection.

      "When I left you": Wiksell to Traubel, December 28, 1903, TC.

271   **"In you I find":** Wiksell to Traubel, June 27, 1897, TC.

      "I feel now": Wiksell to Traubel, [1906], TC.

      "If all the theologies": Percival Wiksell, "If All," *Conservator* 30 (June 1919): 61.

272   **"I say, Walt, dear Walt":** Horace Traubel, "Walt at Bon Echo," in Cyril Greenland and John Robert Colombo, eds., *Walt Whitman's Canada* (Willowdale, ON: Hounslow Press, 1992), 194–95.

273   **"Traubel was born":** Ernest Crosby, "With Walt Whitman in Camden," *Conservator* 19 (September 1908): 105.

      "Thinking comes easy": Traubel to Wallace, July 19, 1893, Bolton.

      Flora MacDonald Denison: The most complete biography of Denison is Deborah Gorham, "Flora MacDonald Denison: Canadian Feminist," in Linda Kealey, ed., *A Not Unreasonable Claim: Women and Reform in Canada, 1880s–1920s* (Toronto: Women's Press, 1979), 47–70. For more on Denison, Traubel, and the Canadian Whitmanites see Greenland and Colombo, *Walt Whitman's Canada* and Michael Lynch, "Walt Whitman in Ontario," in Robert K. Martin, ed., *The Continuing Presence of Walt Whitman* (Iowa City: University of Iowa Press, 1992), 141–51.

275   **"Look, look, Flora":** Flora McDonald Denison, "Horace Traubel," in Greenland and Colombo, *Walt Whitman's Canada*, 198.

      "You're triumphant, Horace": Denison, "Horace Traubel," 199.

276   **"He burned the church":** Stoddard, "Horace Traubel: A Critical Biography," 396.

      "Oh! those blessed old times, Walt!": Traubel, "Walt at Bon Echo," 195–96.

      J. W. Wallace said: Wallace to Traubel, June 30, 1893, TC.

AFTERWORD

277 **"Failing to fetch me":** "Song of Myself," *CPCP* 247.

"seer and philosopher": John Burroughs, "The Poet of the Cosmos," *Accepting the Universe* (1920; New York: Wm. H. Wise, 1924), 317.

278 **"the best loved and best hated":** Edmond Holmes, *Conservator* 12 (November 1901): 138.

"no American poet": Bliss Perry, *Walt Whitman* (Boston: Houghton Mifflin, 1906), 308.

279 **"cult":** Ibid., 263, 286, 303.

"Perry's point of view": Horace Traubel, review of Perry, *Walt Whitman*, *Conservator* 17 (November 1906): 138.

the institutionalization of American literature: See Gerald Graff, *Professing Literature: An Institutional History* (Chicago: University of Chicago Press, 1987).

280 **master narrative of the growth of American democracy:** See Graff, *Professing Literature*, 128–32, 211–16. On the history of Whitman criticism see M. Jimmie Killingsworth, *The Growth of* Leaves of Grass*: The Organic Tradition in Whitman Studies* (Columbia, SC: Camden House, 1993).

"[The disciples] imagine": The newspaper is quoted in Charles B. Willard, *Whitman's American Fame* (Providence: Brown University, 1950), 118.

281 **"the last of the band":** Ibid., 32.

"heroic spiritual grandfather": Bryan K. Garman, *A Race of Singers: Whitman's Working-Class Hero from Guthrie to Springsteen* (Chapel Hill: University of North Carolina Press, 2000), 3.

"cosmic": Langston Hughes, "The Ceaseless Rings of Walt Whitman," in Jim Perlman, Ed Folsom, and Dan Campion, eds., *Walt Whitman: The Measure of His Song*, 2nd ed. (Duluth, MN: Holy Cow! Press, 1998), 187.

Richard Rorty: Richard Rorty, *Achieving Our Country: Leftist Thought in Twentieth-Century America* (Cambridge: Harvard University Press, 1998).

Will Hayes: Will Hayes, *Walt Whitman: The Prophet of the New Era* (London: C. W. Daniel, 1921); Gary David Comstock, preface to Walt Whitman, *Whitman* (Woodstock, VT: SkyLight Paths, 2004).

282 **Dilys Gold:** Dilys Gold, *A Marriage of True Minds: Walt Whitman to Dora* (London: Regency Press, 1990); Philip Akers, *The Principle of*

Life: A New Concept of Reality Based on Walt Whitman's "Leaves of Grass" (New York: Vantage, 1991); Gregory Leifel, *The Day I Met Walt Whitman* (Cary, IL: Thriving Moss, 2001).

285 **"Abstract yourself from this book":** *NUPM* 6:2049–50.

286 **"There was never any more inception":** "Song of Myself," *CPCP* 190.

288 **Paul Salveson:** Paul Salveson, "Loving Comrades: Lancashire's Links to Walt Whitman" was published as a pamphlet in 1984; a revised version was printed in *WWQR* 14 (1996–1997): 57–84.

294 **"extending the globe across":** Traubel to J. W. Wallace, February 12, 1894, Bolton.

295 **"Great Construction of the New Bible":** *NUPM* 1:353.
    "is to me the more I read it": *WWC* 2:284–85.
    "incomparable things": R. W. Emerson, "Letter to Walt Whitman," *CPCP* 1326.
    "Loafe with me on the grass": "Song of Myself," *CPCP* 192.

296 **"I depart as air":** Ibid., *CPCP* 247.
    "I love you": "So Long!" *CPCP* 612.

INDEX

NOTE: *Page numbers in parentheses indicate works quoted but unattributed in the text.*

337

Whitman, Walt (*cont'd*)

democracy, 187, 196, 208, 227, 252; dismissal of from government post, 32–33, 34; and Eagle Street College, 207, 208, 210, 220, 221; egotism of, 93; egotism *vs.* egotheism of, 19; employment of, 23, 32–33, 34; family of, 14; finances of, 17; funeral for, 242–43; in Gilchrist's *The Tea Party*, 79, 80; and homosexuality, 42, 95, 140–43, 144, 160–61, 163–66, 174–75, 194, 196–97, 213–15, 270, 283–84; hospital work of, 22–23, 26, 28, 33–34, 118; illness of, 27, 46, 73, 75, 77, 118, 120, 121, 122, 123, 171, 232, 234, 242, 243; images/photographs of, 6–7, 24, 31, 58, 59, 66, 79, 80, 82, 83–84, 85, 101, 173, 209; and Independent Labour Party, 228; and *In Re Walt Whitman*, 124; and Jesus, 9, 11, 34, 44, 49, 66–67, 69, 99, 115, 117, 118, 119, 127, 146, 171, 183, 216, 217, 221, 222, 294; and labor movement, 227; and masculinity, 187, 191; papers of, 122–23; Perry on, 278–79, 280; persona of, 44, 58, 68, 116, 144, 170, 191; physical appearance of, 25, 42, 45–46, 117, 120, 167–68, 171, 207, 232–33; and political activism, 252; as prophet, 6, 183, 242, 279, 291, 293, 294; and religion, 2–3, 4, 9, 11, 12, 16, 18–22, 114, 150–51; as self-publicist, 15; seventieth birthday celebration of, 240–41; and sexuality, 94–96, 139–43, 144, 167, 194, 236; and socialism, 36, 226, 252; and Traubel-Wiksell relationship, 271; and women, 71–72, 78, 94–96, 135, 140, 266; and working class, 7, 28–30, 135, 171, 177, 178, 189, 208–9; as workingman, 58

CORRESPONDENCE: with Anne Gilchrist, 52, 67, 69–71, 72–74, 84–85, 87; with Beatrice Gilchrist, 87; with Bucke, 106, 111; with Carpenter, 170–71; with Doyle, 30, 77; with Ellen O'Connor, 28; with Emerson, 14–15, 16, 18, 272; with Herbert Gilchrist, 92–93; with Jeff

Whitman, 23; with Johnston, 198–99, 206; with mother, 23; with Rossetti, 69, 75; with Smith, 71–72; with Stafford, 83; with Symonds, 141–43, 153, 160–61, 162, 164, 165, 167, 184; with Wallace, 198–99, 206; with Wilde, 190;

RELATIONSHIPS/CONTACTS: with Bucke, 48–49, 98, 105, 106–7, 111–24, 116, 124, 125–28, 135–36, 171, 243; with Burroughs, 7, 38, 39, 40–50, 214; with Carpenter, 145, 167–68, 170–75, 176, 186–87; with Doyle, 7, 29–30, 31, 47; with Ellen O'Connor, 27–28, 30, 37; with Gilchrist, 8–9, 51, 52, 67–68, 69–86, 88–89, 92–94; with Gilchrist family, 76–77, 78, 79, 81; with Herbert Gilchrist, 82, 83–84, 86, 92–93, 208; with Johnston, 206–8, 211, 221; with O'Connor family, 25–26; with Rossetti, 67, 69, 143, 205; with Sawyer, 29; with Stafford, 47, 83–84; with Symonds, 8, 140–43, 150, 160–61, 162–67; with Traubel, 7, 48–49, 232, 234, 234–37, 241–42, 243, 245, 261; with Wallace, 7, 207, 211, 219–22, 225, 226, 230–31; with Wilde, 7, 144–45, 189–91, 193; with William O'Connor, 7, 24–25, 30, 32–38

RESIDENCES: at George Whitman home, xii–xiii, 46, 74, 77, 79, 83, 112, 113, 171, 189, 234, 235; at Gilchrist home, 77, 79, 83, 113; on Mickle Street, 48, 207, 235, 277; at Riverby, 47, 48; at Stafford home, 83, 84, 113; in Washington, D. C., xii, 23, 25, 77

WORKS: "A Backward Glance o'er Travel'd Roads," (5–6), (14); "Among the Multitude," 68; "**Calamus**," 35; adhesive love in, 166; and Carpenter, 145, 168, 170, 187;